also by america's test kitchen

Dinner Illustrated

Cooking at Home with Bridget and Julia

The Complete Diabetes Cookbook

The Complete Slow Cooker

The Complete Make-Ahead Cookbook

The Complete Mediterranean Cookbook

The Complete Vegetarian Cookbook

The Complete Cooking for Two Cookbook

Just Add Sauce

How to Roast Everything

Nutritious Delicious

What Good Cooks Know

Cook's Science

The Science of Good Cooking

The Perfect Cake

The Perfect Cookie

Bread Illustrated

Master of the Grill

Kitchen Smarts

Kitchen Hacks

100 Recipes: The Absolute Best Ways to Make the True Essentials

The New Family Cookbook

The America's Test Kitchen Cooking School Cookbook

The Cook's Illustrated Meat Book

The Cook's Illustrated Baking Book

The Cook's Illustrated Cookbook

The America's Test Kitchen Family Baking Book

The Best of America's Test Kitchen (2007–2019 Editions)

The Complete America's Test Kitchen TV Show Cookbook 2001–2019

Sous Vide for Everybody

Multicooker Perfection

Food Processor Perfection

Pressure Cooker Perfection

Vegan for Everybody

Naturally Sweet

Foolproof Preserving

Paleo Perfected

The How Can It Be Gluten-Free Cookbook: Volume 2

The How Can It Be Gluten-Free Cookbook

The Best Mexican Recipes

Slow Cooker Revolution Volume 2: The Easy-Prep Edition

Slow Cooker Revolution

The Six-Ingredient Solution

The America's Test Kitchen D.I.Y. Cookbook

THE COOK'S ILLUSTRATED ALL-TIME BEST SERIES

All-Time Best Brunch

All-Time Best Dinners for Two

All-Time Best Sunday Suppers

All-Time Best Holiday Entertaining

All-Time Best Appetizers

All-Time Best Soups

COOK'S COUNTRY TITLES

One-Pan Wonders

Cook It in Cast Iron

Cook's Country Eats Local

The Complete Cook's Country TV Show Cookbook

FOR A FULL LISTING OF ALL OUR BOOKS

CooksIllustrated.com

AmericasTestKitchen.com

praise for other america's test kitchen titles

Selected as the Cookbook Award Winner of 2017 in the Baking Category
INTERNATIONAL ASSOCIATION OF CULINARY PROFESSIONALS (IACP) ON *BREAD ILLUSTRATED*

"With 1,000 photos and the expertise of the America's Test Kitchen editors, this title might be the definitive book on bread baking."
PUBLISHERS WEEKLY ON *BREAD ILLUSTRATED*

"The editors at America's Test Kitchen pack decades of baking experience into this impressive volume of 250 recipes . . . You'll find a wealth of keeper recipes within these pages."
LIBRARY JOURNAL (STARRED REVIEW) ON *THE PERFECT COOKIE*

"A terrifically accessible and useful guide to grilling in all its forms that sets a new bar for its competitors on the bookshelf . . . The book is packed with practical advice, simple tips, and approachable recipes."
PUBLISHERS WEEKLY (STARRED REVIEW) ON *MASTER OF THE GRILL*

"This encyclopedia of meat cookery would feel completely overwhelming if it weren't so meticulously organized and artfully designed. This is *Cook's Illustrated* at its finest."
THE KITCHN ON *THE COOK'S ILLUSTRATED MEAT BOOK*

Selected as one of Amazon's Best Books of 2015 in the Cookbooks and Food Writing Category
AMAZON ON *THE COMPLETE VEGETARIAN COOKBOOK*

"This book is a comprehensive, no-nonsense guide . . . a well-thought-out, clearly explained primer for every aspect of home baking."
THE WALL STREET JOURNAL ON *THE COOK'S ILLUSTRATED BAKING BOOK*

"Cooks with a powerful sweet tooth should scoop up this well-researched recipe book for healthier takes on classic sweet treats."
BOOKLIST ON *NATURALLY SWEET*

"The 21st-century *Fannie Farmer Cookbook* or *The Joy of Cooking*. If you had to have one cookbook and that's all you could have, this one would do it."
CBS SAN FRANCISCO ON *THE NEW FAMILY COOKBOOK*

"The go-to gift book for newlyweds, small families, or empty nesters."
ORLANDO SENTINEL ON *THE COMPLETE COOKING FOR TWO COOKBOOK*

"The sum total of exhaustive experimentation . . . anyone interested in gluten-free cookery simply shouldn't be without it."
NIGELLA LAWSON ON *THE HOW CAN IT BE GLUTEN-FREE COOKBOOK*

"A one-volume kitchen seminar, addressing in one smart chapter after another the sometimes surprising whys behind a cook's best practices . . . You get the myth, the theory, the science, and the proof, all rigorously interrogated as only America's Test Kitchen can do."
NPR ON *THE SCIENCE OF GOOD COOKING*

"The perfect kitchen home companion . . . The practical side of things is very much on display . . . cook-friendly and kitchen-oriented, illuminating the process of preparing food instead of mystifying it."
THE WALL STREET JOURNAL ON *THE COOK'S ILLUSTRATED COOKBOOK*

"Another winning cookbook from ATK . . . The folks at America's Test Kitchen apply their rigorous experiments to determine the facts about these pans."
BOOKLIST ON *COOK IT IN CAST IRON*

"Some 2,500 photos walk readers through 600 painstakingly tested recipes, leaving little room for error."
ASSOCIATED PRESS ON *THE AMERICA'S TEST KITCHEN COOKING SCHOOL COOKBOOK*

"An exceptional resource for novice canners, though preserving veterans will find plenty here to love as well."
LIBRARY JOURNAL (STARRED REVIEW) ON *FOOLPROOF PRESERVING*

the new ESSENTIALS cookbook

A Modern Guide to Better Cooking

America's Test Kitchen

Copyright © 2018
by America's Test Kitchen

Library of Congress Cataloging-in-Publication Data

Names: America's Test Kitchen (Firm)
Title: The new essentials cookbook : a modern guide to better cooking / America's Test Kitchen.
Description: Boston, MA : America's Test Kitchen, [2018] | Includes index.
Identifiers: LCCN 2018017355 | ISBN 9781945256042 (hardcover)
Subjects: LCSH: Cooking. | LCGFT: Cookbooks.
Classification: LCC TX714 .N492 2018 | DDC 641.5--dc23
LC record available at https://lccn.loc.gov/2018017355

America's Test Kitchen
21 Drydock Avenue, Boston, MA 02210
Manufactured in the United States of America
10 9 8 7 6 5 4 3 2 1

Distributed by Penguin Random House Publisher Services
Tel: 800.733.3000

Pictured on front cover **Shrimp Pad Thai** (page 290)
Pictured on title page **Spaghetti with Spring Vegetables (page 278)**
Pictured on introduction page **Olive Oil–Yogurt Bundt Cake (page 414)**

Editorial Director, Books **Elizabeth Carduff**
Executive Editor **Adam Kowit**
Senior Editors **Leah Colins and Sara Mayer**
Associate Editor **Rachel Greenhaus**
Editorial Assistant **Alyssa Langer**
Design Director, Books **Carole Goodman**
Art Director **Lindsey Chandler**
Deputy Art Directors **Allison Boales and Jen Kanavos Hoffman**
Associate Art Director **Katie Barranger**
Production Designer **Reinaldo Cruz**
Photography Director **Julie Bozzo Cote**
Photography Producer **Meredith Mulcahy**
Senior Staff Photographer **Daniel J. van Ackere**
Staff Photographer **Steve Klise**
Additional Photography **Keller + Keller and Carl Tremblay**
Food Styling **Catrine Kelty, Kendra McKnight, Marie Piraino, Elle Simone Scott, and Sally Staub**
Photoshoot Kitchen Team
    Manager **Timothy McQuinn**
    Lead Test Cook **Daniel Cellucci**
    Assistant Test Cooks **Sarah Ewald, Eric Haessler, Mady Nichas, and Jessica Rudolph**
Production Director **Guy Rochford**
Senior Production Manager **Jessica Lindheimer Quirk**
Production Manager **Christine Spanger**
Imaging Manager **Lauren Robbins**
Production and Imaging Specialists **Heather Dube, Dennis Noble, and Jessica Voas**
Copy Editor **Deri Reed**
Proofreaders **Jane Tunks Demel and Elizabeth Wray Emery**
Indexer **Elizabeth Parson**

Chief Creative Officer **Jack Bishop**
Executive Editorial Directors **Julia Collin Davison and Bridget Lancaster**

contents

WELCOME TO AMERICA'S TEST KITCHEN

This book has been tested, written, and edited by the folks at America's Test Kitchen. Located in Boston's Seaport District in the historic Innovation and Design Building, it features 15,000 square feet of kitchen space including multiple photography and video studios. It is the home of *Cook's Illustrated* magazine and *Cook's Country* magazine and the workday destination for more than 60 test cooks, editors, and cookware specialists. Our mission is to test recipes over and over again until we understand how and why they work and until we arrive at the best version for each one.

We start the process of testing a recipe with a complete lack of preconceptions, which means that we accept no claim, no technique, and no recipe at face value. We simply assemble as many variations as possible, test a half-dozen of the most promising, and taste the results blind. We then construct our own recipe and continue to test it, varying ingredients, techniques, and cooking times until we reach a consensus. As we like to say in the test kitchen, "We make the mistakes so you don't have to." The result, we hope, is the best version of a particular recipe, but we realize that only you can be the final judge of our success (or failure). We use the same rigorous approach when we test equipment and taste test ingredients.

All of this would not be possible without a belief that good cooking, much like good music, is based on a foundation of objective technique. Some people like spicy foods and others don't, but there is a right way to sauté, there is a best way to cook a pot roast, and there are measurable scientific principles involved in producing perfectly beaten, stable egg whites. Our ultimate goal is to investigate the fundamental principles of cooking to give you the techniques, tools, and ingredients that you need to become a better cook. It is as simple as that.

To see what goes on behind the scenes at America's Test Kitchen, check out our social media channels for kitchen snapshots, exclusive content, video tips, and much more. You can watch us work (in our actual test kitchen) by tuning in to *America's Test Kitchen* or *Cook's Country* on public television or on our websites. Listen in to test kitchen experts on public radio (SplendidTable.org) to hear insights that illuminate the truth about real home cooking. Want to hone your cooking skills or finally learn how to bake with an America's Test Kitchen test cook? Enroll in one of our online cooking classes. However you choose to visit us, we welcome you into our kitchen, where you can stand by our side as we test our way to the best recipes in America.

facebook.com/AmericasTestKitchen
twitter.com/TestKitchen
youtube.com/AmericasTestKitchen
instagram.com/TestKitchen
pinterest.com/TestKitchen
google.com/+AmericasTestKitchen

AmericasTestKitchen.com
CooksIllustrated.com
CooksCountry.com
OnlineCookingSchool.com

INTRODUCTION

There are plenty of reasons to get more comfortable in the kitchen, develop better skills, and acquire a repertoire of dishes you enjoy making and can confidently cook. First, you'll feed yourself—and others—better food, probably more healthfully and more cheaply than you were before. Second, it's empowering to look at a chicken (or an eggplant or a half-dozen eggs) and know you can turn it into something delicious. Cooking is also one of the simplest ways to share something you've created with others, and the process itself can even become a meditative source of pleasure.

Most of us can cook at least something for ourselves, but what makes a confident cook? You certainly don't need to go to cooking school to cook well, but the way most of us learn to cook—through a combination of helping parents or grandparents, watching random episodes of cooking shows, and/or trying out any recipe that sounds good—can leave our culinary education feeling a bit haphazard. Even those of us who have cooked for years can feel like we don't have a clear handle on certain essentials.

When should you reach for a nonstick skillet, for example? (Whenever you want? Or sometimes not?) How do you cook fish fillets that stay moist, or fry an egg that maintains a runny yolk? And what even counts as essential these days? Making a lasagna, probably, but what about the pad thai you order every week? A perfect steak, sure, but what about having the perfect vegetarian main dish in your back pocket? This book answers these questions and many more. The recipes will help you develop your cooking skills while building a solid set of dishes you can count on—whether for breakfast, Wednesday's dinner, or your first dinner party.

But solid needn't mean boring! Even if you're new to cooking, that's no reason to limit yourself with flavors. You just need an approachable recipe. That's why our new essentials include not only the perfect weeknight roast chicken and a killer banana bread, but also a Turkish-inspired tomato soup, luscious Chinese braised short ribs, and a set of grain bowls that will become regular go-tos. We've got a great burger for you whether you want to use beef, pork, or beans. And if you do think pad thai is out of reach, try our everyday version.

You don't need a kitchen full of fancy equipment to cook great food. In the first part of the book, you'll find the elements of setting up and making use of your kitchen, covering all the equipment you need and the fundamental skills you'll use every time you cook. Try those skills out in the second part, "The Simplest Way to Cook Everything." Here you'll learn to fry that perfect runny egg, braise hearty greens, and sear restaurant-caliber steaks and chops—all building-block dishes that you can serve a new way each time you make them.

From here, chapters become slightly more advanced as they progress. As you move (and cook) through the recipes, you can read about broader aspects of cooking in our "Think Like a Cook" boxes. Learn the connection between salt and moisture, how to properly soften rice noodles, why we love to roast food on a wire rack, and the best way to fix a stew when you went a little overboard on the salt and it's all gone a bit off the rails. This is the kind of thinking used by seasoned cooks, and we hope it serves to give you a deeper understanding about flavor, technique, timing, and the entire experience of cooking.

Of course, to truly become a better cook, you just have to roll up your sleeves and get started. Begin with the very basics or jump to what interests you. Make the supersimple smashed cucumber salad spiked with Sichuan chili oil first if you like. Or skip straight to dessert. Whatever you make, it helps to have a trustworthy guide in the kitchen. We hope to be that for you.

DINNER AT A GLANCE

For quick meal inspiration, here are the book's main dishes and side dishes, by category:

Much as wearing the right pair of shoes can make all the difference as you navigate through your day, having the right equipment, ingredients, and familiarity with some basic techniques puts you on solid footing in the kitchen. Good-quality equipment can repay its value many times over: You'll feel like a superstar chef the first time you chop something with a sharp, sturdy knife if you have previously made do with dull blades. And a wide cutting board that lets you spread out makes that chopping go so much easier. The same holds for good-quality ingredients, which needn't mean pricey or fancy. Here you'll find out how to outfit a kitchen smartly, starting with the true essentials and building from there, as well as the basics of storing food for maximum freshness.

When it comes to techniques, a few will be used so often they will become almost as second nature as tying your shoes (holding a knife, for example). So take the time to learn to do these kitchen tasks the right way. We also show how to prepare a variety of vegetables and fruits and provide an overview of the methods that constitute the basic vocabulary of cooking, from boiling to roasting.

Remember: A recipe is a road map. You're the one making (and eating) the food. And we all have different tastes. An extra sprinkle of salt or squeeze of lemon will ensure food tastes the way you like it. You'll find information and advice here for making a dish your own.

A WALK THROUGH
YOUR KITCHEN

10 HABITS OF A GOOD COOK

1 Read the Recipe Carefully and Follow the Directions—at Least the First Time

Almost everyone has embarked upon preparing a recipe only to realize midway through that the dish needs hours of chilling before it can be served or that it calls for a special pan that you don't own. By reading the recipe through before you start to cook, you will avoid any surprises along the way. We also recommend making the recipe as directed the first time you cook it—once you understand the recipe, you can improvise and make it your own, but first you have to give it a fair shot as written.

2 Be Prepared (It's Not Just for Boy Scouts)

Set out and organize your *mise en place* (see page 24) before you start to cook: Track down all the equipment you will need for the recipe and prep all the ingredients (be sure to prepare the ingredients as instructed—food that is uniformly and properly cut will cook more evenly AND look better). A recipe is a lot simpler to make when all the components and tools you need are at your fingertips. That way your pasta won't overcook when you can't find your colander at the last minute and you won't forget to add the baking soda to your cake.

3 Start with Good Ingredients

Don't expect to turn old eggs into a nicely risen soufflé or make a stunning salad from the wilting greens that have been in your fridge for two weeks. Freshness matters, and the components you use can make or break your dish.

4 Keep Substitutions to a Minimum—No, Seriously

We've all done it—used brown sugar when there's no granulated sugar in the pantry, subbed in whatever cheese we have on hand for the Gruyère in the recipe, poured the batter into a square pan when the round pan was nowhere to be found. There are certain substitutions that can work in a pinch—see page 454 for our list of emergency problem solvers—but in general you should use the ingredients and equipment called for in the recipe. This is especially true in baking, where even the slightest change can spell disaster. And if you use a 10-inch skillet when a 12-inch is called for, you'll never get the sear you're looking for on that chicken.

5 Always Preheat

Most ovens need at least 15 minutes to preheat fully. Plan accordingly. If you don't preheat your oven correctly, then your food will spend more time in the oven and, as a result, will likely be dry and overcooked (and baked goods may suffer more dire consequences). Also, position the racks in the oven as directed—cookies that brown properly on the middle rack may overbrown when baked on the lower rack. These warnings also apply to preheating your pans on the stovetop. The temperature of the cooking surface will drop the minute food is added, so don't rush the preheating step. Wait for the oil to shimmer when cooking vegetables, and wait until you see the first wisps of smoke rise from the oil when you're cooking proteins.

6 Monitor the Dish as It Cooks

Ovens and stovetops can vary in intensity. And maybe you cut those carrots slightly larger than when we prepared the recipe. These little differences are why we often give a range when providing cooking times. You should treat cooking times as solid guidelines, but it is also important to follow the visual cues provided in the recipe. And don't wait until the prescribed time has elapsed to check the doneness of a particular dish: It is good practice to start checking 5 to 10 minutes before the recipe says the food will be done.

7 Taste the Dish Before Serving

Most recipes end by instructing the cook to adjust the seasoning "to taste." This means you actually have to taste the food. We generally write our recipes so you're seasoning the food pretty lightly throughout the cooking process and then adding more as needed at the end. Foods that will be served chilled, such as gazpacho, should be tasted again when they are cold, since cold mutes the effect of seasonings. Don't forget that there are other ways to season besides salt and pepper—see page 46 for some guidelines.

8 Learn from Your Mistakes— Your Education in the Kitchen Is a Lifelong Project

Even the experienced cooks in our test kitchen often turn out less-than-perfect food. (You have to work through the duds to get to the best possible recipes!) A good cook is able to analyze failure, pinpoint the cause, and then avoid that pitfall next time. A good cook also notices when something works particularly well, such as a combination of ingredients or a particular technique. Above all, a good cook is always learning. Don't make a new dish every night of the year; if you find something you like, prepare it again and again until you master it and add it to your regular repertoire.

9 Know the Lingo

Some recipes are precise blueprints, specifying particular sizes, shapes, quantities, and cooking times. Other recipes are rough sketches that leave the cook to fill in the blanks. In addition to the level of detail supplied by the recipe writer, the level of knowledge the cook brings varies tremendously. Unfamiliar terminology can be a big problem, especially for novice cooks trying to work their way through a recipe—if you aren't sure what a word means, check before proceeding with the recipe. Read about common cooking techniques starting on page 40; then see Talk Like a Cook on page 440 for additional often-used terms.

10 Enjoy Yourself. Food Should Be Fun!

In the end, a successful cook is someone who enjoys cooking. Yes, sometimes you just need to feed yourself, and there are plenty of recipes in this book for quick and painless meals when you aren't feeling up to assembling a three-course feast. But even the simplest cooking tasks can be enjoyable. Take pride in your accomplishments. If you enjoy cooking, you will get in the kitchen more often—and practice really does make perfect.

YOUR KITCHEN STARTER KIT

If you're just starting out in the kitchen, it's easy to get overwhelmed by the variety of gear available. Despite the marketing hype, however, you don't actually need a lot of fancy equipment and gadgets in order to cook well. Start with this list of the real basics: You won't be able to tackle every recipe, but you'll have a solid base to work from. See our recommendations for specific brands on pages 443–451.

All-Around Spatulas
Spatulas are your friend for everything from flipping burgers to serving lasagna. You need a plastic spatula to protect nonstick pans and a metal spatula for traditional pans.

Baking Dishes
These versatile dishes are ideal for large casseroles and baked goods. We recommend starting with a 13 by 9-inch porcelain dish; see page 445 for more information.

Can Opener
How else will you open tuna, beans, and SpaghettiOs? Openers that cut into the side of the can (not the top) leave dull edges and save fingers.

Cutting Board
Get a board with plenty of space (at least 20 by 15 inches). Wooden and plastic boards are both great; look for one that's sturdy but still soft enough that it won't beat up your knives.

Dutch Oven
Invest in a big enameled cast-iron Dutch oven and you'll use it forever for everything from stews to frying and even baking bread. Built for both stovetop and oven use, a Dutch oven retains heat well, so it can maintain a low simmer. Choose one with wide handles and a tight-fitting lid.

Instant-Read Thermometer
A fast, accurate digital thermometer is the best way to know when food is done. See pages 20–21 for more information.

Knives
Most knife sets are loaded with superfluous pieces. We consider just three knives essential: a chef's knife, a paring knife, and a serrated knife. For more information see "Cut Out for Greatness," page 23.

Measuring Tools
Essential measuring tools include dry measuring cups, a 2-cup liquid measuring cup, and measuring spoons. See page 448 for more information.

Mixing Bowls
Get bowls in a variety of sizes—at the very least, small (1- to 1½-quart), medium (2½- to 3-quart), and large (4- to 6-quart). Get two sets: stainless steel and glass. Lighter metal is convenient most of the time, but glass is necessary for the microwave.

Pepper Mill
Adding freshly ground pepper is one of the simplest ways to improve your food. Go for a manually operated model with an efficient, comfortable grinding mechanism.

Rimmed Baking Sheets/Wire Rack
We use rimmed baking sheets for everything from roasting vegetables to baking cookies. Fitted with a wire rack, it even becomes a roasting pan. Get at least two: They don't cost much and you'll use them all the time.

Saucepans
Get a 3- to 4-quart saucepan for sauces and vegetables plus a 2-quart nonstick one for foods that stick easily and reheating leftovers.

Silicone Spatula
Nothing is better suited to a multitude of tasks, be it reaching into the corners of bowls and pots, stirring batters, or folding egg whites, than a heatproof silicone spatula.

Skillets
Our best all-purpose skillet pick is a large (12-inch) traditional stainless steel and aluminum skillet. For more information about other options, see "Which Skillet Is Which?"

Tongs
Like an extension of your hand, a sturdy pair of stainless-steel tongs can lift or flip most any type of food.

Wooden Spoon
Basic, yes, but you won't get far without a durable wooden spoon.

which skillet is which?

If you do any amount of serious cooking, you will want at least one traditional and one nonstick skillet (cast iron and carbon steel can also function as nonstick). We recommend owning a smaller (8- or 10-inch) skillet and a large 12-inch skillet, both oven-safe with tight-fitting lids.

Traditional Tri-Ply
We prefer traditional skillets made of stainless steel sandwiched around an aluminum core. The finish (which is NOT nonstick) helps develop fond, the caramelized brown bits that stick to the bottom of the pan.

Nonstick
The coating on nonstick pans helps delicate foods like fish, pancakes, and eggs release easily. The nonstick coating will wear out over time, so choose a relatively inexpensive option.

Cast Iron
A cast-iron skillet (shown on page 444) excels at searing and, if well seasoned, releases food as well as a nonstick surface. However, it does require extra effort to build and maintain its seasoning, so keep that in mind.

Carbon Steel
Carbon steel (shown on page 444) also needs to be seasoned, but once it is, it offers the versatility of a traditional pan, the heat retention of cast iron at a lighter weight, and the slick release of a good nonstick skillet.

pro tools for home cooks

Most gadgets used in a professional kitchen are unnecessary for a home cook, but here a few we find actually pretty useful.

Prep Bowls

A trained chef's *mise en place* includes prepped ingredients corralled into small containers to make them easily accessible. This setup is also a great tool for home cooks. We like small, sturdy glass prep bowls.

Dish Towels

Handy, flexible cotton dish towels can be anything from a potholders to strainers to, yes, dish rags. Keep a stack of clean ones on hand at all times.

Digital Scale

If you're careful (see page 38), you can get pretty accurate results with measuring cups and spoons, but they'll never match the precision of a scale. This is particularly true for baking, where an extra ounce of flour can ruin a recipe.

Honing Steel/Knife Sharpener

Most of the chefs we know are obsessed with keeping their knives sharp. Professional sharpening is an option, but it's a lot more convenient to do it yourself. You can start by using a honing steel. When steeling isn't enough, use a manual or electric sharpener. For more information, see page 23.

TOOLS OF THE TRADE

The items in this section will make your life much easier and more efficient. You should stock your kitchen so it works for you; choose the equipment that you find helpful and skip the rest, no matter the trends. See our recommendations for specific brands in the shopping guide on pages 443–451.

Balloon Whisk
A skinny balloon-style whisk with wires that curve out just a little bit is the best all-purpose tool; it can mix batters, beat eggs or cream, and make a pan sauce on the stove.

Citrus Juicer
While you can juice citrus without a tool (or with a fork), it's much more efficient to use a juicer. Unless you're juicing dozens of oranges every day, you probably only need a manual juicer, not an electric model.

Fat Separator
You can skim fat with a spoon, but a fat separator is more effective. We prefer models that drain from the bottom, since they make it easier to keep any fat from sneaking out with the liquid.

Fine-Mesh Strainer
A fine-mesh strainer is great for rinsing rice, washing vegetables, sifting flour or confectioners' sugar, and straining sauces. Make sure the mesh really is fine, so nothing slips through the holes. You may also want a colander for draining pasta.

Garlic Press
For most home cooks, a garlic press is a much easier way to get a fine, even mince or paste than using a knife. With a good press, you don't even have to peel the cloves first.

Grater
A box grater with a variety of easy-to-use planes can handle almost any task. We also love rasp-style graters. These wand-like tools are ideal for finely grating Parmesan, garlic, nutmeg, chocolate, and citrus zest.

Kitchen Shears
A pair of kitchen shears is one of the best all-around tools, useful for butter-flying chicken, trimming pie dough, shaping parchment paper, snipping herbs, and cutting kitchen twine.

Ladle
A long ladle makes it easier to scoop and serve soup. One with a shallow bowl is also helpful for scraping the bottom of the pot.

Oven Thermometer
We hate to break it to you, but your oven might not be as accurate as you think it is (see page 423). For reliable, consistent results, a good oven thermometer is critical.

Pastry Brush
A sturdy pastry brush with silicone bristles can handle a range of tasks, from spreading thick barbecue sauce on meat to delicately painting egg wash on pastry. Silicone is easy to clean and doesn't hold onto stains or odors.

Potato Masher
While you'll need a ricer or food mill for truly velvety mashed potatoes (see page 208), a classic handheld masher is a solid backup choice.

Rolling Pin
We prefer the classic French-style handle-free wood rolling pins; they easily turn and pivot and allow you to feel the thickness of the dough and apply pressure as needed. Look for a pin that's about 20 inches long.

Salad Spinner
This one-purpose gadget might seem like a waste, but it's really the best way to get greens and other produce clean and dry. Choose one with a large basket and a pump mechanism.

Slotted Spoon
Use this for scooping and draining small or delicate foods from boiling water, hot oil, or sauce. We prefer a no-frills stainless-steel model. A spider skimmer, which is larger with more open area for drainage, can also be useful when blanching and frying.

Vegetable Peeler
A good peeler should be fast and smooth, shaving off just enough of the skin to avoid the need for repeat trips over the same section but not so much that the blade digs deeply into the flesh and wastes food. Look for stainless- or carbon-steel blades.

THE EASY (AND ELECTRONIC) UPGRADES

If you want to cook every recipe in this book successfully, you'll need a few extra items. Most of these aren't things you'll use every day, but when you need them, you'll be glad to have them. That's especially true of the small appliances listed here—in particular, the food processor, which we use for everything from pureeing vegetables to kneading bread and pasta dough. See our recommendations for specific brands in the shopping guide on pages 443–451.

APPLIANCES

Blender
A blender is the only tool that can bring foods (hot or cold) to a uniformly smooth texture, whether you're making milkshakes and frozen drinks or pureeing soups and sauces. You might also consider an immersion blender, which is useful for small jobs like blending salad dressings and pureeing soup right in the pot.

Electric Mixer
A handheld mixer is lightweight, easy to use, and great for most basic tasks, like whipping cream or egg whites, creaming butter and sugar, and making a batter; the only thing it can't handle is kneading dough. But that's no problem for a stand mixer. If you are a serious cook or baker, a stand mixer is simply something you need. If you bake only occasionally, a handheld mixer is fine. Either will work with the recipes in this book.

Electric Spice/Coffee Grinder
Freshly ground whole spices have a superior aroma and roundness of flavor versus preground spices. The test kitchen standard for grinding spices is a blade-type electric coffee grinder.

Food Processor
If you are investing in one big-ticket appliance, it should be a food processor. It can chop foods that blenders can't handle, as well as slice and shred and mix up batters and doughs.

POTS AND PANS

Roasting Pan
This is our go-to for tackling large cuts of meat; its ample size can even accommodate both a roast and side dish. Measure your oven before shopping to ensure a large, tall pan will fit, and make sure the pan has a V-rack.

Stockpot
Pick an all-purpose 12-quart pot that can handle a variety of tasks, from steaming lobsters to canning to making huge batches of homemade stock. We prefer a tall, narrow pot with a thick bottom to prevent scorching.

Muffin Tin
Darker pans produce darker baked goods; lighter pans produce lighter ones. We gravitate to gold-colored muffin tins (and many other pans) for browning that's right in the middle.

Round Cake Pans (9-Inch)
To bake perfect cake layers, look for light-colored pans at least 2 inches tall. Eight-inch pans are also popular.

Baking Pans
We use an 8-inch square baking pan in this book for brownies and bars. A 13 by 9-inch pan is also quite useful.

Loaf Pan
Size matters with loaf pans. We use an 8½ by 4½-inch pan. If yours is 9 by 5 inches, you'll need to adjust the baking time as the recipe indicates.

Bundt Pan
This decorative pan produces cakes that require little adornment. Make sure it's heavy and nonstick.

Springform Pan (9-Inch)
A springform pan's sides release, allowing you to unmold delicate cakes without having to invert them.

Pie Plate
We don't get into pies in this book but do use pie plates in other ways, such as dredging food in bread crumbs and pressing tortillas.

STAPLE INGREDIENTS YOU WILL COUNT ON

Your pantry is an ever-evolving collection of ingredients that reflects the kinds of food you enjoy cooking and eating. There are no hard-and-fast requirements, but this list presents many of the ingredients we most often call for in our recipes and which we think make the basis for a strong, adaptable home pantry. There are bound to be plenty of other foods that you consider must-haves, but you won't get very far into most recipes without at least a few of these staples.

Butter
We like unsalted butter for cooking and baking, but salted butter is great for spreading on toast or homemade Buttermilk Drop Biscuits (page 426).

Cheese
The type(s) depend on your taste, but we recommend at least having Parmesan, which is a common ingredient and also good as a topping. Buy the real thing and grate it yourself. Feta and cheddar are also versatile staples.

Eggs
It's hard to overstate how many things you can do with eggs. They are one of the most versatile and valuable items in your pantry. We always call for large eggs in our recipes.

Milk
Low-fat milk is the most versatile. We often turn to whole milk and buttermilk when baking.

Yogurt
For eating plain and for recipes, we prefer whole-milk yogurt. We're also big fans of Greek yogurt, which has a smooth, thick, decadent texture.

Bacon
From brunch to vegetable sides, bacon livens up pretty much any dish. Good bacon has balanced meaty, smoky, salty, and sweet flavors. We prefer cured, dry-smoked versions.

Lemons and Limes
A squeeze of citrus can be just the thing to brighten up a dish. Keep lemons and limes in the refrigerator until you need them.

Dried Fruit
Almost any fruit can be dried; the drying process concentrates flavor and sugar. Try dried fruit in salads, granola, or baked goods, or on cheese plates.

Garlic
Everyday garlic is the base of a ridiculous number of recipes, in cuisines from Asian to Italian to down-home barbecue. Don't get caught without it.

Onions
Yellow onions are our first choice for cooking for their rich flavor. Red onions are great grilled or raw in salad or salsa (sweet onions are also best raw). White onions are similar to yellow onions but lack their complexity.

Shallots
With a complex, subtly sweet flavor, shallots are ideal in sauces, where they melt into the texture, and in vinaigrettes, where they add gentle heat.

Ginger
Fresh ginger has a bite and pungency that you just can't get from powdered ginger. It also makes up part of the flavor base for many Asian recipes.

Olives
As a pantry staple, we like jarred brine-cured black and green olives. For the best texture, buy unpitted olives and pit them yourself.

Potatoes
These fall into three categories (baking, boiling, and all-purpose) based on their starch levels/textures. Make sure you know which you have, since you can't always use any type and expect great results (see "Choosing the Right Potato," page 211).

Chiles
Dried chiles, chile flakes, and canned chipotle chiles in adobo sauce are all great shelf-stable standbys for when you need to turn up the heat a little.

secret ingredients: take your cooking to the next level

Good old basics are great, but sometimes you need a little something special to jazz up a dish. The ingredients in this list might seem a little unorthodox as pantry staples, but folks in the test kitchen swear by their ability to improve pretty much any food you add them to.

Harissa
A dollop of this bright, spicy North African paste can enliven vegetables, eggs, lamb, and soups. The backbone of harissa—chiles—can vary greatly, as can the heat level, so we prefer to make our own (see page 101).

Tahini
This paste made from ground sesame seeds is most common in Middle Eastern dishes, but its nutty, buttery profile is a welcome addition in salads and grain dishes and on all types of meat and fish. We also love whole sesame seeds as a garnish.

Dukkah
This Egyptian condiment is a blend of nuts, seeds, and spices that adds texture and depth of flavor to dips, salads, and side dishes. (To make your own, see page 215.) Sprinkle it over something as simple as olive oil for dipping bread or yogurt for a leveled-up snack.

Chinese Black Vinegar
This type of vinegar is aged to develop its complex flavor, which contributes earthy notes with hints of warm spice to any dish it's added to. We like it in dipping sauces or simple, high-impact salads like our Smashed Cucumber Salad (page 158).

Miso
Commonly found in Asian cuisines (most notably Japanese), this incredibly versatile ingredient is a fermented paste of soybeans and rice, barley, or rye. It is salty and ranges in strength and color. Lighter misos are typically used in more delicate dishes like soups and salads while darker misos are best in heavier recipes.

Gochujang

Gochujang is a Korean chile bean paste that has a smooth consistency and a rich, spicy flavor. In addition to being made into a sauce for bibimbap (see Korean Chile Sauce, page 103), it can be added to salads, stews, soups, and marinades.

Fish Sauce

This salty liquid is made from fermented fish and is used as an ingredient and a condiment in Southeast Asian cuisines. In small amounts, it adds a well-rounded, salty flavor to sauces, soups, and marinades.

Pomegranate Molasses

Made by reducing pomegranate juice down to a syrup, pomegranate molasses has a unique, sweet-sour flavor. Use it to add complex tanginess to grain salads, glazed meats, and more.

Smoked Paprika

A Spanish favorite, smoked paprika is produced by drying peppers (either sweet or hot) over smoldering oak embers. Since smoked paprika has a deep, musky flavor all its own, it is best used to season grilled meats or to add a smoky aroma to boldly flavored dishes (even if they've never been near an open flame).

Dried Porcini Mushrooms

We often turn to dried porcini to add potent savory flavor to dishes. Because the mushrooms are dried, their flavor is concentrated and they are conveniently shelf-stable. You can grind the porcini into a fine powder using a spice grinder or mortar and pestle and then sprinkle this savory magic dust on pretty much anything you can think of to give it a meaty boost.

Canned Tomatoes

Since canned tomatoes are processed at the height of freshness, they deliver more flavor than off-season fresh tomatoes. We rely on them in a variety of contexts. Canned whole tomatoes, diced tomatoes, crushed tomatoes, pureed tomatoes, and tomato paste all have their place; see page 319 for more information.

Frozen Vegetables

Many kinds of frozen vegetables make solid stand-ins for fresh. Frozen peas can even be sweeter than fresh ones, since they are frozen at the very peak of ripeness. For more information, see "When Frozen Vegetables Are the Best Choice," page 125.

Oil

Vegetable oil (we prefer canola) is a workhorse because of its neutral taste. Extra-virgin olive oil is great for cooking, as a condiment, or in a vinaigrette. Peanut oil works well for frying. Many other cooking and finishing oils are available, depending on your tastes and needs.

Vinegar

The types you should keep in your cupboard depend on what you like to use. We recommend having at least three: white wine vinegar, red wine vinegar, and balsamic vinegar.

Broth

In the test kitchen we rarely go a day without using chicken broth, and not just in soup. We also recommend keeping vegetable broth and beef broth on hand. Homemade is great (see our recipes starting on page 270), but store-bought works perfectly well in most applications.

Beans

When beans are the star of a dish, we prefer the superior flavor and texture of dried beans, but nine times out of ten, we rely on the convenience of canned beans. Our staples are black beans, cannellini beans, pinto beans, red kidney beans, and chickpeas.

Hot Sauce

Even cooks who don't crave spicy foods should keep a bottle of hot sauce on hand to give recipes a little kick. Find a brand that you enjoy. We like one with a little sugar in it to balance the heat with sweetness (see page 289 for more information).

Ketchup

We prefer ketchups made with sugar instead of high-fructose corn syrup; they have a cleaner, purer sweetness and fewer off-flavors.

Mayonnaise

A good supermarket mayonnaise can rival homemade and certainly keeps for much longer. The best-tasting brands have the fewest ingredients.

Mustard

Mild yellow mustard is the most popular in American cupboards, but we use Dijon more frequently in recipes. You may also want spicy brown, whole-grain, or honey mustard.

Soy Sauce

This dark, salty fermented liquid is a common ingredient and condiment in Asian cuisines that enhances umami flavor and contributes complexity.

Tuna

For a basic everyday canned tuna, look for wild albacore packed in water. If you like a fancier option (that actually tastes like fish), try fillets packed in olive oil.

Anchovies

Even if you're not the type to eat these tiny fish right out of the tin, we recommend keeping some on hand. We use anchovies in a surprising number of recipes to build a strong umami (but not superfishy) base.

Panko Bread Crumbs

We prefer homemade bread crumbs, but for a convenient store-bought option, Japanese-style panko bread crumbs have superior crunch.

Pasta

There are many different shapes and sizes of dried pasta. We recommend stocking a few favorites for quick, no-fuss dinners. Dried Asian noodles also make a great pantry standby.

Rice and Grains

White rice is a classic staple but we also love nutty whole-grain brown rice. We also suggest you stock at least one other grain. We're partial to quinoa because it's quick-cooking, but there's a world of options.

Nuts

Keep a couple of your favorite nuts on hand for baking, granola, topping salads, and snacking. Store them in the freezer to prevent rancidity.

Peanut Butter

Not just for sandwiches, peanut butter is useful in baking and in sauces. Texture matters most here, so we prefer creamy traditional peanut butter to grittier "natural" versions.

Flour

There are many types of flour, and each has its place and uses. As its name suggests, all-purpose flour is the most versatile. We also call for whole-wheat flour, bread flour, and cake flour in certain recipes.

Cornmeal

For a basic baking cornmeal, look for fine-ground whole-grain yellow corn-meal. We recommend stone ground over commercially processed.

Baking Soda

This leavener is used to provide lift to baked goods that also contain an acidic ingredient (such as sour cream, buttermilk, or brown sugar).

Baking Powder

Baking powder provides leavening for baked goods that have no natural acidity in the batter (or to add extra lift alongside baking soda).

Yeast

We prefer instant (aka rapid-rise) yeast, which is the easiest to use; it can be added directly to the dry ingredients.

Sugar

White granulated sugar, brown sugar (light and dark can pretty much be used interchangeably), and confectioners' sugar are the most common sugars for baking and beyond.

Maple Syrup

Opt for 100 percent maple syrup rather than one blended with corn syrup (see page 139 for more information).

---

herbal how-tos

We frequently use a sprinkling of minced herbs to give dishes a fresh finish, or employ whole herb leaves to brighten salads or sandwiches. Parsley, cilantro, and basil are the ones we use most often. Try growing them in small pots in your kitchen so you always have them on hand. This can also help you avoid the all-too-common tragedy of buying a bunch of herbs and having almost all of it turn slimy before you can use it. If you're not up for gardening, proper storage is key: To get the most out of fresh herbs, gently rinse and dry them (a salad spinner works well), wrap in a damp paper towel, and place in a partially open zipper-lock bag in the crisper drawer. Basil is an exception; don't wash it until just before you need to use it.

Buy Fresh Only

For leafy herbs (basil, parsley, chives, mint, cilantro), fresh is the best option.

Dried Is Okay

If you're making a long-cooked recipe using heartier herbs (rosemary, oregano, sage, thyme), dried herbs can work. If you do substitute dried for fresh, you only need to use one-third as much of the dried version.

Freshness Matters for Dried Herbs, Too

Check dried herbs for freshness by crumbling a small amount between your fingers and taking a whiff. If they release a strong aroma, they're still good to go. If the smell and the color have faded, it's time to restock.

Honey

Try different honeys to see what you like. Strongly flavored varieties such as buckwheat honey are too assertive for cooking—save them for your tea.

Chocolate

Chocolate chips are probably the most convenient form, but we also like bars. We stock a dark chocolate with 60 percent cacao in addition to unsweetened baker's chocolate.

Cocoa Powder

You will find cocoa powder in both Dutch-processed and natural versions. Dutch-processed cocoa has been treated with alkali to neutralize the powder's acidity and mellow its astringent notes (it also darkens the color). Both types will work in most recipes, although Dutch-processed cocoa will produce baked goods with a darker color and moister texture.

Vanilla Extract

Get the real thing. Real vanilla extract has around 250 flavor compounds compared with imitation vanilla's one, giving it a unique complexity.

Black Peppercorns

Peppercorns' scent and flavor start to fade as soon as they're ground, so buy whole peppercorns and grind them as you use them.

Salt

Table salt is our go-to for most applications, while kosher salt is great for seasoning meat. Flaky sea salt is best reserved for finishing dishes. Because of varying crystal sizes, do not substitute one kind for another without using the chart on page 454.

your spice rack starter kit

If you're only buying a handful of spices to start your pantry, we recommend these (in addition to salt and pepper, of course!).

Cayenne Pepper

This fiery spice made from ground dried chiles has enough heat that you'll usually only need to use a pinch at a time.

Chili Powder

This blend of ground dried chiles, garlic powder, oregano, and cumin has not just heat but also multidimensional complexity.

Cinnamon

Ground cinnamon is a key ingredient for many baking recipes. Whole stick cinnamon can be used to infuse flavor into wine, cider, and even sauces.

Cumin

This earthy, warming spice is common in a wide variety of world cuisines.

Curry Powder

We prefer the mild formulation of this blend of spices, herbs, and seeds; it works equally well in recipes from traditional curries to baked goods.

spice smarts

» Spices start losing flavor as soon as you grind them, so buy them whole, not preground, whenever possible, and grind just before using, either with a small coffee grinder or a mortar and pestle.

» Label your herbs and spices with the purchase date and then regularly purge your pantry of jars that are more than 12 months old. Store in a cool, dark place to prolong freshness.

» Bulk spices aren't necessarily the freshest, but they can be useful if you need just a tiny amount of a very particular spice for one recipe.

refrigerator storage tips

Storing Meat
Storing meat on a rimmed baking sheet helps keep refrigerator shelves sanitary and allows other food items, such as fruits and vegetables, to be stored on the same shelf without risk of cross-contamination.

Storing Cheese
Wrap cheese first in parchment paper and then in aluminum foil. Store the wrapped cheese in the crisper or in an airtight plastic bag or container.

Storing Greens
To prevent bacterial growth, greens must be completely dried before being stored. Store washed and dried greens in paper towels in a zipper-lock bag left slightly open.

ANATOMY OF YOUR REFRIGERATOR

Your refrigerator is more than a box of cold air. There are actually different microenvironments inside a refrigerator and understanding how they work can help you use the various zones to your advantage and keep your meat, dairy, and produce fresh and flavorful.

COLD ZONE

Back, Top to Bottom

The area of the shelves at the back of the fridge (and the bottom of the door) are normally the coldest areas (around 33 degrees). Meat, dairy, and produce that is not prone to chilling injury (apples, cherries, grapes) should be stored in these areas. This is also the best place for prepared foods and leftovers.

MODERATE ZONE

Front, Top to Bottom

The areas at the front of the refrigerator, from the top to the bottom shelves, are generally moderate, with temperatures above 37 degrees. Put eggs, butter, and fruits and vegetables that are sensitive to chilling injury (berries, citrus, corn on the cob, melons) in this area. This also includes the top shelves on the door, which can be warmer and should therefore be reserved for items like beverages and condiments.

HUMID ZONE

Crisper Drawer

The crisper drawer provides a humid environment that helps keep produce with a high water content (artichokes, asparagus, beets, broccoli, cabbage, carrots, cauliflower, celery, chiles, cucumbers, eggplant, fresh herbs, green beans, leafy greens, leeks, lettuce, mushrooms, peppers, radishes, scallions, summer squash, turnips, zucchini) from shriveling and rotting. However, if the humidity is too high, water can accumulate and hasten spoilage. You can regulate the humidity by adjusting the vents; the more cold air that is let in, the less humid the environment will be. (If your crisper doesn't have a slide control, it is always at the highest humidity level of which it is capable.)

what not to store in the fridge

Some produce is sensitive to chilling injury and should be stored on the counter.

Apricots, Bananas*, Kiwis*, Mangos, Nectarines, Papayas, Peaches, Pears*, Pineapples, Plums, Tomatoes

*Once ripe, these can be refrigerated to avoid overripening. Some discoloration may occur.

Some produce also needs to be kept away from light and heat. Store these in the pantry at cool room temperature in a basket or other ventilated container.

Garlic, Onions, Potatoes, Shallots, Sweet Potatoes, Winter Squash

Storing bread in the refrigerator may seem like a good idea, but the cold speeds up the staling process. We store bread on the counter or in a bread box; otherwise we freeze it. The same is true for most baked goods.

FOOD SAFETY IN 10 EASY STEPS

Food safety may seem like a drag, but it can be a matter of life and death—or at least, life and extreme gastrointestinal discomfort. Luckily, it's actually pretty easy to keep your kitchen clean and safe. Most of our cleaning protocols are based on the judicious application of hot water, soap, and the occasional splash of bleach solution. Following basic sanitation practices can dramatically reduce the risk of foodborne illness for you and everyone else you're feeding.

1 Wash Your Hands

Washing your hands is one of the best (and easiest) ways to stop the spread of foodborne pathogens that can make you sick. Wash before and during cooking, especially after touching raw meat or poultry. The U.S. Food and Drug Administration (FDA) recommends washing for at least 20 seconds in warm, soapy water, i.e., for at least the length of the Happy Birthday song. So get scrubbing (and singing).

2 Sanitize Your Sink

Studies have found that the kitchen sink is crawling with even more bacteria than the garbage bin. The faucet handle, which can reintroduce bacteria to your hands after you've washed them, is a close second. Though we've found that hot, soapy water is amazingly effective at eliminating bacteria, for added insurance you should clean these areas frequently with a solution of 1 tablespoon bleach per quart of water.

3 Clean Your Gear

In terms of bacteria, your sponge is right up there with your sink. A wet sponge is an ideal host for bacteria, so whenever possible, use a paper towel or dishcloth instead. If you do use a sponge, disinfect it. Microwaving and boiling are effective ways to clean a sponge but since sponges have been known to catch fire in high-powered microwaves, we prefer to boil them for 5 minutes. Cutting boards are another key location for bacteria in the kitchen. We have found that cutting boards of all materials are best cleaned by a thorough scrub with hot, soapy water.

4 Season Safely

Though most bacteria can't live for more than a few minutes in direct contact with salt, it can live on the edges of a box or shaker. To avoid contamination, grind pepper into a clean small bowl and then mix it with salt. You can reach into the bowl for seasoning without washing your hands every time. At the end of meal prep, discard any leftover seasoning and wash the bowl.

5 Separate Raw and Cooked Foods
Keep raw and cooked foods separate to prevent the spread of bacteria. Never place cooked food on a plate or cutting board that came into contact with raw food (meat or not), and wash any utensil (including a thermometer) that comes in contact with raw food before reusing it.

6 Put Up Barriers
Items that come in contact with both raw and cooked food, like scales and platters, should be covered with aluminum foil or plastic wrap to create a protective barrier. Once the item has been used, the protective layer should be discarded—taking any bacteria with it. Similarly, wrapping your cutting board with plastic wrap before pounding meat and poultry on it will limit the spread of bacteria.

7 Don't Rinse Raw Meat and Poultry
Avoid rinsing raw meat and poultry. Contrary to what some cookbooks (or your grandmother) might advise, rinsing is more likely to spread contaminants around your sink than send them down the drain. Cooking food to a safe internal temperature will kill surface bacteria more effectively than rinsing, and we've found no difference in flavor between rinsed and unrinsed meat.

8 Defrost in the Fridge
Always defrost in the refrigerator. On the counter, the temperature is higher and bacteria multiply rapidly. Place food on a plate or in a bowl to collect any liquid it releases. Most food will take 24 hours to thaw. (Larger items, like whole turkeys, can take far longer, about 6 hours per pound.)

9 Cool on the Counter
Don't put hot food in the fridge right away. This will cause the temperature in the refrigerator to rise, potentially making it hospitable to the spread of bacteria. The FDA recommends cooling foods to 70 degrees within the first 2 hours after cooking, and to 40 degrees within another 4 hours. We cool food on the counter for about an hour and then put it in the fridge.

10 Reheat Rapidly
When food is reheated, it should be brought through the danger zone (the temperature range from 40 to 140 degrees, where bacteria thrive) as rapidly as possible—don't let it come slowly to a simmer. Bring leftover sauces, soups, and gravies to a boil and make sure casseroles reach at least 165 degrees.

WHEN IS FOOD DONE?

There's nothing like a spectacular kitchen failure featuring leathery meat, disintegrated vegetables, or, worse yet, billowing smoke to drive home the importance of timing in cooking. Don't just glance at the clock or assume your internal timekeeping will be reliable enough; always set a timer. You can get a special timer specifically designed for use in the kitchen, but you can also use a microwave timer, oven timer, or the timer on your phone; just make sure you have some way of keeping time. All that being said, don't rely solely on timing to guide your cooking—other types of cues are also incredibly important. And if a recipe presents a range of time for a step, always start checking for doneness at the early end of the range. Trust your senses and your common sense alongside your reading of the recipe.

USE YOUR EYES

Food changes color and appearance as it cooks; the difference between a crisp-tender, bright green piece of broccoli and a dull gray-green piece of overcooked broccoli is easy to see. And if you want good flavor on your chicken, don't take it out of the pan until it has good golden-brown color all over it.

USE YOUR NOSE

Many foods have a distinct aroma when they're done, such as toasted nuts, baked goods, or caramelized onions. And unless you're making a recipe that's purposefully blackened or charred, if you can smell something burning, you should check on it, even if the timer says you still have 20 minutes left.

USE A THERMOMETER— ESPECIALLY FOR MEAT

When it comes to final doneness, numbers don't lie; the best and most foolproof way to determine when food is done is to use a thermometer, not only for proteins but also bread and custardy desserts. A good one is vital for ensuring success in the kitchen. See page 449 for our brand recommendations.

USE A PARING KNIFE

The texture of most foods changes during cooking. In order to gauge these changes, use a sharp paring knife to test foods for doneness cues; do the potatoes yield easily or does the blade meet resistance? When you nick a piece of fish or thin cut of meat, is it still raw inside?

USE DOWNTIME

Don't forget about the magic of carry-over cooking and the importance of resting meat (see page 83 for much more information). Finished food often needs to rest after cooking in order for temperatures to equalize, juices to redistribute, and ingredients to cool enough that you won't burn your mouth. Your food isn't really done until this step is!

Slip a paring knife into food to "feel" for doneness; a vegetable is tender when it meets with little resistance.

CHECKING DONENESS

Always take the temperature of the area that will finish cooking last, which is the thickest part or, in some cases, the center. Bones conduct heat, so make sure the thermometer doesn't touch them. We recommend taking more than one reading to confirm doneness. For specific doneness temperatures, see the chart below.

Steaks, Chops, and Small Roasts

Use tongs to hold the meat, then insert the thermometer sideways into the center. You can also use this technique for pork tenderloin or rack of lamb; just lift the meat with a pair of tongs and insert the thermometer into the end.

Burgers

Leave the burger in the pan or on the grill (so it won't fall apart), slide the tip of the thermometer into the burger at the top edge, and push it toward the center, making sure to avoid hitting the pan (or grill) with the probe.

Poultry

Because breast meat cooks faster than thigh meat, you must take the temperature of both. Try to avoid hitting bones, cavities, or the surface of the pan, as this will result in an inaccurate reading. When temping a whole bird, use the following methods:

For Thigh Meat Insert the thermometer at an angle into the area between the drumstick and the breast, taking care not to hit the bone. It should register 175 degrees.

For Breast Meat Insert the thermometer from the neck end into a breast, holding the thermometer parallel to the bird. It should register 160 degrees.

If cooking chicken or turkey pieces, use the same techniques described above, while lifting the piece with tongs and inserting the thermometer sideways into the thickest part of the meat, taking care to avoid bones.

MEAT DONENESS TEMPERATURES

Since the temperature of meat will continue to rise as it rests, it should be taken off the heat just before it reaches the desired temperature. Note that this does not apply to poultry, which should be fully cooked before it is removed from the heat. For more information, see page 83.

TYPE OF MEAT	COOK UNTIL IT REGISTERS
Beef, Veal, Lamb	
Rare	115° to 120° (120° to 125° after resting)
Medium-Rare	120° to 125° (125° to 130° after resting)
Medium	130° to 135° (135° to 140° after resting)
Medium-Well	140° to 145° (145° to 150° after resting)
Well-Done	150° to 155° (155° to 160° after resting)
Pork	
Chops and Tenderloin	145° (150° after resting)
Loin Roasts	140° (145° after resting)
Chicken and Turkey	
White Meat	160°
Dark Meat	175°

checking your thermometer's accuracy

Even our favorite instant-read digital thermometer is not infallible—sometimes it needs to be recalibrated. Check that your thermometer takes accurate readings when you first buy it and then again periodically over time. Here's how.

Put a mixture of ice and cold tap water in a glass or bowl; allow this mixture to sit for several minutes to let the temperature stabilize. Put the probe in the slush, being careful not to touch the sides or bottom of the glass or bowl. On a digital thermometer, press the "calibrate" button to 32 degrees; on a dial-face thermometer, turn the dial to 32 degrees (the method differs from model to model; you may need pliers to turn a small knob on the back).

KNIFE SCHOOL 101

HOLDING YOUR KNIFE

We get it—this sounds too basic to even discuss. You just hold it how you hold it, right? You don't have to think about it. But what you don't think about can still hurt you. Much as how a Major League Baseball star holds a bat, how you hold a knife makes a difference in terms of control and force. And don't forget about the other hand—the one that holds the food securely in place while you cut. How you hold the food steady makes a difference in terms of fingertip safety.

Control Grip
For more control, choke up on the handle and actually grip the blade of the knife between your thumb and forefinger. This will be the most common grip you use for ingredient prep.

Force Grip
Holding the knife on the handle allows you to use more force and is helpful when cutting through hard foods or bone. Most ingredients don't require that much force, however.

Protect Your Fingertips
Use the "bear claw" grip to hold food in place and minimize danger. Tuck your fingertips in, away from the knife, and rest your knuckles against the blade. During the upward motion of slicing, reposition your guiding hand for the next cut.

MOVING YOUR KNIFE

For Small Items, Keep the Tip Down
To cut small items, push the blade forward and down, using its curve to make smooth strokes. With each cut, move the knife (not the food). The blade should touch the board at all times when cutting small food.

For Large Items, Lift Blade Up
To cut large items, such as an eggplant, lift the entire blade off the board to help make smooth strokes.

For Tough Items, Use the Heel
To cut through tough foods, use one hand to grip the handle and place your flat palm on top of the blade. Cut straight down, pushing the blade gently. Make sure your hand and the knife are both dry to prevent slippage.

KEEPING KNIVES SHARP

A sharp knife is a fast knife, and a dull knife is an accident waiting to happen. Dull knives are dangerous because they require more force to do the job and so there is a higher chance of the knife slipping and missing the mark. Even the best knives will dull over time with regular use.

A honing steel (also called a sharpening steel, though that's a misnomer), the metal rod sold with most knife sets, doesn't really sharpen knives. Instead, it trues the edge of a slightly dulled blade. Over time, the sharp cutting edge of a knife blade can turn to the side, making the blade seem dull. A knife that feels dull may need only a few light strokes across a steel to correct its edge and restore sharpness without the need to run it through a sharpener. The honing process is also faster than sharpening a knife (about 1 minute to hone versus 5 minutes to sharpen) and doesn't remove metal from the blade.

Here's How to Use a Honing Steel

1. Place the tip of the honing steel on the counter and place the heel of the blade against the other end of the steel, pointing the knife tip slightly upward. Hold the blade at a 15-degree angle to the steel.

2. Maintaining light, consistent pressure and a 15-degree angle between the knife blade and steel, slide the blade down the length of the steel in a sweeping motion, pulling the knife toward your body so that the entire edge of the blade makes contact.

3. Repeat this motion on the other side of the blade. Four or five strokes on each side of the blade (a total of eight to ten alternating passes) should realign the edge.

THE PAPER TEST

To determine if your knife is sharp, put it to the paper test: Holding a sheet of paper (basic printer/copy paper is best) firmly at the top with one hand, draw the blade down through the paper, heel to tip, with the other hand. The knife should glide through the paper and require only minimal pushing. If it snags, try realigning the blade's edge using a honing steel and then repeat the test. If the knife still doesn't cut the paper cleanly, use your sharpener.

cut out for greatness

Knives are some of the most basic and essential tools you'll use in the kitchen. Here are the basics on our three favorite types.

Chef's Knife

From chopping onions to mincing herbs to butchering a chicken, this knife will handle 90 percent of your ingredient prep. If you buy only one knife, make it a reliable chef's knife.

Paring Knife

A paring knife is key for tasks that require more dexterity than a chef's knife can provide: peeling and coring apples, deveining shrimp, cutting citrus segments, and more.

Serrated Knife

The pointed serrations of a good serrated knife glide through crusty breads, bagels, and the tough skins of tomatoes to produce neat slices.

AT THE CUTTING BOARD

The cutting board is the center of a cook's work. If your board is in order, your cooking is off to a good start.

Set Up Your Board

First, make sure the board isn't going to slide around the counter as you work. Some boards have nonslip grips on the bottom or sides. If yours doesn't, place either a square of damp paper towel or small pieces of shelf liner between the counter and the cutting board to firmly anchor it before you do anything else.

A Place for Everything

Organizing your prepared ingredients into little bowls isn't just for TV chefs— it's actually really useful. This setup makes it easy to grab an ingredient and add it to a hot pan at just the right moment, and it keeps the prepped ingredients from crowding your cutting board.

Keep It Clean

As you're prepping your ingredients, don't just push the trimmings and skins to the side; this reduces the usable area on your board, and those trimmings have a way of getting back into the mix. Instead, place a small bowl or plastic grocery bag at the side of your board for everything that's destined for the trash or compost.

KNOW YOUR CUTS

The language of cutting can seem mystifying—chopping, dicing, mincing. What exactly is the difference? It may not seem like it would matter that much, but because cooking times are calibrated for ingredients cut to a particular size, food that's cut incorrectly won't cook right. Here are some explanations for a few common and sometimes confusing prep terms that you should know.

"chopped fine" / "chopped" / "chopped coarse"

Chopping is the most general word for cutting food into small pieces, but the size designations have pretty specific meanings. "Chopped fine" corresponds to food cut into ⅛- to ¼-inch pieces, "chopped" to ¼- to ½-inch pieces, and "chopped coarse" to ½- to ¾-inch pieces.

"diced"

We don't call for dicing ("chopped" works fine for us) but if you see the term, it refers to food cut into uniform cubes, which can be large or small. Since most ingredients don't have right angles, not every piece will be a perfect cube; just do your best.

"minced"

Minced ingredients are cut into ⅛-inch pieces or smaller; this is likely the smallest cut most recipes will call for. Pungent ingredients such as garlic and herbs are often minced to make them easier to evenly distribute throughout a dish.

"sliced"

In general, slicing calls for cutting food into pieces with two flat edges (the thickness will depend on the recipe). Orb-shaped foods like onions are difficult to slice whole because they do not sit on a flat side. Unless whole sliced onion rings are the goal, halve an onion pole to pole, peel it, sit it on a cut side, and then slice.

"matchsticks"

Also known as "julienne," this refers to cutting food into matchstick-size pieces, ¼ inch thick (or less) and 2 inches long, unless otherwise specified. Start by cutting the ingredient into 2-inch-long segments, then cut each segment into ¼-inch-thick planks. Working with a few planks at a time, stack the planks and cut them into ¼-inch-thick matchsticks.

BASIC VEGETABLE PREP

Whether you are simply steaming a vegetable or using it as one component of a more involved recipe, usually some basic vegetable prep is required. After years of peeling, seeding, and chopping vegetables in the test kitchen, we've found the following methods are the easiest and most efficient ways to prepare a number of vegetables for myriad uses.

ASPARAGUS: TRIMMING

1. Remove one stalk of asparagus from bunch and bend it at thicker end until it snaps.

2. With broken asparagus as guide, trim tough ends from remaining asparagus bunch, using chef's knife.

AVOCADOS: CUTTING UP

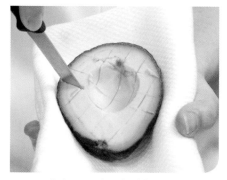

1. After slicing avocado in half around pit with chef's knife, lodge edge of knife blade into pit and twist to remove.

2. Use dish towel to hold avocado steady. Make ½-inch crosshatch incisions in flesh of each avocado half with knife, cutting down to, but not through, skin.

3. Insert soupspoon between skin and flesh and gently scoop out avocado cubes.

BELL PEPPERS: PREPARING

1. Slice off top and bottom of pepper and remove seeds and stem.

2. Slice down through side of pepper.

3. Lay pepper flat, trim away remaining ribs and seeds, then cut into pieces or strips as desired.

BOK CHOY: PREPARING

1. Trim bottom 1 inch from head of bok choy. Wash and pat leaves and stalks dry. Cut leafy green portion away from either side of white stalk.

2. Cut each white stalk in half lengthwise, then crosswise into thin strips.

3. Stack leafy greens and slice crosswise into thin strips. Keep sliced stalks and leaves separate.

BROCCOLI: CUTTING UP

1. Place head of broccoli upside down on cutting board and use chef's knife to trim off florets very close to heads. Cut florets into 1-inch pieces.

2. After cutting away tough outer peel of stalk, square off stalk, then slice into ¼-inch-thick pieces.

CABBAGE: SHREDDING

1. Cut cabbage into quarters, then trim and discard hard core.

2. Separate cabbage into small stacks of leaves that flatten when pressed.

3. Use chef's knife to cut each stack of leaves into thin shreds (you can also use slicing disk of food processor to do this).

CARROTS: CUTTING ON BIAS AND INTO MATCHSTICKS

1. Slice carrot on bias into 2-inch-long oval-shaped pieces.

2. For matchsticks, lay ovals flat on cutting board, then slice into 2-inch-long matchsticks, about ¼ inch thick.

CAULIFLOWER: CUTTING UP

1. Pull off any leaves, then cut out core of cauliflower using paring knife.

2. Separate florets from inner stem using tip of paring knife.

3. Cut larger florets into smaller pieces by slicing through stem.

CHILES: STEMMING AND SEEDING

1. Using sharp knife, trim and discard stem end. Slice chile in half lengthwise.

2. Use spoon to scrape out seeds and ribs (reserve if desired). Prepare seeded chile as directed.

CORN: STRIPPING

After removing husk and silk, stand ear upright in large bowl and use paring knife to slice kernels off of cob.

CUCUMBERS AND ZUCCHINI: SEEDING

Halve vegetable lengthwise. Run spoon inside each half to scoop out seeds.

FENNEL: PREPARING

1. Cut off stems and fronds. Trim thin slice from base. Remove any tough or blemished outer layers from bulb.

2. Cut bulb in half through base, then use paring knife to remove core.

3. Slice each half into thin strips, cutting from base to stem end.

GARLIC: MINCING

1. Trim off root end, then crush clove between side of knife and cutting board to loosen and remove skin.

2. Resting fingers on top of knife blade, use rocking motion to mince garlic, pivoting knife as you work.

MINCING TO A PASTE

Sprinkle minced garlic with salt, then scrape blade of knife back and forth over garlic until it forms sticky paste.

GINGER: PREPARING

1. To peel ginger, hold it firmly against cutting board and use edge of dinner spoon to scrape away skin.

2A. To grate ginger, peel small section then grate peeled portion with rasp-style grater.

2B. To mince ginger, slice peeled ginger into thin rounds, cut rounds into thin strips, and mince strips.

GREEN BEANS: TRIMMING

Line beans up on cutting board and trim ends with one slice.

GREENS: WASHING

Fill salad spinner with cool water, add cut greens, swish them around. Let grit settle to bottom, then lift greens out and drain water. Repeat until greens no longer release dirt.

HEARTY GREENS (SWISS CHARD, KALE, COLLARD GREENS): PREPARING

1. Cut away leafy portion from stalk or stem using chef's knife.

2. Stack several leaves and either slice crosswise or chop into pieces according to recipe.

3. If using chard stems, cut into pieces as directed. (Discard collard and kale stems.)

HERBS: PREPARING

A. To remove leaves, hold sprig by top of stem then run thumb and forefinger down stem to release leaves. Tender tips can be left intact and chopped along with leaves.

B. To shred (or chiffonade) leaves, stack several clean leaves on top of one another. Roll them up, then slice roll crosswise into shreds.

C. To mince fresh herbs, place one hand on handle of chef's knife and rest fingers of your other hand lightly on top of knife blade. Use rocking motion to mince, pivoting knife as you work.

LEEKS: PREPARING

1. Trim and discard root and dark green leaves.

2. Cut trimmed leek in half lengthwise, then slice crosswise.

3. Rinse cut leeks thoroughly using salad spinner or bowl of water.

MUSHROOMS: PREPARING

1. Rinse mushrooms just before cooking. Or, if mushrooms will be eaten raw, simply brush dirt away with soft pastry brush or cloth.

2. Tender white button and cremini stems can simply be trimmed. Tough, woody shiitake and portobello stems should be removed.

OLIVES: PITTING

Place olive on work surface and hold flat edge of knife over olive. Press blade firmly with your hand to loosen olive meat from pit.

ONIONS: CHOPPING

1. Halve onion through root end, then peel and trim top. Make several horizontal cuts from one end of onion to other but don't cut through root end.

2. Make several vertical cuts. Be sure to cut up to but not through root end.

3. Rotate onion so root end is in back; slice onion thinly across previous cuts. As you slice, onion will fall apart into chopped pieces.

SNOW PEAS: TRIMMING

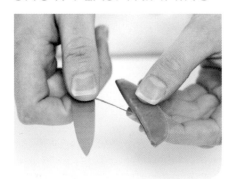

Use paring knife and thumb to snip off tip of pod and pull along flat side to remove string at same time.

POTATOES: CUTTING

1. Cut thin sliver from one side of potato to create stable base. Set on cut side and slice potato crosswise into even planks.

2. Stack several planks and cut crosswise, then rotate 90 degrees and cut crosswise again to create even pieces as directed in recipe.

SHALLOTS: MINCING

1. Make closely spaced horizontal cuts through peeled shallot, leaving root end intact.

2. Next, make several vertical cuts through shallot.

3. Finally, thinly slice shallot crosswise, creating fine mince.

TOMATOES: CORING AND DICING

1. Remove core of tomato using paring knife.

2. Slice tomato crosswise with sharp chef's knife or serrated knife.

3. Stack several slices of tomato, then slice into pieces as desired.

WINTER SQUASH (BUTTERNUT SQUASH): CUTTING UP

1. After peeling squash, use chef's knife to trim off top and bottom and then cut squash in half where narrow neck and wide curved bottom meet.

2. Cut strip from neck to create stable base. Set neck on base and cut into planks, then into pieces. (Or halve neck lengthwise and slice each into half moons.)

3. Cut base in half lengthwise, and scoop out and discard seeds and fibers. Slice each base half into even lengths and then into pieces according to recipe.

BASIC FRUIT PREP

Whether you are cutting up fruit for a simple fruit salad or making a more involved recipe with a lot of prep work, it helps to know the most efficient way to peel, pit, core, stem, juice, or zest the fruit involved. After years of making fruit desserts in the test kitchen, we've found the following methods to be the easiest.

APPLE: CORING

1A. If you don't have a corer, cut sides of apple squarely away from core. Cut each piece of apple into slices according to recipe.

1B. Or, for less waste, cut apple in half. Make diagonal slices with paring knife partway into apple half on either side of core and remove it.

2. Place each piece on its flat side. Cut straight down to make slices or at an angle toward center for wedges.

BERRIES: WASHING

1. Place berries in colander and rinse them gently under running water.

2. To dry, line salad spinner with layers of paper towels and carefully disperse berries. Spin gently until dry, about 20 seconds.

CHERRIES: PITTING

Using cherry pitter, punch stone from flesh of cherry.

CITRUS: SECTIONING

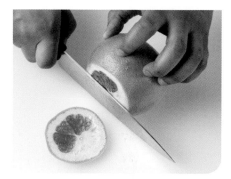

1. Cut thin slice from top and bottom of fruit.

2. Use sharp knife to slice off rind, including white pith, following contours of the fruit.

3. Insert blade of paring knife between membrane and section and slice to center of fruit. Turn blade outward, then slice along membrane on other side until section falls out.

CITRUS: ZESTING

Rub fruit against holes of rasp-style grater, grating over same area of fruit only once or twice to avoid grating bitter white pith beneath skin.

CITRUS: JUICING

1. Roll fruit vigorously on hard surface to tear juice sacs for maximum extraction of juice.

2. Slice fruit in half, then use reamer or citrus juicer to extract juice.

KIWI: PEELING

1. Trim ends of kiwi, then insert small spoon between skin and flesh. Gently slide spoon around fruit, separating flesh from skin.

2. Pull loosened skin away from flesh, then chop or slice according to recipe.

MANGO: CUTTING UP

1. Cut thin slice from one end of mango so it sits flat on counter. Resting mango on trimmed end, cut off skin in thin strips from top to bottom.

2. Cut down along each side of flat pit to remove flesh.

3. Trim around pit to remove any remaining flesh. Chop or slice according to recipe.

PEACH (FREESTONE): HALVING AND PITTING

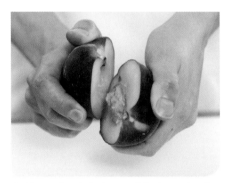

1. Cut peach in half, pole to pole around pit, using crease in peach skin as guide.

2. Grasp both halves of fruit and twist apart. Remove pit.

PEAR: CORING

1. Use melon baller to cut around central core of halved pear with circular motion and remove core.

2. Draw melon baller from central core to top of pear, removing interior stem. Then remove blossom end.

PINEAPPLE: CUTTING UP

  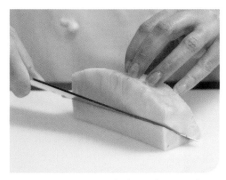

1. Trim off bottom and top of pineapple so it sits flat on counter.

2. Rest pineapple on trimmed bottom and cut off skin in thin strips from top to bottom.

3. Quarter pineapple lengthwise, then cut tough core from each quarter. Slice pineapple according to recipe.

RHUBARB: PEELING

1. Trim both ends of stalk. Partially slice thin disk from bottom end, being careful not to cut through stalk entirely. Pull partially attached disk away from stalk to remove outer peel.

2. Make second cut partway through bottom of stalk in reverse direction. Pull back peel on other side and discard. Slice or chop according to recipe.

STRAWBERRIES: HULLING

A. Use serrated tip of grapefruit spoon to cut around leafy stem and remove white core and stem.

B. Alternately, push plastic straw into bottom of berry and up through leafy steam end to remove core as well as leafy top.

HOW TO MEASURE

Accurate measuring is often the difference between success and failure in the kitchen. In an ideal world, everyone would measure all ingredients by weight at all times, but we are realists. Even though weight is a more accurate way to measure than volume, we know that most cooks rely on measuring cups and spoons, not scales, so here are some ways to increase your accuracy when using volume measures. Our biggest piece of advice: Don't use liquid and dry measuring cups interchangeably—if you do, your ingredient amounts may be significantly off.

MEASURING DRY INGREDIENTS

For absolute accuracy, always weigh flour and sugar when baking. Otherwise, for dry ingredients we recommend the "dip and sweep" method, which reliably yields a 5-ounce cup of unbleached all-purpose flour and a 7-ounce cup of granulated sugar. Dip the measuring cup into the container and scoop up the ingredient in a heaping mound. Use a straight edge, like the back of a knife, to sweep the excess back into the container. We also use dip and sweep with measuring spoons when meting out small amounts of dry ingredients like baking powder.

MEASURING BROWN SUGAR

Brown sugar is clumpy, so it must be packed into a measuring cup to get an accurate reading. To do this, use your fingers or the bottom of a smaller cup to press the sugar into the measuring cup.

MEASURING LIQUID INGREDIENTS

For liquid ingredients, use a liquid measuring cup set on the counter and lean down to read the measurement at eye level. Make sure the meniscus—the bottom of the curved surface line of the liquid—aligns with the measurement you're aiming for. When emptying the cup, use a rubber spatula to scrape it clean.

MEASURING IN-BETWEEN INGREDIENTS

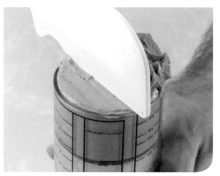

For sticky and/or semisolid ingredients such as mayonnaise, peanut butter, sour cream, and honey, we prefer an adjustable measuring cup. An adjustable measuring cup has a clear cylinder with volume markings and a plunger insert. You withdraw the plunger to the desired measurement and then fill the cylinder, level it off, and plunge to empty it. This design makes it easy to push out every last bit of the ingredient. If you don't own an adjustable measuring cup, a dry measuring cup is the next most consistent tool.

when to measure

In addition to how you measure, it matters *when* you measure. For instance, "1 cup walnuts, chopped" is not the same as "1 cup chopped walnuts." In the first example, the cook should measure out the whole walnuts and then chop them. In the second example, the cook should chop first, and then measure out a cup of the already-chopped walnuts. One cup of unchopped walnuts weighs 4 ounces, while one cup of chopped walnuts weighs 4.8 ounces—that's 20 percent more nuts. Apply this principle to other ingredients (such as "sifted flour" versus "flour, sifted") and you can see how this makes a significant difference in the final outcome of a recipe.

whether to weigh

A digital scale is critical for baking recipes, where measuring dry ingredients by weight is the only way to guarantee accuracy. Our testing has found that there can be up to a 20 percent variance in the weight between cups of flour measured by different cooks using a dry measuring cup—a range that can mean the difference between a cake that's squat and dense and one that's fluffy and tender. Scales have many applications in cooking, too. Using one to portion burgers, for example, means no more guessing if the patties are the same size and will thus cook at the same rate. Weighing ingredients may sound like a chore but is actually easier than measuring by volume, especially with a hyperprecise digital scale.

WAYS TO COOK: IN LIQUID

Cooking is simply the process of transferring heat to food. At a basic level, the process is the same whether food is being cooked over an open fire à la caveman or via one of our slightly more sophisticated modern equivalents. All of the cooking we do uses elemental mediums—liquid, fat, air, and fire—for their heat energy. And while there are multiple techniques that rely on each energy source, they tend to behave in similar ways. So it can be helpful to think of the cooking within these groups, as we do here. We'll start with cooking in liquid, which is one of the most common techniques we use.

Cooking food in liquid or steam offers even heat (since the food is fully enveloped) and plenty of moisture. But there's an exchange: As water hydrates food, food gives particles and flavors back to water. We use this to our advantage when simmering a broth or drawing meat's gelatin into a rich braise. While boiling cooks food rapidly, at lower temperatures water can be the gentlest of cooking methods.

Boil
To cook foods in boiling liquid in a pot set on a hot burner.
Water boils at 212 degrees at sea level. It's an efficient heat conductor; vigorously bubbling water can cook food very quickly, making it ideal for pasta and sturdy foods like potatoes, and for flash-cooking vegetables as when blanching. The jostling also helps to prevent sticking.

Blanch
To quickly immerse food in boiling water, then transfer to an ice bath.
We like to blanch green vegetables—such as green beans, broccoli rabe, and snap peas—to help set their color and remove any bitterness. Blanching also helps loosen the skins of nuts and soft fruits. The ice bath quickly stops the cooking in order to get just the right crisp-tender results.

Simmer
To cook foods in liquid that is just below the boiling point.
Simmering generally happens between 180 and 205 degrees. At these temperatures, meat become tender without drying out and flavors blend. Simmering is invaluable for broths, soups, and sauces. To get a good simmer, we usually bring liquid to a boil and then reduce the heat.

Steam
To cook foods suspended over simmering liquid in a covered pot.
Steaming is an especially gentle cooking method. Unlike other moist-heat cooking methods, steaming does not wash away flavor. It is an excellent choice for vegetables, fish, and delicate foods like dumplings.

Poach
To cook foods in liquid that is well below boiling point in a covered pot.
Poaching is related to simmering: The temperature of the liquid is lower (no bubbles are breaking the surface) and the pot is generally covered to create a constant, gentle cooking environment. Poaching is best used for chicken, delicate fish, and fruits.

Braise
To cook foods by first sautéing them and then adding liquid, covering the pan, and simmering.
Braising is most often used for tough cuts of meat that need to cook gently until tender. Braising liquid is typically wine or stock infused with aromatics. Braising is usually a low-and-slow approach, but depending on the ingredients involved, it doesn't have to be an all-day affair.

When a liquid boils, large bubbles energetically break the surface at a rapid and constant pace. It's simmering when small bubbles gently break the surface of the liquid at a variable and infrequent rate.

WAYS TO COOK: WITH FAT

Cooking with fat encourages browning and adds richness. A lot of the cooking we do involves some kind of fat, whether it is vegetable oil, olive oil, butter, or fat rendered from meat (yay, bacon fat!). The difference between various cooking techniques that use fat mostly has to do with how much fat you're using. It can range from 1 to 2 tablespoons in the whole recipe for a sauté to multiple cups for deep frying. Most cooking methods that use fat also rely on high heat, which limits the types of fat that can be used; you need one with a high smoke point that won't break down and cause off-flavors, especially when deep frying (we like peanut oil). Frying causes moisture to flee the food once it lands in hot oil. As the food cooks and more moisture escapes, the food's exterior dries out and you achieve the final goal: a crisp crust.

Sear

To cook food in a small amount of fat over high heat without moving the food in order to develop a flavorful, well-browned crust.
Searing is frequently used to create a browned crust on proteins like steaks, chops, fish, or poultry before the interior of the food is finished with a gentler cooking method. Preheat the pan properly before searing; it should be very hot and the fat should just start to smoke before you add the ingredient to be seared. Make sure to pat the food dry before searing it; moisture can interfere with getting a good sear. And don't move the food around at all during the first few minutes of searing or worry if it seems to be sticking; wait until it releases from the pan by itself before you flip it or move it.

Sauté

To quickly cook food in a small amount of fat over moderately high heat while frequently moving it around the pan.
The moderate heat of a sauté ensures that the food won't overcook. Stirring and/or shaking the pan helps make sure all the ingredients are equally exposed to the heat. Make sure the pan and any fat are properly heated before adding your ingredients.

Stir-Fry

To quickly cook thinly cut food in oil over high heat.
Traditionally, stir-fried food is constantly flipped and turned, but we find that you get better browning if you actually let the food stay put, stirring just once or twice. And by the way, you don't need a wok to stir-fry; on a home stove, you'll get better results with a regular old skillet.

Shallow-Fry

To cook in hot oil deep enough to partially surround the food.
Also called pan frying, shallow frying uses much less oil than deep frying and can be done in a skillet. It works best for thinner ingredients like cutlets that don't have to be fully submerged in oil in order to cook through.

Deep-Fry

To cook in hot oil deep enough to fully surround the food.
The key to crispy, browned deep-fried food is keeping the oil at the right temperature. Oil that's too cool will yield pale, greasy food. Too hot, and you'll get bitter, blackened food. The proper frying temperature is usually between 325 and 375 degrees (but check your recipe for specifics). Use a digital thermometer to check the temperature before adding the first batch of food to be fried.

Strike when the pan is hot; the temperature of the cooking surface will drop the minute food is added so don't rush preheating. When the oil starts to shimmer, it's the right temperature to sauté vegetables that don't need to be browned. For proteins, wait until the oil lets off wisps of smoke.

WAYS TO COOK: WITH DRY HEAT

Cooking with dry heat, as opposed to in fat or water, is a way to cook food without introducing distracting flavors from fats or excess moisture from water. In roasting and baking, the two most common dry-heat techniques, what you're actually cooking with is essentially hot air, aka convective heat, as well as radiant heat from the oven's walls. Air is a relatively inefficient conductor, however, which makes baking and roasting fairly slow cooking methods. This is also why dry-heat cooking is frequently used as a component step in a larger, more complex recipe; we frequently combine stovetop searing with oven roasting, as in Slow-Roasted Beef (page 82). This allows us to get the quick high-heat browning of cooking with fat as well as the gentler, more forgiving convective heat of roasting.

Roast
To cook food in a pan in a hot oven.

Bake
To cook by convective heat in a hot oven.

The terms "roast" and "bake" mean essentially the same thing but are commonly used to refer to different types of recipes. As a category, "baking" involves a lot of chemistry that happens in the oven because of the ingredients used in baking recipes. However, there is nothing different in the way the heat itself is applied to the food. A baked potato and a roasted potato are the same thing.

Toast
To brown food by dry heat—and without adding fat—using an oven or skillet.

Toasting causes browning reactions and chemical changes in ingredients. Ingredients that are commonly toasted include nuts, seeds, and whole spices.

Spacing food out when roasting allows the hot air to wash over the food, cooking it more evenly and drying the surface, which helps to develop a nice crust.

WAYS TO COOK: WITH AN OPEN FLAME

Despite today's fancy gear, grilling remains a basic—primitive, even—technique: Go outside, put food over hot coals or an open flame, and cook until it's done, with the added bonus of flavors created by the smoke and fire. Not everyone has year-round access to outdoor cooking methods, but if you do, they are some of the most flavorful ways to cook food. Broiling brings the flame indoors and approximates the effect of grilling from above.

Broil

To cook by direct exposure to a heating element in an oven. While roasting relies on convective heat of air molecules surrounding the food, a broiler cooks food primarily with radiant heat, a form of invisible light waves. Their intense heat, whether from an actual flame or heated coil, makes them ideal for creating browned crusts, as in our Macaroni and Cheese (page 286), and cooking food through in minutes. But not all broilers operate the same way, which can make them tricky until you understand how yours works. So follow the manufacturer's instructions. See page 61 for more on using your broiler.

Grill

To cook relatively small, individual-size, and quick-cooking foods directly over an outdoor fire. Grilling is the speediest and simplest open-flame cooking method and typically uses high or moderate heat between 400 and 600 degrees. Most grilling takes place directly over the fire and the lid is often not used. Grilled foods derive their "grilled" flavor from dripping fat that hits the heat source, creating smoke.

Barbecue

To cook large, tough cuts of meat using indirect, gentle heat from an outdoor fire. Barbecuing is the lowest and slowest open-flame cooking method. It uses temperatures of 250 to 300 degrees, and cooking times often exceed 3 hours as the meat is cooked past the point of what's considered well done, until its proteins break down to a meltingly tender texture. Barbecued foods derive their "barbecued" flavor from wood chips or chunks that create smoke.

The distance of an inch or two can mean the difference between perfectly charred and burnt, so read the recipe to be sure your rack is properly spaced from the broiler's heat source.

HOW TO SEASON FOOD

You can follow a recipe to the letter and still end up with food that doesn't taste good to you; everyone's palate is different. We have tastebuds for salty, sweet, bitter, sour, and savory (or umami) distributed all over our tongues and the rest of our mouths. Thanks to genetic variation, different individuals taste things differently, so what the recipe developer thought was perfect may not be your cup of tea. It's important to understand how to make seasoning work for you.

While adding salt and pepper "to taste" is almost always the final step of a recipe, you can also use a whole range of other ingredients to bring a dish into balance. Just a small quantity of one of these finishing touches (from a pinch to ½ teaspoon) is a good starting place.

SALTINESS

Salt, soy sauce, fish sauce, feta cheese, Parmesan

What It Does	Adds depth and offsets sweetness; tempers acidity and bitterness
Suggested Uses	Chocolate desserts, soups and stews, pasta, grains, fruit salads, dipping sauces

SWEETNESS

Granulated or brown sugar, honey, maple syrup, mirin, sweet wine or liqueur, jam or jelly

What It Does	Rounds out sharp, bitter, or salty flavors
Suggested Uses	Salsas, sauces, bitter greens, vinaigrettes, relishes

SOURNESS

Vinegar, citrus juice, pickled vegetables (such as jalapeños)

What It Does	Adds brightness to flat-tasting dishes, cuts through richness or sweetness
Suggested Uses	Meaty stews and soups, creamy sauces and condiments, braised or roasted meats

BITTERNESS

Dry or prepared mustard, beer, fresh ginger, chili powder, unsweetened cocoa powder, dark chocolate, horseradish, cayenne pepper, coffee, citrus zest

What It Does	Cuts sweetness
Suggested Uses	Barbecued meats, slaws, chopped salads, chili

UMAMI

Worcestershire sauce, soy sauce, fish sauce, miso, Parmesan cheese, anchovies, tomato paste, mushrooms, sherry

What It Does	Adds meatiness, depth, or earthiness; boosts dishes that taste a bit flat
Suggested Uses	Bolognese or other meaty sauces, hearty vegetarian sauces, soups, deli sandwich fillings such as tuna salad

RICHNESS

Heavy cream, butter, olive oil

What It Does	Rounds out flavors, adds viscosity
Suggested Uses	Lean vegetable-based soups, sauces

5 EYE-OPENING PRINCIPLES OF HOW FLAVOR WORKS

1 Cold Dulls Flavor
The microscopic receptors in your taste buds are extremely temperature-sensitive. They work much better at warm temperatures than at cooler ones; when you eat cold food, they barely open, minimizing flavor perception. However, when food is hot, their sensitivity increases more than a hundredfold, making food taste way more flavorful. Cold food also has fewer aromas, which makes them taste less flavorful. So, dishes meant to be served hot should be reheated, and dishes served chilled must be aggressively seasoned to make up for the flavor-dulling effects of cold temperatures.

2 Fat Carries Flavor
Fat is not only an efficient carrier of flavor, it also dissolves flavor components, carrying them into sauce and other surrounding ingredients. Some meat scientists claim that if you removed all of the fat from meat you could not tell the difference between, say, pork and beef because so many of the flavor components reside in the fat. Fat also gives flavors roundness and, by coating your mouth, lets you savor them. This is why adding a fat (such as butter, sour cream, cheese, or oil) to an overly spicy dish can help counteract the offending ingredient and balance out the flavors.

3 Brown Is the Color of Flavor
Whether from caramelization of sugars or the browning of proteins called the Maillard reaction, when a food turns brown during cooking, that indicates chemical changes that cause the development of tons of new flavor, color, and aroma compounds.

4 Flavor Changes over Time
Have you ever noticed how some soups and stews taste better the day after you make them? In addition to the changes that occur with temperature, there are many other chemical reactions that continue to take place even after cooking ends. The sugars in dairy break down, the carbohydrates in onions develop into sugars, the starches in potatoes convert into flavorful compounds, and you end up with a deeper, more richly flavored dish. Flavors that may seem harsh at first, like chile peppers, mellow with time. If a recipe specifically calls for you to let the dish sit so the flavors can meld, do it; it will result in a more balanced dish.

5 Salt Is Magic
Salt may well be the most important ingredient in cooking. It is one of our five basic tastes and it adds an essential depth of flavor to food. Salt also has the ability to change the molecular makeup of food and is used to preserve and to add moisture to meat. For more information, see page 81 and page 93.

---

5 never-fail strategies for making food taste better

1. SPICE UP SPICES To intensify the flavor of preground spices, cook them briefly in a little butter or oil before adding liquid to the pan. If the recipe calls for sautéing aromatics, add the spices to the pan when the aromatics are nearly cooked.

2. MAKE NUTS NUTTIER Toasting nuts brings out their aromatic oils, contributing to a stronger, more complex flavor and aroma. See page 157 for more information.

3. YOU'RE THE SAUCE BOSS Almost any dish can be improved with the addition of a sauce. Sauce is your secret weapon: Dollop it on vegetables, drizzle it on steak, or smear it on a sandwich. See some of our favorites on pages 100–103.

4. JUST A SPOONFUL OF SUGAR Browned food tastes better, and the best way to accelerate browning is with a pinch of sugar sprinkled on lean proteins (such as chicken and seafood) or over vegetables before sautéing.

5. FINISH WITH ACID AND HERBS One of the easiest fixes for a dish that needs a little more life is a dash of brightness from something acidic, such as lemon juice or vinegar, and a sprinkle of freshness from minced herbs.

One of the basic foundations of good cooking is knowing which methods are best for common ingredients, so if you find yourself with a whole chicken or a bag of potatoes or even just a dozen eggs, you know one or two simple, foolproof ways to turn that ingredient into something delicious. Of course, there are many different ways to use any ingredient, but in this section, we've collected some of our favorite methods for preparing the staples. While this isn't a definitive list of ways to use salmon or greens or tofu, they are fresh, interesting basic recipes for foods you actually want to eat.

Consider these the building blocks for becoming a capable, confident, and comfortable cook. Some can be prepared in just a few minutes, and most can be made and then stored in the refrigerator so that you never lack for something homemade to eat. Many of these recipes also offer ideas for varying the flavors and suggestions for pairing with the sauces and condiments at the end of the chapter. Once you've mastered them, your options for improvising multiply exponentially, and you also always have a set of delicious and reliable basics to come back to when you just really need a simple, perfectly cooked roast chicken, a no-fuss veggie side dish, or the perfect herb sauce to drizzle over anything.

THE SIMPLEST WAY TO COOK EVERYTHING

Green Salad with Foolproof Vinaigrette

Serves 4; Total Time 10 minutes

1 tablespoon wine vinegar

1½ teaspoons minced shallot

½ teaspoon mayonnaise

½ teaspoon Dijon mustard

⅛ teaspoon salt

Pepper

3 tablespoons extra-virgin olive oil

8 ounces (8 cups) lettuce

½ garlic clove, peeled

1. Combine vinegar, shallot, mayonnaise, mustard, salt, and pepper to taste in small bowl. Whisk until mixture is milky in appearance and no lumps of mayonnaise remain.

2. Place oil in small measuring cup so that it is easy to pour. Whisking constantly, slowly drizzle oil into vinegar mixture. If pools of oil gather on surface as you whisk, stop addition of oil and whisk mixture well to combine, then resume whisking and drizzling in oil in slow stream. Vinaigrette should be glossy and lightly thickened, with no pools of oil on its surface. (Vinaigrette can be refrigerated for up to 2 weeks.)

3. Fill salad spinner bowl with cool water, add lettuce, and gently swish leaves around. Let grit settle to bottom of bowl, then lift lettuce out and drain water. Repeat until lettuce no longer releases any dirt.

4. Dry greens using salad spinner, stopping several times to dump out excess water. Blot with paper towels to remove any remaining moisture. Tear dried greens into bite-size pieces. Rub inside of salad bowl with garlic. Add lettuce.

5. Rewhisk dressing and drizzle small amount over greens. Toss greens with tongs, taste, and add more dressing if desired. Serve.

why this recipe works

Most cooks, even good ones, don't do a very good job when it comes to making a simple green salad. The key is coating the greens evenly but lightly with a properly mixed dressing. Because oil and vinegar naturally repel each other, vinaigrettes tend to separate, leading to a dressing that is harsh and acidic in one bite, then dull and oily in the next. Whisking slowly and steadily helps break the vinegar into tiny droplets that become dispersed in the oil, creating a smooth mixture called an emulsion. To make a more stable emulsion, we added mustard and mayonnaise, which help to bond the vinegar and oil together. Rubbing the salad bowl with half a peeled garlic clove provides just a hint of garlic flavor. This is a basic formula for vinaigrette; red wine, white wine, sherry, or champagne vinegar will all work here, so use whichever you like best.

variation

Lemon Vinaigrette

Substitute lemon juice for vinegar and omit shallot. Add ¼ teaspoon finely grated lemon zest and pinch sugar with salt and pepper.

PAIRING GREENS WITH DRESSING

A leafy green salad is a vital recipe to have in your arsenal. It might not seem like the most exciting dish in the world, but it's a perfect pairing with almost any meal. Keeping your salads varied is as easy as changing the greens, the dressing, or both. Most salad greens fall into one of two categories: mellow or assertive. Choose your dressing to complement the greens you are using.

Mellow Greens

Boston, Bibb, mâche, mesclun, red and green leaf, red oak, and flat-leaf spinach are relatively mellow. Their easily overpowered flavors are best complemented by a simple dressing such as a classic vinaigrette. Sturdy lettuces such as romaine and iceberg are also mellow but have a crisp texture that pairs well with creamy dressings such as blue cheese (see page 168).

Assertive or Spicy Greens

For greens with a bit more personality, try arugula, escarole, chicory, Belgian endive, radicchio, frisée, or watercress. These greens can easily stand up to strong flavors like balsamic vinegar.

Vinaigrette Beyond Salad

Vinaigrette can also be used to dress cooked vegetables: asparagus, green beans, and cauliflower are excellent this way. Stir with grains and vegetables to make grain salads or bowls. Or serve it over simple cooked chicken or fish. Mix up the flavorings of the vinaigrette to match your recipe by changing the acid, oil, or seasonings.

Braised Winter Greens

Serves 4; Total Time 1 hour

2 pounds kale or collard greens

3 tablespoons extra-virgin olive oil

1 onion, chopped fine

5 garlic cloves, minced

⅛ teaspoon red pepper flakes

1 cup vegetable broth

1 cup water

Salt and pepper

2 teaspoons lemon juice

1. Cut leafy portions of greens from either side of stems. Discard stems. Stack several leaves and chop them into 3-inch pieces. Rinse chopped greens until they no longer release any dirt and dry thoroughly in salad spinner.

2. Heat 2 tablespoons oil in Dutch oven over medium heat until shimmering. Add onion and cook until softened and beginning to brown, 4 to 5 minutes. Stir in garlic and pepper flakes and cook until fragrant, about 1 minute. Stir in half of greens and cook until beginning to wilt, 1 minute. Stir in remaining greens, broth, water, and ¼ teaspoon salt. Quickly cover pot and reduce heat to medium-low. Cook, stirring occasionally, until greens are tender, 25 to 35 minutes for kale and 35 to 45 minutes for collards.

3. Remove lid and increase heat to medium-high. Cook, stirring occasionally, until most of liquid has evaporated (bottom of pot will be almost dry and greens will begin to sizzle), 8 to 12 minutes. Off heat, stir in lemon juice and remaining 1 tablespoon oil. Season with salt and pepper. Transfer to bowl and serve.

why this recipe works

Braised hearty greens, such as kale or collards, are excellent as a side dish or stirred into pasta or grains. Don't be afraid of braising; it's a very approachable and forgiving cooking method. The challenge is getting the sturdy greens tender but not washed out and dull. Cooking the greens in just a cup each of broth and water—which we simply seasoned with garlic, onion, and red pepper flakes—allowed the greens to absorb all the flavorful liquid. Most of the liquid was absorbed or evaporated by the time the greens became tender. A squeeze of fresh lemon juice at the end brightened and balanced the dish. Don't be alarmed by the volume of raw greens: They cook down a lot, and wilting half of them in the pan first makes room for the rest. For best results, be sure the greens are fully cooked and tender in step 2 before moving on to step 3.

variations

Braised Winter Greens with Chorizo

Cut 8 ounces chorizo sausage into ¼-inch-thick half-moons. Add chorizo to shimmering oil in step 2 and cook until lightly browned, 4 to 6 minutes. Using slotted spoon, transfer chorizo to paper towel–lined plate. Proceed with recipe, cooking onion and garlic in remaining oil and substituting 1½ teaspoons ground cumin for red pepper flakes. Stir reserved chorizo into greens before serving.

Braised Winter Greens with Coconut and Curry

Substitute 2 teaspoons grated fresh ginger and 1 teaspoon curry powder for red pepper flakes and 1 (14-ounce) can coconut milk for water. Substitute 1 tablespoon lime juice for lemon juice and sprinkle greens with ⅓ cup toasted cashews before serving.

think like a cook

CONQUERING HEARTY GREENS

Hearty greens have moved from fancy farmers' markets into major grocery stores across the country. They offer earthy flavor and texture plus nutrients, but they do require a little extra work to make them palatable. If you're using kale or collard greens, you'll want to remove the tough, woody stems. Baby kale is tender enough to eat raw, but mature kale requires cooking or at least a soak in warm water to tenderize the leaves (see page 154). Swiss chard stems, by contrast, are tender and delicious when cooked; just make sure you separate them from the quicker-cooking leaves, as they need a head start. Don't skip prep steps like rinsing or stemming or you'll end up with tough, gritty results. The greens will reduce dramatically when cooked, so don't be intimidated by the giant bunches you find at the store. To preserve freshness, store greens in a dry plastic bag in the refrigerator. Kept this way, they can last five to seven days.

Sautéed Green Beans with Garlic and Herbs
Serves 4; Total Time 20 minutes

1 tablespoon unsalted butter, softened

3 garlic cloves, minced

1 teaspoon chopped fresh thyme

1 teaspoon extra-virgin olive oil

1 pound green beans, trimmed and cut into 2-inch lengths

Salt and pepper

¼ cup water

2 teaspoons lemon juice

1 tablespoon chopped fresh parsley

1. Combine butter, garlic, and thyme in small bowl; set aside. Heat oil in 12-inch nonstick skillet over medium heat until just smoking. Add green beans, ¼ teaspoon salt, and ⅛ teaspoon pepper; cook, stirring occasionally, until spotty brown, 4 to 6 minutes. Add water, cover, and cook until green beans are bright green but still crisp, about 2 minutes.

2. Remove cover, increase heat to high, and cook until water evaporates, 30 to 60 seconds. Add butter mixture and continue to cook, stirring frequently, until green beans are crisp-tender, lightly browned, and beginning to wrinkle, 1 to 3 minutes longer. Off heat, toss with lemon juice and parsley and season with salt and pepper to taste. Serve.

variations
Sautéed Green Beans with Paprika and Almonds
Substitute ¼ teaspoon smoked paprika for thyme. Omit parsley garnish, but sprinkle cooked green beans with ¼ cup toasted slivered almonds before serving.

Sautéed Green Beans with Ginger and Sesame
Combine 1 teaspoon toasted sesame oil, 1 teaspoon grated fresh ginger, and 1 tablespoon Asian chili-garlic sauce in small bowl and substitute for butter mixture. Substitute 2 teaspoons vegetable oil for olive oil. Omit lemon juice and parsley. Sprinkle cooked green beans with 2 teaspoons toasted sesame seeds before serving.

why this recipe works
Sautéing is not as simple as it seems, especially when it comes to fresh vegetables. When we just cooked fresh green beans in hot oil, it resulted in blackened exteriors and under-cooked interiors. For more even cooking, once the beans were spotty brown, we added water and covered the pan to let them steam. When the beans were cooked through, we lifted the lid to evaporate any remaining water and continue browning. Garlic-thyme butter added flavor and promoted further browning and fresh lemon juice brightened things up. This recipe yields crisp-tender beans. If you prefer a more tender texture (or are using large, tough beans), increase the water by a tablespoon and increase the covered cooking time by 1 minute. You will need a 12-inch nonstick skillet with a tight-fitting lid for this recipe.

Sautéed Green Beans with Roasted Red Peppers and Basil

Combine 2 teaspoons olive oil, ⅓ cup jarred roasted red peppers, cut into ½-inch pieces, 1 minced shallot, and ⅛ teaspoon red pepper flakes in small bowl and substitute for butter mixture. Substitute 1 teaspoon red wine vinegar for lemon juice and 2 tablespoons chopped fresh basil for parsley.

Sautéed Green Beans with Tarragon and Lime

Substitute 2 thinly sliced scallions and ½ teaspoon grated lime zest for the garlic and thyme. Substitute 1½ teaspoons lime juice for lemon juice and 2 teaspoons chopped fresh tarragon for parsley.

think like a cook

DRESSING UP VEGETABLES

A few flavorings can go a long way to prevent simply prepared vegetables from getting too boring. We typically season vegetables with salt and pepper at two points in the process (during cooking, when the salt has a chance to be absorbed, and at the end, when we can taste to be sure we've got it right). Aromatics such as garlic commonly get cooked with the vegetables so they have time to soften and add complexity. But it's the end point that offers the most room to be creative—a spoonful of this or that can totally change the flavor of your dish. Start with a simple squeeze of citrus. More easy ideas follow. Use these flavor boosters with simple roasted, boiled, steamed, or microwaved vegetables or any other vegetable dish.

» Cook butter in a small skillet over medium heat until it browns, then drizzle over the vegetables and sprinkle with toasted nuts.
» Dot with a flavored butter (see page 329).
» Sprinkle with chopped fresh herbs.
» Sprinkle with fruity extra-virgin olive oil, grated Parmesan cheese, and a few red pepper flakes.
» Sprinkle with soy sauce or toasted sesame oil.
» Toss with a vinaigrette (see page 50), pesto (see page 100) or green sauce (see page 101).
» Drizzle with a creamy tahini- (see page 60) or yogurt-based sauce (see page 102).
» Sprinkle with a flavorful spice mixture such as *za'atar* or *dukkah* (see page 215).

Pan-Roasted Potatoes
Serves 4; Total Time 35 minutes

2 pounds small or medium red potatoes, unpeeled
3 tablespoons olive oil
Salt and pepper

1. Halve or quarter potatoes into 1-inch pieces. Toss potatoes with 1 tablespoon oil and ¼ teaspoon salt in bowl. Microwave until potatoes soften but still hold their shape, about 10 minutes, gently stirring twice during microwaving. Drain potatoes thoroughly in colander.

2. Heat remaining 2 tablespoons oil in 12-inch nonstick skillet over medium-high heat until shimmering. Add potatoes cut side down in single layer; cook, without stirring, until golden brown, 5 to 7 minutes.

3. Using tongs, turn potatoes skin side down if using halved small potatoes or second cut side down if using quartered medium potatoes; cook, without stirring, until deep golden brown, 5 to 6 minutes longer. Season with salt and pepper to taste, and serve.

why this recipe works

The key to roasting potatoes is achieving a crisp exterior and perfectly done interior at the same time. The process typically takes a while, especially with sturdy potatoes. To speed things up, some recipes call for partially boiling the potatoes before roasting, but we found that zapping them in the microwave proved even faster and more convenient. Once partially cooked, they needed only 10 minutes in a hot skillet to crisp up and become tender. We found that low-starch, high-moisture red potatoes yielded crisp yet delicate crusts and moist, dense interiors. These potatoes are great served either plain or with one of the simple herb, spice, or aromatic variations listed. We prefer to use small or medium potatoes (1½ to 3 inches in diameter) here because they are easier to cut into uniform pieces, either halved or quartered depending on their size.

variations

Pan-Roasted Potatoes with Lemon and Chives

Toss potatoes with 2 tablespoons minced fresh chives and 2 teaspoons grated lemon zest before serving.

Pan-Roasted Potatoes with Southwestern Spices

Combine ½ teaspoon chili powder, ½ teaspoon paprika, ¼ teaspoon ground cumin, and ⅛ teaspoon cayenne pepper in bowl. Toss pinch of spice mixture with potatoes before microwaving. Stir remaining spice mixture into potatoes before browning on second side.

Pan-Roasted Potatoes with Garlic and Rosemary

Combine 1 teaspoon olive oil, 2 minced garlic cloves, and 2 teaspoons minced fresh rosemary in bowl. After browning potatoes, push potatoes to sides of skillet, add garlic mixture, and cook, mashing garlic into skillet, until fragrant, about 30 seconds. Stir garlic mixture into potatoes.

think like a cook

MAKE FRIENDS WITH THE MICROWAVE

Microwaving is easily dismissed as a nonserious way to cook food, but there's more to this appliance than reheating leftovers. We frequently use it as a shortcut to jump-start ingredients that will finish cooking on the stove or in the oven. For our quick Pan-Roasted Potatoes, starting in the microwave helped ensure the potatoes fully cooked through and that they browned quickly in the pan. It also helped us get perfectly crisp potatoes: Before the exterior of the potatoes can brown, excess moisture has to be driven off. Thanks to the microwave, the potatoes cooked through and crisped up in less than 15 minutes in the pan.

After many years of working with the microwave, we've also come up with a couple best practices to help ensure even cooking. First, be sure to stir or flip the food often during microwaving. We also recommend resting foods for a few minutes after microwaving to allow hot and cold spots to even out.

Roasted Root Vegetables

Serves 4; Total Time 1 hour

12 ounces carrots, peeled and cut into 1¼-inch pieces

12 ounces red potatoes, unpeeled and cut into 1¼-inch pieces

12 ounces turnips, peeled and cut into 1¼-inch pieces

4 shallots, halved and peeled

2 tablespoons unsalted butter, melted

Salt and pepper

1 garlic head, cloves separated and peeled

1. Adjust oven rack to middle position and heat oven to 400 degrees. Toss carrots, potatoes, turnips, shallots, butter, ¾ teaspoon salt, and ¼ teaspoon pepper together in bowl.

2. Spread vegetables into single layer on rimmed baking sheet and roast until vegetables are tender and well browned, about 45 minutes, adding garlic cloves during final 20 minutes.

3. Season with salt and pepper to taste, and serve warm or at room temperature.

why this recipe works

Few techniques transform humble root vegetables into something rich and complex more effectively than roasting, and this recipe provides an easy way to roast several kinds at once. Roasting vegetables is a lot like roasting meat: You need high, dry heat and a low-sided pan large enough to accommodate the food without crowding, which would inhibit browning. You also need some fat. We liked butter for its great flavor, but you can also use vegetable oil or a combination of butter and oil. (Chicken or duck fat, if you have any, is also wonderful.) We also added whole garlic cloves and halved shallots, which added deep flavor to the finished dish. We liked a mix of hearty potatoes, sweet carrots, and peppery turnips in this recipe, but you can substitute other root vegetables such as parsnips, sweet potatoes, or rutabagas; just make sure you cut them into even pieces (see "Shape Matters" for more information).

variations

Roasted Carrots and Red Onion with Balsamic Vinegar

Omit red potatoes and turnips. Increase carrots to 2 pounds. Substitute 1 medium red onion, peeled and cut into 1-inch wedges through root end, for shallots. Add 3 tablespoons balsamic vinegar to carrots with butter.

Roasted Turnips, Shallots, and Garlic with Rosemary

Omit red potatoes and carrots. Increase turnips to 1½ pounds. Add 2 teaspoons minced fresh rosemary to turnips with butter.

think like a cook

SHAPE MATTERS

Ingredients cut into even pieces produce more attractive dishes, but it's not all about looks; this also helps the food cook evenly so you don't end up with both charred and raw bits. For our Roasted Root Vegetables, we cut the roots into 1¼-inch pieces—bite-size but still big enough to get good browning.

What's the best way to cut a vegetable? That depends on its shape and size. With oblong carrots and parsnips, crosswise cuts are often sufficient, but the fatter ends may need to be cut in half lengthwise to match the skinnier bottoms. With round vegetables such as turnips and potatoes, we typically cut them in half to create a stable base, cut the halves lengthwise into planks, then cut the planks into pieces. If they are small enough, however, as with some shallots or potatoes, you can simply halve or quarter them, or even leave them whole, depending on their size. For more information on prepping specific vegetables, see page 26.

Broiled Eggplant with Basil and Tahini Sauce

Serves 4; Total Time 1 hour

why this recipe works

Many people complain that eggplant is either tough, bitter, or oily. This is not inevitable. The challenge is dealing with eggplant's texture; it contains a lot of water but is also porous and drinks up oil, causing the exterior to become greasy and charred while the interior remains tough and bitter. A simple fix was salting: The salt drew water to the eggplant's surface, where it could be wiped away so the eggplant only needed a few minutes per side under a blazing hot broiler. Broiling rather than frying meant we could use just a light brushing of oil for less greasy results. While it's good simply seasoned with basil, broiled eggplant really shines with our Tahini Sauce, which perfectly complements the eggplant's concentrated roasted flavor. Make sure to slice the eggplant thin so that the slices will cook through by the time the exterior is browned.

TAHINI SAUCE
¼ cup tahini

¼ cup water

2 tablespoons lemon juice

1 clove garlic, minced

Salt and pepper

EGGPLANT
1½ pounds eggplant, sliced into ¼-inch-thick rounds

1 tablespoon kosher salt

3 tablespoons extra-virgin olive oil

Pepper

2 tablespoons chopped fresh basil

1. FOR THE TAHINI SAUCE Whisk tahini, water, lemon juice, and garlic in bowl until smooth (mixture will appear broken at first). Season with salt and pepper to taste. Let sit at room temperature for at least 30 minutes to allow flavors to meld. (Sauce can be refrigerated for up to 4 days; bring to room temperature before serving.)

2. FOR THE EGGPLANT Arrange eggplant on baking sheet lined with paper towels, sprinkle both sides with kosher salt, and let stand for 30 minutes.

3. Adjust oven rack 4 inches from broiler element and heat broiler. Thoroughly pat eggplant dry, arrange on aluminum foil–lined baking sheet, and brush both sides with oil. Broil eggplant until tops are mahogany brown, 4 to 6 minutes. Flip slices over and broil until second sides are brown, 4 to 6 minutes.

4. Transfer eggplant to platter and season with pepper to taste. Sprinkle with basil, drizzle with sauce, and serve.

BROIL IT LIKE YOU MEAN IT

To use a broiler effectively, it's important to understand how it differs from regular oven cooking. While roasting relies on convective heat (air molecules surround the food), a broiler cooks food primarily with radiant heat, a form of invisible infrared light waves. The broiler element can reach 2,000 degrees, making it a powerful but challenging cooking tool to use with precision. The way most broilers operate doesn't make it any easier.

Waves Must Hit the Food

The waves should directly hit the food. The food should be just far enough away from the element that the heat is intense but also evenly hitting the food. Pay close attention to recipe instructions about how to position your oven rack in relation to the broiler.

Preheating Is Unreliable

Most broilers have no ready signal, so you're left guessing when the broiler is preheated. Those that heat quickly may cycle off during cooking, while slow-to-heat broilers will be too cool and won't cook the food in the given time. Getting to know your broiler takes time and experience.

If a Broiler Cycles Off, Browning Suffers

If the broiler is on for too long, most ovens will exceed a maximum air temperature and the broiler will temporarily switch off. The food will continue to cook by convection, but without radiant heat, browning will slow dramatically. Take that into account and keep an eye on your food when cooking with the broiler.

White Beans with Tomatoes, Garlic, and Sage

Serves 6; Total Time 2 hours 30 minutes

1 pound (2½ cups) dried cannellini, great Northern, or navy beans, rinsed and picked over to remove any small stones and beans that are broken or shriveled

1 onion, unpeeled and halved through root end

1 carrot, cut into 2-inch lengths

1 garlic head, outer papery skins removed and top third of head cut off and discarded, plus 4 cloves, sliced thin

Salt and pepper

2 bay leaves

6 cups water

¼ cup extra-virgin olive oil, plus extra for drizzling

¼ cup chopped fresh sage

1 (28-ounce) can diced tomatoes, drained

2 tablespoons minced fresh parsley

1. Bring beans, onion, carrot, garlic head, 1 teaspoon salt, bay leaves, and water to boil in large saucepan or Dutch oven over medium-high heat. Reduce heat to low, partially cover, and simmer, stirring occasionally, until beans are almost tender, 1 to 1¼ hours, adding more liquid if necessary. Remove pot from heat, completely cover, and let stand until beans are fully tender, 30 to 60 minutes. Drain beans in colander, reserving 1 cup cooking liquid. Discard onion, carrot, and bay leaves. With a slotted spoon, transfer head of garlic to cutting board. Using tongs, squeeze cloves out of skins and return softened cloves to pot with beans; discard skins.

2. Heat oil, thinly sliced garlic, and sage in 12-inch skillet over medium heat. As oil begins to sizzle, shake pan back and forth so that garlic does not stick (stirring with wooden spoon will cause garlic to clump). Cook until garlic turns very pale gold and sage darkens, about 4 minutes. Add tomatoes and ½ teaspoon salt and simmer, stirring occasionally, until tomato juices have evaporated and tomatoes look shiny, about 10 minutes.

3. Stir in beans and reserved cooking liquid. Simmer, stirring occasionally, until liquid has evaporated, 18 to 20 minutes. Off heat, stir in parsley and season with salt and pepper to taste. Serve immediately, accompanied by extra-virgin olive oil for drizzling at table.

why this recipe works

Dried beans come in a range of color, shapes, and sizes, with flavors from earthy to nutty. They have a far superior texture and better flavor than canned beans, but while it's not difficult to cook dried beans, it does take some time. For a simple but hearty bean recipe, we started by giving dried white beans a gentle simmer on the stove and then letting them sit off heat to finish cooking for a perfectly creamy texture. Onion, carrot, and bay leaves simmered with the beans to help impart a subtle flavor. Simmering a whole head of garlic also gave us softened cloves with a mild, sweet garlic flavor that we then stirred into the beans. Sautéing more garlic and sage in olive oil before adding tomatoes gave us a potently flavored base. Adding the cooked beans and simmering let the traditional Italian flavors meld into a simple and satisfying dish.

think like a cook

WHEN DRIED BEANS ARE WORTH IT

The biggest considerations when choosing whether to use dried or canned beans for a recipe are how much time you have and how central the beans are to the dish. Canned beans are undeniably convenient, but when the beans are the star of a dish, we prefer the firmer texture and cleaner flavor of dried beans. In long-cooked, slow-simmered applications, dried beans also help create their own broth, as they do in our White Beans with Tomatoes, Garlic, and Sage. Canned beans are a great option for quicker recipes and dishes where texture is less important, such as when the beans will be pureed.

Buy "Fresh" Dried Beans

When shopping for beans, it's essential to select the freshest dried beans available. Buy those that are uniform in size and have a smooth exterior. When dried beans are fully hydrated and cooked, they should be plump, with taut skins, and have creamy insides; spent beans will have wrinkled skin and a dry, almost gritty texture.

Make Dried Beans a Pantry Staple

Uncooked beans should be stored in a cool, dry place in a sealed plastic or glass container. Beans are less susceptible than rice and grains to pests and spoilage, but it is still best to use them within a month or two. Always pick over dried beans to remove stones and debris, and rinse them before cooking to wash away any dust or impurities.

Substitute Canned Beans with Caution

Most recipes that call for dried beans require the beans to cook slowly with the other ingredients so that they release their starches and thicken the dish. When you replace dried beans with canned beans and shorten the cooking time (canned beans are fully cooked and need to cook only long enough to warm through and soak up flavor), you sacrifice both the flavor and the texture of the finished dish. But if you're short on time and need to swap in canned beans, a general rule of thumb is that 1 cup of dried beans equals 3 cups of canned beans.

Crispy Tofu Fingers with Sweet Chili Sauce

Serves 4; Total Time 45 minutes

28 ounces soft tofu

4 teaspoons plus ¾ cup cornstarch

½ cup water

½ cup rice vinegar

6 tablespoons sugar

2 tablespoons Asian chili-garlic sauce

¼ cup cornmeal

Salt and pepper

¾ cup vegetable oil

1. Slice tofu crosswise into ¾-inch-thick slabs, then slice each slab into 3 fingers. Arrange tofu on paper towel–lined baking sheet and let sit for 20 minutes to drain, then gently pat tofu dry with paper towels.

2. Meanwhile, whisk 4 teaspoons cornstarch, water, vinegar, sugar, and chili-garlic sauce together in small saucepan. Bring to simmer over medium-high heat and cook, whisking constantly, until thickened, about 4 minutes. Remove sauce from heat and cover to keep warm.

3. Set wire rack in rimmed baking sheet. Combine remaining ¾ cup cornstarch and cornmeal in shallow dish. Season tofu with salt and pepper. Coat tofu thoroughly with cornstarch mixture a few pieces at a time, pressing gently to adhere. Transfer to prepared rack.

4. Heat oil in 12-inch nonstick skillet over medium-high heat until shimmering. Working in 2 batches, fry tofu, turning as needed, until crisp and golden on all sides, about 4 minutes. Gently lift tofu from oil, letting excess oil drip back into skillet, and transfer to paper towel–lined plate to drain. Serve with sauce.

why this recipe works

Pan frying is one of our favorite ways to prepare tofu. It becomes crispy on the outside and creamy within, perfect for dipping into a sauce, as we do here, or adding to salads (see the variation). To ensure the tofu got nice and crisp, we first drained it thoroughly. A coating of cornstarch and cornmeal gave us a crunchy, golden-brown crust that paired perfectly with a quick spicy-sweet chili sauce. We prefer the softer, creamier texture of soft tofu here for the perfect contrast between creamy interior and crispy exterior. Medium-firm, firm, or extra-firm tofu will also work, but will taste drier. You can find Asian chili-garlic sauce in Asian markets or the international aisle of most supermarkets. Be sure to handle the tofu gently and pat it dry thoroughly before seasoning and coating.

variation

Crispy Tofu and Warm Cabbage Salad

Skip step 2, omitting dipping sauce. Instead, whisk 3 tablespoons vegetable oil, 5 tablespoons rice vinegar, 2 tablespoons soy sauce, 2 tablespoons sugar, and 1–2 teaspoons Asian chili-garlic sauce in bowl, cover, and microwave until simmering, 1 to 2 minutes. Reserve

2 tablespoons dressing and toss remainder with 1 (14-ounce) bag green coleslaw mix, ¾ cup chopped dry-roasted peanuts, 4 thinly sliced scallions, ½ cup fresh cilantro leaves, and ½ cup chopped fresh mint. Drizzle tofu with reserved dressing; serve with salad.

think like a cook

SECRETS OF TERRIFIC TOFU

Most tofu comes stored in water, and since it's quite porous, it needs to be drained before cooking. You could just pat tofu dry, but taking time to drain it for 20 minutes removes excess moisture that can make dishes bland and watery. Plus, the more water you remove, the more flavor the tofu can soak up from sauces or other ingredients added during cooking. Coating the tofu in cornstarch helps absorb exuded moisture and ensures a crispy exterior and better browning.

As an ingredient, tofu takes to a wide variety of preparations. Crispy tofu stars in our Farro Bowls with Tofu, Mushrooms, and Spinach (page 186), and Tofu Banh Mi (page 304). We scramble it like eggs in Tofu Scramble with Herbs (page 120), and stir-fry it to make Stir-Fried Tofu and Bok Choy (page 66) and Spicy Tofu and Basil Lettuce Cups (page 306). It even tastes great raw if marinated first in a flavorful dressing, as in our Marinated Tofu and Vegetable Salad (page 170).

Stir-Fried Tofu and Bok Choy
Serves 4; Total Time 45 minutes

SAUCE

½ cup chicken broth

¼ cup Chinese rice wine or dry sherry

3 tablespoons hoisin sauce or oyster-flavored sauce

1 tablespoon soy sauce

2 teaspoons cornstarch

1 teaspoon toasted sesame oil

STIR-FRY

14 ounces extra-firm tofu, cut into 1-inch cubes

1 small head bok choy (about 1 pound)

3 scallions, minced

3 garlic cloves, minced

1 tablespoon grated fresh ginger

2 tablespoons vegetable oil

⅓ cup cornstarch

2 carrots, peeled and cut into matchsticks (see page 28)

why this recipe works

You don't need sous chef–level skills or a fancy wok to make a great tofu and vegetable stir-fry at home. To create an easy stir-fry where all the components are properly cooked, we were careful about preparing the ingredients and adding each one at the right time. For perfectly crispy tofu with a creamy interior, we cooked the tofu first, giving it plenty of room to brown in the hot pan, and then set it aside until we were ready to finish the dish. Coating the tofu with a thin layer of cornstarch helped it to develop a browned crust with a minimum of oil; the coating also helped the stir-fry sauce cling to the tofu cubes for lots of flavor in every bite. Tougher bok choy stems and carrots were added before the quicker-cooking bok choy greens. The delicate aromatics, ginger and garlic, were only added near the end of cooking, followed by the flavorful sauce. Serve with white or brown rice (see page 74).

1. **FOR THE SAUCE** Whisk all ingredients together in bowl.

2. **FOR THE STIR-FRY** Arrange tofu on rimmed baking sheet lined with several layers of paper towels and let sit for 20 minutes to drain.

3. While tofu drains, remove greens from stems of bok choy by cutting along either side of stems. Slice stalks thin on bias and slice greens thin. Combine scallions, garlic, ginger, and 1 teaspoon oil in bowl.

4. Gently pat tofu dry with paper towels. Place cornstarch in medium bowl. Working with a few pieces at a time, toss tofu gently in cornstarch to coat, then transfer to plate.

5. Heat 1 tablespoon oil in 12-inch nonstick skillet over high heat until just smoking. Add tofu and cook, turning occasionally, until crisp and browned on all sides, about 8 minutes. Transfer to bowl (do not cover) and set aside.

6. Add remaining 2 teaspoons oil to skillet and return to high heat until shimmering. Add bok choy stalks and carrots and cook until vegetables are crisp-tender, about 4 minutes.

7. Clear center of skillet, add scallion mixture, and cook, mashing mixture into pan, until fragrant, 15 to 30 seconds. Stir into vegetables.

8. Return tofu to skillet and stir in bok choy greens. Whisk sauce to recombine, then add to skillet. Simmer, tossing constantly, until tofu is heated through and sauce is thickened, 30 seconds to 2 minutes. Serve.

think like a cook

STIR-FRY LIKE A PRO

No matter which ingredients you're stir-frying, follow these guidelines to ensure success.

Prep Everything Before Cooking

A stir-fry cooks within a matter of minutes, so have everything fully prepped (including the sauce) before you begin.

Use a 12-Inch Skillet and Get It Smoking Hot

A broad, searing hot surface is crucial for ingredients to brown rather than steam. (Don't bother with a wok; its curved sides won't get hot enough on a home stove.)

Don't Overstir

Despite the technique's name, food browns when in undisturbed contact with a hot surface; with too much actual stirring, you won't get good browning.

Stagger the Vegetables

Add longer-cooking vegetables first, then more delicate ones, to ensure everything ends up crisp-tender.

Clear the Center of the Pan for Your Aromatics

Ingredients like minced garlic and ginger quickly scorch over high heat. To avoid this, add them in a centralized space with a little oil and quickly mash them using a wooden spoon until they are fragrant.

Finish with Sauce

Whisk the sauce to recombine, add it, and simmer until it has thickened and coated the food.

Perfect Scrambled Eggs
Serves 4; Total Time 10 minutes

8 large eggs plus 2 large yolks
¼ cup half-and-half
Salt and pepper
1 tablespoon unsalted butter, chilled

1. Beat eggs, yolks, half-and-half, ⅜ teaspoon salt, and ¼ teaspoon pepper with fork until eggs are thoroughly combined and color is pure yellow; do not overbeat.

2. Heat butter in 10-inch nonstick skillet over medium-high heat until foaming just subsides (butter should not brown), swirling to coat pan. Add egg mixture and, using rubber spatula, constantly and firmly scrape along bottom and sides of skillet until eggs begin to clump and spatula just leaves trail on bottom of pan, 1½ to 2½ minutes. Reduce heat to low and gently but constantly fold eggs until clumped and just slightly wet, 30 to 60 seconds. Immediately transfer eggs to warmed plates and season with salt to taste. Serve immediately.

why this recipe works
Turning out rich and creamy—not dry and rubbery—scrambled eggs makes the simplest of all meals something special. Adding a couple extra yolks and ¼ cup half-and-half ensures rich flavor, and the added fat prevents over-cooking, as does seasoning the raw eggs with salt, which tenderizes them. To create large, even curds, we used a smaller (10-inch) skillet so we'd have a thicker layer of eggs. Stirring constantly (scraping along both the sides and bottom) helped the eggs coagulate evenly, and dropping the heat partway through gave us more control over doneness. Follow the visual cues, as pan thickness will affect cooking times. (If using an electric stove, heat one burner on low and a second on medium-high; move the skillet between burners for temperature adjustment.) To dress up the eggs, add 2 tablespoons minced fresh parsley, chives, basil, or cilantro, or 1 tablespoon minced fresh dill or tarragon after reducing the heat to low.

variations
Perfect Scrambled Eggs for Two
Use 4 large eggs plus 1 large yolk, 2 tablespoons half-and-half, ⅛ teaspoon salt, ⅛ teaspoon pepper, and 1½ teaspoons butter. Cook eggs in 8-inch skillet for 45 to 75 seconds over medium-high heat and then 30 to 60 seconds over low heat.

Perfect Scrambled Eggs for One
Use 2 large eggs plus 1 large yolk, 1 tablespoon half-and-half, pinch salt, pinch pepper, and ¾ teaspoon butter. Cook eggs in 8-inch skillet for 30 to 60 seconds over medium-high heat and then 30 to 60 seconds over low heat.

Smoked Salmon Scrambled Eggs with Chive Butter
Mash 3 tablespoons softened unsalted butter with 3 tablespoons minced fresh chives. Toast 4 (1-inch-thick) slices rustic white bread, then spread with 2 tablespoons chive butter. Cook eggs as directed, using remaining chive butter. Immediately spoon eggs on top of buttered toasts, top with 3 ounces smoked salmon, and serve. Garnish with extra chives if desired.

think like a cook

THE CLEANEST BREAK

There are best practices for even the simplest kitchen tasks. For example: cracking an egg. Do it thoughtlessly and you'll end up with annoying bits of shell in the bowl. For the cleanest break, crack eggs against a flat surface, rather than the edge of the counter or a mixing bowl.

Once you can crack an egg correctly, separating them is easy. We separate eggs if we need just the yolk or white (as in our scrambled eggs, which uses additional yolks) or if the two will be used in different ways. Separate eggs when they're cold: Cold yolks are less apt to break into the whites. To separate an egg, hold the halves of the cracked shell over a bowl and gently transfer the yolk back and forth between them, letting the white fall into the bowl; drop the yolk into a second bowl. (Alternatively, open the cracked egg into your cupped palm and slowly separate your fingers to allow the white to slide into the bowl, leaving the yolk intact in your palm.) If you plan on whipping the egg whites, use three bowls: Separate each egg over the first bowl and let the white fall in. Slide the yolk into the second bowl and then move the white to the third bowl before starting over with the next egg. That way, if one yolk breaks into the white, it doesn't contaminate the whole batch of whites. Even the tiniest amount of fat from the egg yolks can undermine the stability of the beaten whites.

Fried Eggs

Serves 2; Total Time 15 minutes

2 teaspoons vegetable oil

4 large eggs

Salt and pepper

2 teaspoons unsalted butter,
cut into 4 pieces and chilled

1. Heat oil in 12-inch nonstick skillet over low heat for 5 minutes. Meanwhile, crack 2 eggs into small bowl and season with salt and pepper. Repeat with remaining 2 eggs and second small bowl.

2. Increase heat to medium-high and heat until oil is shimmering. Add butter to skillet and quickly swirl to coat pan. Working quickly, pour 1 bowl of eggs in 1 side of pan and second bowl of eggs in other side. Cover and cook for 1 minute. Remove skillet from burner and let stand, covered, 15 to 45 seconds for runny yolks (white around edge of yolk will be barely opaque), 45 to 60 seconds for soft but set yolks, and about 2 minutes for medium-set yolks. Slide eggs onto plates and serve.

why this recipe works

This method produces diner-style fried eggs with crisp edges and a runny yolk. If, like us, you have struggled with whites that never fully set up or yolks that overcook, it's a game changer. The first thing to do is to reach for a nonstick skillet; there's no point in frying eggs in anything else. Next, don't skip preheating: It ensures the pan's surface will be evenly hot, which is extra important for quick-cooking foods like eggs. Once you raise the heat, don't dawdle: Each step from here takes under a minute. When checking the eggs for doneness, lift the lid just a crack to prevent loss of steam should they need further cooking. To fry just two eggs, use an 8-inch nonstick skillet and halve the amounts of oil and butter. You can use this method with extra-large or jumbo eggs without altering the timing.

variation
Egg in a Hole

Use 6 eggs. Adjust oven racks to lowest and top positions, place rimmed baking sheet on lower rack, and heat oven to 500 degrees. Spread 2½ tablespoons softened unsalted butter evenly over 1 side of 6 slices hearty white sandwich bread. Using 2½-inch biscuit cutter, cut out and remove circle from center of each piece of buttered bread. Remove hot sheet from oven, add 2½ tablespoons softened unsalted butter, and let melt, tilting sheet to let butter cover sheet evenly. Place bread circles down center of sheet and bread slices on either side of circles, buttered side up. Return sheet to lower rack and bake until bread is golden, 3 to 5 minutes, flipping bread and rotating sheet halfway through baking. Remove sheet from oven and set inside second (room temperature) rimmed baking sheet. Crack 1 egg into each bread hole. Season eggs with salt and pepper. Bake on upper rack until whites are barely set, 4 to 6 minutes, rotating sheet halfway through baking. Transfer sheets to wire rack and let eggs sit until whites are completely set, about 2 minutes. Serve. Makes 6 toasts.

think like a cook

PUT AN EGG ON IT

Adding a fried egg on top of pretty much any dish makes it richer, heartier, and more luxurious. In addition to bulking up the protein content of your meal, a fried egg also comes with its own built-in sauce from the silky, runny yolk. This makes it a great topping for simple pasta dishes (try it on top of our Pasta with Garlic and Oil on page 78) or for salad greens to turn them into a light meal (spinach is especially nice).

Other recipes in this book that feature fried eggs as their finishing touch are our Bacon and Cheddar Breakfast Sandwiches (page 116), Brown Rice Bowls with Roasted Carrots, Kale, and Fried Eggs (page 180), and Vegetable Bibimbap (page 188). We also recommend trying one on top of Hash Browns (page 132), mixed into Faster Steel-Cut Oatmeal (page 108) for a savory take on breakfast porridge, or as the ultimate decadent topping for The Burger Lover's Burger (page 296).

Easy-Peel Hard-Cooked Eggs

Makes 6 eggs; Total Time 35 minutes

6 large eggs

1. Bring 1 inch water to rolling boil in medium saucepan over high heat. Place eggs in steamer basket. Transfer basket to saucepan. Cover, reduce heat to medium-low, and cook eggs for 13 minutes.

2. When eggs are almost finished cooking, combine 2 cups ice cubes and 2 cups cold water in medium bowl. Using tongs or spoon, transfer eggs to ice bath; let sit for 15 minutes.

3. Crack wide end of each egg against a hard, flat surface. Starting at wide end of each egg, peel away shell. When done, dunk peeled egg back into ice bath to remove any stray bits of shell (if necessary).

variation
Soft-Cooked Eggs

With a set white and fluid yolk, these have the appeal of poached eggs but are less fussy and can be eaten out of the shell. Precise timing is critical, so use a digital timer. You can use this method for one to six large, extra-large, or jumbo eggs without altering the timing. We recommend serving these eggs in egg cups and with buttered toast sticks, or soldiers, for dipping, or simply use the dull side of a butter knife to crack the egg along the equator, break the egg in half, and scoop out the insides with a teaspoon and serve as you would a poached egg—over toast, salad, or cooked vegetables.

After adding steamer basket with eggs to saucepan of boiling water, reduce heat to medium-high and cook for 6½ minutes. Remove cover, transfer saucepan to sink, and place under cold running water for 30 seconds. Remove eggs from saucepan and serve, seasoning with salt and pepper to taste.

why this recipe works

A hard-cooked egg that's just cooked through, with no chalkiness (or greenish tinge) to the yolk, is plenty good on its own sprinkled with salt, and it can also be used in myriad other ways. Cooking methods abound, but we found that steaming, followed by an ice bath to halt the cooking, not only guarantees perfect eggs but also results in shells that slip off easily. Why? Hot steam hitting cold eggs rapidly cooks the outermost egg white proteins, which shrink away from the membrane. Be sure to use large, cold eggs that have no cracks. You can cook fewer than six eggs without altering the timing, or more eggs as long as your pot and steamer basket can hold them in a single layer. If you don't have a steamer basket, use a spoon or tongs to gently place the eggs in the water. It does not matter if the eggs are above the water or partially submerged. Unpeeled cooked eggs can be stored in their shells in the refrigerator for up to 3 days.

THE EGG-DONENESS CONTINUUM

The fundamental challenge in egg cookery is that an egg is not really one ingredient but two: the white and the yolk. And each solidifies at different temperatures: Whites start to thicken at 145 degrees and are fully set at 180. Yolks begin to thicken at 150 degrees and are fully set at 158; this narrow range means that just a minute or two of timing can completely change the consistency of your eggs, from creamy to fully set to overdone, as the photos below show. Our steaming method ensures a consistent temperature, allowing us to nail down more precise timing than boiling would, since adding eggs to a pot of boiling water lowers the temperature of the water. Just make sure to set a timer!

Soft-Cooked Egg

Perfect Hard-Cooked Egg

Overcooked Egg

Foolproof Baked Brown Rice

Serves 4 to 6; Total Time 1 hour 30 minutes

2⅓ cups boiling water

1½ cups long-grain, medium-grain, or short-grain brown rice, rinsed

2 teaspoons extra-virgin olive oil

Salt and pepper

1. Adjust oven rack to middle position and heat oven to 375 degrees. Combine boiling water, rice, oil, and ½ teaspoon salt in 8-inch square baking dish.

2. Cover dish tightly with double layer of aluminum foil. Transfer dish to oven and bake until liquid is absorbed and rice is tender, about 1 hour.

3. Remove dish from oven, uncover, and fluff rice with fork, scraping up any rice that has stuck to bottom. Cover dish with clean dish towel and let rice sit for 5 minutes. Uncover and let rice sit 5 minutes longer. Season with salt and pepper to taste, and serve.

why this recipe works

Brown rice is ultimately satisfying, with nutty flavor and serious textural personality. While it's often steamed, baking it in an aluminum foil–covered dish ensures more even cooking and makes it a simple, hands-off endeavor. We found that we needed less liquid than the 2:1 water-to-rice ratio usually advised by rice producers and recipes. Adding boiling water jump-started the cooking process. A small amount of oil complemented the flavor while keeping the rice fluffy. For an accurate measurement of boiling water, bring a full kettle to a boil, then measure out the desired amount. If your baking dish has a lid, it may be used instead of the aluminum foil. To double the recipe, use a 13 by 9-inch baking dish; the baking time does not need to be increased. You can use long-, medium-, or short-grain brown rice. This method also works for long-grain white rice with a few modifications; see the variation.

variation
Foolproof Baked White Rice

Basmati, jasmine, or Texmati rice can also be used in this recipe.

Adjust oven rack to middle position and heat oven to 450 degrees. Combine 2¾ cups boiling water, 1⅓ cups rinsed long-grain white rice, 1 tablespoon extra-virgin olive oil, and ½ teaspoon salt in 8-inch square baking dish. Cover dish tightly with double layer of aluminum foil. Transfer dish to oven and bake until liquid is absorbed and rice is tender, about 20 minutes. Remove dish from oven, uncover, and fluff rice with fork, scraping up any rice that has stuck to bottom. Cover dish with clean dish towel and let rice sit for 10 minutes. Season with salt and pepper to taste and serve.

JAZZING UP PLAIN RICE

To add some oomph to plain rice, try one of these ideas to turn it into a flavorful side dish in no time.

» Add butter, minced fresh herbs, and/or citrus zest.

» Stir in a compound butter (see page 329).

» Mix in heartier ingredients for a more substantial side dish to match the flavors of your meal. Some combinations we like are chopped dried fruit, toasted nuts, and goat cheese, or sliced olives, feta, and pine nuts. Or use black beans, cilantro, and lime juice for a Latin-inspired dish.

» Let the rice cool, then toss with a vinaigrette (see page 50) to make rice salad.

Quinoa Pilaf with Herbs and Lemon

Serves 4 to 6; Total Time 50 minutes

1½ cups prewashed white quinoa

2 tablespoons unsalted butter or extra-virgin olive oil

1 small onion, chopped fine

¾ teaspoon salt

1¾ cups water

3 tablespoons chopped fresh cilantro, parsley, chives, mint, or tarragon

1 tablespoon lemon juice

1. Toast quinoa in medium saucepan over medium-high heat, stirring frequently, until quinoa is very fragrant and makes continuous popping sound, 5 to 7 minutes; transfer to bowl.

2. Melt butter in now-empty saucepan over medium-low heat. Add onion and salt and cook until onion is softened and light golden, 5 to 7 minutes. Stir in water and toasted quinoa, increase heat to medium-high, and bring to simmer. Cover, reduce heat to low, and simmer until grains are just tender and liquid is absorbed, 18 to 20 minutes, stirring once halfway through cooking.

3. Remove saucepan from heat and let sit, covered, for 10 minutes. Fluff quinoa with fork, stir in herbs and lemon juice, and serve.

why this recipe works

While in theory this "supergrain" should be appealingly nutty and crunchy, cooked quinoa often ends up a mushy mess with washed-out flavor and an underlying bitterness. For a simple quinoa pilaf with light, distinct grains and great flavor, we used less water than most quinoa recipes to avoid any mushiness. We also toasted the quinoa to develop its natural nuttiness before simmering. We flavored our pilaf with onion sautéed in fat and finished it with herbs and a squeeze of lemon juice. Quinoa is also easily adapted to a variety of other flavor profiles as in the variations. We like the convenience of prewashed quinoa; rinsing removes the quinoa's bitter protective coating (called saponin). If you buy unwashed quinoa (or if you are unsure whether it's washed), rinse it and then spread it out over a clean dish towel to dry for 15 minutes before cooking.

variations

Quinoa Pilaf with Goat Cheese and Chives

Substitute 4 minced garlic cloves for onion; cook until fragrant, about 30 seconds, before adding toasted quinoa. Use chives for chopped herbs. Sprinkle with ½ cup crumbled goat cheese before serving.

Quinoa Pilaf with Olives, Raisins, and Cilantro

Add ¼ teaspoon ground cumin, ¼ teaspoon dried oregano, and ⅛ teaspoon ground cinnamon to saucepan with onion. Stir in ¼ cup golden raisins halfway through cooking quinoa. Substitute ⅓ cup coarsely chopped pimento-stuffed green olives and 3 tablespoons chopped fresh cilantro for chopped fresh herbs, and 4 teaspoons red wine vinegar for lemon juice.

Quinoa Pilaf with Apricots, Aged Gouda, and Pistachios

Add ½ teaspoon grated lemon zest, ½ teaspoon ground coriander, ¼ teaspoon ground cumin, and ⅛ teaspoon pepper to saucepan with onion. Stir in ½ cup coarsely chopped dried apricots before letting quinoa sit for 10 minutes in step 3. Substitute ½ cup shredded aged gouda; ½ cup shelled pistachios, toasted and chopped coarse; and 2 tablespoons chopped fresh mint for herbs.

think like a cook

WHAT IS A PILAF?

You may associate pilaf with rice, but the pilaf method can be used to cook any grain. It is a simple but elegant approach where the grain is toasted before being simmered slowly in liquid until it's tender and super-flavorful. We use the pilaf method for many grains, including rice, bulgur, quinoa, barley, and millet, as well as pasta and couscous. It produces grains with a light, fluffy texture and an extra layer of nutty, toasted flavor that you don't get from just boiling the grains.

Many pilaf recipes also add sautéed aromatics like onion, garlic, or shallot to the grain for an extra-flavorful dish. Other ways to build complex flavor in this simple preparation include swapping in chicken broth for water and stirring in chopped fresh herbs, dried fruit, cheese, or other additions before serving, as in the variations here.

Make sure you use a sturdy, heavy-bottomed saucepan with a tight-fitting lid for any pilaf recipe so the rice or grain will cook evenly and not scorch or stick to the pan.

Pasta with Garlic and Oil (Aglio e Olio)
Serves 4 to 6; Total Time 30 minutes

6 tablespoons extra-virgin olive oil

12 garlic cloves, minced (4 tablespoons)

Salt and pepper

3 tablespoons minced fresh parsley

2 teaspoons lemon juice

¾ teaspoon red pepper flakes

1 pound spaghetti

Grated Parmesan cheese

1. Cook 3 tablespoons oil, 3 tablespoons garlic, and ½ teaspoon salt in 10-inch nonstick skillet over low heat, stirring often, until garlic foams and is sticky and straw-colored, about 10 minutes. Off heat, stir in parsley, lemon juice, pepper flakes, remaining 3 tablespoons oil, and remaining 1 tablespoon garlic.

2. Meanwhile, bring 4 quarts water to boil in large pot. Add pasta and 1 tablespoon salt and cook, stirring often, until almost al dente. Reserve ½ cup cooking water, then drain pasta in colander and return it to pot.

3. Stir 2 tablespoons reserved cooking water into garlic sauce to loosen, then add sauce to pasta and toss to combine. Season with salt and pepper to taste and add remaining reserved cooking water as needed to adjust consistency. Serve with Parmesan.

why this recipe works

Call it the simplest spaghetti dish, a pantry dinner mainstay, or a favorite midnight meal among Italians, but don't call it plain. Our take on *aglio e olio* is packed with flavor, thanks to a whopping 12 cloves of garlic. Cooking most of the garlic slowly over low heat softened its edge, turning it golden, nutty-tasting, and subtly sweet. Stirring in raw garlic off the heat delivered some bite to the sauce, while lemon juice balanced the oil's richness. With such a minimal sauce, getting perfectly al dente pasta is critical, as its texture can make or break the dish. So taste often to avoid overcooking. And reserve some of the cooking water before draining the pasta; the water is used to loosen the texture of the sauce. For a twist on this dish, try sprinkling toasted bread crumbs over the individual serving bowls. For a quick way to peel the garlic, see page 351.

variation
Pasta with Garlic, Oil, and Artichokes

Transfer cooked garlic mixture to bowl before combining with other ingredients at end of step 1. Heat 2 teaspoons extra-virgin olive oil in now-empty skillet over medium-high heat until shimmering. Add 9 ounces frozen artichoke hearts, thawed and patted dry, and ⅛ teaspoon salt and cook until artichokes are lightly browned and tender, 4 to 6 minutes. Add cooked artichokes to pasta with garlic sauce.

PASTA PERFECT

Pasta is one of those things that is easy to cook, but hard to cook just right. We prefer pasta cooked al dente, with a little bite left in the center (al dente is Italian for "to the tooth"). Follow these simple steps for perfect pasta every time.

Use Plenty of Water

Pasta leaches starch as it cooks; without plenty of water to dilute the starch, it will coat the noodles and they will stick together. We recommend 4 quarts of water for 1 pound of pasta. Use a pot with at least a 6-quart capacity, and fill it with cold tap water; warm water can pick up off-flavors from your water heater. Make sure to bring the water to a rolling boil over high heat; pasta cooks best (and fastest) in boiling, not simmering, water.

Salt the Water, Don't Oil It

Once the water is boiling, add 1 tablespoon of salt to flavor the pasta. Don't add oil: It does nothing for the pasta and also prevents the sauce from adhering.

When You Add the Pasta, Give It a Stir

Stirring the pasta when you first add it to the water, and occasionally as it cooks, will prevent it from sticking.

Check Often for Doneness

Several minutes before the pasta should be done, begin tasting it—that's really the only way to know when it's ready. When the pasta is almost al dente, remove the pot from heat. Because the pasta continues to cook after it is drained, you need to compensate by draining when it is just a little underdone.

Reserve Some Cooking Water Before Draining

Get in the habit of saving about ½ cup of the cooking water before you drain the cooked pasta. Then, when you add your sauce to the pasta, add some (or all) of the starchy reserved water. This helps spread the sauce and gets it to the proper consistency.

Sauce in the Pot

Returning the drained pasta to the pot and then saucing it ensures evenly coated, hot pasta.

Butter-Basted Rib-Eye Steak
Serves 2 to 3; Total Time 30 minutes (plus 45 minutes for salting)

1 (1-pound) rib-eye steak, about 1½ inches thick, trimmed

2 teaspoons kosher salt

3 tablespoons vegetable oil

Pepper

4 tablespoons unsalted butter

1 large shallot, peeled and quartered lengthwise (root end attached)

2 garlic cloves, peeled

5 sprigs fresh thyme

1. Sprinkle steak evenly on both sides with salt and place on wire rack set in rimmed baking sheet. Let sit for at least 45 minutes or up to 3 hours (if waiting more than 1 hour, transfer steak to refrigerator, uncovered, until you are ready to cook).

2. Heat oil in 10-inch skillet over high heat until just smoking. Pat steak dry with paper towels and season liberally on both sides with pepper. Place steak in skillet and cook for 30 seconds. Flip steak using tongs and continue to cook for 30 seconds longer. Continue flipping steak every 30 seconds for 3 more minutes.

3. Slide steak to back of skillet, opposite handle, and add butter to front of skillet. Once butter has melted and begun to foam, add shallot, garlic, and thyme sprigs. Holding skillet handle, tilt skillet so butter pools near base of handle. Use metal spoon to continuously spoon butter and aromatics over steak, concentrating on areas where crust is less browned. Baste steak, flipping it every 30 seconds, until thermometer inserted into center registers 120 to 125 degrees (for medium-rare), 1 to 2 minutes.

4. Remove skillet from heat and transfer steak to cutting board; let steak rest for 10 minutes. Discard aromatics from pan and transfer butter mixture to small bowl. Slice steak crosswise ½ inch thick. Serve immediately with butter mixture.

why this recipe works

Steaks can be cooked every which way, but one of the most satisfying methods we've found is pan-searing and butter-basting a thick-cut rib eye. This cut is tender and juicy—it's essentially a boneless piece of prime rib—so it works best with a simple preparation that lets its beefy flavor shine through. Butter basting involves continuously spooning hot fat over an item as it cooks. Adding aromatics to the butter infused the whole dish with subtle savory flavor. In addition to butter-basting, we also flipped the steak throughout the entire cooking process. This technique gave us a great crust on both sides of the steak and evenly cooked the meat all the way through. Salting the steak at least 45 minutes before cooking increases its tenderness and juiciness (see "Salt + Time = Better Meat") though you can skip the wait if you don't have time. While not very complicated, this recipe calls for your full attention in order to be successful, so don't be distracted while cooking this one.

SEASONING MEAT

No matter how well cooked the meat is, it won't taste very good if it's not properly seasoned.

Season Early

For the most well-rounded flavor, we encourage seasoning meat before cooking. This gives the salt time to migrate into the food and allows heat to tame the punch of pepper. Seasoning properly at the start is especially important with steaks, chops, and roasts since you won't be able to season them to taste after cooking without cutting off a piece!

Salt + Time = Better Meat

You can certainly season with salt right before cooking for flavor, but you can also use salt (and time) in advance of cooking to improve the texture of many cuts of meat. When salt is applied to raw meat, juices inside the meat are drawn to the surface. The salt then dissolves in the exuded liquid, forming a brine that is eventually reabsorbed by the meat, creating juicier and more flavorful results. But you do have to wait until the brine is reabsorbed; if you try to pan-sear the meat too soon, the liquid will inhibit browning in the skillet. We prefer to use kosher salt for salting meat because it's easier to distribute the salt evenly. See page 454 for information about converting measurements if you want to use sea salt or table salt instead.

Seasoning with Flair (and a Purpose)

In recipes that call for seasoning meat with a specified amount of salt, it can be tempting to sprinkle very close to the meat so that none of the salt is lost to the cutting board. Unfortunately, this leads to an uneven distribution of salt. There's a reason that chefs tend to season food by sprinkling the seasoning from a good foot above the counter, and it's not just kitchen theatrics: The higher the starting point, the more evenly the seasoning will be distributed. The more evenly distributed the seasoning, the better the food tastes. So next time you have to season a steak, place the meat on a rimmed baking sheet and sprinkle with the specified amount of salt from up high. Then simply pick up each piece of meat and roll it in any salt that has landed on the baking sheet.

Slow-Roasted Beef
Serves 6 to 8; Total Time 2 hours 30 minutes (plus 18 hours for salting)

BEEF
1 (3½- to 4½-pound) boneless eye-round roast, trimmed

4 teaspoons kosher salt

2 teaspoons plus 1 tablespoon vegetable oil

2 teaspoons pepper

HORSERADISH CREAM SAUCE
½ cup heavy cream

½ cup prepared horseradish, drained

1 teaspoon salt

⅛ teaspoon pepper

1. FOR THE BEEF Rub roast thoroughly with salt, wrap in plastic wrap, and refrigerate for 18 to 24 hours.

2. Adjust oven rack to middle position and heat oven to 225 degrees. Pat roast dry with paper towels, rub with 2 teaspoons oil, and sprinkle with pepper.

3. Heat remaining 1 tablespoon oil in 12-inch skillet over medium-high heat until just smoking. Brown roast well on all sides, 12 to 16 minutes; reduce heat if pan begins to scorch. Transfer roast to wire rack set in rimmed baking sheet and roast until thermometer inserted into center of meat registers 115 degrees (for medium-rare), 1¼ to 1¾ hours, or 125 degrees (for medium), 1¾ to 2¼ hours.

4. FOR THE SAUCE Meanwhile, whisk cream in bowl until thickened but not yet stiff, 1 to 2 minutes. Gently fold in horseradish, salt, and pepper. Transfer to serving bowl and refrigerate for at least 30 minutes or up to 1 hour before serving.

5. Turn oven off and leave roast in oven, without opening door, until meat registers 130 degrees (for medium-rare) or 140 degrees (for medium), 30 to 50 minutes.

6. Transfer roast to carving board, tent with aluminum foil, and let rest for 15 minutes. Slice meat crosswise as thinly as possible and serve with sauce.

why this recipe works

Without proper preparation, inexpensive beef roasts can turn out tough and flavorless. To transform an affordable boneless eye-round roast into a centerpiece-worthy dish, we started by salting the meat and then searing it before roasting. We also roasted it at a very low 225 degrees and then turned off the oven toward the end of cooking. This allowed the meat's enzymes to break down the roast's tough connective tissue. Open the oven as little as possible, and remove the roast from the oven (and close the oven door) while taking the meat's temperature. If the roast has not reached the desired temperature in the time specified in step 5, reheat the oven to 225 degrees for 5 minutes, then shut it off and continue to cook the roast to the desired temperature. We don't recommend cooking this roast past medium. Buy refrigerated prepared horseradish, not the shelf-stable kind, which contains preservatives and additives.

HOT FOOD KEEPS COOKING

To get a cut of meat to the table cooked just right, you have to know a little bit about physics. The temperature of meat keeps rising even after you stop cooking it. This is an effect called carryover cooking, and it happens for two reasons: First, the exterior of a large roast gets hot much more quickly than the interior. Second, because heat always moves from a hotter to a cooler area, as long as there is a difference in temperature between two areas of the meat (the very-hot outside and the less-hot inside), heat will keep moving from one to the other, even after you remove the meat from the heat source. Eventually the inside and outside will reach equilibrium, but before they get to that point, the carryover cooking can cause a significant increase in temperature at the center of a large roast, bringing it from a perfect pink to a disappointing gray. This means that if you wait until your meat is at your desired doneness before you take it out of the oven, it'll probably be overdone by the time you sit down to eat.

Timing Is Everything

So when, exactly, should you remove meat from the heat source to ensure it finishes at the perfect temperature? Both the size of the food and the heat level during cooking will affect the answer. A large roast will absorb more heat than a thin steak, which means that there will be more heat in the meat and therefore a greater amount of carryover cooking. Similarly, carryover cooking is greater in a roast cooked in a hotter oven. In general, however, meat should be removed from the oven when it's 5 to 10 degrees below the desired serving temperature. For more information about doneness temperatures, see page 21.

Exceptions to the Rule: Poultry and Fish

Carryover cooking also applies to poultry and fish, although they don't retain heat as well as beef, lamb, and pork, which have denser muscle structure. For this reason and for optimal food safety, poultry and fish should be cooked to the desired serving temperatures. Cooking loosely structured proteins like fish at lower temperatures is a good way to avoid overcooking; the hotter the oven, the more dramatic the effect of carryover cooking.

Pan-Seared Thick-Cut Pork Chops

Serves 4; Total Time 1 hour (plus 45 minutes for salting)

4 (12-ounce) bone-in pork rib chops, 1½ inches thick, trimmed
Kosher salt and pepper
1–2 tablespoons vegetable oil

1. Adjust oven rack to middle position and heat oven to 275 degrees. Pat chops dry with paper towels. Using sharp knife, cut 2 slits, about 2 inches apart, through outer layer of fat and silverskin around edge of each chop. (This membrane contracts faster than rest of meat and can cause buckling if left intact.) Sprinkle entire surface of each chop with 1 teaspoon salt. Place chops on wire rack set in rimmed baking sheet and let stand at room temperature for 45 minutes.

2. Season chops liberally with pepper; transfer baking sheet to oven. Cook until thermometer inserted into centers of chops and away from bones registers 120 to 125 degrees, 30 to 45 minutes.

3. Heat 1 tablespoon oil in 12-inch heavy-bottomed skillet over high heat until just smoking. Place 2 chops in skillet and sear until well browned and crusty, 1½ to 3 minutes, lifting once halfway through to redistribute fat underneath each chop. (Reduce heat if browned bits in pan bottom start to burn.) Using tongs, turn chops and cook until well browned on second side, 2 to 3 minutes. Transfer chops to plate and repeat with remaining 2 chops, adding extra tablespoon oil if pan is dry.

4. Reduce heat to medium. Use tongs to stand 2 pork chops on their sides. Holding chops together with tongs, sear sides of chops (with exception of bone side) until browned and chops register 140 to 145 degrees, about 1½ minutes. Repeat with remaining 2 chops. Let chops rest, tented with aluminum foil, for 10 minutes.

why this recipe works

Thick-cut chops are decadent, restaurant-style fare, but come with the challenge of cooking the inside without overcooking the exterior. For perfect chops, we flip-flopped conventional logic and started them in a low oven, letting the meat gently tenderize before finishing by searing them in a hot pan to create a beautifully caramelized exterior. Buy chops of similar thickness so that they cook at the same rate. We prefer the flavor of natural chops over that of enhanced chops (which have been injected with a salt solution and sodium phosphate to increase moistness and flavor), but if processed pork is all you can find, skip the salting step in step 1. Serve the chops with Salsa Verde (page 101) or your favorite applesauce.

think like a cook

A REVERSE SEAR

It's difficult to cook thicker steaks (1½ to 1¾ inches thick) such as filets mignons and pork chops entirely on the stovetop; you often end up with a burnt exterior and a raw center. Even if you can manage to avoid burning the exterior, the meat around the perimeter is usually over-cooked by the time the center comes to temperature. The secret to getting a great crust on extra-thick chops and steaks without making them tough is to cook them in a very low oven, then quickly sear them. This is called reverse searing. The gentle oven heat minimizes mois-ture loss and promotes a natural enzymatic reaction that breaks down connective tissue in the meat and makes it especially tender. We also roast the meat on a wire rack, which allows the hot air to circulate and dry the surface of the mat. The drier surface helps the meat brown even better in the skillet. After their time in the oven, the chops brown in record time, and since the meat is in the pan for just a few minutes, there isn't time for it to lose much moisture or become overcooked.

Oven-Roasted Pork Tenderloin with Shallot-Balsamic Pan Sauce

Serves 4; Total Time 45 minutes

why this recipe works

Pork tenderloin is a superfriendly cut to experiment with in the kitchen; it's easy to prepare and cooks quickly. One of our favorite ways to cook it is a two-step pan-searing, oven-roasting technique, which gives the meat a golden crust and an evenly cooked, juicy interior. To punch up the mild pork, we used the fond left behind in the pan to build a deeply flavored pan sauce when we transferred the meat to the oven. We prefer natural pork tenderloin to enhanced pork tenderloin (which has been injected with a salt solution). This recipe calls for cooking two tenderloins at the same time in the same skillet, so be sure to buy tenderloins that are roughly the same size. This recipe will work in a nonstick or a traditional skillet. You will make the pan sauce while the tenderloins roast, so be sure to prepare all of the sauce ingredients before searing the pork.

PORK

2 (12- to 16-ounce) pork tenderloins, trimmed

1¼ teaspoons kosher salt

¾ teaspoon pepper

2 teaspoons vegetable oil

SHALLOT-BALSAMIC PAN SAUCE

4 tablespoons unsalted butter, cut into 4 pieces and chilled

2 shallots, sliced thin

2 tablespoons water

1 teaspoon packed light brown sugar

¾ cup balsamic vinegar

2 teaspoons chopped fresh rosemary

1 tablespoon Dijon mustard

Salt and pepper

1. FOR THE PORK Adjust oven rack to middle position and heat oven to 400 degrees. Sprinkle tenderloins with salt and pepper and rub into meat. Heat oil in 12-inch skillet over medium-high heat until just smoking. Place both tenderloins in skillet; cook until well browned, about 3 minutes. Using tongs, rotate tenderloins one-quarter turn; cook until well browned, 1 to 2 minutes. Repeat until all sides are browned. Transfer tenderloins to rimmed baking sheet and place in oven; roast until thermometer inserted into center of tenderloins registers 145 degrees, 10 to 16 minutes.

2. FOR THE PAN SAUCE Meanwhile, immediately after placing pork in oven, melt 1 tablespoon butter in still-hot skillet. Add shallots, water, and sugar and cook over medium-low heat, stirring frequently, until shallots are browned and caramelized, 7 to 10 minutes; remove skillet from heat and set aside.

3. Transfer tenderloins to cutting board and tent with aluminum foil; let rest for 10 minutes.

4. While pork rests, set skillet over medium-low heat and add vinegar; simmer, scraping up any browned bits, until mixture is slightly thickened, 5 to 7 minutes. Add rosemary and any juices from resting pork; continue to simmer until syrupy and reduced to about ⅓ cup, about 2 minutes longer. Off heat, whisk in mustard and remaining 3 tablespoons butter, 1 piece at a time. Season with salt and pepper to taste.

5. Slice tenderloins ½ inch thick and serve with sauce.

think like a cook

IMPROVING A PAN SAUCE

So you just pan-seared a steak, chop, or chicken breast, and have a pan full of browned, stuck-on bits. But wait! Don't clean that pan! Pan sauces take advantage of that fond to create a rich, deeply flavored accompaniment for the meat. Although the ingredients can change depending on the sauce, the steps are the same.

Pour Off Excess Fat
If there's more than a tablespoon of fat in the pan, pour off the excess or the sauce will be greasy. If there's very little fat in the pan, add a little vegetable oil or butter.

Add Aromatics
Aromatics like shallot, garlic, or onion will enhance the flavor of a quick pan sauce and give it depth.

Deglaze the Pan
Add liquid to the pan and use a wooden spoon to scrape up the browned bits. The fond dissolves as the liquid simmers, adding meaty flavor.

Simmer and Reduce
You want to reduce the liquid to both concentrate flavors and change its consistency. Don't shortcut this process, or your sauce will be too watery.

Add Meat Juices
As the meat rests, it will exude juices. Add these juices to the skillet and simmer to reduce. Add robust seasonings such as rosemary or capers so they can cook a bit.

Whisk in Butter
Off heat, whisk in chilled unsalted butter, 1 tablespoon at a time, to make the sauce thick and glossy. To finish, add seasonings such as leafy herbs, salt, and pepper. If the pan sauce isn't vinegar- or citrus-based, add a splash of vinegar or lemon juice to brighten it up.

Roasted Chicken Parts with Lemon and Herbs

Serves 4 to 6; Total Time 1 hour

4 pounds bone-in chicken pieces (split breasts, whole legs, thighs, and/or drumsticks), trimmed of excess fat and skin

3 tablespoons unsalted butter, softened, plus 2 tablespoons melted

1 tablespoon minced fresh thyme, rosemary, tarragon, or sage

1 teaspoon grated lemon zest

Salt and pepper

1. Adjust oven rack to upper-middle position and heat oven to 450 degrees. Line rimmed baking sheet with aluminum foil and set wire rack in baking sheet.

2. Mix softened butter with herbs, lemon zest, ¼ teaspoon salt, and ¼ teaspoon pepper in small bowl.

3. Pat chicken dry with paper towels. Use your fingers to carefully separate skin from meat on chicken pieces. Rub butter mixture underneath skin of chicken. Arrange chicken, skin side up, on prepared wire rack. Brush chicken with melted butter and season with salt and pepper.

4. Roast until thermometer inserted into breasts registers 160 degrees, about 30 minutes, and legs, thighs, and/or drumsticks register 175 degrees, about 30 minutes for drumsticks and 45 minutes for legs and thighs. Transfer chicken to cutting board and let rest for 5 minutes.

why this recipe works

A chicken needn't be roasted whole. Often, we turn to roasting individual parts—a largely walkaway approach that allows you to use whatever combination of parts you want. To encourage crispy skin and avoid the flabbiness that plagues some recipes, we brushed the parts with melted butter and roasted them in a 450-degree oven, elevating them on a wire rack to let the fat render away. Using bone-in, skin-on parts insulated the meat, ensuring it would stay juicy in the hot oven. Because dark meat cooks slower than white meat (and should be cooked to 175 degrees rather than 160 degrees for white), be prepared to remove different cuts at different times, or simply roast all breasts, or all thighs, and so on. Rubbing herb butter under the skin adds incredible flavor, but you can skip it if you prefer. Serve with lemon wedges.

variations

Roasted Chicken Parts with Honey and Mustard

Instead of lemon-herb-butter mixture, mix ¼ cup Dijon mustard, 2 tablespoons honey, and 1 teaspoon packed brown sugar together in bowl. Brush over chicken several times during last 5 minutes of cooking.

Roasted Chicken Parts with Five-Spice Powder and Ginger

Instead of lemon-herb-butter mixture, mix 3 tablespoons softened unsalted butter with 1 tablespoon grated fresh ginger, 1 teaspoon five-spice powder, ¼ teaspoon salt, and ¼ teaspoon pepper in bowl. Rub butter mixture underneath skin of chicken.

think like a cook

(POULTRY) SKIN IN THE GAME

When cooking poultry, we recommend that you either make sure the skin ends up nice and crispy or remove it before serving. Flabby chicken or turkey skin is unappealing and unattractive; it isn't something anyone wants to eat or see on the plate. But the crisp, well-browned skin on a great roast chicken can be the best part of the dish. That's because when you sauté or roast the skin and it reaches temperatures over 300 degrees, a set of reactions take place in its fats and proteins to produce hundreds of deeply flavorful compounds.

The Keys to Crisp Skin

In order to get the skin as crisp as possible, you need to render all the fat between the skin and the meat. Tricks like elevating the poultry on a rack while cooking in the oven help with this, as does cutting slashes in the skin. You can also brown the skin in a hot skillet and then finish cooking the chicken in the skillet over a lower temperature, or in the even heat of the oven (this has the added benefit of creating flavorful browned bits—fond—in the skillet, great for making a pan sauce). When the skin is fully cooked it will not only turn a lovely golden-brown color, it will also get supercrispy, almost like a potato chip. When you're trying to gauge doneness, watch for both the color and the texture of the skin to change.

Shedding the Skin

Chicken skin is like a raincoat: It's an effective barrier, keeping what's outside out and what's inside in. This is especially important in oven-roasted recipes, where the skin helps protect delicate white meat in the hot oven, but if you don't want to serve the skin you can remove and discard it before serving. Chicken skin is slippery; to simplify the task, use a paper towel to provide extra grip when pulling off the skin. For stews and braises, if you don't crisp the skin and render the fat, you should typically discard the skin before cooking. If you don't, the fat will render into the stew or sauce, which could make it overly greasy.

Weeknight Whole Roast Chicken with Tarragon-Lemon Pan Sauce

Serves 4; Total Time 1 hour 30 minutes

why this recipe works

Few dishes are more impressive than a roast chicken—or more rewarding. While there is no single perfect way to make one, there are factors to consider, chiefly that different parts cook at different rates, and that chicken is prone to drying out. Ideally, you'd salt or brine the bird, but that takes time. This recipe uses a creative, weeknight-friendly approach: We start with a preheated skillet to give the slower-cooking thighs a jump-start and then literally turn the oven off halfway through cooking. This helps the meat finish cooking gently and slows the evaporation of juices as the oven cools. We prefer to use a 3½- to 4-pound chicken; if roasting a larger bird, increase the time when the oven is on in step 2 to 35 to 40 minutes. Prep all sauce ingredients while the chicken is in the oven and make the sauce itself while the chicken rests.

CHICKEN

1 tablespoon kosher salt

½ teaspoon pepper

1 (3½- to 4-pound) whole chicken, giblets discarded

1 tablespoon olive oil

TARRAGON-LEMON PAN SAUCE

1 shallot, minced

1 cup chicken broth

2 teaspoons Dijon mustard

2 tablespoons unsalted butter

2 teaspoons minced fresh tarragon

2 teaspoons lemon juice

Pepper

1. FOR THE CHICKEN Adjust oven rack to middle position, place 12-inch ovensafe skillet on rack, and heat oven to 450 degrees. Combine salt and pepper in bowl. Pat chicken dry with paper towels. Rub oil all over chicken. Sprinkle salt mixture evenly over surface of chicken, then rub mixture in with your hands to coat evenly. Tie legs together with kitchen twine and tuck wingtips behind back.

2. Transfer chicken, breast side up, to skillet in oven. Roast until thermometer inserted into breast registers 120 degrees and thighs register 135 degrees (taking care not to hit bone), 25 to 35 minutes. Turn off oven and leave chicken in oven, opening door as little as possible, until breast registers 160 degrees and thighs register 175 degrees, 25 to 35 minutes longer. Transfer chicken to carving board and let rest, uncovered, for 20 minutes.

3. FOR THE PAN SAUCE Meanwhile, using large spoon, carefully remove all but 1 tablespoon fat from skillet (handle will be hot), leaving any browned bits and jus in skillet. Place skillet over medium-high heat, add shallot, and cook until softened, about 2 minutes. Stir in broth and mustard, scraping up any browned bits. Simmer until reduced to ¾ cup, about 3 minutes. Off heat, whisk in butter, tarragon, and lemon juice. Season with pepper to taste. Carve chicken and serve with sauce.

variation
Thyme–Sherry Vinegar Pan Sauce

Add 2 minced garlic cloves and 2 teaspoons chopped fresh thyme to skillet with shallot. Omit tarragon and substitute sherry vinegar for lemon juice.

think like a cook

WHOLE CHICKEN CHALLENGES

The natural shape of a chicken creates certain challenges when you try to roast it whole. Within a whole chicken there are actually two different types of meat: dark meat (thighs and drumsticks) and white meat (breast). Dark meat cooks more slowly than white meat. This is mainly due to the fact that dark meat is denser because it has more fat and proteins. To account for this difference, we cook the bird thigh side down in a preheated skillet to give the dark meat a head start. To prevent it from drying out while ensuring it is safe to eat, white meat should be cooked to an internal temperature of 160 degrees and dark meat should be cooked to 175 degrees. Having a good instant-read thermometer is essential for perfectly cooked chicken.

Another challenge with whole chickens is getting crisp skin. Make sure to blot the chicken dry with paper towels before cooking to eliminate excess moisture that can cause the skin to steam and become flabby.

Roast Turkey Breast

Serves 8 to 10; Total Time 2 hours 10 minutes
(plus 3 hours for brining)

½ cup salt

1 (6- to 7-pound) bone-in turkey breast, trimmed

4 tablespoons unsalted butter, softened

¼ teaspoon pepper

1. Dissolve salt in 1 gallon cold water in large container. Submerge turkey in brine, cover, and refrigerate for 3 to 6 hours.

2. Adjust oven rack to middle position and heat oven to 425 degrees. Set V-rack inside roasting pan and spray with vegetable oil spray. Combine butter and pepper in bowl.

3. Remove turkey from brine and pat turkey dry with paper towels. Using your fingers, gently loosen skin covering each side of breast. Place butter mixture under skin, directly on meat in center of each side of breast. Gently press on skin to distribute butter mixture over meat.

4. Place turkey, skin side up, on prepared V-rack and add 1 cup water to pan. Roast turkey for 30 minutes.

5. Reduce oven temperature to 325 degrees and continue to roast until thermometer inseted into thickest part of turkey registers 160 degrees, about 1 hour longer.

6. Transfer turkey to carving board and let rest for 20 minutes. Carve turkey and serve.

why this recipe works

You don't have to roast a whole turkey to get holiday-worthy moist meat and crisp skin. A whole breast is a great, manageable alternative. We started by brining the breast, which flavored the mild white meat and helped it hold moisture. Loosening the skin and rubbing the meat underneath with softened butter promoted browner, crispier skin. We found that a dual-temperature approach to cooking was best: Starting the turkey breast in a 425-degree oven jump-started browning, and reducing the heat to 325 degrees after 30 minutes allowed the meat to finish cooking gently. If you're using a self-basting turkey breast or a kosher turkey, skip the brining in step 1. Pair this roast with cranberry sauce (see page 330) for a classic complement.

variations
Roast Turkey Breast with Orange and Rosemary

Add 3 minced garlic cloves, 1 tablespoon minced fresh rosemary, 1 teaspoon grated orange zest, and ¼ teaspoon red pepper flakes to butter mixture.

Roast Turkey Breast with Southwestern Flavors

Add 3 minced garlic cloves, 1 tablespoon minced fresh oregano, 2 teaspoons ground cumin, 2 teaspoons chili powder, ¾ teaspoon unsweetened cocoa powder, and ½ teaspoon cayenne pepper to butter mixture.

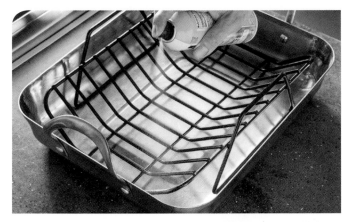

think like a cook

BRINING MAKES IT BETTER

We often rely on one of two methods to boost flavor and juiciness when cooking meat and poultry: brining or salting. Brining works faster and is best for lean cuts like turkey breast because it adds, rather than merely retains, moisture. As it soaks, the meat absorbs the brine and retains it during cooking. The result? The juiciest, best-tasting meat you have ever eaten. All you need is refrigerator space, a little time, and a big container.

How to Brine

Follow the chart below; dissolve salt and sugar in the water in a container large enough to hold the brine and meat. Submerge the meat completely. Cover and refrigerate for the specified time (no longer or the meat will be too salty and may be mushy). Remove the meat and pat it dry with paper towels before proceeding. We prefer table salt for brining because it dissolves easily. If you use kosher salt, adjust the amount using the chart on page 454. Do not brine kosher birds or enhanced pork, since they've already been treated with salt.

PROTEIN	BRINE	TIME
Boneless, Skinless Chicken Breasts (up to 6)	1½ quarts water, 3 tablespoons salt, 3 tablespoons sugar (optional)	½ to 1 hour
Bone-In Parts (4 pounds)	2 quarts water, ½ cup salt, ½ cup sugar (optional)	½ to 1 hour
1 Whole Chicken (3–8 pounds)	2 quarts water, ½ cup salt, ½ cup sugar (optional)	1 hour
1 Whole Turkey (12–17 pounds)	2 gallons water, 1 cup salt	6 to 12 hours
1 Whole Turkey (18–24 pounds)	3 gallons water, 1½ cups salt	6 to 12 hours
Bone-In Turkey Breast (6–7 pounds)	4 quarts water, ½ cup salt	3 to 6 hours
Pork Chops (up to 6)	1½ quarts water, 3 tablespoons salt, 3 tablespoons sugar (optional)	½ to 1 hour
Boneless Pork Roast (3–6 pounds)	2 quarts water, ¼ cup salt, ¼ cup sugar (optional)	1½ to 2 hours
Pork Tenderloins (up to 2)	2 quarts water, ¼ cup salt, ¼ cup sugar (optional)	½ to 1 hour

Oven-Roasted Salmon

Serves 4; Total Time 25 minutes

1 (1¾- to 2-pound) skin-on salmon fillet, 1½ inches thick
2 teaspoons extra-virgin olive oil
Salt and pepper
Lemon wedges

1. Adjust oven rack to lowest position, place rimmed baking sheet on rack, and heat oven to 500 degrees.

2. Meanwhile, cut salmon crosswise into 4 fillets. Make 4 or 5 shallow slashes, about 1 inch apart, on skin side of each fillet, being careful not to cut into flesh. Pat salmon dry with paper towels, rub with oil, and season with salt and pepper.

3. Reduce oven temperature to 275 degrees and remove baking sheet. Carefully place salmon, skin side down, on rimmed baking sheet. Roast until centers are still translucent when checked with tip of paring knife and thermometer inserted into salmon registers 125 degrees (for medium-rare), 9 to 13 minutes. Transfer salmon to plates and serve with lemon wedges.

why this recipe works

Oven roasting is a simple, hands-off way to tackle fish, which can be intimidating to inexperienced cooks. To get a browned exterior and perfectly cooked interior on salmon fillets, we used a method where we preheat the oven and a baking sheet to 500 degrees, then turn down the heat just before placing the fish on the sheet. The initial blast of high heat firms up the exterior of the fish, which then gently cooks as the temperature in the oven slowly drops. To ensure uniform pieces of fish, start with a whole center-cut fillet and cut it yourself. Cutting several slits in the skin helps the fat render. If your knife is not sharp enough to cut through and slash the skin easily, try a serrated knife. It's important to keep the skin on the fillets during cooking; remove it afterward if you want. For information on removing pinbones from salmon, see page 371.

variation
Oven-Roasted Salmon with Grapefruit and Basil Relish

Omit lemon wedges. Cut away peel and pith from 2 red grapefruit, then separate segments and cut into ½-inch pieces. Place grapefruit pieces in fine-mesh strainer set in a bowl and drain for 15 minutes. Pour off and discard all but 1 tablespoon grapefruit juice from bowl; whisk ½ minced small shallot, 2 tablespoons chopped fresh basil, 2 teaspoons lemon juice, and 2 teaspoons extra-virgin olive oil into juice in bowl. Stir in grapefruit segments and season to taste with salt and pepper. Serve with salmon.

SHOPPING FOR SALMON

When you see the labels "Atlantic" and "Pacific" on salmon, you probably assume they refer to the places the fish were caught, but those names are a little misleading. Once upon a time, Atlantic salmon did originate in the Atlantic Ocean. But nowadays most Atlantic salmon sold in the United States is raised on farms in Norway, Scotland, Chile, and Canada. The fish called Pacific salmon—which includes sockeye, coho, and Chinook (also called king)—originated in the North Pacific Ocean. Most Pacific salmon sold in this country is still wild-caught in the American Northwest, British Columbia, and Alaska. Pacific salmon has a more assertive flavor and a lower fat content than farmed Atlantic salmon. With its naturally firmer flesh and lower fat content, wild Pacific salmon is better cooked to a slightly lower temperature than farmed Atlantic salmon (120 degrees versus 125 degrees) for the ideal tender, moist texture.

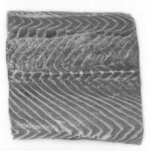

Wild Salmon
Pacific salmon has less fat and more flavor.

Farmed Salmon
Atlantic salmon has more fat and a mild flavor.

Sautéed White Fish Fillets
Serves 4; Total Time 25 minutes

½ cup all-purpose flour
4 (6-ounce) skinless thick white fish fillets, ½ to 1 inch thick,
or 8 (3-ounce) skinless thin white fish fillets, ¼ to ½ inch thick
Salt and pepper
2 tablespoons vegetable oil
Lemon wedges

1. Place flour shallow dish. Pat fish dry with paper towels. Season both sides of each fillet with salt and pepper; let stand until fillets are glistening with moisture, about 5 minutes. If using any tail-end fillets, tuck thin, tapered end under to create even thickness. Coat both sides of fillets with flour, shake off excess, and place in single layer on baking sheet.

2. Heat 1 tablespoon oil in 12-inch nonstick skillet over high heat until shimmering. Place half of fillets in skillet in single layer and immediately reduce heat to medium-high.

3A. FOR THICK FILLETS Cook, without moving fish, until edges of fillets are opaque and bottoms are golden brown, 3 to 4 minutes. Using 2 spatulas, gently flip fillets. Cook on second side until thickest part of fillets is firm to touch and fish flakes easily, 2 to 3 minutes.

3B. FOR THIN FILLETS Cook, without moving fish, until edges of fillets are opaque and bottoms are lightly browned, 2 to 3 minutes. Using 2 spatulas, gently flip fillets. Cook on second side until thickest part of fillets is firm to touch and fish flakes easily, 30 to 60 seconds.

4. Transfer fillets to serving platter and tent with aluminum foil. Repeat steps 2 and 3 with remaining 1 tablespoon oil and remaining fillets.

5. Place second batch of fillets on platter with first batch; tilt platter to discard any accumulated liquid. Serve fish immediately with lemon wedges.

why this recipe works

Sautéed fish fillets seem simple, but in reality they are rarely executed well. Attempts often result in dry, overcooked fillets, especially with thinner cuts. Yet sautéing adds a delicate, crispy texture and flavor to fish fillets that you can't get with other techniques. The trick to our method was to brown the fillets undisturbed on the first side, in the fat and with assertive heat, until the edges and a thin border turned opaque, resisting the temptation to check doneness constantly. (All that activity can cool down the food, meaning the fish won't brown and will be more likely to stick to the pan.) Thickness determines in part how long fillets must cook. This recipe gives cooking times for both thin and thick fillets. Do not use fillets thinner than ¼ inch, as they will overcook very quickly. These fish fillets can also be served with Grapefruit and Basil Relish (page 94), Cherry Tomato Salsa (page 102), Salsa Verde (page 101), or one of the savory compound butters on page 329.

ONE FISH, TWO FISH, WHAT IS WHITE FISH?

White fish is a marketing term that encompasses many species of deepwater saltwater fish, all of which are mild-flavored and white-fleshed. It's a big group (sometimes lumped together under the label "scrod") that includes cod, flounder, grouper, haddock, hake, halibut, pollack, sole, and many others. The term "white fish" is often used to differentiate these species from oily fish, a designation that includes meatier, moister fish such as salmon, swordfish, and tuna. (Confusingly, "whitefish" is used for a second and entirely different sort of freshwater fish—which we're not referring to here—that is often smoked and used for whitefish salad at delis.)

Because of its flaky flesh, white fish can be tricky to cook. Here are some tips for keeping it from falling apart when cooking on the stovetop:

» Always use a nonstick skillet to keep the fish from sticking, and be sure to preheat it properly so that the oil is just shimmering before you add the fish to the pan.

» We recommend a two-spatula turning method, which supports the fillets as you flip them. We like slotted fish spatulas for this job. They have long, thin, pliable metal blades that can easily shimmy underneath delicate fillets. And these spatulas are good for way more than just fish; they're actually our favorite all-purpose spatulas in the test kitchen.

» Overcooked fish is more likely to fall apart, so check the temperature of your fish at the start of the time range and immediately transfer the fish to plates once it's done.

Pan-Seared Shrimp with Lemon Butter

Serves 4; Total Time 30 minutes

2 pounds extra-large shrimp (21 to 25 per pound)

⅛ teaspoon sugar

Salt and pepper

2 tablespoons vegetable oil

2 tablespoons unsalted butter

1 tablespoon lemon juice, plus lemon wedges for serving

1 tablespoon minced fresh parsley

1. Peel and devein shrimp. Pat dry with paper towels and season with sugar, ¼ teaspoon salt, and ¼ teaspoon pepper. Heat 1 tablespoon oil in 12-inch nonstick skillet over high heat until just smoking. Add half of shrimp to skillet in single layer and cook, without stirring, until spotty brown and edges turn pink, about 1 minute.

2. Remove skillet from heat, flip shrimp, and let sit until opaque in very center, about 30 seconds; transfer to bowl. Repeat with remaining 1 tablespoon oil and shrimp.

3. Off heat, return first batch of shrimp and any accumulated juices to skillet. Add butter, lemon juice, and parsley and toss to coat until butter melts. Cover and let sit until shrimp are cooked through, 1 to 2 minutes. Season with salt and pepper to taste. Serve with lemon wedges.

why this recipe works

Pan searing is one of the quickest, easiest ways to get moist, tender shrimp with browned exteriors. But a good recipe for pan-seared shrimp is hard to find. The majority result in either dry and flavorless or pale, tough, and gummy shrimp. We started by seasoning the shrimp with salt, pepper, and sugar, which brought out their natural sweetness and aided in browning. We cooked the shrimp in batches in a large, piping hot skillet and then tossed them with butter, lemon juice, and fresh parsley. We also like pairing these shrimp with a glaze-like sauce with plenty of acidity as a foil for their richness; see the variations. The cooking time is for extra-large shrimp. If using smaller or larger shrimp, be sure to adjust the cooking time as needed. For more information on how to prepare shrimp, see "Peel-It-Yourself Shrimp."

variations

Pan-Seared Shrimp with Chipotle-Lime Glaze

Substitute following mixture for butter, lemon juice, and parsley in step 3: 2 tablespoons lime juice, 2 tablespoons chopped fresh cilantro, 4 teaspoons packed brown sugar, 1 teaspoon minced canned chipotle chile in adobo sauce, and 2 teaspoons adobo sauce.

Pan-Seared Shrimp with Ginger-Hoisin Glaze

Omit pepper. Add ¼ teaspoon red pepper flakes with salt and sugar in step 1. Substitute following mixture for butter, lemon juice, and parsley in step 3: 2 tablespoons hoisin sauce, 1 tablespoon rice vinegar, 2 teaspoons water, 1½ teaspoons soy sauce, 2 teaspoons grated fresh ginger, and 2 thinly sliced scallions.

PEEL-IT-YOURSELF SHRIMP

Many cooks buy peeled shrimp, and they are making a big mistake before they even get in the kitchen. The machines that peel shrimp rough up these delicate crustaceans and the end results are miserable. A far better option in terms of convenience is to keep frozen shell-on shrimp in your freezer. Frozen shrimp are actually better than "fresh," which are almost always thawed previously frozen shrimp that are past their prime. Simply thaw frozen shrimp in a colander under cool running water for about 10 minutes, depending on their size. Thoroughly dry them before proceeding. Break the shrimp's shell on the underside, under the swimming legs; it will peel off easily. Leave the tail end intact if desired, or tug it to remove the shell. Use a paring knife to make a shallow cut along the back of the shrimp to expose the vein. (The vein doesn't affect flavor, but removing it improves the appearance of cooked shrimp.) Use the tip of a knife to lift the vein out. Discard it by wiping the knife against a paper towel.

SAUCES AND CONDIMENTS TO SERVE WITH EVERYTHING

Once you have a few basic recipes and techniques mastered, the next step is adding flavor. An easy way to do that is with a sauce. All the sauces here are quick to prepare and packed with flavor; any one of them can be used numerous ways to spice up your cooking. We've provided some suggestions for using them here (you'll find more ideas in the chapters that follow), but consider them jumping-off points for your own culinary exploration and creativity.

Classic Basil Pesto
Makes about ¾ cup
Toast garlic cloves, unpeeled, in a skillet over medium heat until softened and spotty brown, 8 minutes.

Lightly bruise 2 cups fresh basil leaves in 1-gallon zipper-lock bag with rolling pin. Process basil, ¼ cup toasted pine nuts (see page 157), 3 toasted and minced garlic cloves, and ½ cup extra-virgin olive oil in food processor until smooth, about 1 minute, scraping down sides of bowl with rubber spatula as needed. Transfer pesto to bowl, stir in ¼ cup grated Parmesan, and season with salt and pepper to taste. (Pesto can be refrigerated for up to 3 days. To prevent browning, press plastic wrap on surface or top with thin layer of olive oil.)

Sun-Dried Tomato Pesto
Makes about ¾ cup
To toast garlic, see Classic Basil Pesto. We prefer oil-packed sun-dried tomatoes over dried.

Drain, pat dry, and chop 1 cup oil-packed sun-dried tomatoes. Process chopped tomatoes, ¼ cup toasted walnuts (see page 157), 3 toasted and minced garlic cloves, ½ cup extra-virgin olive oil, ½ cup grated Parmesan, and ½ teaspoon salt in food processor until smooth, about 1 minute, scraping down sides of bowl with rubber spatula as needed. Season with salt and pepper to taste. (Pesto can be refrigerated for up to 3 days. To prevent browning, press plastic wrap on surface or top with thin layer of olive oil.)

Mango-Mint Salsa
Makes about 3 cups
This sweet-spicy salsa is the perfect complement to pork, shrimp, and meaty fish. Try it on Oven-Roasted Salmon (page 94). Or stir it into cooked quinoa and vegetables for a simple grain salad. For a spicier salsa, add the jalapeño seeds.

Peel and pit 2 ripe but firm mangos (see page 36) and cut into ¼-inch pieces. Stem, seed, and mince 2 jalapeños. Combine mangos and jalapeños with 3 minced shallots, 6 tablespoons lime juice (from 3 limes), 6 tablespoons chopped fresh mint, 3 tablespoons extra-virgin olive oil, 3 minced garlic cloves, and ½ teaspoon salt in bowl. (Salsa can be refrigerated for up to 2 days.)

Salsa Verde

Makes about 1 cup

This Italian herb-based green sauce brings vibrancy to just about anything.

Pulse 3 cups fresh parsley leaves, 1 cup fresh mint leaves, ½ cup extra-virgin olive oil, 3 tablespoons white wine vinegar, 2 tablespoons rinsed capers, 3 rinsed anchovy fillets (optional), 1 minced garlic clove, and ⅛ teaspoon salt in food processor until finely chopped (mixture should not be smooth), about 10 pulses, scraping down sides of bowl with rubber spatula as needed. Transfer salsa to bowl. (Salsa can be refrigerated for up to 2 days.)

variation
Lemon-Basil Salsa Verde
Use only 1 cup parsley and add 2 cups fresh basil leaves. Increase garlic to 2 cloves and add 1 teaspoon grated lemon zest.

Harissa

Makes about ½ cup

We use this potent North African sauce to flavor lamb (see page 394). It is also nice stirred into soups and drizzled on hummus, eggs, and sandwiches. If you can't find Aleppo pepper, substitute ¾ teaspoon paprika plus ¾ teaspoon finely chopped red pepper flakes.

Combine 6 tablespoons extra-virgin olive oil, 6 minced garlic cloves, 2 tablespoons paprika, 1 tablespoon ground coriander, 1 tablespoon ground dried Aleppo pepper, 1 teaspoon ground cumin, ¾ teaspoon caraway seeds, and ½ teaspoon salt in bowl. Microwave until bubbling and very fragrant, about 1 minute, stirring halfway through microwaving; let cool to room temperature. (Sauce can be refrigerated for up to 4 days.)

think like a cook

MAKING THE MOST OF SAUCES

A sauce can instantly transform a dish from boring to best in show. Here are some of our favorite ways to use the sauces on these pages.

» Toss pesto, Salsa Verde, or Harissa with boiled sliced potatoes for an instant potato salad. Or serve boiled potatoes with Garlic Aïoli.

» Drizzle pesto, Harissa, or Mexican Crema onto soups.

» Spoon pretty much any sauce on top of roasted or grilled poultry, meat, or seafood, or brush onto roasted, grilled, or steamed vegetables.

» Combine pesto, Salsa Verde, or Harissa with mayonnaise and sour cream to make a dip for crudités or potato chips. (Salsa, Garlic Aïoli, Lemon-Yogurt Sauce, Chipotle Mayonnaise, Curried Peanut Sauce, and Cilantro-Mint Chutney all make great dips as is.)

» Spread pesto, Garlic Aïoli, or Chipotle Mayonnaise onto sandwiches.

» Toss any cooked vegetables (Roasted Root Vegetables, page 58, and Pan-Roasted Potatoes, page 56, would both be great) with pesto, Harissa, Salsa Verde, Curried Peanut Sauce, or Cilantro-Mint Chutney. Or dollop with Lemon-Yogurt Sauce, Garlic Aïoli, or Chipotle Mayonnaise.

» Drizzle a sauce over a grain bowl, matching the sauce to the other flavors in the dish (see "Anatomy of a Great Grain Bowl," page 179).

» Use pesto, Salsa Verde, Mango-Mint Salsa, or Cilantro-Mint Chutney to flavor fresh cheeses such as mozzarella or ricotta—or add to a cheese plate.

» Top grilled or toasted bread with pesto, Cherry Tomato Salsa, or Salsa Verde for a quick bruschetta appetizer.

Quick Tomato Sauce

Makes about 4 cups

To freeze, cool the sauce completely and transfer to a freezer-safe container. Press a layer of plastic wrap directly on the surface, cover the container, and freeze for up to 3 months. Defrost in the microwave, or in the refrigerator overnight.

Cook 3 tablespoons extra-virgin olive oil and 3 minced garlic cloves in medium saucepan over medium heat, stirring often, until garlic is fragrant but not browned, about 2 minutes. Stir in one 28-ounce can crushed tomatoes and one 14.5-ounce can diced tomatoes and their juice. Bring to simmer and cook until slightly thickened, about 20 minutes. Stir in 3 tablespoons chopped fresh basil and ¼ teaspoon sugar and season with salt to taste. (Sauce can be refrigerated for up to 4 days.)

Cherry Tomato Salsa

Makes about 1 cup

Combine 6 ounces quartered cherry tomatoes, 1 tablespoon extra-virgin olive oil, 1 tablespoon minced fresh cilantro, and 1½ teaspoons lime juice in bowl and season with salt and pepper to taste. (Salsa can be refrigerated for up to 24 hours.)

Quick Mexican Crema

Makes about 1¼ cups

Whisk ½ cup mayonnaise, ½ cup sour cream, 2 tablespoons lime juice, and 2 tablespoons milk together in bowl. (Crema can be refrigerated for up to 2 days.)

Garlic Aïoli

Makes about 1¼ cups

Process 2 large egg yolks, 2 teaspoons Dijon mustard, 2 teaspoons lemon juice, and 1 minced garlic clove in food processor until combined, about 10 seconds. With processor running, slowly drizzle in ¾ cup vegetable oil. Transfer mixture to medium bowl and whisk in 1 tablespoon water, ½ teaspoon salt, and ¼ teaspoon pepper. Whisking constantly, slowly drizzle in ¼ cup extra-virgin olive oil until emulsified. (Aïoli can be refrigerated for up to 4 days.)

Lemon-Yogurt Sauce

Makes about 1 cup

Use whole-milk yogurt or low-fat yogurt in this recipe (not nonfat).

Whisk 1 cup plain yogurt, 1 tablespoon minced fresh mint, 1 teaspoon grated lemon zest, 2 tablespoons lemon juice, and 1 minced garlic clove together in bowl until combined. Season with salt and pepper to taste. Let sit until flavors meld, about 30 minutes. (Sauce can be refrigerated for up to 2 days.)

Chipotle Mayonnaise

Makes about ½ cup

You can vary the spiciness of this sauce by adjusting the amount of chipotle.

Whisk 3 tablespoons mayonnaise, 3 tablespoons sour cream, 2 tablespoons minced canned chipotle chile in adobo sauce, 1 minced garlic clove, and ⅛ teaspoon salt together in small bowl. Cover and refrigerate for at least 1 hour. (Sauce can be refrigerated for up to 24 hours.)

Pub-Style Burger Sauce

Makes about 1 cup

Whisk ¾ cup mayonnaise, 2 tablespoons soy sauce, 1 tablespoon packed dark brown sugar, 1 tablespoon Worcestershire sauce, 1 tablespoon minced fresh chives, 1 minced garlic clove, and ¾ teaspoon pepper together in bowl. (Sauce can be refrigerated for up to 4 days.)

Curried Peanut Sauce
Makes about 1 cup
For a spicier sauce, add the jalapeño seeds.

Heat 1 tablespoon vegetable oil in medium saucepan over medium heat until shimmering. Stir in 2 stemmed, seeded, and minced jalapeño chiles, 3 minced garlic cloves, 1 tablespoon grated fresh ginger, and 1½ teaspoons curry powder and cook until fragrant, about 30 seconds. Stir in ½ cup water, ⅓ cup creamy peanut butter, 3 tablespoons seasoned rice vinegar, 2 tablespoons soy sauce, and 1 tablespoon sugar and bring to simmer. Cook, stirring occasionally, until slightly thickened and flavors meld, about 2 minutes. Adjust consistency as needed with additional water. (Sauce can be refrigerated for up to 24 hours; whisk to recombine before serving.)

Scallion Dipping Sauce
Makes about ¾ cup
Mirin can be found in most supermarkets; if you cannot find it, substitute 2 tablespoons dry white wine mixed with 1 teaspoon sugar. For a milder sauce, omit the chili oil.

Combine 1 minced scallion, ¼ cup soy sauce, 2 tablespoons rice vinegar, 2 tablespoons mirin, 2 tablespoons water, 1 teaspoon chili oil, and ½ teaspoon toasted sesame oil in bowl. (Sauce can be refrigerated for up to 8 hours; whisk to recombine before serving.)

think like a cook

WHEN LIFE GIVES YOU LEMONS . . . PRESERVE THEM!
It's not exactly a sauce, but this Moroccan condiment is one of our favorite magic ingredients to put in anything. Add preserved lemon to vinaigrettes, pan sauces, grain salads, roasted vegetables, chicken, fish, pasta dishes, and anything else that could use a bright, briny pop of lemon flavor. We like Meyer lemons here because they are thin-skinned and mellower. When using regular lemons, choose smaller fruits with thin skin. Because regular lemons have thicker peels, they may take 2 to 4 weeks longer to soften. It's important to wash, scrub, and dry the lemons well before preserving.

Preserved Lemons
Makes 4 preserved lemons
Wash and dry 4 lemons, then cut each lengthwise into quarters, stopping 1 inch from bottom so lemon stays intact at base. Juice 8 more lemons to yield 1½ cups juice; reserve extra juice to use as needed. Working over bowl, gently stretch 1 cut lemon open and pour 2 tablespoons salt into center. Gently rub cut surfaces of lemon together, then place in 1-quart jar. Repeat with remaining cut lemons and 6 more tablespoons salt. Add any accumulated salt and juice in bowl to jar. Pour 1½ cups lemon juice into jar and press gently to submerge lemons. (Add more lemon juice if needed to cover lemons completely.) Cover jar tightly with lid and shake. Refrigerate lemons, shaking jar once per day for first 4 days to redistribute salt and juice. Let lemons cure in refrigerator until glossy and softened, 6 to 8 weeks. (Preserved lemons can be refrigerated for at least 6 months.) To use, cut off desired amount of preserved lemon. Rinse if desired. Using knife, remove pulp and while pith from rind and discard. Slice, chop, or mince rind as desired.

Korean Chile Sauce
Makes about ½ cup
This sauce is the classic topping for Vegetable Bibimbap (page 188). Gochujang, a Korean chile paste, is sold in Asian markets and some supermarkets. If you can't find gochujang, an equal amount of Sriracha sauce can be substituted. Because Sriracha is more watery than gochujang, omit the water if you use this substitution.

Whisk ¼ cup gochujang, 3 tablespoons water, 2 tablespoons toasted sesame oil, and 1 teaspoon sugar together in bowl until well combined. (Sauce can be refrigerated for up to 24 hours.)

Cilantro-Mint Chutney
Makes about 1 cup
Combine 2 cups fresh cilantro leaves, 1 cup fresh mint leaves, ⅓ cup plain whole-milk yogurt, ¼ cup finely chopped onion, 1 tablespoon lime juice, 1½ teaspoons sugar, ½ teaspoon ground cumin, and ¼ teaspoon salt in food processor. Process until smooth, about 20 seconds, scraping down sides of bowl as needed. (Chutney can be refrigerated for up to 2 days.)

The notion of what constitutes a meal is pretty broad, which can be freeing but also overwhelming. These chapters seek to help, offering recipes for busy days when you just need to put food on the table as well as for days when you can spend a bit more time in the kitchen.

Breakfast provides an opportunity to set the tone for your day with care, flavor, and sustenance and is a quick way to expand your kitchen skills. Make-ahead options satisfy when you have only minutes to spare, as do the basic egg dishes previously covered in "The Simplest Way to Cook Everything." Then there are the leisurely brunches where you can relax and explore the possibilities of the morning meal.

A salad can be so much more than a pile of lettuce on a plate. Any salad brings color and freshness to a meal, but the heartiest salads and bowls help us reimagine the way a meal can look, moving away from the meat-centric plate. Side dishes are the spice of life—simple ways to incorporate a variety of flavors and nutritious vegetables and grains. Equally simple are soups and stews, the original one-pot meals, which offer lessons in building layers of flavor and easy ways to sample cuisines from around the world.

Many recipes in this book could work as dinner; the ones in "Week-night Dinners" offer smart ways to get great flavor in limited time. And many include a built-in side dish. Of course, sometimes you want to dig in, linger in the kitchen, and show off a little. The recipes in "Sunday Suppers" illustrate how a dish can be complex without being complicated. Finally, our last chapter tackles the mysteries of flour, butter, and yeast to prove anyone can be a baker with back-pocket ideas that bring new flavors and simple approaches to cookies, breads, and cakes.

RECIPES FOR EVERY OCCASION

breakfast and brunch

Faster Steel-Cut Oatmeal

Serves 4; Total Time 15 minutes (plus overnight soaking)

4 cups water

1 cup steel-cut oats

¼ teaspoon salt

1. Bring 3 cups water to boil in large saucepan over high heat. Remove pan from heat; stir in oats and salt. Cover pan and let stand overnight.

2. Stir remaining 1 cup water into oats and bring to boil over medium-high heat. Reduce heat to medium and cook, stirring occasionally, until oats are softened but still retain some chew and mixture thickens and resembles warm pudding, 4 to 6 minutes. Remove pan from heat and let stand for 5 minutes. Stir and serve.

variations
Apple-Cinnamon Steel-Cut Oatmeal
Increase salt to ½ teaspoon. Substitute ½ cup apple cider and ½ cup whole milk for water in step 2. Stir ½ cup peeled, grated sweet apple, 2 tablespoons packed dark brown sugar, and ½ teaspoon ground cinnamon into oatmeal with cider and milk. Sprinkle each serving with 2 tablespoons coarsely chopped toasted walnuts.

Banana-Coconut Steel-Cut Oatmeal
Increase salt to ½ teaspoon. Substitute 1 cup canned coconut milk for water in step 2. Stir ½ cup toasted shredded coconut, 2 diced bananas, and ½ teaspoon vanilla extract into oatmeal before serving.

Carrot-Spice Steel-Cut Oatmeal
Increase salt to ¾ teaspoon. Substitute ½ cup carrot juice and ½ cup whole milk for water in step 2. Stir ½ cup finely grated carrot, ¼ cup packed dark brown sugar, ⅓ cup dried currants, and ½ teaspoon ground cinnamon into oatmeal with carrot juice and milk. Sprinkle each serving with 2 tablespoons coarsely chopped toasted pecans.

Cranberry-Orange Steel-Cut Oatmeal
Increase salt to ½ teaspoon. Substitute ½ cup orange juice and ½ cup whole milk for water in step 2. Stir ½ cup dried cranberries, 3 tablespoons packed dark brown sugar, and ⅛ teaspoon ground cardamom into oatmeal with orange juice and milk. Sprinkle each serving with 2 tablespoons toasted sliced almonds.

why this recipe works
Oatmeal can be so much better than the gluey, artificially flavored packets of the instant stuff that have given this nourishing breakfast a bad name. Most oatmeal fans agree that the steel-cut version of the grain offers the best flavor and texture, but the 40-minute cooking time doesn't exactly make it a quick and convenient option. We were able to decrease the day-of active cooking time to only 10 minutes by stirring steel-cut oats into boiling water the night before. This enabled the grains to hydrate and soften overnight. In the morning, we added more water and simmered the mixture for 4 to 6 minutes, until it was thick and creamy. A brief resting period off the heat ensured the perfect consistency. The oatmeal will continue to thicken as it cools; if you prefer a looser consistency, thin the oatmeal with more boiling water. Customize your oatmeal with toppings such as brown sugar, toasted nuts, maple syrup, or dried fruit, or try the variations.

think like a cook

KNOW YOUR OATS

We found that only steel-cut oats (also known as Scottish or Irish oats) worked for our ideal bowl of breakfast oatmeal, but rolled oats are our top choice for baking recipes. And they are only two of the many oat products you're likely to see at the supermarket.

Groats
Whole oats that have been hulled and cleaned. They are the least processed oat product, but we find them too coarse for oatmeal.

Steel-Cut Oats
Groats cut crosswise into coarse bits. We strongly prefer them in oatmeal; they cook up creamy yet chewy with rich, nutty flavor.

Rolled Oats
Groats steamed and pressed into flat flakes, also known as old-fashioned oats. They cook faster than steel-cut but make for a gummy, lackluster bowl of oatmeal. These are our go-to for baking. Quick oats and instant oats are also rolled; quick oats are rolled extra-thin and instant oats are precooked. We don't like quick oats or instant oats for cereal or baking.

Almond Granola with Dried Fruit

Makes about 9 cups; Total Time 1 hour 55 minutes

⅓ cup maple syrup

⅓ cup packed (2⅓ ounces) light brown sugar

4 teaspoons vanilla extract

½ teaspoon salt

½ cup vegetable oil

5 cups (15 ounces) old-fashioned rolled oats

2 cups (10 ounces) whole almonds, chopped coarse

2 cups (10 ounces) raisins or other dried fruit, chopped

1. Adjust oven rack to upper-middle position and heat oven to 325 degrees. Line rimmed baking sheet with parchment paper.

2. Whisk maple syrup, sugar, vanilla, and salt together in large bowl. Whisk oil into maple syrup mixture, then fold in oats and almonds until thoroughly coated.

3. Transfer oat mixture to prepared sheet and spread into thin, even layer (about ⅜ inch thick). Using stiff metal spatula, compress oat mixture until very compact. Bake until lightly browned, 40 to 45 minutes, rotating sheet halfway through baking. Transfer sheet to wire rack and let cool completely, about 1 hour. Break granola into pieces of desired size. Stir in raisins. (Granola can be stored at room temperature for up to 2 weeks.)

why this recipe works

Store-bought granola suffers from many short-comings. It's often loose and gravelly and/or infuriatingly expensive, and it never has exactly the balance of ingredients that you wish it had. We wanted to make our own granola at home, with big, satisfying clusters and a crisp texture. The secret was to firmly pack the granola mixture into a rimmed baking sheet before baking. Once it was baked, we had a granola "bark" that we could break into crunchy clumps of any size. We liked using maple syrup as a sweetener for its mild character, especially when balanced with the molasses notes of light brown sugar. The best way to incorporate dried fruit was to keep it away from the heat altogether, stirring it in once the granola was cool. Do not substitute quick or instant oats.

variations

Hazelnut Granola with Dried Pear

Substitute skinned and coarsely chopped toasted hazelnuts for almonds. Use 2 cups chopped dried pear for dried fruit.

Pecan-Orange Granola with Dried Cranberries

Add 2 tablespoons finely grated orange zest and 2½ teaspoons ground cinnamon to maple syrup mixture in step 2. Substitute coarsely chopped pecans for almonds. Use 2 cups dried cranberries for dried fruit.

Spiced Walnut Granola with Dried Apple

Add 2 teaspoons ground cinnamon, 1½ teaspoons ground ginger, ¾ teaspoon ground allspice, ½ teaspoon ground nutmeg, and ½ teaspoon pepper to maple syrup mixture in step 2. Substitute coarsely chopped walnuts for almonds. Use 2 cups chopped dried apple for dried fruit.

Tropical Granola with Dried Mango

Decrease vanilla extract to 2 teaspoons and add 1½ teaspoons ground ginger and ¾ teaspoon ground nutmeg to maple syrup mixture in step 2. Substitute coarsely chopped macadamia nuts for almonds and 1½ cups unsweetened shredded coconut for 1 cup oats. Use 2 cups chopped dried mango or pineapple for dried fruit.

think like a cook

DIY GRANOLA

Our basic recipe is very adaptable; just keep a few rules in mind as you mix and match.

The Base

The ratio of oats to other ingredients in our granola is slightly more than 1:1 by volume. You want a bit more base than mix-ins, but that base doesn't have to be just oats; try replacing 1 cup of the oats with 1–1½ cups unsweetened shredded coconut or even quinoa flakes.

The Nuts

Almost any type of nuts will work. We like chopped nuts for a more even distribution, but if you choose a smaller nut or like the texture of bigger pieces, try whole nuts. Or replace half of the nuts with seeds.

The Oil

Fat is essential for a substantial, crisp texture. Fat and liquid sweeteners form a fluid emulsion that thoroughly coats ingredients, creating crunch as the granola bakes. Without any fat, the texture is bound to be dry and fragile. We prefer the neutral taste of vegetable oil.

The Fruit

Dried fruit has already had most of its moisture pulled out, so exposing it to the heat of the oven is going to turn it leathery and overcooked. Save the fruit to add after cooking the other ingredients.

The Salt

Don't skip the salt! A half teaspoon may not seem like much, but it adds essential depth of flavor, accenting both the sweet and savory, toasted elements of the granola.

All-Morning Energy Bars
Makes 10 bars; Total Time 2 hours 15 minutes

½ cup whole raw almonds

½ cup raw cashews

⅓ cup raw pepitas

¼ cup raw sunflower seeds

2 tablespoons flaxseeds

1 tablespoon sesame seeds

3 ounces pitted dates, chopped (½ cup)

2 tablespoons warm tap water

2 tablespoons maple syrup

1 large egg white

¾ teaspoon kosher salt

why this recipe works

Sometimes you can't avoid eating breakfast on the run, but that doesn't mean you have to resort to something that tastes bad or won't nourish you. We wanted our homemade energy bars to be full of hearty, nutritious nuts and seeds. Toasting the nuts and seeds before pulsing them in the food processor gave the bars a pleasant roasted flavor. Dates and maple syrup not only added satisfying sweetness but also aided in binding the bars together. We found that processing some of the dates with the maple syrup, warm water, and an egg white gave the bars a slight chew while still allowing the nuts and seeds to remain crisp. We stirred the remaining chopped dates into the mixture for textural contrast; tasters also liked the little bursts of sweetness. A two-step baking process gave us bars with the perfect balance of crunchiness and chewiness. Be sure not to overbake the nuts and seeds in step 2; they will continue to toast while the bars bake.

1. Adjust oven rack to middle position and heat oven to 300 degrees. Line baking sheet with aluminum foil. Make foil sling for 8-sinch square baking pan by folding 2 long sheets of aluminum foil so each is 8 inches wide. Lay sheets of foil in pan perpendicular to each other, with extra foil hanging over edges of pan. Push foil into corners and up sides of pan, smoothing foil flush to pan. Grease foil with vegetable oil spray.

2. Spread almonds, cashews, pepitas, sunflower seeds, flaxseeds, and sesame seeds on prepared baking sheet. Bake, stirring occasionally, until pale golden and fragrant, 15 to 20 minutes. Transfer nut mixture to food processor and let cool slightly, then pulse until coarsely chopped, about 5 pulses; transfer to large bowl.

3. Process ¼ cup dates, warm water, maple syrup, egg white, and salt in now-empty processor until smooth, about 30 seconds, scraping down sides of bowl with rubber spatula as needed. Stir processed date mixture and remaining ¼ cup chopped dates into nut mixture until well combined. Spread mixture in prepared baking pan and press firmly into even layer using greased metal spatula. Bake until golden brown, 20 to 25 minutes, rotating pan halfway through baking. Do not turn off oven.

4. Let bars cool in pan for 15 minutes. Using foil overhang, lift bars out of pan; transfer to cutting board and cut into 10 bars. Space bars evenly on parchment paper–lined baking sheet and bake until deep golden brown, 10 to 15 minutes. Let bars cool completely on wire rack, about 1 hour. Serve. (Bars can be stored at room temperature for up to 1 week.)

think like a cook

GETTING SEEDY

You may think seeds belong in the garden, but one look around a well-stocked kitchen proves otherwise. We use them to lend richness, protein, and crunch to baked goods, salads, and more. They will keep for months in a bag in the freezer, making them a reliable pantry staple.

Chia Seeds

Mild, nutty chia seeds are a popular health food due to their high fiber content. The seeds can be used dry, ground and used as a powder, or combined with water to create a tapioca-like gel.

Flaxseeds

Flaxseeds can be toasted, sprouted, or ground; they're most easily digested when eaten ground. We prefer the milder flavor of golden flaxseeds, but you can use brown and golden varieties interchangeably. Flaxseeds have a wheaty, earthy flavor, making them a nice addition to whole-grain breads. Store them in the refrigerator or freezer.

Poppy Seeds

Poppy seeds are used for their peppery, smoky-sweet flavor. Try them in baked goods, coleslaw, egg noodles, and salad dressing.

Pumpkin Seeds

Whole white pumpkin seeds are sold for snacking and have a pleasant vegetal taste, but we usually turn to green hulled pumpkin seeds (pepitas). Toss them in salads or try them in these energy bars.

Sesame Seeds

Sesame seeds add a nutty, subtle flavor to both sweet and savory recipes. They star in our Sesame Noodles with Shredded Chicken (page 288), where we grind them into a rich paste.

Sunflower Seeds

Sunflower seeds are mildly sweet and creamy. They are usually sold hulled, but if you buy them unhulled, make sure to remove the black-and-white shells. Try them in salads and bowls such as our Buckwheat Bowls with Snow Peas, Avocado, and Yogurt Sauce (page 178).

Strawberry-Peach Smoothies
Serves 2; Total Time 5 minutes

1 ripe banana, peeled and halved lengthwise

2 tablespoons honey

⅛ teaspoon salt

1 cup frozen strawberries

1 cup frozen peaches

1 cup plain whole-milk yogurt

¼ cup orange juice

Process banana, honey, and salt in blender until smooth, about 10 seconds. Add strawberries, peaches, yogurt, and orange juice and blend until smooth, scraping down sides of blender with rubber spatula as necessary, about 1 minute. Serve.

variations
Cherry-Almond Smoothies
Add ¼ cup almond butter to blender with banana, honey, and salt. Substitute 2 cups frozen sweet cherries for strawberries and peaches. Substitute whole milk for orange juice.

Kale-Pineapple Smoothies
Substitute frozen pineapple chunks for strawberries and 1 cup frozen chopped kale for peaches.

Mixed Berry Smoothies
Substitute 2 cups frozen mixed berries for strawberries and peaches.

Tropical Fruit Smoothies
Substitute frozen mango chunks for strawberries, frozen pineapple chunks for peaches, and pineapple juice for orange juice.

why this recipe works
Sure, you could buy a smoothie for an exorbitant price at your local coffee shop or juice bar, but why would you, when it's so easy to make them at home? We replaced the ice called for in most smoothie recipes with frozen fruit to avoid diluting the flavors. We found that bananas are the secret weapon for smooth smoothies. Blending them creates a substantive (but not stiff) base, and their flavor is mild enough to play well with many different ingredient combinations. Pureeing a banana with honey and a pinch of salt before adding the other ingredients guaranteed an even level of sweetness throughout. The salt also helped bring out the fruit flavors. We love using Greek yogurt, but for these smoothies we preferred regular whole-milk yogurt because of its looser texture. Once you have this basic formula down, try the fruit combination that best fits your mood and tastes. You can substitute low-fat for whole-milk yogurt here, but your smoothies will be much less creamy.

think like a cook

SMOOTHIE PRO TIPS

Washing the blender jar after you make your morning smoothie can be a real chore. Get a head start on the cleaning process by following this method: Fill the dirty blender halfway with hot water and add a couple of drops of liquid dish soap. With the top firmly in place, turn the blender on high for 30 seconds, then empty the blender jar. Most of the residue pours right out with the soapy water, and the jar need only be rinsed or lightly washed by hand. Another advantage to this technique: It keeps your fingers out of the jar and away from the sharp blades.

Stock your freezer for smoothie success by preparing smoothie packs in advance. Peel and cut up all the fruit for a week's worth of smoothies and then portion enough for one smoothie into each of five zipper-lock freezer bags. Freeze the portioned fruit and then simply pull out a bag and blend its contents with yogurt, juice, and/or milk as needed.

Bacon and Cheddar Breakfast Sandwiches

Serves 4; Total Time 35 minutes

4 English muffins, split

3 tablespoons unsalted butter, softened

¼ cup mayonnaise

1 tablespoon hot sauce

4 large eggs

Salt and pepper

6 slices bacon

4 ounces sharp cheddar cheese, shredded (1 cup)

1½ ounces (1½ cups) baby spinach

4 thin tomato slices

1. Adjust oven rack 5 inches from broiler element and heat broiler. Spread insides of muffins evenly with butter and arrange split side up on rimmed baking sheet. Combine mayonnaise and hot sauce in bowl; set aside. Crack 2 eggs into small bowl and season with salt and pepper. Repeat with remaining 2 eggs and second small bowl.

2. Cook bacon in 12-inch nonstick skillet over medium heat until crispy, 7 to 9 minutes; transfer to paper towel–lined plate. When cool enough to handle, break each slice in half. Broil muffins until golden brown, 2 to 4 minutes, rotating sheet halfway through broiling. Flip muffins and broil until just crisp on second side, 1 to 2 minutes; set aside while cooking eggs.

3. Pour off all but 1 tablespoon fat from skillet and heat over medium-high heat until shimmering. Working quickly, pour 1 bowl of eggs in 1 side of pan and second bowl of eggs in other side. Cover and cook for 1 minute.

4. Working quickly, top each egg with 3 pieces bacon and ¼ cup cheddar. Cover pan, remove from heat, and let stand until cheddar is melted and egg whites are cooked through, about 2 minutes.

5. Spread mayonnaise mixture on muffin bottoms and place 1 bacon-and-cheese-topped egg on each. Divide spinach evenly among sandwiches, then top with tomato slices and muffin tops. Serve.

why this recipe works

No portable breakfast is as satisfying as the breakfast sandwich. You can buy one almost anywhere—a fast-food drive-through, corner bodega, or school cafeteria—but unless you like soggy bread, cold cheese, and rubbery eggs, your best option might be to make them at home. We started with our tried and true fried eggs, cooked in bacon fat for a great flavor bonus. After a minute over the heat, the eggs got topped with bacon and cheddar cheese. Covering the pan and letting it sit off the heat let the eggs cook through gently and gave the cheese time to melt. Tomato and baby spinach added freshness, and a simple mixture of mayonnaise and hot sauce gave our sandwiches just the right amount of richness and tang. If there's not enough fat left in the skillet after cooking the bacon in step 2, add enough vegetable oil to measure 1 tablespoon.

variation
Sausage and American Cheese Breakfast Sandwiches
Substitute ketchup for hot sauce. Substitute 8 ounces bulk breakfast sausage, formed into four 4-inch patties, for bacon. Melt 1 tablespoon butter in 12-inch nonstick skillet over medium heat. Add sausage patties and cook until well browned and cooked through, 3 to 5 minutes per side; transfer to paper towel–lined plate. Substitute 4 slices deli American cheese (4 ounces) for shredded cheddar cheese.

think like a cook

DIY BREAKFAST SAUSAGE
You can absolutely use store-bought sausage to make our Sausage and American Cheese Breakfast Sandwiches—and it's definitely a faster option—but if you want to make your own, it's supersimple. We start with ground pork, then amp up its mild flavor with classic breakfast sausage flavors: garlic, sage, thyme, and cayenne pepper. A spoonful of maple syrup sweetens the patties nicely. Avoid lean or extra-lean ground pork; it makes the sausage dry, crumbly, and less flavorful. This sausage also makes a great accompaniment to other breakfast classics, such as Perfect Scrambled Eggs (page 68) or Overnight Yeasted Waffles (page 136).

Homemade Breakfast Sausage
Makes 16 patties
Combine 2 pounds ground pork, 1 tablespoon maple syrup, 1 minced garlic clove, 2 teaspoons dried sage, 1½ teaspoons pepper, 1 teaspoon salt, ½ teaspoon dried thyme, and ⅛ teaspoon cayenne pepper in large bowl. Gently mix with hands until well combined. Using greased ¼-cup measure, divide mixture into 16 patties and place on rimmed baking sheet. Cover with plastic wrap, then gently flatten each one until ½ inch thick. Melt 1 tablespoon butter in 12-inch nonstick skillet over medium heat. Cook half of patties until well browned on both sides and cooked through, turning once, 6 to 10 minutes. Transfer to paper towel–lined plate and tent with aluminum foil. Wipe out skillet. Repeat with 1 tablespoon butter and remaining patties. (Uncooked patties can be refrigerated for up to 24 hours or frozen and stored in a zipper-lock bag for up to 1 month. For frozen patties, increase cooking time to 14 to 18 minutes.)

Egg and Black Bean Breakfast Burritos

Serves 6; Total Time 30 minutes

2 tablespoons vegetable oil

1 red bell pepper, stemmed, seeded, and chopped into ¼-inch pieces

1 (15-ounce) can black beans, rinsed

3 scallions, sliced thin

⅛ teaspoon cayenne pepper

12 large eggs

¼ cup half-and-half

Salt and pepper

4 ounces sharp cheddar cheese, shredded (1 cup)

3 tablespoons minced fresh cilantro

6 (10-inch) flour tortillas

why this recipe works

Breakfast burritos are a supersatisfying (and eminently portable) morning meal. We built our version on hearty black beans and fluffy, tender scrambled eggs that made it filling but not heavy. To freshen things up, we added sweet, bright bell pepper, cilantro, and sliced scallions. Sharp cheddar cheese added richness and bold flavor, and a little cayenne pepper provided just the right amount of balancing heat. To make this an easy one-dish meal, we cooked the bell pepper and beans in the skillet before scrambling the eggs, then folded them into the eggs with the cheese and cilantro. You can substitute whole milk for the half-and-half in this recipe, but the eggs will be less rich and less tender. Serve with hot sauce or salsa, sour cream, and sliced avocado.

1. Heat 1 tablespoon oil in 12-inch nonstick skillet over medium-high heat until shimmering. Add bell pepper and cook until softened and beginning to brown, about 5 minutes. Stir in beans, scallions, and cayenne and cook until heated through, about 1 minute; transfer to bowl.

2. Beat eggs, half-and-half, ½ teaspoon salt, and ¼ teaspoon pepper with fork in bowl until thoroughly combined. Wipe out now-empty skillet with paper towels, add remaining 1 tablespoon oil, and return to medium heat. Add egg mixture and cook, using heat-resistant rubber spatula to push mixture back and forth, until curds begin to form. Continue to cook, lifting and folding curds from side to side, until they clump in single mound but are still very moist, about 3 minutes. Off heat, gently fold in bell pepper–bean mixture, cheddar, and cilantro. Season with salt and pepper to taste.

3. Stack tortillas between paper towels on plate and microwave until hot and pliable, 30 to 60 seconds. Divide egg mixture evenly across center of each tortilla, close to bottom edge. Fold sides then bottom of tortilla over filling, pulling back on it firmly to tighten it around filling, then continue to roll tightly into burritos. Serve.

think like a cook

AROMATICS: KITCHEN SUPERSTARS

In this breakfast burrito recipe, the bell pepper, scallions, and cayenne pepper are all aromatics. Aromatics are the flavorful building blocks that form the base of countless savory recipes. They are also often quite fragrant, which is where they get their name. Without aromatics, the flavor of most dishes would be much less deep and complex.

The particular aromatics that are used in a recipe vary from cuisine to cuisine. In French cooking, you will see recipes built on a combination of onion, carrot, and celery (see page 273 for more on this trio, called *mirepoix*); in Chinese cuisine, most recipes have a backbone of garlic, ginger, and scallions. Other common aromatics include chiles, herbs, and spices.

We almost always start a recipe by sautéing aromatics in fat: Because many herbs and spices are fat-soluble, cooking them in fat, or "blooming" them, helps their flavor compounds dissolve more effectively. Doing this at the beginning of a recipe gives these potent ingredients time to really build up flavor, which then gets infused throughout the whole dish.

Tofu Scramble with Herbs
Serves 4; Total Time 35 minutes

14 ounces soft tofu

1½ teaspoons vegetable oil

1 shallot, minced

¼ teaspoon curry powder

¾ teaspoon salt

⅛ teaspoon pepper

2 tablespoons finely chopped fresh basil, parsley, tarragon, or marjoram

1. Crumble tofu into ¼- to ½-inch pieces. Spread tofu on paper towel–lined baking sheet and let drain for 20 minutes, then gently press dry with paper towels.

2. Heat oil in 10-inch nonstick skillet over medium heat until shimmering. Add shallot and cook until softened, about 2 minutes. Stir in crumbled tofu, curry powder, salt, and pepper and cook until tofu is hot, about 2 minutes. Off heat, stir in basil and serve.

why this recipe works

Eggs are not the only thing you can scramble (for that, see page 68). Soft tofu can be cooked in a similar way to produce a quick, hearty, egg-free breakfast. When crumbled up and sautéed, the tofu yielded smooth, creamy pieces very much like curds of scrambled egg. Tofu scramble is a great option if you're cooking for a vegan or if you're just looking for a change. We added a small amount of curry powder to our version for a touch of flavor and color, plus a sautéed shallot and chopped fresh herbs. This simple preparation is perfect for a basic approach, but it's also very easy to add other ingredients into the mix for a more substantial variation. Do not substitute firm tofu for the soft tofu in this recipe. Be sure to press the tofu completely dry before cooking.

variations

Tofu Scramble with Spinach and Feta
Before adding tofu to skillet, add 4 cups baby spinach and cook until wilted, about 1 minute. Add ½ cup crumbled feta to skillet with tofu.

Tofu Scramble with Tomato, Scallions, and Parmesan
Add 1 seeded and finely chopped tomato and 1 minced garlic clove to pan with shallot; cook until tomato is no longer wet, 3 to 5 minutes. Add ¼ cup grated Parmesan and 2 tablespoons minced scallions to skillet with tofu.

Tofu Scramble with Shiitakes, Red Bell Pepper, and Goat Cheese
Before adding shallot to skillet, cook 4 ounces stemmed and thinly sliced shiitake mushrooms, 1 finely chopped small red bell pepper, and pinch red pepper flakes, covered, until mushrooms have released their liquid, about 5 minutes. Uncover, add shallot, and continue to cook until mushrooms are dry and shallot is softened, about 2 minutes. Add ¼ cup crumbled goat cheese to skillet with tofu.

think like a cook

REDEEMING TOFU

To many people, tofu is the quintessential tasteless, unappealing health food: the punch line of a million vegan jokes and probably to be avoided at all costs. But we want to change the way you think about this maligned ingredient, and that starts with understanding exactly what it is and how to make it shine in recipes.

Tofu comes in a variety of textures based on how much liquid has been pressed out of the soy curds: silken, soft, medium-firm, firm, and extra-firm. In general, firmer varieties maintain their shape when cooking, while softer varieties do not. We prefer extra-firm or firm tofu for stir-fries and noodle dishes, as they hold together during high heat cooking and when tossed with noodles. These two varieties of tofu are also great marinated (they absorb marinade better than softer varieties) or tossed raw into salads—try our Marinated Tofu and Vegetable Salad (page 170). Medium and soft tofu boast a creamy texture; we love to pan-fry them (see page 64). The crispy crust that develops makes a nice textural contrast to the silky interior. Soft tofu is also great scrambled like eggs, as in this recipe. Silken tofu has a soft, ultracreamy texture and is often used as a base for smoothies and dips, in desserts such as puddings, or as an egg replacement in vegan baked goods.

Classic Cheese Omelet
Serves 2; Total Time 15 minutes

6 large eggs

Salt and pepper

1 tablespoon unsalted butter, plus 1 tablespoon melted

6 tablespoons finely shredded Gruyère cheese

1. Place 3 eggs in small bowl, season with salt and pepper, and beat with fork until combined. Repeat with remaining 3 eggs in separate bowl.

2. Melt 1½ teaspoons butter in 10-inch nonstick skillet over medium-high heat. Add 1 bowl of egg mixture and cook until edges begin to set, 2 or 3 seconds. Using heat-resistant rubber spatula, stir eggs in circular motion until slightly thickened, about 10 seconds. Use spatula to pull cooked edges of eggs in toward center, then tilt skillet to 1 side so that uncooked eggs run to edge of skillet. Repeat until omelet is just set but still moist on surface, 20 to 25 seconds. Sprinkle 3 tablespoons Gruyère across center of omelet.

3. Off heat, use spatula to fold lower third (portion nearest you) of omelet over filling; press gently with spatula to secure seams, maintaining fold.

4. Run spatula between outer edge of omelet and skillet to loosen. Pull skillet sharply toward you a few times so omelet slides up lip of far edge of pan. Use spatula to fold far edge of omelet toward center. Press to secure the seam. Invert omelet onto warm plate. Tidy edges with spatula, brush with half of melted butter, and serve immediately.

5. Wipe out skillet and repeat with remaining 1½ teaspoons butter, remaining egg mixture, remaining 3 tablespoons Gruyère, and remaining melted butter.

why this recipe works

A quick and creamy cheese omelet makes the perfect breakfast for two (or an easy dinner!), and once you master the basic technique of cooking the eggs and shaping the omelet, you can vary the filling to suit any taste. A good nonstick skillet is essential for perfectly stick-free omelets, since the eggs need to move freely so that the omelet can be folded over itself. To ensure the cheese melted before the eggs overcooked, we finely shredded it and removed the pan from the heat after adding the cheese to the eggs. The residual heat was enough to melt the cheese without overcooking the omelet. This technique gave us the results we had been looking for: moist and creamy eggs, with plenty of perfectly melted cheese. You can substitute cheddar, Monterey Jack, or any semisoft cheese for the Gruyère. Making perfect omelets takes some practice, so don't be disappointed if your first effort fails to meet your expectations.

variations
Asparagus and Smoked Salmon Filling

Heat 1 teaspoon olive oil in skillet over medium-high heat until shimmering. Add 1 thinly sliced shallot and cook until softened and starting to brown, about 2 minutes. Add 5 ounces trimmed asparagus, cut on bias into ¼-inch lengths; pinch salt; and pepper to taste. Cook, stirring frequently, until asparagus is crisp-tender, 5 to 7 minutes. Transfer asparagus mixture to bowl and stir in 1 ounce chopped smoked salmon and ½ teaspoon lemon juice. Add half of filling with Gruyère in step 2 and remaining filling to second omelet with Gruyère in step 5.

Mushroom Filling

Melt 1 tablespoon unsalted butter in 10-inch skillet over medium heat. Add 1 minced small shallot and cook until softened, about 2 minutes. Add 2 ounces white mushrooms, trimmed and sliced ¼ inch thick, and cook until lightly browned, about 3 minutes. Transfer to bowl and stir in 1 teaspoon minced fresh thyme and season with salt and pepper to taste. Add half of filling with Gruyère in step 2 and remaining filling to second omelet with Gruyère in step 5.

think like a cook

TRADITIONAL VS. NONSTICK SKILLETS: WHEN TO USE WHICH FOR WHAT?

One of the big differences between types of skillets is whether the surface is traditional or nonstick. Traditional skillets are made from materials that allow food to adhere slightly, which is ideal for creating the browned bits of fond that are the foundation of a great seared steak or pan sauce. Nonstick skillets, on the other hand, have a coating that keeps food from sticking to minimize the need for lubricating fat. This makes it easier to cook delicate foods and also facilitates cleanup (see page 5 for more information about types of skillets). A nonstick skillet is particularly useful in a recipe like this one since you need to be able to move the cooked omelet around in the pan to successfully fold it; however, we don't think you need a specially designed omelet pan for this task. We also prefer nonstick skillets for stir-fries; they're actually better suited to this task on most home stovetops than a wok would be. Other delicate ingredients that are well suited to nonstick are fish and seafood, and lean meats like chicken, turkey, and pork (as long as you're not making a pan sauce that requires a fond).

Baked Eggs Florentine
Serves 6; Total Time 1 hour

10 ounces frozen spinach, thawed

2 tablespoons unsalted butter

1 large shallot, minced

1 tablespoon all-purpose flour

¾ cup half-and-half

2 ounces Parmesan cheese, grated (1 cup)

Salt and pepper

⅛ teaspoon dry mustard

⅛ teaspoon ground nutmeg

Pinch cayenne pepper

Vegetable oil spray

6 large eggs

1. Adjust oven rack to middle position and heat oven to 500 degrees. Transfer thawed spinach to piece of cheesecloth and squeeze firmly to remove excess water.

2. Melt butter in medium saucepan over medium heat. Add shallot and cook, stirring occasionally, until softened, about 3 minutes. Stir in flour and cook, stirring constantly, for 1 minute. Gradually whisk in half-and-half; bring mixture to boil, whisking constantly. Simmer, whisking frequently, until thickened, 2 to 3 minutes. Remove pan from heat and stir in spinach, Parmesan, ¾ teaspoon salt, ½ teaspoon pepper, mustard, nutmeg, and cayenne.

3. Lightly spray six 6-ounce ramekins with oil spray. Evenly divide spinach filling among ramekins. Using back of spoon, push filling 1 inch up sides of ramekins to create ⅛-inch-thick layer. Shape remaining filling in bottom of ramekin into 1½-inch-diameter mound, then make a shallow indentation in center of mound large enough to hold yolk. Place filled ramekins in 13 by 9-inch glass baking dish. Bake until filling just starts to brown, about 7 minutes, rotating dish halfway through baking.

4. While filling is heating, crack eggs (taking care not to break yolks) into individual cups or bowls. Remove baking dish with ramekins from oven and place on wire rack. Gently pour eggs from cups into hot ramekins, centering yolk in filling. Lightly spray surface of each egg with oil spray and sprinkle each evenly with pinch salt. Return baking dish to oven and bake until whites are just opaque but still tremble (carryover heat will cook whites through), 6 to 8 minutes, rotating dish halfway through baking.

why this recipe works

Almost any food is more appealing when it comes in a neatly packaged individual serving. This recipe reimagines eggs Florentine, with its hearty spinach and creamy sauce, as a simple baked egg dish; no tricky poaching or last-minute assembly required. To achieve the elegant ideal of a perfect-set-white, runny-yolk egg, we added raw eggs to preheated ramekins, ensuring that the egg whites cooked before the yolks had a chance to lose their runniness. The spinach sauce, which we used to line each ramekin, provided a buffer between the eggs and the scorching ramekin walls. Use 6-ounce ramekins with 3¼-inch diameters, measured from the inner lip. It is imperative to remove the eggs from the oven just after the whites have turned opaque but are still jiggly—carryover cooking will finish the job. We developed this recipe using a glass baking dish; if using a metal baking pan, reduce the oven temperature to 425 degrees.

5. Remove dish from oven and, using tongs, transfer ramekins to wire rack. Let stand until whites are firm and set (yolks should still be runny), about 10 minutes. Serve immediately.

variation
Baked Eggs Lorraine
Slice white and green parts of 1 pound leeks thin and wash thoroughly. Cook 2 slices bacon, cut into ½-inch pieces, in medium saucepan over medium heat until crisp, about 10 minutes. Transfer bacon to paper towel–lined plate. Add leeks to pan and cook until softened, about 10 minutes. Transfer leeks to plate with bacon. Proceed with recipe, omitting shallot and reducing butter to 1 tablespoon. Substitute bacon and leek mixture for spinach and ½ cup shredded Gruyère cheese for Parmesan.

think like a cook

WHICH FROZEN VEGETABLES ARE BEST?
Frozen vegetables can be a great option; besides being convenient, vegetables are often frozen at the peak of freshness. However, some vegetables freeze better than others. As a rule, vegetables with a lower moisture content generally freeze well, while their high-moisture counterparts turn mushy and develop off-flavors. (High-moisture spinach is an exception because it doesn't need to retain its shape in most cooked dishes.) Taking that into consideration, here are the frozen vegetables we like best, as well as the ones we don't recommend.

First-Rate: Corn, Lima Beans, Pearl Onions, Peas, and Spinach
Frozen versions of these vegetables can even be preferable to fresh versions, depending on the season.

Acceptable in Some Situations: Broccoli, Carrots, Cauliflower, and Green Beans
These are acceptable options for soups, stews, and long-cooked dishes, where their less-than-crisp texture isn't a factor. But we always prefer fresh when these vegetables are the main component of a dish.

Just Skip: Asparagus, Bell Peppers, Mushrooms, and Snow Peas
These high-moisture vegetables do not freeze well, and you should avoid them both on their own and in frozen vegetable medleys.

Shakshuka

Serves 4; Total Time 1 hour

3 tablespoons vegetable oil

2 onions, chopped fine

2 yellow bell peppers, stemmed, seeded, and cut into ¼-inch pieces

4 garlic cloves, minced

2 teaspoons tomato paste

1 teaspoon ground cumin

1 teaspoon ground turmeric

Salt and pepper

⅛ teaspoon cayenne pepper

1½ cups jarred piquillo peppers or Roasted Red Peppers (see right), chopped coarse

1 (14.5-ounce) can diced tomatoes

¼ cup water

2 bay leaves

⅓ cup chopped fresh cilantro

8 large eggs

2 ounces feta cheese, crumbled (½ cup)

why this recipe works

Shakshuka is a Tunisian one-pan dish featuring eggs poached in a spiced tomato, onion, and pepper sauce. It's great for a savory breakfast or when you're looking to dress up some eggs for dinner. The beauty of shakshuka is that rather than fussing with poaching individual eggs and adding them to a dish, you poach eight eggs right in the flavorful sauce for a fully integrated meal. The key to great shakshuka is balancing the piquancy, acidity, richness, and sweetness of its ingredients. Roasted peppers make the perfect base. We finished our shakshuka with a sprinkling of bright cilantro and salty feta cheese. Jarred or homemade roasted red peppers can be substituted for the piquillo peppers. Serve with pita or crusty bread to mop up the sauce. You will need a 12-inch skillet with a tight-fitting lid for this recipe.

1. Heat oil in 12-inch skillet over medium-high heat until shimmering. Add onions and bell peppers and cook until softened and beginning to brown, 8 to 10 minutes. Add garlic, tomato paste, cumin, turmeric, 1½ teaspoons salt, ¼ teaspoon pepper, and cayenne and cook, stirring frequently, until tomato paste begins to darken, about 3 minutes.

2. Stir in piquillo peppers, tomatoes and their juice, water, and bay leaves and bring to simmer. Reduce heat to medium-low and cook, stirring occasionally, until sauce is slightly thickened, 10 to 15 minutes.

3. Off heat, discard bay leaves and stir in ¼ cup cilantro. Transfer 2 cups sauce to blender and process until smooth, about 60 seconds. Return puree to skillet and bring sauce to simmer over medium-low heat.

4. Off heat, make 4 shallow indentations (about 2 inches wide) in surface of sauce using back of spoon. Crack 2 eggs into each indentation and season eggs with salt and pepper. Cover and cook over medium-low heat until egg whites are just set and yolks are still runny, 5 to 10 minutes. Sprinkle with feta and remaining cilantro and serve.

think like a cook

HOMEMADE ROASTED RED PEPPERS

Sweet red bell peppers take on a whole new layer of complex, smoky flavor when roasted. Jarred roasted red peppers are definitely a convenient alternative to roasting them at home, but you can also roast your own with just a little extra effort. Our preferred method uses the broiler. Cooking times vary depending on the broiler, so watch the peppers carefully. You can substitute yellow or orange bell peppers here, but note that they roast faster than red ones; decrease the cooking time by 2 to 4 minutes. Roasted peppers make a great topping for a pizza or addition to scrambled eggs or antipasto spread. You will need two bell peppers if you want to use them in place of the jarred piquillo peppers in this Shakshuka recipe. Store extra peppers in the refrigerator for up to 3 days.

Roasted Red Peppers

Makes 3 cups

Adjust oven rack 2½ to 3½ inches from broiler element and heat broiler. Cut off top and bottom of 4 red bell peppers, then remove cores and stems. Slice down through sides of peppers, lay them flat on cutting board and trim away any remaining ribs. Place flattened peppers, pepper tops, and pepper bottoms skin side up on aluminum foil–lined baking sheet. Broil peppers until skin is charred and puffed but flesh is still firm, 8 to 10 minutes, rotating sheet halfway through broiling. Transfer broiled peppers to bowl, cover with plastic wrap, and let steam until skins peel off easily, 10 to 15 minutes.

Breakfast Pizza
Serves 6; Total Time 1 hour

3 tablespoons extra-virgin olive oil, plus extra for drizzling

6 slices bacon

8 ounces mozzarella cheese, shredded (2 cups)

1 ounce Parmesan cheese, grated (½ cup)

4 ounces (½ cup) small-curd cottage cheese

¼ teaspoon dried oregano

Salt and pepper

Pinch cayenne pepper

1 pound store-bought pizza dough, room temperature

6 large eggs

2 scallions, sliced thin

2 tablespoons minced fresh chives

why this recipe works

Although it sounds like a bad Saturday morning commercial (Pizza?! For breakfast?!!), it turns out breakfast pizza is just a creative version of the classic bread-eggs-cheese-meat combo. It makes an ideal dish for a brunch crowd and isn't difficult if you start with store-bought pizza dough. Our challenge was getting a crisp crust without overcooking the eggs. To get there, we pressed room-temperature dough into a lightly oiled baking sheet and parbaked it for 5 minutes to give the crust a head start before we added the toppings. The remaining minutes in the oven cooked the eggs just right. The surprising addition of cottage cheese tethered all the ingredients together with a silky creaminess. Room-temperature dough is much easier to shape than cold, so pull the dough from the fridge about 1 hour before you start cooking. If you want to make your own dough, use the recipe on page 344.

1. Adjust oven rack to lowest position and heat oven to 500 degrees. Grease rimmed baking sheet with 1 tablespoon oil.

2. Cook bacon in 12-inch skillet over medium heat until crisp, 7 to 9 minutes. Transfer to paper towel–lined plate; when cool enough to handle, crumble bacon. Combine mozzarella and Parmesan in bowl; set aside. Combine cottage cheese, oregano, ¼ teaspoon pepper, cayenne, and 1 tablespoon oil in separate bowl; set aside.

3. Sprinkle counter lightly with flour. Roll dough into 15 by 11-inch rectangle with rolling pin, pulling on corners to help make distinct rectangle. Transfer dough to prepared sheet and press to edges of sheet. Brush edges of dough with remaining 1 tablespoon oil. Bake dough until top appears dry and bottom is just beginning to brown, about 5 minutes.

4. Remove crust from oven and, using spatula, press down on any air bubbles. Spread cottage cheese mixture evenly over top, leaving 1-inch border around edges. Sprinkle bacon evenly over cottage cheese mixture.

5. Sprinkle mozzarella mixture evenly over pizza, leaving ½-inch border. Create 2 rows of 3 evenly spaced small wells in cheese, each about 3 inches in diameter (6 wells total). Crack 1 egg into each well, then season each egg with salt and pepper.

6. Return pizza to oven and bake until crust is light golden around edges and eggs are just set, 9 to 10 minutes for slightly runny yolks or 11 to 12 minutes for soft-cooked yolks, rotating sheet halfway through baking.

7. Transfer pan to wire rack and let pizza cool for 5 minutes. Transfer pizza to cutting board. Sprinkle with scallions and chives and drizzle with extra oil. Slice and serve.

variation
Chorizo and Manchego Breakfast Pizza

Substitute 6 ounces chorizo sausage, halved lengthwise and cut into ½-inch slices, for bacon and 1 cup shredded Manchego cheese for Parmesan. Cook chorizo in 12-inch skillet over medium heat until lightly browned, 7 to 9 minutes. Let cool completely before proceeding.

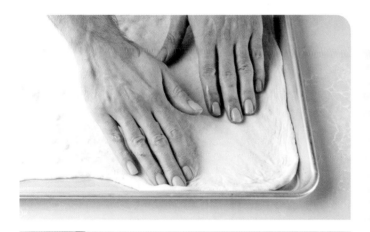

think like a cook

PANTRY POWER MOVE: FROZEN PIZZA DOUGH

Pizza dough is nothing more than bread dough with oil added for softness and stretchiness. While in most cases homemade dough is worth the modest effort, we have to admit that prepared dough can be a great time-saving option for a weeknight pizza made at home (or breakfast pizza made first thing in the morning). Many supermarkets and pizzerias sell dough for just a few dollars a pound, and the dough can be easily frozen. We found that store-bought dough and refrigerated pop-up canisters of pizza dough worked well and tasted fine, but we recommend buying dough from a pizzeria, where it is more likely to be fresh. Supermarket pizza dough is frequently unlabeled, so there's no way to know how long it has been sitting in the refrigerated case or how much dough is in the bag.

Of course, you can also make your own pizza dough and store it in the freezer. Our favorite basic pizza dough recipe is included as part of our Skillet Pizza (page 344). Once the dough has fully risen and doubled in size, shape it into a ball, wrap it in plastic wrap coated with vegetable oil spray, place it in a zipper-lock bag, and freeze it. The best way to defrost dough is to let it sit on the counter for a couple of hours or overnight in the refrigerator. (Thawing pizza dough in a microwave or low oven isn't recommended as it will dry the dough out.)

Sweet Potato Hash

Serves 4; Total Time 45 minutes

why this recipe works

Traditional potato hash is a delicious dish of crispy pan-fried potatoes. Pressing the spuds against the hot pan creates a perfectly browned crust; top it off with an egg and you have a classic diner-style breakfast. For a fresher spin on hash, we replaced half of the russet potatoes with sweet potatoes. The combination of starchy russets and softer sweet potatoes gave us just the right texture to bind the hash together. To speed things up, we parcooked both types of potatoes in the microwave, then moved them to the skillet to brown and crisp. We rounded out the flavors with onion, garlic, thyme, chili powder, and a dash of hot sauce, plus heavy cream for richness. As with our Shakshuka (page 126), we cooked the eggs right in the pan with the rest of the dish. If the potatoes aren't getting brown in step 3, turn up the heat (but don't let them burn). You will need a 12-inch nonstick skillet with a tight-fitting lid for this recipe.

12 ounces russet potatoes, peeled and cut into ¼-inch pieces

12 ounces sweet potatoes, peeled and cut into ¼-inch pieces

2 tablespoons vegetable oil

Salt and pepper

1 onion, chopped fine

2 garlic cloves, minced

½ teaspoon minced fresh thyme or ¼ teaspoon dried

½ teaspoon chili powder

⅓ cup heavy cream

¼ teaspoon hot sauce

8 large eggs

1. Microwave russets, sweet potatoes, 1 tablespoon oil, ½ teaspoon salt, and ¼ teaspoon pepper in covered bowl until potatoes are translucent around edges, 5 to 8 minutes, stirring halfway through microwaving.

2. Meanwhile, heat remaining 1 tablespoon oil in 12-inch nonstick skillet over medium-high heat until shimmering. Add onion and cook until softened and lightly browned, 5 to 7 minutes.

3. Stir in garlic, thyme, and chili powder and cook until fragrant, about 30 seconds. Stir in hot potatoes, cream, and hot sauce. Using back of spatula, gently pack potatoes into pan and cook undisturbed for 2 minutes. Flip hash, 1 portion at a time, and lightly repack into pan. Repeat flipping process every few minutes until potatoes are nicely browned, 6 to 8 minutes.

4. Off heat, make 4 shallow indentations (about 2 inches wide) in surface of hash using back of spoon. Crack 2 eggs into each indentation and season eggs with salt and pepper. Cover and cook over medium-low heat until egg whites are just set and yolks are still runny, 5 to 10 minutes. Serve.

variation
Sweet Potato–Red Flannel Hash
Beets will not brown like potatoes; they will burn if the pan gets too dry.

Reduce russet potatoes and sweet potatoes to 8 ounces each. Microwave 8 ounces beets, peeled and cut into ¼-inch pieces, with potatoes. Add ¼ teaspoon Worcestershire sauce to skillet with cream.

think like a cook

SIDE OF BACON (HOLD THE MESS)

A couple strips of bacon are a welcome accompaniment to a pan of hash and eggs or any breakfast, but bacon requires frequent monitoring when cooked on the stovetop, and the grease can be messy. Microwaving isn't any better, producing unevenly cooked and flavorless strips. Instead, we prefer to use the oven. You have a larger margin of error than in the skillet when it comes to timing (a couple of minutes instead of just a few seconds). The oven also cooks the bacon strips more consistently and your stovetop is saved from splatters and stains. A rimmed baking sheet is necessary to contain the rendered bacon fat. If you're cooking more than one sheet of bacon, switch their positions once about halfway through cooking. You can use thin- or thick-cut bacon here, though cooking times will vary.

Oven-Fried Bacon

Serves 4 to 6

Adjust oven rack to middle position and heat oven to 400 degrees. Arrange 12 bacon slices in rimmed baking sheet. Bake until fat begins to render, 5 to 6 minutes; rotate sheet. Continue cooking until bacon is crisp and brown, 5 to 6 minute for thin-cut bacon, 8 to 10 minutes for thick-cut bacon. Transfer bacon to paper towel–lined plate, drain, and serve.

Hash Browns

Serves 4; Total Time 25 minutes

1 pound russet potatoes, peeled and shredded

Salt and pepper

2 tablespoons unsalted butter

1. Wrap shredded potatoes in clean dish towel and squeeze thoroughly to remove excess moisture. Toss potatoes with ¼ teaspoon salt and season with pepper.

2. Melt 1 tablespoon butter in 10-inch skillet over medium-high heat until it begins to brown, swirling to coat skillet. Scatter potatoes evenly over entire skillet and press to flatten. Reduce heat to medium and cook until dark golden brown and crisp, 7 to 8 minutes.

3. Slide hash browns onto large plate. Melt remaining 1 tablespoon butter in now-empty skillet, swirling to coat pan. Invert hash browns onto second plate and slide, browned side up, back into skillet. Continue to cook over medium heat until bottom is dark golden brown and crisp, 5 to 6 minutes longer.

4. Fold hash brown cake in half; cook for 1 minute. Slide onto plate or cutting board, cut into wedges, and serve immediately.

why this recipe works

Cooked in a sizzling hot pan with melted butter, these are the very best of what hash browns have to offer. In well-made hash browns, the thinly shredded potatoes cook up browned and crispy for the perfect complement to all kinds of breakfast menus. We found that high-starch russet potatoes worked best; the starch helped them stick together and they had the most pronounced potato flavor. We squeezed as much moisture as possible out of the raw grated potatoes before cooking for the best browning and crispy edges. An innovative method using two plates made flipping the hash browns foolproof. We prefer to prepare these hash browns using potatoes that have been cut with the large shredding disk of a food processor, but a box grater can also be used. To prevent the potatoes from turning brown, grate them just before cooking. You can garnish the hash browns with chopped scallions or chives before serving, if desired.

variation

Hash Brown "Omelet" with Cheddar, Tomato, and Basil

After melting butter in step 3 and sliding potatoes back into skillet, top hash browns with 1 seeded and finely chopped tomato, ¼ cup shredded cheddar cheese, and 1 tablespoon chopped fresh basil. Proceed with recipe, folding potato cake in half and cooking until cheese melts.

think like a cook

DON'T FLIP OUT

While certain professional chefs (or particularly buff individuals) may think nothing of flipping over a full, piping hot skillet to turn a hash brown or frittata out onto a serving plate, it can be a scary endeavor for mere mortals. A slipped grip or faltering wrist can send your meal crashing to the floor.

Fortunately, there is a safer and less intimidating way to turn something over in a large skillet. Working with two plates, slide whatever you wish to flip onto one plate and top it with the other. Then, holding the two plates together, flip them over and slide the inverted food back into the pan to finish cooking. This trick also comes in handy for foods such as roesti, Spanish tortilla, and other egg dishes.

100 Percent Whole-Wheat Pancakes

Makes 15 pancakes; Serves 6; Total Time 40 minutes

2 cups (11 ounces) whole-wheat flour

2 tablespoons sugar

1½ teaspoons baking powder

½ teaspoon baking soda

¾ teaspoon salt

2¼ cups buttermilk

5 tablespoons plus 2 teaspoons vegetable oil

2 large eggs

1. Adjust oven rack to middle position and heat oven to 200 degrees. Spray wire rack set in rimmed baking sheet with vegetable oil spray; place in oven.

2. Whisk flour, sugar, baking powder, baking soda, and salt together in medium bowl. Whisk buttermilk, 5 tablespoons oil, and eggs together in second medium bowl. Make well in center of flour mixture and pour in buttermilk mixture; whisk until smooth. (Mixture will be thick; do not add more buttermilk.)

3. Heat 1 teaspoon oil in 12-inch nonstick skillet over medium heat until shimmering. Using paper towels, carefully wipe out oil, leaving thin film on bottom and sides of pan. Using ¼-cup dry measuring cup or 2-ounce ladle, portion batter into pan in 3 places. Gently spread each portion into 4½-inch round. Cook until edges are set, first side is golden brown, and bubbles on surface are just beginning to break, 2 to 3 minutes. Using thin, wide spatula, flip pancakes and continue to cook until second side is golden brown, 1 to 2 minutes longer. Serve pancakes immediately or transfer to wire rack in oven. Repeat with remaining batter, using remaining 1 teaspoon oil as necessary.

why this recipe works

Robust whole-wheat flour is the perfect match for the caramel notes of maple syrup. An all-whole-wheat pancake might sound like a recipe for a tough hockey puck, but to our surprise, when we baked a batch they turned out light and fluffy. Unlike white flour, whole-wheat flour inhibits development of gluten, the protein that gives bread structure and chew. (For more on gluten, see page 435.) Since you don't want those qualities in a pancake anyway, less gluten is a big advantage. That said, without the right amount of liquid, whole-wheat flour can make foods dense and dry. We used a generous amount of buttermilk for light, fluffy, and tender results. Use recently purchased whole-wheat flour or flour that has been stored in the freezer for less than 12 months; otherwise it can turn rancid. An electric griddle set at 350 degrees can be used in place of a skillet.

think like a cook

WHOLE-WHEAT RULES

These pancakes are a bit of an exception; usually you won't be making recipes that use only whole-wheat flour. This is because of certain properties of whole-wheat flour that make it much more difficult to get good results. Whole-wheat flour is ground from the entire wheat berry—the outer bran layer, the germ, and the endosperm (the heart of the berry)—whereas all-purpose flour is ground from just the endosperm. While the germ layer gives whole-wheat flour more protein than all-purpose flour, it also inhibits the formation of gluten, which is what provides lift and structure to baked goods. Less gluten results in a denser crumb. Additionally, the germ and bran particles in whole-wheat flour contribute to greater dryness and chewiness, since they absorb more moisture from the recipe. Thus, if you simply replace all the all-purpose flour in a recipe with whole-wheat flour without making other modifications, you'll end up with dense, tough, chewy baked goods. That doesn't mean you can't use any whole-wheat flour at all; we've found you can replace about 25 percent of the all-purpose flour in a recipe with whole-wheat flour without any adverse effects. However, if you want to bake with more whole-wheat flour than that, we recommend that you seek out recipes specifically designed for that ingredient (like the one here).

Overnight Yeasted Waffles

Serves 4; Total Time 45 minutes (plus 12 hours to refrigerate batter)

1¾ cups milk

8 tablespoons unsalted butter, cut into 8 pieces

2 cups (10 ounces) all-purpose flour

1 tablespoon sugar

1½ teaspoons instant or rapid-rise yeast

1 teaspoon salt

2 large eggs

1 teaspoon vanilla extract

1. Heat milk and butter in small saucepan over medium-low heat until butter is melted, 3 to 5 minutes. Let mixture cool until warm to touch.

2. Whisk flour, sugar, yeast, and salt together in large bowl. In small bowl, whisk eggs and vanilla together. Gradually whisk warm milk mixture into flour mixture until smooth, then whisk in egg mixture. Scrape down bowl with rubber spatula, cover tightly with plastic wrap, and refrigerate for at least 12 hours or up to 24 hours.

3. Adjust oven rack to middle position and heat oven to 200 degrees. Set wire rack in rimmed baking sheet and place in oven. Heat waffle iron according to manufacturer's instructions. Remove batter from refrigerator when waffle iron is hot (batter will be foamy and doubled in size). Whisk to recombine (batter will deflate).

4. Cook waffles according to manufacturer's instructions (use about ½ cup batter for 7-inch round iron and about 1 cup batter for 9-inch square iron). Serve immediately or transfer to wire rack in oven to keep warm while cooking remaining waffles.

why this recipe works

You probably don't think of waffles as a recipe that needs yeast. Adding yeast to what's supposed to be a simple breakfast food might even sound fussy, but in fact yeasted waffles are very easy to prepare and have a tangy, complex flavor that makes them worth the minor effort of planning ahead. The concept is simple enough: Mix together a yeasted batter the night before you plan to make the waffles, then leave it in the fridge overnight to slow the fermentation and develop tangy, complex flavor and creamy, airy texture. All you have to do in the morning is heat up the waffle iron. While the waffles can be eaten as soon as they are removed from the iron, they will have a crispier exterior if rested in a warm oven for 10 minutes. (This method also makes it possible to serve everyone at the same time.) This batter must be made 12 to 24 hours in advance.

variation

Blueberry Yeasted Waffles

We found that frozen wild blueberries—which are smaller—work best here. Larger blueberries release too much juice.

After removing waffle batter from refrigerator in step 3, gently fold 1½ cups frozen blueberries into batter.

think like a cook

KEEPING WAFFLES WARM AND CRISP

When you've got a bunch of people all sitting down to a meal together, you want all the food to be ready at the same time, and at the right temperature. But that can be tricky, especially with food that's cooked in batches, like pancakes and waffles. To avoid having to force your friends and family to eat in lonely shifts or endure lukewarm breakfasts, try this trick: Turn your oven on to a very low temperature—we like 200 degrees—before you start cooking and put a wire rack in a rimmed baking sheet on the middle oven rack. Then transfer the finished food to the rack as it comes out of the pan. The oven's heat keeps the food warm and the elevation of the rack helps avoid sogginess. This also works with pretty much any food that you need to hold while the rest of the meal comes together. Bonus tip: Warm food is even better on warm dishes. Run dishes through the dishwasher on the dry cycle to warm them up just in time for the meal.

French Toast Casserole

Serves 6 to 8; Total Time 1 hour 5 minutes

1 tablespoon unsalted butter, softened, plus 6 tablespoons, melted

¾ cup packed (5¼ ounces) brown sugar

1 tablespoon ground cinnamon

½ teaspoon ground nutmeg

⅛ teaspoon salt

18 slices potato sandwich bread

2½ cups whole milk

6 large eggs

¼ cup sliced almonds, toasted (see page 157)

Confectioners' sugar

why this recipe works

French toast is great, but it's a tricky dish to make for a crowd; someone is pretty much guaranteed to get a cold, soggy breakfast, and the cook has to labor over the hot stove right up until the food is served. We fixed that by translating all the best aspects of French toast into a casserole. We layered potato bread (which held up better than regular sandwich bread) with a gooey brown sugar–cinnamon mixture and butter and then poured a creamy custard over the top. We finished by sprinkling the casserole with sliced almonds. The result? A 13 by 9-inch dish filled with layers of tender, sweet French toast—ready all at once. Serve with maple syrup.

1. Adjust oven rack to middle position and heat oven to 350 degrees. Grease 13 by 9-inch baking dish with softened butter. Mix brown sugar, cinnamon, nutmeg, and salt together in bowl.

2. Sprinkle 3 tablespoons brown sugar mixture evenly over bottom of prepared dish. Place 6 bread slices (use bread heels here) in even layer in bottom of dish. Brush bread with 1½ tablespoons melted butter and sprinkle with 3 tablespoons sugar mixture.

3. Arrange 6 bread slices over first layer, brush with 1½ tablespoons melted butter, then sprinkle with 3 tablespoons sugar mixture. Place remaining 6 bread slices over previous layer and brush with 1½ table-spoons melted butter.

4. In separate bowl, whisk milk and eggs together until well combined. Pour milk mixture over bread and press lightly to submerge. Sprinkle with almonds and remaining heaping 3 tablespoons sugar mixture.

5. Bake until casserole is slightly puffed and golden brown and bubbling around edges, about 30 minutes. Transfer casserole to wire rack, brush with remaining 1½ tablespoons melted butter, and let cool for 15 minutes. Sprinkle with confectioners' sugar and serve.

think like a cook

THE MAGIC OF MAPLE SYRUP

What is breakfast without maple syrup? On pancakes, waffles, French toast, or even for dipping sausages in, this all-natural nectar is a must-have. Pure maple syrup is simply sap from sugar maple trees that is collected and boiled to concentrate its sugar, with no additives or preservatives. Commercial maple syrup comes in various grades, although there is no universal system for grading. International grading uses color and flavor combinations to label syrup; if you're looking for a syrup to use in baking or cooking, look for labels that say "dark." The lighter the color, the more delicate the flavor.

During a recent tasting of eight pure maple syrups, we found that they all tasted similar, so our advice is to buy the cheapest all-maple product you can find. We do not recommend pancake syrup, which is artificially flavored corn syrup that often contains no real maple syrup at all. Because of its high moisture level and lack of preservatives, maple syrup is susceptible to the growth of yeasts, molds, and bacteria, so we recommend refrigerating it. Once opened, maple syrup will keep six months to a year in the refrigerator. For longer storage, keep it in the freezer. It will never freeze solid because of the high sugar concentration; at most, the syrup will become thick, viscous, or crystallized during freezing, but a quick zap in the microwave will restore it.

Lemon-Blueberry Muffins
Makes 12 muffins; Total Time 50 minutes

3 cups (15 ounces) all-purpose flour

1 cup (7 ounces) sugar

1 tablespoon baking powder

½ teaspoon baking soda

½ teaspoon salt

1½ cups plain whole-milk or low-fat yogurt

2 large eggs

1 teaspoon grated lemon zest

8 tablespoons unsalted butter, melted and cooled

7½ ounces blueberries (1½ cups)

1. Adjust oven rack to middle position and heat oven to 375 degrees. Spray 12-cup muffin tin with vegetable oil spray.

2. Whisk flour, sugar, baking powder, baking soda, and salt together in large bowl. In separate bowl, whisk yogurt, eggs, and lemon zest together until smooth. Gently fold yogurt mixture into flour mixture with rubber spatula until just combined, then fold in melted butter; do not overmix. Gently fold in blueberries.

3. Using greased ⅓-cup measure, portion batter into prepared muffin cups. Bake until golden brown and toothpick inserted in center comes out clean, 20 to 25 minutes, rotating muffin tin halfway through baking. Let muffins cool in tin for 5 minutes before removing. Serve warm or at room temperature.

why this recipe works
Why are bakery muffins always so much bigger and fluffier than the ones we make at home? For a homemade muffin that got closer to that big, beautiful bakery ideal, we started with all-purpose flour, which gave the muffins plenty of structure and a nice contrast between crust and crumb. For a liquid, we tested all manner of dairy and liked yogurt the best; it kept our batter thick and produced muffins with rounded, textured tops. For bakery-style muffin tops, we increased the amount of all the ingredients to ensure there was enough batter to fill the muffin cups to the brim. A hit of lemon zest took these beyond basic blueberry. We prefer not to use paper liners, since peeling them off takes off some of the tasty browned exterior of the muffin; simply grease the muffin tin (inside and between the cups) and you'll be able to enjoy every crumb. Frozen blueberries can be substituted for fresh; rinse and dry the frozen berries (do not thaw) before tossing with the flour.

variation
Apricot-Almond Muffins
Substitute ½ teaspoon almond extract for lemon zest and 1 cup finely chopped dried apricots for blueberries. Sprinkle with ¼ cup sliced almonds before baking.

think like a cook

ANATOMY OF A MUFFIN

All cooking involves some elements of science, but baking, in particular, is chemistry in action. Every key ingredient has a role to play in creating the flavor and texture of a great baked good. Let's look at muffins as an example: What goes into making tall, fluffy muffins with a tender crumb, crisp crust, and rich flavor?

All-Purpose Flour

All-purpose flour has enough protein to provide structure in our oversize muffins but not so much that they get tough or chewy.

Granulated Sugar

Besides adding sweetness, the sugar in our muffins also helps create a tender texture by retaining water, which keeps the muffins moist and weakens the gluten structure that would otherwise make the muffins tough.

Baking Soda and Baking Powder

These leaveners both form carbon dioxide, which causes the muffin batter to rise, but they react in different ways. The baking soda is activated by the moisture and acidity in the yogurt, while the baking powder is activated first by the moisture in the yogurt and then again by the heat of the oven. Using them in combination means we get an extra-high, fluffy dome on our muffins and great browning on the tops.

Butter and Yogurt

The fat from these ingredients coats the flour proteins, preventing them from linking up and forming gluten, which means our muffins stay tender. (The yogurt also adds moisture and tang.) Fat also carries flavor, which is why we like using full-fat yogurt in baking. You can use low-fat yogurt but the muffins will not be as rich. Do not use nonfat yogurt.

Eggs

Egg yolks add density and richness to baked goods, and the whites also contribute to their structure. Using whole eggs here means our muffins take advantage of both of these benefits.

Ultimate Banana Bread

Makes 1 loaf; Serves 10; Total Time 2 hours

1¾ cups (8¾ ounces) all-purpose flour

1 teaspoon baking soda

½ teaspoon salt

6 very ripe large bananas (2¼ pounds), peeled

8 tablespoons unsalted butter, melted and cooled

2 large eggs

¾ cup packed (5¼ ounces) light brown sugar

1 teaspoon vanilla extract

½ cup walnuts, toasted (see page 157) and chopped coarse (optional)

2 teaspoons granulated sugar

1. Adjust oven rack to middle position and heat oven to 350 degrees. Grease 8½ by 4½-inch loaf pan. Whisk flour, baking soda, and salt together in large bowl.

2. Place 5 bananas in separate bowl, cover, and microwave until bananas are soft and have released liquid, about 5 minutes. Drain bananas in fine-mesh strainer set over medium bowl, stirring occasionally, for 15 minutes; you should have ½ to ¾ cup liquid.

3. Transfer drained liquid to medium saucepan and cook over medium-high heat until reduced to ¼ cup, about 5 minutes. Return drained bananas to bowl. Stir reduced liquid into bananas and mash with potato masher until mostly smooth. Whisk in melted butter, eggs, brown sugar, and vanilla.

4. Pour banana mixture into flour mixture and stir until just combined, with some streaks of flour remaining. Gently fold in walnuts, if using. Scrape batter into prepared loaf pan and smooth top. Slice remaining banana on bias into ¼-inch slices and shingle down both sides of loaf pan, leaving center clear to ensure even rise. Sprinkle granulated sugar over top.

5. Bake until skewer inserted in center comes out clean, 55 minutes to 1¼ hours, rotating pan halfway through baking. Let loaf cool in pan for 15 minutes, then turn out onto wire rack and continue to cool. Serve warm or at room temperature.

why this recipe works

Banana bread is comfortable, familiar, and in most cases, pretty mediocre. We wanted a more impressive version of this classic that would have tons of banana flavor, with a light, fluffy texture. We started with five bananas, which we microwaved to draw out as much moisture as possible. We then reduced the banana liquid before incorporating it into the batter along with the banana solids. As a final embellishment, we sliced a sixth banana and shingled it on top of the loaf with a sprinkle of sugar to help it caramelize. Be sure to use very ripe, heavily speckled (or even black) bananas. You can freeze overly ripe bananas and save them for this recipe. Thawed frozen bananas will release their liquid without the need for microwaving, so skip that step and put them directly into the fine-mesh strainer to drain, then continue as directed. The test kitchen's preferred loaf pan measures 8½ by 4½ inches; if you use a 9 by 5-inch loaf pan, start checking for doneness 5 minutes early.

think like a cook

JUDGING DONENESS IN QUICK BREADS AND CAKES

The top looks browned, the aroma coming from the oven smells heavenly, and the timer is counting down the last few seconds . . . but is your baking masterpiece really done? There are two ways to judge doneness in most quick breads and cakes. First, use your sense of touch. Fully baked items will feel springy and resilient when the center is gently pressed. If your finger leaves an impression—or if the center jiggles—it's not done. (Custardy cakes follow different rules: A slight jiggle in the center of a cheesecake indicates perfect doneness.)

The other option is to insert a wooden skewer or toothpick into the center; it should emerge clean or with just a few crumbs attached. If you see moist batter, the item needs to bake longer. This test works well with cakes, muffins, and loaf-style quick breads. If a particular recipe gives specific instructions for determining doneness, always follow those.

British-Style Currant Scones
Makes 12 scones; Total Time 45 minutes

3 cups (15 ounces) all-purpose flour

⅓ cup (2⅓ ounces) sugar

2 tablespoons baking powder

½ teaspoon salt

8 tablespoons unsalted butter,
cut into ½-inch pieces and softened

¾ cup dried currants

1 cup whole milk

2 large eggs

1. Adjust oven rack to upper-middle position and heat oven to 500 degrees. Line rimmed baking sheet with parchment paper. Pulse flour, sugar, baking powder, and salt in food processor until combined, about 5 pulses. Add butter and pulse until fully incorporated and mixture looks like very fine crumbs with no visible butter, about 20 pulses. Transfer mixture to large bowl and stir in currants.

2. In separate bowl, whisk milk and eggs together. Reserve 2 tablespoons milk mixture for brushing. Add remaining milk mixture to flour mixture and gently fold together until almost no dry bits of flour remain.

3. Transfer dough to well-floured counter and gather into ball. With floured hands, knead until dough is smooth and free of cracks, 25 to 30 times. Press gently to form disk. Using floured rolling pin, roll disk into 9-inch round, about 1 inch thick.

4. Cut out 8 rounds using 2½-inch biscuit cutter, dipping cutter in flour as needed. Place scones on prepared sheet. Gather dough scraps, form into ball, and knead gently until surface is smooth. Roll dough to 1-inch thickness and cut out 4 additional scones. Discard remaining dough.

5. Brush tops of scones with reserved milk mixture. Reduce oven temperature to 425 degrees and bake scones until risen and golden brown, 10 to 12 minutes, rotating sheet halfway through baking. Transfer scones to wire rack and let cool for at least 10 minutes. Serve warm or at room temperature.

why this recipe works
Teatime! British scones are not as sweet or as rich as their American counterparts, and that makes them more suitable for serving with butter and jam. To make the lightest, fluffiest scones, we added more than the usual amount of leavener. Rather than leave flakes of cold butter in the dough, as we would for American-style scones, we worked softened butter into the flour until it was fully integrated. This protected more of the flour granules from moisture, which in turn limited gluten development and kept the crumb tender and cake-like. We added currants for tiny bursts of fruit flavor and brushed some milk and egg on top for enhanced browning. We prefer whole milk in this recipe, but low-fat milk can be used. The dough will be quite soft and wet; dust your work surface and your hands liberally with flour. For a tall, even rise, use a sharp-edged biscuit cutter and push straight down; do not twist the cutter. Serve with jam, salted butter, or clotted cream.

think like a cook

I DON'T HAVE A BISCUIT CUTTER, BUT I WANT TO MAKE SCONES

You don't absolutely need a biscuit cutter to make scones and biscuits. We know that not everyone is going to have this specialty baking tool on hand. If you find yourself cutter-less, try a clean, empty aluminum can, Mason jar ring, or overturned juice glass. Just ensure whatever tool you use matches the size of cutter called for in your recipe and remember to dip your makeshift cutter in flour just like you would with a real cutter in order to minimize sticking.

All that being said, a biscuit cutter is the secret to tall, symmetrical scones and biscuits. They're inexpensive and their sharp edges are really the best tool for cutting dough, so it's definitely worth it if you want to make these baked goods a regular part of your rotation.

Make-Ahead Coffee Cake

Serves 12; Total Time 1 hour 30 minutes

why this recipe works

Fresh, hot coffee cake for breakfast or brunch is undeniably appealing. But waking up extra early to whip up batter? Not so much. So we developed a simple, convenient coffee cake batter that you can make the night before, pour into a cake pan, and then simply stick in the fridge until you're ready to bake it. You can even freeze it. For our make-ahead cake, we used a reverse creaming method where you cut the butter into the dry ingredients. Because less air was worked into the batter, there was less deflation as the batter sat overnight. This recipe produces two small coffee cakes, which can be baked on different days if desired (unbaked cakes can be frozen for up to 1 month). If you don't have two 9-inch round pans, use two 8-inch square pans instead. We prefer to use a stand mixer for this recipe but a handheld mixer will also work.

STREUSEL

⅔ cup packed (4⅔ ounces) light brown sugar

⅔ cup (4⅔ ounces) granulated sugar

⅔ cup (3⅓ ounces) all-purpose flour

1½ tablespoons ground cinnamon

8 tablespoons unsalted butter, cut into ½-inch pieces and chilled

½ cup chopped pecans

CAKE

3½ cups (17½ ounces) all-purpose flour

1 cup packed (7 ounces) light brown sugar

1 cup (7 ounces) granulated sugar

2 teaspoons baking powder

1 teaspoon baking soda

1½ teaspoons ground cinnamon

½ teaspoon salt

12 tablespoons unsalted butter, softened

3 large eggs

1¾ cups sour cream

1. FOR THE STREUSEL Pulse brown sugar, granulated sugar, flour, cinnamon, and butter in food processor until mixture resembles coarse meal. Divide streusel in half. Stir pecans into one half and reserve separately.

2. FOR THE CAKE Grease two 9-inch round cake pans with vegetable oil spray. With electric mixer on medium-low speed, mix flour, sugars, baking powder, baking soda, cinnamon, and salt in large bowl until combined. Add butter, 1 tablespoon at a time, and mix until only pea-sized pieces remain, 1 to 2 minutes. Add eggs, one at a time, and beat until combined. Add sour cream in 3 additions, using rubber spatula to scrape down bowl as needed. Increase speed to medium-high and beat until batter is light and fluffy, about 2 minutes.

3. Divide batter in half. Scrape one half into prepared pans, dividing batter as evenly as possible. Sprinkle streusel without nuts evenly over each pan. Divide remaining batter evenly between pans and top with nutty streusel. Wrap pans with plastic wrap and refrigerate for up to 24 hours or freeze for up to 1 month.

4. WHEN READY TO BAKE Adjust oven rack to middle position and heat oven to 350 degrees. Unwrap cakes and bake until golden brown and toothpick inserted in center comes out with few dry crumbs attached, about 45 minutes (about 55 minutes if frozen). Cool on wire rack at least 15 minutes. Serve.

variation
Make-Ahead Apple-Walnut Coffee Cake
Substitute ½ cup chopped walnuts for pecans in streusel. Spread ⅓ cup apple butter over top of each cake before adding nutty streusel in step 3 (⅔ cup apple butter total).

think like a cook

DO THE REVERSE CREAM
Many traditional cake (and cookie) recipes require that you cream butter and sugar together, or beat until pale and fluffy. This makes the butter malleable and helps incorporate air into the batter, giving the cake lift. But when a tender texture is the most important thing, as in this coffee cake, we turn to a method known as reverse creaming. Here, softened butter is beaten into the dry ingredients, coating the flour with fat. The fat-coated flour can't readily combine with water to form gluten, which results in a cake that's tender and fine-crumbed, though not as tall since less air was beaten into the batter. (For more information about gluten, see page 435.)

salads and bowls

Summer Vegetable Chopped Salad

Serves 4; Total Time 30 minutes

3 cucumbers, peeled, halved lengthwise, seeded (see page 29), and cut into ½-inch pieces

1½ pounds cherry tomatoes, quartered

Salt and pepper

¼ cup red wine vinegar

1 garlic clove, minced

¼ cup extra-virgin olive oil

1 yellow bell pepper, stemmed, seeded, and cut into ½-inch pieces

1 small red onion, chopped fine

8 ounces radishes, trimmed and sliced thin

¾ cup chopped fresh parsley

1 romaine lettuce heart (6 ounces), cut into 1-inch pieces

1. Toss cucumbers and tomatoes with 1 teaspoon salt and let drain in colander for 15 minutes.

2. Whisk vinegar, garlic, ¼ teaspoon salt, and ⅛ teaspoon pepper together in large bowl. Whisking constantly, drizzle in oil. Add drained cucumbers and tomatoes, bell pepper, onion, radishes, and parsley and toss to coat. Let salad sit for at least 5 minutes or up to 20 minutes.

3. Add lettuce and gently toss to combine. Season with salt and pepper to taste, and serve.

why this recipe works

A chopped salad, where every ingredient is cut into pieces of about the same size, offers the perfect mixture of flavors and textures in every bite. However, some vegetables get watery and soggy when you chop and dress them, and require extra attention. In this summery salad, we first salted the tomatoes and cucumbers to draw out their excess moisture before adding them to the salad. Seeding the cucumbers and quartering the tomatoes exposed more surface area to the salt for even better results. Letting all the vegetables marinate in the vinaigrette for a few minutes before adding the lettuce intensified their flavor. Along with cucumbers and tomatoes, we chose sweet yellow bell pepper, red onion, and peppery radishes and tossed them all with chopped romaine lettuce hearts. Be sure to add the lettuce just before serving, or it will turn soggy.

variations

Mediterranean Chopped Salad

Reduce cucumber to 1 cucumber and substitute 10 ounces grape tomatoes for cherry tomatoes. Reduce vinegar to 3 tablespoons and olive oil to 3 tablespoons. Omit bell pepper and radishes. Reduce onion to ½ onion and parsley to ½ cup. Add 1 (15-ounce) can chickpeas, rinsed, and ½ cup chopped pitted kalamata olives with cucumber and tomatoes in step 2. Add 1 cup crumbled feta with lettuce.

Pear and Cranberry Chopped Salad

Omit tomatoes. Reduce cucumber to 1 cucumber. Substitute 3 table-spoons sherry vinegar for red wine vinegar and reduce olive oil to 3 tablespoons. Substitute red bell pepper for yellow bell pepper. Omit radishes and parsley. Reduce onion to ½ onion. Add 1 ripe but firm pear, halved, cored, and cut into ¼-inch pieces, and ½ cup dried cranberries with cucumber in step 2. Add 1 cup crumbled blue cheese and ½ cup chopped, toasted pistachios with lettuce.

think like a cook

NO MORE WATERY, BLAND VEGETABLES

Tossing watery vegetables like tomatoes, cucumbers, and zucchini with salt before using them not only seasons them but also draws water out of the vegetables so it can be drained away. (Salting is also an important pre-cooking step for eggplant—see page 285.) Use this trick to avoid salad disaster; an unsalted tomato will break down and its liquid will wash out your dressing. Salting vegetables also draws out their flavor molecules. Many of these are trapped within the vegetables' cell walls and tightly bound to proteins that make them inaccessible to our tastebuds without some kind of chemical intervention. With time, the salt draws the flavor compounds out of the cell walls while forcing the proteins to separate from these molecules. The upshot? You get less watery produce with more intense flavors.

Our general formula is for every pound of vegetables, add ½ to 1 teaspoon of table salt and toss in a large bowl. Transfer the vegetables to a colander and let drain for at least 15 minutes (or up to an hour depending on the vegetables and how they are cut). To remove even more liquid, pat the vegetables dry before using.

Arugula Salad with Figs, Prosciutto, Walnuts, and Parmesan

Serves 6; Total Time 25 minutes

¼ cup extra-virgin olive oil

2 ounces thinly sliced prosciutto, cut into ¼-inch-wide ribbons

3 tablespoons balsamic vinegar

1 tablespoon raspberry jam

½ cup dried figs, stemmed and chopped into ¼-inch pieces

1 small shallot, minced

Salt and pepper

8 ounces (8 cups) baby arugula

½ cup walnuts, toasted (see page 157) and chopped

2 ounces Parmesan cheese, shaved

1. Heat 1 tablespoon oil in 10-inch nonstick skillet over medium heat. Add prosciutto and cook, stirring often, until crisp, about 7 minutes. Using slotted spoon, transfer to paper towel–lined plate; let cool.

2. Meanwhile, whisk vinegar and jam together in medium bowl. Stir in figs, cover, and microwave until figs are plump, 30 to 60 seconds. Whisk in remaining 3 tablespoons oil, shallot, ¼ teaspoon salt, and ⅛ teaspoon pepper; let cool.

3. Toss arugula with cooled vinaigrette in large bowl and season with salt and pepper to taste. Divide salad among individual plates and top with prosciutto, walnuts, and Parmesan. Serve.

why this recipe works

Unlike everyday lettuce, arugula is more than just a leafy backdrop for salad garnishes and dressing. But arugula's complex, peppery flavor also makes it something of a challenge to pair with other ingredients. For a truly outstanding arugula-based salad we picked co-starring ingredients that could stand up to these spicy greens. A fruit-nut-cheese pairing was a classic route. Dried figs had mellow sweetness, while toasted walnuts provided just the right amount of crunch. Shaved Parmesan had the perfect salty-savory balance, and that got even better when we added crispy prosciutto strips. A spoonful of jam added to the vinaigrette helped to emulsify the dressing and provided an additional sweet contrast to arugula's peppery bite.

variation

Arugula Salad with Pears, Almonds, Goat Cheese, and Dried Apricots

Omit prosciutto. Substitute white wine vinegar for balsamic and apricot jam for raspberry. Substitute dried apricots for figs and ¼ cup thinly sliced red onion for shallot. Add 1 ripe but firm pear, halved, cored, and sliced ¼ inch thick, to cooled vinaigrette with arugula. Substitute ⅓ cup toasted sliced almonds for walnuts and ¾ cup crumbled goat cheese for Parmesan.

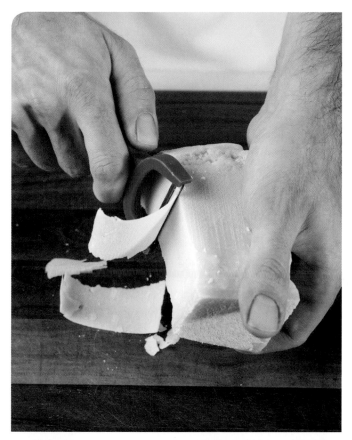

think like a cook

WAYS TO USE UP A JAR OF JAM

We use a tablespoon of raspberry jam in the vinaigrette for this salad to add sweetness and depth. This is also just a great way to use up the dregs of a jar of fancy jam when there isn't enough for your morning toast but you don't want it to go to waste. Below are some other ideas for cleaning out those mostly empty jars of jam, jelly, preserves, or marmalade.

» Take advantage of the jar itself: Add olive oil, vinegar, Dijon mustard, salt, and pepper to a nearly empty jar of jam or jelly, screw on the lid, and shake away. In seconds you have dressing in a ready-made container! (This works with a jar of mustard, too.)

» Mix a spoonful into plain yogurt, cottage cheese, or your morning oatmeal. Top with nuts or seeds.

» Swirl into the batter of your next muffins or quick bread.

» Heat with maple syrup to make flavored syrup.

» Fold some into frosting for cakes, cupcakes, or cookies.

» Use as a glaze for roasted or grilled poultry or meat.

» Use to flavor a pan sauce for pork. See "Improvising a Pan Sauce" (page 87).

» Melt in a small saucepan and use it as an ice cream topping.

» Serve with cheese, crackers, and charcuterie as part of a simple cheese plate.

» Add a spoonful to a cocktail for a sweetener and a boost of fruit flavor.

» Spice up a savory sandwich with a smear of jam and a touch of mustard.

Kale Caesar Salad

Serves 4 to 6; Total Time 45 minutes

SALAD

12 ounces curly kale, stemmed and cut into 1-inch pieces (16 cups)

1 ounce Parmesan cheese, grated (½ cup)

1 recipe Homemade Croutons (see right)

DRESSING

½ cup mayonnaise

¼ cup grated Parmesan cheese

2 tablespoons lemon juice

1 tablespoon white wine vinegar

1 tablespoon Worcestershire sauce

1 tablespoon Dijon mustard

3 anchovy fillets, rinsed

1 garlic clove, minced

½ teaspoon salt

½ teaspoon pepper

¼ cup extra-virgin olive oil

why this recipe works

It's no wonder that kale Caesar has become just as well loved and ubiquitous as the classic: The powerful flavors of earthy kale and tangy Caesar dressing are a great match. However, uncooked kale needs a little special treatment to temper its bitterness and soften its texture so it can work in a salad. A popular method for this is massaging, but applying this hands-on technique to 16 cups of kale took too much work. Instead, we turned to another method: a brief warm water bath. Soaking the kale for 10 minutes broke down the cell walls and mellowed the flavor as well. Plus, this doubled as the washing step and also gave us time to prepare the croutons and dressing. Marinating the soaked and dried kale in the Caesar dressing in the refrigerator allowed time for the greens to cool down and the flavors to meld together. The kale leaves must be dressed at least 20 minutes (or up to 6 hours) before serving.

1. FOR THE SALAD Place kale in large bowl and cover with warm tap water (110 to 115 degrees). Swish kale around to remove grit. Let kale sit in warm water bath for 10 minutes. Remove kale from water and spin dry in salad spinner in multiple batches. Pat leaves dry with paper towels if still wet.

2. FOR THE DRESSING Process mayonnaise, Parmesan, lemon juice, vinegar, Worcestershire, mustard, anchovies, garlic, salt, and pepper in blender until pureed, about 30 seconds. With blender running, slowly add oil until emulsified.

3. Toss kale with ¾ cup dressing in large bowl. Refrigerate dressed kale for at least 20 minutes or up to 6 hours. Toss Parmesan and croutons with dressed kale. Serve, passing remaining ¼ cup dressing at table.

think like a cook

CROUTONS CAN BE DELICIOUS

The carb element of your salad doesn't have to taste like oily cardboard. Homemade croutons are easy to make and taste way better than anything you can buy in the supermarket. Making them is also a great way to repurpose stale bread. We like to use a baguette here, but most any savory bread will work. Pro tip: These are great on soups as well as salads.

Homemade Croutons

Makes about 3 cups

Adjust oven rack to middle position and heat oven to 350 degrees. Toss 3 ounces baguette, cut into ¾-inch cubes (3 cups); 2 tablespoons extra-virgin olive oil; ¼ teaspoon pepper; and ⅛ teaspoon salt together in bowl. Bake on rimmed baking sheet until golden and crisp, about 15 minutes. Let croutons cool completely on sheet. (Cooled croutons can be stored in airtight container at room temperature for up to 24 hours.)

Brussels Sprout Salad

Serves 8; Total Time 1 hour

2 pounds Brussels sprouts

3 tablespoons lemon juice

2 tablespoons Dijon mustard

1 small shallot, minced

1 garlic clove, minced

Salt and pepper

6 tablespoons extra-virgin olive oil

3 ounces Pecorino Romano cheese, shredded (1 cup)

½ cup pine nuts, toasted (see right)

1. Trim Brussels sprouts, then halve each sprout and slice very thin.

2. Whisk lemon juice, mustard, shallot, garlic, and ½ teaspoon salt together in large bowl. Slowly whisk in oil until incorporated. Toss Brussels sprouts with vinaigrette and let sit for at least 30 minutes or up to 2 hours.

3. Fold in Pecorino and pine nuts. Season with salt and pepper to taste, and serve.

why this recipe works

There are many cooking methods that play to the strengths of Brussels sprouts (see Roasted Brussels Sprouts on page 198), but one preparation you may not have thought of is to skip cooking them altogether. Raw Brussels sprouts can be extremely appealing as long as they are treated correctly. We found that shredding the sprouts superthin was key, and letting them sit in the dressing for at least 30 minutes softened them fully and seasoned them deeply. We chose a simple lemon vinaigrette to flavor the salad, rounding it out with shallot and mustard. Crunchy nuts and salty cheese were the perfect finishing touches for this light, fresh alternative to basic green salads. Slice the sprouts as thin as possible; to streamline the process, we recommend first trimming all the sprouts, then halving them all, and then shredding them one by one. When trimming the sprouts, cut off enough so each is roughly as tall as it is wide. Shred the Pecorino Romano on the large holes of a box grater.

variations

Brussels Sprout Salad with Cheddar, Hazelnuts, and Apple

Substitute 1 cup shredded sharp cheddar for Pecorino and ½ cup hazelnuts, toasted, skinned, and chopped, for pine nuts. Add 1 Granny Smith apple, cored and cut into ½-inch pieces.

Brussels Sprout Salad with Smoked Gouda, Pecans, and Dried Cherries

Substitute 1 cup shredded smoked gouda for Pecorino and ½ cup pecans, toasted and chopped, for pine nuts. Add ½ cup chopped dried cherries.

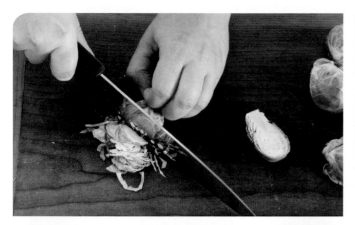

think like a cook

TOASTING NUTS AND SEEDS AND MORE

We almost always toast nuts and seeds (as well as whole spices and shredded coconut) before using them in order to bring out their flavors and aromas and to maximize crunch.

To Toast Small Batches of Nuts and Seeds

If you have less than 1 cup of nuts or seeds, toast them in a dry skillet (i.e., without oil) over medium heat, shaking the pan occasionally, until lightly browned and fragrant, 2 to 5 minutes. Watch them closely as they can go from golden to burnt quickly, especially delicate pine nuts and sesame seeds. Whole spices can be toasted the same way; they may need only a minute or two.

To Toast Large Batches of Nuts and Seeds

For larger amounts, spread nuts and seeds in a single layer on a rimmed baking sheet and toast in a 350-degree oven for 5 to 10 minutes, shaking the pan every few minutes.

To Toast Coconut

We like to toast shredded coconut in the microwave as it can easily burn when not closely monitored. Spread coconut evenly on a large plate and microwave until the coconut is golden brown, stirring every 30 seconds. It takes a couple of minutes.

Smashed Cucumber Salad

Serves 4; Total Time 30 minutes

why this recipe works

This simple salad may not sound like much on paper, but its crunchy, pickle-like texture, slight acidity, and sweet-salty dressing make it a standout on the plate. Smashed cucumbers, or *pai huang gua,* is a Sichuan dish that is typically served with rich, spicy food. Why smash cukes? First, the irregular pieces crisp up faster during salting. They also do a better job of holding onto dressing than clean slices. The Chinese black vinegar used in the dressing may be unfamiliar but is worth seeking out for its malty, smoky notes. (And a recipe this easy is a great opportunity to try a new ingredient.) If you can't find it, substitute 2 teaspoons rice vinegar and 1 teaspoon balsamic vinegar. A rasp-style grater makes quick work of turning the garlic into a paste. We like to drizzle the cucumbers with Sichuan Chili Oil (see right) when serving them with milder dishes like Oven-Roasted Salmon (page 94).

2 English cucumbers

1½ teaspoons kosher salt

4 teaspoons Chinese black vinegar

1 teaspoon garlic, minced to paste

1 tablespoon soy sauce

2 teaspoons toasted sesame oil

1 teaspoon sugar

1 teaspoon sesame seeds, toasted (see page 157)

Sichuan Chili Oil (optional; see right)

1. Trim and discard ends from cucumbers. Cut each cucumber crosswise into three equal lengths. Place pieces in large zipper-lock bag and seal bag. Using small skillet or rolling pin, firmly but gently smash cucumbers until flattened and split lengthwise into 3 or 4 spears each. Tear spears into rough 1- to 1½-inch pieces and transfer to colander set in large bowl. Toss cucumbers with salt and let stand for at least 15 minutes or up to 30 minutes.

2. While cucumbers sit, whisk vinegar and garlic together in small bowl; let stand for at least 5 minutes or up to 15 minutes.

3. Whisk soy sauce, oil, and sugar into vinegar mixture until sugar has dissolved. Transfer cucumbers to medium bowl (discard any extracted liquid). Add dressing and sesame seeds to cucumbers and toss to combine. Serve immediately with Sichuan Chili Oil, if using.

think like a cook

DIY SICHUAN CHILI OIL

If you like spicy food, you should definitely add this homemade Sichuan chili oil to your pantry. We like to drizzle it over our Smashed Cucumber Salad to add an extra dimension when the salad is paired with milder dishes. It's also great on dumplings or as a finishing oil for soups. The hallmark of Sichuan chili oil is a balance between *la*—the concentrated heat from dried chiles—and *ma*—the numbing effect of Sichuan peppercorns. Blooming the aromatics in vegetable oil builds a pungent base. Asian chili powder is similar to red pepper flakes but is milder and more finely ground. A Sichuan chili powder is preferred, but Korean red pepper flakes, called *gochugaru*, are a good alternative.

Sichuan Chili Oil

Makes about 1½ cups

Place ½ cup Asian chili powder, 2 tablespoon sesame seeds, 1 tablespoon crushed Sichuan peppercorns, and ½ teaspoon salt in heatproof bowl. Heat 1 cup vegetable oil; one 1-inch piece unpeeled ginger, sliced into ¼-inch rounds and smashed; 2 bay leaves; 3 star anise pods; 5 crushed cardamom pods; and another 1 tablespoon crushed Sichuan peppercorns in small saucepan over low heat. Cook, stirring occasionally, until spices have darkened and mixture is very fragrant, 25 to 30 minutes. Strain oil mixture through fine-mesh strainer into bowl with chili powder mixture (it may bubble slightly); discard solids in strainer. Stir well to combine. Once cool, transfer mixture to airtight container and let stand for at least 12 hours before using. (Oil can be stored at room temperature for up to 1 week or refrigerated for up to 3 months.)

French Potato Salad with Dijon Mustard and Fines Herbes

Serves 6; Total Time 45 minutes

2 pounds small red potatoes (1 to 2 inches in diameter), unpeeled and sliced ¼ inch thick

2 tablespoons salt

1 garlic clove, peeled and threaded on skewer

1½ tablespoons Champagne vinegar or white wine vinegar

2 teaspoons Dijon mustard

¼ cup olive oil

½ teaspoon pepper

1 small shallot, minced

1 tablespoon minced fresh chervil

1 tablespoon minced fresh parsley

1 tablespoon minced fresh chives

1 teaspoon minced fresh tarragon

1. Place potatoes and salt in large saucepan and add water to cover by 1 inch. Bring to boil over high heat, then reduce heat to medium. Lower skewered garlic into simmering water and cook for 45 seconds. Immediately run garlic under cold running water to stop cooking; set aside to cool. Continue to simmer potatoes, uncovered, until tender but still firm (thin-bladed paring knife can be slipped into and out of center of potato slice with no resistance), about 5 minutes. Reserve ¼ cup cooking water, then drain potatoes. Arrange hot potatoes close together in single layer on rimmed baking sheet.

2. Remove garlic from skewer and mince. Whisk garlic, reserved cooking water, vinegar, mustard, oil, and pepper together in bowl, then drizzle evenly over warm potatoes. Let potatoes stand for 10 minutes, then transfer to large serving bowl. (Salad can be refrigerated for up to 24 hours. Return salad to room temperature before continuing.)

3. Combine shallot, chervil, parsley, chives, and tarragon in bowl, then mix gently into potatoes with rubber spatula. Serve.

why this recipe works

Unlike American potato salads, which are usually smothered in heavy mayonnaise-based dressings, classic French potato salad is tossed with a lively herb and mustard vinaigrette for a lighter, brighter dish. It's a refreshing change from the usual picnic fare. We started by slicing the potatoes before boiling them, which eliminated torn skins and broken slices. We dressed the potatoes on a sheet pan while they were still warm to evenly infuse them with the clean, light champagne-vinegar dressing. This style of potato salad is served warm or at room temperature, with no flavor-dulling trip to the fridge. The combination of herbs that make up *fines herbes* is a hallmark of French cuisine; if fresh chervil isn't available, substitute an additional 1½ teaspoons minced parsley and an additional ½ teaspoon minced tarragon.

variation
French Potato Salad with Arugula, Roquefort, and Walnuts

Omit herbs and toss dressed potatoes with ½ cup walnuts, toasted and coarsely chopped, 1 cup crumbled Roquefort cheese, and 3 ounces baby arugula, torn into bite-size pieces (3 cups), along with shallot in step 3.

think like a cook

WASTE NOT, WANT NOT: HERBS EDITION

When preparing a recipe, we rarely use an entire bunch of herbs. Inevitably, a few days later the leftovers look less than fresh and we end up throwing them away and buying a new bunch. But it doesn't have to be that way! First, always store your herbs properly (see page 14). If you have fresh herbs that have seen better days, trim the stems and soak them for 10 minutes in cold water to perk up their look and texture. An even better option is to use the herbs before they have a chance to wilt. (Make one of the herb sauces on pages 100–101, or make Roast Chicken Parts with Lemon and Herbs, page 88.) You can also add the whole leaves to a green salad, use them to infuse fresh flavor into homemade drinks, or dry them for longer-term storage. To dry, place the herbs on a paper towel and microwave for 30 to 40 seconds, then crumble the dried herbs and store in an airtight container for up to 3 months.

Farro Salad with Sugar Snap Peas and White Beans

Serves 4 to 6; Total Time 1 hour

12 ounces sugar snap peas, strings removed, cut into 1-inch lengths

Salt and pepper

1½ cups whole farro

3 tablespoons extra-virgin olive oil

2 tablespoons lemon juice

2 tablespoons minced shallot

1 teaspoon Dijon mustard

1 (15-ounce) can cannellini beans, rinsed

6 ounces cherry tomatoes, halved

⅓ cup chopped pitted kalamata olives

2 tablespoons chopped fresh dill

1. Bring 4 quarts water to boil in large pot. Add snap peas and 1 tablespoon salt and cook until crisp-tender, about 2 minutes. Using slotted spoon, transfer snap peas to large plate and let cool completely, about 15 minutes.

2. Add farro to water, return to boil, and cook until grains are tender with slight chew, 15 to 30 minutes. Drain farro, spread on rimmed baking sheet, and let cool completely, about 15 minutes. (Cooled farro can be refrigerated for up to 3 days.)

3. Whisk oil, lemon juice, shallot, mustard, ¼ teaspoon salt, and ¼ teaspoon pepper together in large bowl. Add cooled snap peas, cooled farro, beans, tomatoes, olives, and dill and toss to combine. Season with salt and pepper to taste, and serve.

why this recipe works

Grain salads offer a heartier way to eat your vegetables and can work as a substantial side or a light meal on their own. Farro is a widely adaptable grain that's a favorite in Italian cuisine. It has a sweet, nutty flavor and a chewy bite. Here, we let the cooked farro cool quickly on a rimmed baking sheet and then tossed it with snap peas that we had cooked first in the boiling water to bring out their vibrant color and crisp-tender bite. For a hearty finish, we added cherry tomatoes, meaty kalamata olives, and creamy cannellini beans. We prefer the flavor and texture of whole farro; pearled farro can be used, but the texture may be softer. We found a wide range of cooking times among various brands of farro, so start checking for doneness after 10 minutes. Do not use quick-cooking farro in this recipe.

variation

Farro Salad with Cucumber, Yogurt, and Mint

Omit snap peas. Substitute 2 tablespoons plain Greek yogurt for Dijon mustard in dressing. Omit cannellini beans and olives and substitute 2 tablespoon chopped fresh mint for dill. Halve 1 English cucumber lengthwise, seed, cut into ¼-inch pieces, and add to farro with tomatoes along with 1 cup baby arugula.

think like a cook

THE PASTA METHOD

You may have noticed that the cooking method for the farro in this recipe is different from what you might see on the grain's package. Rice and other grains are often cooked using what we call the absorption method: The grain simmers in a small, precise amount of a liquid and absorbs almost all of that liquid by the time it becomes fully cooked. This can lead to uneven results, however, since only the grains that fully hydrate at the start will completely soften, while the grains that didn't initially absorb enough liquid will remain relatively firm. (One solution for this is to use the gentle heat of the oven; see Foolproof Baked Brown Rice, page 74.) Simmering also requires that you know the proper ratio of water to grain, which differs from one type of grain to another and so can be hard to keep track of. And the cooking can be slow going for firmer grains.

For grains that take a relatively long time to cook, we have found that boiling them in an abundance of water, as you would pasta (thus we call it the pasta method), cooks them not only more evenly, but also more quickly. With a large volume of boiling water in the pot (which is drained off after cooking), the liquid can penetrate the individual grains evenly from all sides, so their starches gelatinize more uniformly and in much less time. We tend to avoid the pasta method for white rice. Being mostly unprotected starch, white rice is less able to handle such agitation, which causes its starches to release and make the rice gummy. But it's an excellent and speedy alternative for cooking farro, barley, wheat berries, whole-grain rices (see Black Rice Bowls with Salmon, page 182), and other sturdy grains.

North African Cauliflower Salad with Chermoula

Serves 4 to 6; Total Time 40 minutes

why this recipe works

Chermoula is a traditional Moroccan marinade and sauce made with hefty amounts of cilantro, lemon, and garlic. While it is traditionally used on meat and fish (and is wonderful that way), we love it as the dressing for this roasted cauliflower salad, where it zests up a relatively bland vegetable. Because cauliflower can over-brown in the oven before it cooks through, we started it on a baking sheet covered with aluminum foil and let it steam until barely tender. Then we removed the foil, added sliced onion, and returned the sheet to the oven to let both vegetables caramelize. Shredded carrots and raisins, two traditional North African ingredients, highlighted the sweetness of the cooked vegetables. Use the large holes of a box grater to shred the carrot.

SALAD

1 head cauliflower (2 pounds), cored and cut into 2-inch florets

2 tablespoons extra-virgin olive oil

Salt and pepper

½ red onion, sliced ¼ inch thick

1 cup shredded carrot (about 2 carrots)

½ cup raisins

2 tablespoons chopped fresh cilantro

2 tablespoons sliced almonds, toasted (see page 157)

CHERMOULA

¾ cup fresh cilantro leaves

¼ cup extra-virgin olive oil

2 tablespoons lemon juice

4 garlic cloves, minced

½ teaspoon ground cumin

½ teaspoon paprika

¼ teaspoon salt

⅛ teaspoon cayenne pepper

1. FOR THE SALAD Adjust oven rack to lowest position and heat oven to 475 degrees. Toss cauliflower with oil and season with salt and pepper. Arrange cauliflower in single layer in parchment paper–lined rimmed baking sheet. Cover tightly with aluminum foil and roast until softened, 5 to 7 minutes. Remove foil and spread onion evenly in pan. Roast until vegetables are tender, cauliflower is deep golden brown, and onion slices are charred at edges, 10 to 15 minutes, stirring halfway through roasting. Let cool slightly, about 5 minutes.

2. FOR THE CHERMOULA Process all ingredients in food processor until smooth, about 1 minute, scraping down sides of bowl as needed. Transfer to large bowl.

3. Gently toss cauliflower-onion mixture, carrots, raisins, and cilantro with chermoula until coated. Transfer to serving platter and sprinkle with almonds. Serve warm or at room temperature.

think like a cook

WHAT IS THIS FRUIT DOING IN MY SALAD?

Raisins and cauliflower, apples and Brussels sprouts, figs and arugula . . . you'll find all of these fruit and veggie combinations (and more) in this salad chapter, even though there is no recipe for traditional fruit salad. These pairings may not sound completely intuitive, but we love playing around with the possibilities of adding fruits, both dried and fresh, to recipes that might traditionally seem like exclusively savory territory. We particularly like to use dried fruit in salads with fresh vegetables for the textural interest and pop of sweetness they add. It can be just the thing to bring the flavors of a dish into balance, and other common salad components (such as high-acid vinaigrettes, salty cheeses, and toasted nuts) all interact differently with fruits than they do with vegetables, making for a more complex and enjoyable dish.

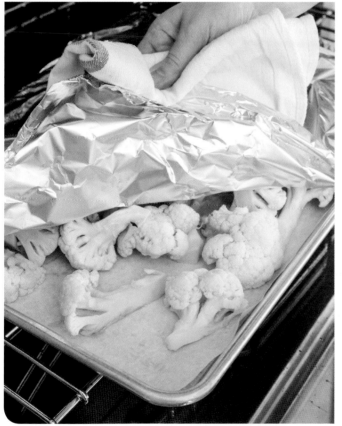

Chinese Chicken Salad
Serves 6; Total Time 1 hour

3 oranges

⅓ cup rice vinegar

3 tablespoons soy sauce

3 tablespoons grated fresh ginger

1 tablespoon Asian chili-garlic sauce

1 tablespoon honey

3 tablespoons vegetable oil

2 teaspoons toasted sesame oil

1 boneless, skinless chicken breast, trimmed

1 small head napa cabbage (1½ pounds),
cored and sliced thin

2 red bell peppers, stemmed, seeded,
and cut into 2-inch-long matchsticks

1 cup fresh cilantro leaves

6 scallions, sliced thin

½ cup salted dry-roasted peanuts, chopped

why this recipe works

Although you may be enamored with your takeout and restaurant favorites, homemade versions are often worlds better (not to mention more healthful). With its juicy oranges, tender chicken, and crunchy topping, Chinese chicken salad has the perfect balance of flavors and textures. But many versions lose their way with gloppy sauces, lackluster chicken, sugary canned orange segments, and watery greens. To recast this salad in a new light, we turned to fresh ingredients. We cut out fresh orange segments to top our salad and used the juice as the basis for a bright dressing, which we also used as a simmering liquid for the chicken breast. For the salad's base, we chose napa cabbage, red bell peppers, cilantro, and scallions. Crunchy roasted peanuts were the perfect finishing touch. You can substitute 1 minced garlic clove and ¼ teaspoon cayenne pepper for the Asian chili-garlic sauce. To learn how to cut peel from an orange, see page 35.

1. Cut away peel and pith from oranges. Holding fruit over large bowl, use paring knife to slice between membranes to release segments; transfer segments to second bowl and set aside. Squeeze juice from membrane into first bowl (juice should measure 6 tablespoons).

2. Whisk vinegar, soy sauce, ginger, chili-garlic sauce, and honey into orange juice in large bowl; transfer ½ cup orange juice mixture to 12-inch skillet and set aside. Whisking constantly, slowly drizzle vegetable oil and sesame oil into remaining orange mixture in bowl; set aside.

3. Bring orange juice mixture in skillet to boil over medium-high heat. Add chicken, reduce heat to medium-low, cover, and simmer, flipping halfway through cooking, until meat registers 160 degrees, 10 to 15 minutes.

4. Transfer chicken to plate and let cool slightly. Using 2 forks, shred chicken into bite-size pieces. Off heat, return shredded chicken and any accumulated juices to skillet and let sit for 10 minutes.

5. Add cabbage, bell peppers, cilantro, and scallions to vinaigrette in bowl and toss to combine. Transfer to serving platter and top with shredded chicken, orange segments, and peanuts. Serve.

think like a cook

STORING AND USING CITRUS

Unlike bananas or peaches, which ripen at room temperature, citrus fruits stop ripening the moment they are picked, thus beginning a slow and steady decline in texture and flavor. To improve their shelf life, commercially grown citrus are buffed with a thin layer of food-safe wax that prevents moisture from escaping through the fruits' porous rind. To test how well the wax coating works, we bought lemons, limes, and oranges and stored half in the refrigerator and half at room temperature. The fruit that was refrigerated remained firm and juicy for about three weeks, while citrus that was left at room temperature began to discolor and dehydrate in as little as five days. Ultimately, the only downside to storing citrus in the fridge is that it's more difficult to squeeze juice from a cold citrus fruit. But that's easy to fix: Simply let your citrus sit at room temperature for about 15 minutes before juicing. For more details on which produce to store where, see page 17.

Wedge Salad with Steak Tips

Serves 4; Total Time 45 minutes

4 slices bacon, cut into ½-inch pieces

¾ cup plain yogurt

1 teaspoon red wine vinegar

3 ounces Stilton cheese, crumbled (¾ cup)

1 garlic clove, minced

Salt and pepper

1½ pounds sirloin steak tips, trimmed and cut into 2-inch pieces

1 head iceberg lettuce (9 ounces)

10 ounces cherry tomatoes, halved

2 tablespoons minced fresh chives

1. Cook bacon in 12-inch skillet over medium heat, stirring frequently, until crisp and well rendered, 6 to 8 minutes. Using slotted spoon, transfer bacon to paper towel–lined plate and remove skillet from heat, leaving rendered bacon fat in skillet.

2. Whisk yogurt, vinegar, ½ cup Stilton, garlic, ¼ teaspoon salt, and ¼ teaspoon pepper in bowl to combine.

3. Pat steak dry with paper towels and season with salt and pepper. Heat bacon fat in skillet over medium-high heat until just smoking. Add steak and cook until well browned on all sides and meat registers 120 to 125 degrees (for medium-rare), about 7 minutes. Transfer to plate, tent with aluminum foil, and let rest for 5 to 10 minutes.

4. While steak rests, cut lettuce into 8 wedges and remove cores.

5. Arrange lettuce wedges and steak tips on individual serving dishes and drizzle with dressing. Top with tomatoes, bacon, and remaining ¼ cup Stilton. Sprinkle with chives and season with salt and pepper to taste. Serve.

why this recipe works

There's a reason that the wedge salad is such a classic and enduring menu item at American restaurants; the combo of crunchy iceberg lettuce, tangy blue cheese, and crispy bacon has a lot to recommend it. To turn the salad into a bona fide dinner, we added meaty steak tips in a nod to its steakhouse roots. Since the flavor of the cheese is front and center, this is a time to spring for a good one. We prefer Stilton, but you can substitute any high-quality blue cheese. This salad is best when the iceberg wedges are cold, so leave the lettuce in the fridge until the steak is done cooking. Sirloin steak tips, also known as flap meat, can be sold as whole steaks, cubes, and strips. To ensure uniform pieces, we prefer to purchase whole steaks and cut them ourselves.

think like a cook

MIXING AND MATCHING SALAD GREENS

In a salad rut? It's easy to default to buying the same kind of lettuce every week. For variety, try combining several kinds of greens to create a salad with a mix of textures and flavors.

Mild Greens

All-purpose, ruffly red leaf and green leaf lettuces pair well with almost anything. Soft, buttery Boston and Bibb lettuces pair with fresh herbs like chives or tarragon as well as watercress and endive. Earthy sweet spinach pairs well with other mild greens as well as arugula and watercress.

Crunchy Greens

Crisp Romaine and iceberg lettuce can be chopped or torn and tossed with tender greens for textural interest.

Bitter Greens

Escarole, endive, frisée, and raddichio, when used sparingly, add punch to milder greens. Or mix several to make a bitter greens salad.

Peppery Greens

Watercress and arugula make salads with bite. (Baby arugula and kale offer a gentler bite.) Combine arugula, endive, and radicchio for a classic tricolor salad.

Marinated Tofu and Vegetable Salad

Serves 4; Total Time 30 minutes

28 ounces firm tofu

¼ cup seasoned rice vinegar

3 tablespoons toasted sesame oil

2 tablespoons Sriracha sauce

2 teaspoons honey

Salt and pepper

2 tablespoons sesame seeds

½ small head napa cabbage, cored and sliced thin (4 cups)

6 ounces snow peas, strings removed

1 red bell pepper, stemmed, seeded, and cut into ½-inch pieces

2 scallions, sliced thin on bias

1. Cut tofu into ¾-inch cubes. Gently press tofu cubes dry with paper towels.

2. Whisk vinegar, oil, Sriracha, honey, and ¼ teaspoon salt together in large bowl. Gently toss tofu in dressing until evenly coated, then cover and refrigerate for 20 minutes.

3. While tofu marinates, toast sesame seeds in 10-inch skillet over medium heat, shaking pan occasionally, until golden and fragrant, 3 to 5 minutes. Set aside to cool.

4. Add cabbage, snow peas, and bell pepper to bowl with tofu and gently toss to combine. Season with salt and pepper to taste and sprinkle with sesame seeds and scallions. Serve.

why this recipe works

There's more to raw salads than leafy greens and basic vinaigrettes. This light and easy Asian-inspired salad boasts a bright and refreshing dressing over fresh, crunchy cabbage, snow peas, and bell pepper, plus a hefty dose of protein from quick-marinated tofu. Tofu takes particularly well to marinating, so is a great way to add flavor to recipes where the tofu is served raw. A Sriracha-based sauce does double duty in this recipe as both a marinade for the tofu and a dressing for the salad, adding a touch of heat and tons of flavor. Seasoned rice vinegar, which contains added sugar and salt, is one of our favorite shortcut ingredients and helps round out our marinade-dressing. Firm tofu is tender and supple when eaten raw, but still sturdy. Do not substitute other varieties in this recipe.

think like a cook

ASIAN PANTRY INGREDIENTS

While the universe of Asian ingredients is vast, we turn to certain staples on a regular basis. We've discussed soy sauce, fish sauce, and miso on pages 12–13. Here are more staples worth stocking.

Chili Sauce

Used both in cooking and as a condiment, chili sauce comes in many styles. For heat along with garlicky flavor, opt for smooth Sriracha or chunky chili-garlic sauce. Sambal oelek offers pure chile flavor. And *gochujang*, made from chiles, rice, soybeans, and salt, forms the savory base for Korean sauces and marinades.

Hoisin Sauce

A thick, reddish-brown mixture of soybeans, sugar, vinegar, garlic, and chiles, hoisin sauce is used in many classic Chinese dishes.

Oyster Sauce

Made from a reduction of boiled oysters, this adds salty sweetness (not fishiness) and body to stir-fries.

Mirin

This Japanese rice wine adds sweetness and acidity to sauces and glazes like teriyaki.

Chinese Rice Wine (Shaoxing)

Like mirin, Shaoxing is made from fermented rice, but its flavor is deeper, more aromatic, and not as sweet. It is a staple in stir-fries, sauces, and glazes.

Rice Vinegar

Not to be confused with rice wine, rice vinegar has malty sweetness and mild acidity. It is used to season sushi rice and stir-fries and makes a less-sharp alternative to other vinegars in dressings. You can also find seasoned rice vinegar, which contains salt and sugar.

Toasted Sesame Oil

While plain sesame oil has very little color, smell, or flavor, toasted (or roasted) sesame oil boasts deeper color and much stronger, richer flavor. We've found that a little goes a long way in dressings, dipping sauces, and stir-fries in Chinese, Korean, and Japanese recipes.

Quinoa Taco Salad

Serves 4; Total Time 1 hour 10 minutes

why this recipe works

This is taco salad for the 21st century. We've replaced the usual beef with quinoa, which gets simmered in a flavorful broth doctored with chipotle chile in adobo, tomato paste, and cumin to give it deep, spiced flavor. Using complex, slightly bitter escarole for our greens provides the perfect base for the rich quinoa, black beans, and cheese. We found this salad so hearty that it didn't need tortilla chips (or a deep-fried tortilla bowl, for that matter), but if you prefer, serve with your favorite chip for added crunch. We like the convenience of prewashed quinoa; rinsing removes the quinoa's bitter protective coating (called saponin). If you buy unwashed quinoa (or if you are unsure whether it's been washed), rinse it and then spread it out on a clean dish towel to dry for 15 minutes before cooking.

¾ cup prewashed white quinoa

3 tablespoons extra-virgin olive oil

1 small onion, chopped fine

Salt and pepper

2 teaspoons minced canned chipotle chile in adobo sauce

2 teaspoons tomato paste

1 teaspoon anchovy paste (optional)

½ teaspoon ground cumin

1 cup chicken or vegetable broth

2 tablespoons lime juice

1 head escarole (1 pound), trimmed and sliced thin

2 scallions, sliced thin

½ cup chopped fresh cilantro

1 (15-ounce) can black beans, rinsed

8 ounces cherry or grape tomatoes, quartered

1 ripe avocado, halved, pitted, and chopped (see page 26)

2 ounces queso fresco, crumbled (½ cup)

1. Toast quinoa in medium saucepan over medium-high heat, stirring frequently, until quinoa is very fragrant and makes continuous popping sounds, 5 to 7 minutes; transfer to bowl.

2. Heat 1 tablespoon oil in now-empty saucepan over medium heat until shimmering. Add onion and ¼ teaspoon salt and cook until onion is softened and lightly browned, 5 to 7 minutes.

3. Stir in chipotle; tomato paste; anchovy paste, if using; and cumin and cook until fragrant, about 30 seconds. Stir in broth and toasted quinoa, increase heat to medium-high, and bring to simmer. Cover, reduce heat to low, and simmer, stirring once halfway through cooking, until quinoa is tender and liquid has been absorbed, 18 to 22 minutes. Remove pan from heat and let sit, covered, for 10 minutes. Spread quinoa onto rimmed baking sheet and let cool for 20 minutes.

4. Whisk remaining 2 tablespoons oil, lime juice, ¼ teaspoon salt, and ¼ teaspoon pepper together in large bowl. Add escarole, scallions, and ¼ cup cilantro and toss to combine. Gently fold in beans, tomatoes, and avocado. Transfer to serving platter and top with quinoa, queso fresco, and remaining ¼ cup cilantro. Serve.

think like a cook

HOW TO BE AN AVOCADO WHISPERER

You may have heard that you can tell how ripe an avocado is by squeezing it. While it's true that avocados do get softer as they ripen, bruised avocados are also soft, and in fact you might actually bruise the fruit (ripe or not) in the process of squeezing it. To avoid all that, our preferred method for identifying a ripe avocado is to try to flick the small stem off the fruit. If it comes off easily and you can see green underneath, the avocado is ripe. If it does not come off easily or you see brown underneath, the avocado is not yet ripe, or it's overripe and therefore unusable.

If you do have an unripe avocado and don't mind waiting longer, we recommend ripening it in the fridge for a few days. It will soften a little more slowly than on the counter, but the ripening will be more even. Either way, a fully ripe avocado will last longer if stored in the fridge— for a full 5 days, as opposed to 2 days on the countertop.

Pork and Broccoli Noodle Bowls

Serves 4; Total Time 40 minutes

¼ cup hoisin sauce

3 tablespoons soy sauce

2 teaspoons cornstarch

1 (12-ounce) pork tenderloin, trimmed, halved lengthwise, and sliced crosswise ¼ inch thick

2¼ cups chicken broth

2 tablespoons vegetable oil

4 ounces white mushrooms, trimmed and sliced thin

1 tablespoon grated fresh ginger

2 garlic cloves, minced

3 (3-ounce) packages ramen noodles, seasoning packets discarded

12 ounces broccoli florets, cut into 1-inch pieces

3 scallions, sliced thin on bias

why this recipe works

For Asian-style noodle bowls mounded high with deeply seasoned meat and vegetables that don't require every pan in the kitchen to prepare, we started with ramen noodles. These incredibly quick-cooking noodles were the perfect choice for this easy one-pan dish. We ditched the seasoning packets and created a rich broth by browning sliced mushrooms to concentrate their flavor and then adding aromatic garlic, grated ginger, chicken broth, hoisin sauce, and soy sauce. The noodles cooked in the broth until the liquid was completely absorbed, and the broccoli steamed atop the noodles until it was bright green and tender. We then flash-seared pork with soy sauce, hoisin sauce, and a bit of cornstarch (to encourage the sauce to cling to the meat). We finished the noodle bowls with a sprinkle of aromatic scallions. Serve with Sriracha.

1. Whisk 1 tablespoon hoisin, 1 tablespoon soy sauce, and cornstarch together in bowl. Add pork and toss to coat; set aside. Whisk broth, remaining 3 tablespoons hoisin, and remaining 2 tablespoons soy sauce together in second bowl; set aside.

2. Heat 1 tablespoon oil in 12-inch nonstick skillet over medium-high heat until shimmering. Add mushrooms and cook until browned, about 5 minutes. Add ginger and garlic and cook until fragrant, about 30 seconds.

3. Add broth mixture and bring to boil. Arrange noodles in skillet in single layer; cover and reduce heat to medium. Cook until noodles have softened on bottoms (tops will still be dry), about 3 minutes.

4. Uncover skillet and, using tongs, flip noodles and stir to separate. Spread noodles in even layer and scatter broccoli over top. Cover and cook until noodles and broccoli are tender, about 3 minutes, tossing halfway through cooking. Divide noodle mixture evenly among individual bowls; tent with aluminum foil.

5. Wipe skillet clean with paper towels. Heat remaining 1 tablespoon oil in now-empty skillet over high heat until just smoking. Add pork in single layer, breaking up any clumps, and cook without stirring until browned on bottom, about 1 minute. Stir pork and continue to cook until pork is no longer pink, about 1 minute longer. Divide pork among bowls. Sprinkle with scallions and serve.

think like a cook

ASIAN NOODLE BASICS

This recipe uses the ubiquitous ramen noodle packages that you are probably familiar with as a college dorm diet staple. Ramen noodles are fried in oil and then dried, so they're superconvenient and only take a few minutes to cook, which is perfect for this noodle bowl. But they're far from the only option when it comes to Asian noodles. Here are some other popular types.

Rice Noodles

Used in a variety of dishes in Southeast Asia and southern China, rice noodles should be steeped in hot water to soften them, as boiling them will make them mushy. (See "Soaking Rice Noodles," page 177.) Rice noodles come in flat and round versions and a variety of widths.

Fresh Chinese Noodles

The texture of fresh Chinese noodles is starchier and chewier than that of dried noodles, and their flavor is milder and less wheaty than that of Italian pasta.

Soba Noodles

Soba noodles get their nutty flavor and delicate texture from buckwheat flour. They are traditionally served chilled, although we also like them warm.

Udon Noodles

Thick, chewy Japanese udon noodles can be purchased both fresh and dried. They are typically used in soups, but their hearty texture also works especially well in ultrarich, savory dishes.

Spicy Peanut Noodle Bowls
Serves 4 to 6; Total Time 40 minutes

1 cup shredded carrots (about 2 carrots)

2 tablespoons seasoned rice vinegar

12 ounces (¼-inch-wide) rice noodles

3 tablespoons vegetable oil

1 cup frozen shelled edamame

1 recipe Curried Peanut Sauce (page 103)

1 cup shredded red cabbage

⅓ cup dry-roasted peanuts, chopped

2 tablespoons torn fresh Thai basil

Lime wedges

1. Combine carrots and vinegar in small bowl; set aside. Cover noodles with very hot tap water in large bowl and stir to separate. Let noodles soak until softened, pliable, and limp but not fully tender, about 20 minutes. Drain noodles.

2. Heat 1 tablespoon oil in 12-inch nonstick skillet over medium-high heat until just smoking. Add edamame and cook until spotty brown but still bright green, about 2 minutes; transfer to bowl. In now-empty skillet, heat remaining 2 tablespoons oil over medium heat until shimmering. Add drained noodles, 1¼ cups water, and ½ cup peanut sauce and cook until sauce has thickened slightly and noodles are well coated and tender, about 1 minute.

3. Divide noodles among individual serving bowls, then top with carrots, edamame, and cabbage. Drizzle with remaining peanut sauce, sprinkle with peanuts and basil, and serve with lime wedges.

why this recipe works

A well-assembled noodle or grain bowl may be one of the most satisfying self-contained meals you can make. This one is inspired by the sweet, savory, and spicy flavors of Southeast Asia, with tender rice noodles, savory edamame, tangy pickled carrots, and crunchy cabbage, all draped in a rich spicy-sweet peanut sauce. For a shortcut version of pickled carrots, we simply added seasoned rice vinegar to shredded carrots and let them sit briefly. We quickly sautéed edamame just until it was speckled brown and then cooked the noodles in the same pan. Cooking the noodles in the sauce lightly glazed and flavored them. After topping our noodle bowls with the veggies, we added plenty of garnishes—fragrant Thai basil, chopped peanuts, lime wedges, and a light pour of additional sauce were the perfect finish. If you can't find Thai basil, you can use regular basil. Be sure to use seasoned rice vinegar to pickle the carrots in this recipe.

think like a cook

SOAKING RICE NOODLES

In Southeast Asia and southern regions of China, a delicate-textured noodle made from rice flour and water is used in an array of dishes including soups, stir-fries, and salads. Unlike Italian pasta, you don't want to boil these delicate noodles because they have a tendency to very quickly overcook into a mushy, sticky mess. Instead, soak them in hot water. Here are the most common rice noodles you'll find.

Thin Rice Noodles or Vermicelli

These angel-hair-width noodles will become fully tender when steeped in boiling water for 5 minutes. Rinse soaked noodles under water to remove excess starch.

Stir-Fry Noodles

Wider rice noodles, also called rice sticks, are used in stir-fries, such as Shrimp Pad Thai (page 290), and in this noodle bowl. This type of noodle is often soaked only until partially cooked, as it will continue to cook and become fully tender when it is tossed with the sauce and other ingredients in the skillet.

To prepare stir-fry noodles, cover in very hot tap water, stir to separate, and let soak just until pliable but not fully tender. This will take about 20 minutes for ¼-inch-wide rice noodles or 35 to 40 minutes for ⅜-inch-wide rice noodles. Drain the noodles. They should remain separated. Undersoaked noodles will still be firm and rigid, while oversoaked noodles will be soft and gummy and stick together. When properly presoaked, these noodles will turn out pleasantly tender but still resilient.

Buckwheat Bowls with Snow Peas, Avocado, and Yogurt Sauce

Serves 4; Total Time 40 minutes

1½ cups buckwheat groats

Salt and pepper

¼ cup extra-virgin olive oil

¾ teaspoon ground coriander

8 ounces snow peas, strings removed and halved

¼ cup raw sunflower seeds

⅛ teaspoon ground cumin

1 teaspoon grated lemon zest plus 2 tablespoons juice

1 tablespoon minced fresh mint

½ teaspoon Dijon mustard

1 avocado, halved, pitted, and cut into ½-inch pieces (see page 26)

1 recipe Lemon-Yogurt Sauce (page 102)

1. Bring 2 quarts water to boil in large pot. Add buckwheat and 1 teaspoon salt and cook until tender, 10 to 12 minutes; drain and transfer to large bowl.

2. Meanwhile, heat 1½ teaspoons oil in 12-inch nonstick skillet over medium-high heat until just smoking. Stir in ½ teaspoon coriander and cook until fragrant, about 20 seconds. Add snow peas and ¼ teaspoon salt and cook until snow peas are spotty brown, about 3 minutes; transfer to bowl with buckwheat.

3. Add 1½ teaspoons oil, sunflower seeds, cumin, remaining ¼ teaspoon coriander, and ¼ teaspoon salt to skillet and cook over medium heat until seeds are toasted, about 2 minutes; transfer to plate and let cool.

4. In separate bowl, whisk lemon zest and juice, mint, and mustard together. Whisking constantly, drizzle in remaining 3 tablespoons oil. Season with salt and pepper to taste, pour over buckwheat mixture, and toss to coat. Portion buckwheat into individual bowls, top with avocado and spiced sunflower seeds, and drizzle with yogurt sauce. Serve.

why this recipe works

For a fresh, whole-grain meal in a bowl, we looked past familiar rice options and toward whole buckwheat groats, which have an earthy, toasty flavor. We paired the grain with snow peas, chunks of avocado, and toasted, spiced sunflower seeds. To keep the cooking method easy, we simply boiled the buckwheat in a large pot of water until it was tender; it was no harder than making rice or any other common grain. We then tossed the cooked buckwheat with a bright lemon-mint dressing. While the buckwheat cooked, we sautéed the snow peas with some coriander and toasted the sunflower seeds with lots of warm spices. Lastly, we drizzled a quick yogurt sauce over the top, which perfectly balanced the flavors and elements of the bowl.

think like a cook

ANATOMY OF A GREAT GRAIN BOWL

There's more to a really complex and flavorful grain bowl than just throwing together a bunch of random ingredients. In the course of developing the grain and noodle bowls in this chapter, we came up with a few general guidelines. Use our recipes, but also follow these rules to build your own bowls for endless delicious flavor combinations.

Step 1: Lay the Base

Our bowls start with a warm, hearty grain or noodle. Quinoa, brown rice, barley, buckwheat, and farro are all good choices. Don't be afraid to try something unfamiliar here; most grains have a fairly neutral flavor profile that can be adapted to many different uses.

Step 2: Bulk It Up

Grains are filling, but usually we want a little more heft. Meat, beans, tofu, nuts, and seeds are all great protein-packed options to make your bowl more of a meal. Seasoning your protein, rather than adding it plain, brings another dimension of flavor to your bowl.

Step 3: Pick Your Produce

Unlike a leafy salad, the vegetables in a bowl aren't the base but are instead toppings that enliven the grains. We like to use a couple of vegetables that have different qualities, including a mix of raw and cooked, leafy and starchy, mild and more assertive. (Here we pair crisp snow peas with buttery avocado.) Vegetables also make a great base for further seasoning.

Step 4: Drizzle It

We've developed an arsenal of flavor-packed sauces to add richness to bowls and other dishes (see pages 100–103). Drizzle one on top, mix up the ingredients, and enjoy your artfully composed bowl.

Bonus: Top It Off

If you've gotten this far, you already have a balanced, filling bowl. The rest is fun: Add pickled vegetables or chopped herbs for final hits of texture and flavor that make your bowl special. And of course another option is to put a runny fried egg on it (it even comes with its own built-in sauce).

Brown Rice Bowls with Roasted Carrots, Kale, and Fried Eggs

Serves 4; Total Time 1 hour 15 minutes

2 cups boiling water

1 cup long-grain brown rice, rinsed

Salt and pepper

5 carrots, peeled, halved crosswise, then halved or quartered lengthwise to create uniformly sized pieces

⅓ cup extra-virgin olive oil

2 teaspoons za'atar

8 ounces kale, stemmed and sliced into 1-inch-wide strips

2 tablespoons red wine vinegar

1 small shallot, minced

4 large eggs

why this recipe works

This hearty rice bowl pairs nutty brown rice with roasted vegetables, plus a fried egg on top for a protein bonus. We started by tossing carrots with *za'atar*, a bold Middle Eastern spice blend, and roasting them until tender and spotty brown. We also roasted some chopped kale, which gave it a crispy texture. Taking advantage of the vegetables' time in the oven, we baked the rice in there too, using a hands-off method based on our Foolproof Baked Brown Rice (page 74). A simple red wine vinaigrette contributed brightness and complexity. Finally, we topped each bowl with a fried egg, which, when broken, added an instant rich sauce to the dish. Medium-grain or short-grain brown rice can be substituted for the long-grain rice. For an accurate measurement of boiling water, bring a full kettle of water to a boil and then measure out the desired amount.

1. Adjust oven racks to upper-middle and lower-middle positions and heat oven to 375 degrees. Combine boiling water, rice, and ¾ teaspoon salt in 8-inch square baking dish and cover tightly with aluminum foil. Bake rice on lower rack until tender, 45 to 50 minutes. Remove rice from oven, uncover, and fluff with fork. Cover with dish towel and let sit for 5 minutes.

2. Meanwhile, toss carrots, 1 tablespoon oil, za'atar, ¼ teaspoon salt, and ⅛ teaspoon pepper together in bowl. Spread carrots onto parchment paper–lined rimmed baking sheet, cover with foil, and roast on upper rack for 20 minutes.

3. Toss kale, 1 tablespoon oil, ¼ teaspoon salt, and ⅛ teaspoon pepper together in bowl. Remove foil from carrots and spread kale over top. Continue to roast vegetables, uncovered, until carrots are spotty brown and tender and edges of kale are lightly browned, about 15 minutes.

4. Portion brown rice into individual bowls and top with roasted vegetables. Whisk vinegar, shallot, and 3 tablespoons oil together in bowl and season with salt and pepper to taste. Drizzle vinaigrette over rice and vegetables; cover and set aside.

5. Heat remaining 1 teaspoon oil in 12-inch nonstick skillet over low heat for 5 minutes. Crack eggs into 2 small bowls (2 eggs per bowl) and season with salt and pepper. Increase heat to medium-high and heat until oil is

shimmering. Working quickly, pour eggs into skillet, cover, and cook for 1 minute. Remove skillet from burner and let sit, covered, 15 to 45 seconds for runny yolks, 45 to 60 seconds for soft but set yolks, and about 2 minutes for medium-set yolks. Top each bowl with fried egg and serve immediately.

think like a cook

HERB AND SPICE BLENDS

A number of the jars in your pantry are actually blends of multiple herbs and/or spices, including the *za'atar* used in this recipe. These blends can be great flavor-boosting shortcuts, but it's important to understand what's in them. (See the entries for curry powder and chili powder on page 15 as well.)

Za'atar

Za'atar contains thyme, oregano, sesame seeds, citrusy sumac, and salt. Sprinkle it on kebabs and vegetables.

Herbes de Provence

As the name suggests, herbs de Provence are commonly found and used in southern France. The blend combines dried lavender flowers with herbs such as rosemary, sage, thyme, marjoram, and fennel. It's a natural partner for poultry and pork.

Italian Seasoning

This blend is chock-full of the Italian mainstays: oregano, marjoram, rosemary, basil, sage, thyme, and savory.

Chinese Five-Spice Powder

The five spices in this aromatic blend are cinnamon, clove, fennel seeds, Sichuan peppercorn, and star anise. It can be used for both sweet and savory dishes.

Ras el Hanout

This North African seasoning combines some 25 spices, seeds, dried flowers, berries, and nuts, including cumin, saffron, rose petals, galangal, and paprika. Use it in tagines and hearty meat dishes.

Garam Masala

Garam masala is an Indian seasoning made from warm spices like cloves, cinnamon, peppercorns, cardamom, and cumin. Add it to couscous or use in a tagine.

Black Rice Bowls with Salmon

Serves 4; Total Time 1 hour

RICE AND DRESSING
1½ cups black rice

Salt and pepper

¼ cup rice vinegar

¼ cup mirin

1 tablespoon white miso

1 teaspoon grated fresh ginger

½ teaspoon grated lime zest plus 2 tablespoons juice

SALMON AND VEGETABLES
4 (4- to 6-ounce) skin-on salmon fillets, 1 inch thick

1 teaspoon vegetable oil

Salt and pepper

1 (8 by 7½-inch) sheet nori, crumbled (optional)

4 radishes, trimmed, halved, and sliced thin

1 avocado, halved, pitted, and sliced thin

1 cucumber, halved lengthwise, seeded (see page 29), and sliced thin

2 scallions, sliced thin

why this recipe works

Black rice is an ancient grain that was once reserved for the emperors of China. In addition to its striking color, it contains more protein, fiber, and iron than other rice varieties. Here it is the perfect base for a Japanese-style rice bowl. To ensure well-seasoned grains with a bit of chew, we boiled the rice like we would pasta and then drizzled it with a mix of rice vinegar, mirin, miso, and ginger. We roasted salmon fillets until medium-rare and then arranged them atop the rice before garnishing our bowls with radishes, avocado, cucumber, nori, and scallions. Skin-on salmon fillets hold together best during cooking, and the skin helps keep the fish moist. If your salmon is less than 1 inch thick, start checking for doneness early. Nori is seaweed that has been dried and pressed into sheets for rolling sushi; you can find it in the international foods aisle of the supermarket. For information on removing pinbones from salmon, see page 371.

1. FOR THE RICE AND DRESSING Bring 4 quarts water to boil in Dutch oven over medium-high heat. Add rice and 1 teaspoon salt and cook until rice is tender, 20 to 25 minutes. Drain rice and transfer to large bowl.

2. Whisk vinegar, mirin, miso, ginger, and lime zest and juice together in small bowl until miso is fully incorporated. Season with salt and pepper to taste. Measure out ¼ cup vinegar mixture and drizzle over rice. Let rice cool to room temperature, tossing occasionally, about 20 minutes. Set remaining dressing aside for serving.

3. FOR THE SALMON AND VEGETABLES While rice is cooking, adjust oven rack to lowest position, place aluminum foil–lined rimmed baking sheet on rack, and heat oven to 500 degrees. Pat salmon dry with paper towels, rub with oil, and season with salt and pepper.

4. Once oven reaches 500 degrees, reduce oven temperature to 275 degrees. Remove sheet from oven and carefully place salmon skin-side down on hot sheet. Roast until center is still translucent when checked with tip of paring knife and thermometer inserted into salmon registers 125 degrees (for medium-rare), 4 to 6 minutes. Slide fish spatula under fillets and transfer to large plate; discard skin.

5. Portion rice into 4 individual serving bowls and sprinkle with some of nori, if using. Top with salmon, radishes, avocado, and cucumber. Sprinkle with scallions and drizzle with reserved dressing. Serve, passing remaining nori separately.

think like a cook

JUDGING DONENESS IN FISH

Checking doneness of a piece of delicate fish such as salmon is similar to checking the doneness of a steak, whole chicken, or large roast, but there are a few differences to keep in mind. The trick to perfectly cooked fish is knowing when to remove it from the heat so that it is just slightly underdone and then allowing the residual heat to finish the cooking. This is carryover cooking (see page 83), and it can have a dramatic effect on fish and its loosely structured flesh. The extent of carryover cooking will vary depending on the type (and thickness) of the fish. Using the gentle heat of a low oven to cook the fish, as we do here, can help to mitigate the effect of carryover cooking and ensure that the fish stays near the ideal doneness temperature until it's served.

As with meat and poultry, the most accurate way to make sure that thicker fish fillets and steaks are properly cooked is to use an instant-read thermometer. However, if you don't have an instant-read thermometer (or if you want a visual cue as well as a number to follow), try peeking inside the piece of fish with a paring knife. Exactly what you're looking for will depend on the specific recipe; the visual cue in this recipe is to remove the fish from the oven when the center is still translucent. As it sits, the flesh finishes cooking through and becomes fully opaque.

The following temperatures should be used to determine when to stop the cooking process (remove the fish from the heat).

DONENESS	TEMPERATURE
Rare	110 degrees (for tuna only)
Medium-Rare	120 degrees (for wild salmon)
	125 degrees (for tuna or farmed salmon)
Medium	140 degrees (for white-fleshed fish)

Skillet Burrito Bowls
Serves 4; Total Time 45 minutes

3 tablespoons extra-virgin olive oil

1½ cups frozen corn

Salt and pepper

1 onion, chopped fine

4 garlic cloves, minced

1 tablespoon minced canned chipotle chile in adobo sauce

1 teaspoon ground cumin

2 (15-ounce) cans black beans, rinsed

1 cup long-grain white rice

2 cups water

10 ounces cherry or grape tomatoes, quartered

¼ cup minced fresh cilantro

¼ teaspoon grated lime zest plus 1 tablespoon lime juice, plus lime wedges for serving (2 limes)

1 avocado, halved, pitted, and cut into ½-inch pieces (see page 26)

½ cup sour cream

why this recipe works

A good burrito is all about the filling; layers of spicy, smoky flavors work together in a cohesive whole. The tortilla? We can take it or leave it, and if we're trying to wrap a hefty amount of filling at home, we'll probably leave it. For a hearty bowl with everything we love in a burrito and none of the fuss, we started with a base of classic rice and beans. Cooking a chopped onion with bloomed cumin, garlic, and chipotle chile created an intense base that infused the bowl with flavor. Sautéed frozen corn added layers of toasty sweetness. A fresh, zingy topping made with simple tomatoes, lime, and cilantro plus cubes of avocado and mounds of sour cream added richness and tang to the bowl. You can substitute fresh corn for frozen corn but the cooking time in step 1 will be shorter. You will need a 12-inch nonstick skillet with a tight-fitting lid for this recipe.

1. Heat 1 tablespoon oil in 12-inch nonstick skillet over medium-high heat until shimmering. Add corn and cook, stirring occasionally, until kernels begin to brown and pop, 6 to 8 minutes. Transfer corn to bowl and season with salt and pepper to taste.

2. Heat 1 tablespoon oil in now-empty skillet over medium-high heat until shimmering. Add onion and ½ teaspoon salt and cook until softened, about 5 minutes. Stir in garlic, chipotle, and cumin and cook until fragrant, about 30 seconds.

3. Stir beans, rice, and water into skillet and bring to simmer. Cover, reduce heat to low, and simmer gently, stirring occasionally, until liquid is absorbed and rice is tender, about 15 minutes.

4. Meanwhile, combine tomatoes, cilantro, lime zest and juice, and remaining 1 tablespoon oil in bowl and season with salt and pepper to taste.

5. Off heat, sprinkle corn over rice and beans. Cover and let sit for 5 minutes. Gently fluff rice and beans with fork and season with salt and pepper to taste; scoop into individual bowls. Sprinkle tomato mixture and avocado over bowls and serve with sour cream and lime wedges.

think like a cook

DON'T SKIP THE STEMS

Usually, stems are the part of an herb that you throw away, but we were curious whether you can use the stems as well as the leaves with leafy herbs like parsley and cilantro. We asked tasters to eat the herbs by the sprig, from the tender leaf to the fat tip of the stem. It turns out that the stems have more flavor, but that's not always good news. While the parsley leaves were fresh and herbal, we were surprised by how intense the flavor became as we traveled down the stems. By the time we reached the stem ends, tasters were complaining (loudly) about bitterness.

Cilantro, however, was another story. Sure, the leaves were tasty, but the great flavor found in the stems caught us all off guard. Sweet, fresh, and potent, the flavor intensified as we traveled down the stem but never became bitter. The moral? If a recipe calls for cilantro and a crunchy texture isn't an issue, use the stems as well as the leaves. But when it comes to parsley—unless you'll be using it in a soup or stew where its strong flavor won't be out of place—be picky and use just the leaves. Similarly, you can use basil stems in recipes that call for fresh basil, but only the younger, tender stems close to the leaves, not the thicker, older portions of the stem, where bitter flavors begin to dominate.

Farro Bowls with Tofu, Mushrooms, and Spinach

Serves 4 to 6; Total Time 1 hour

why this recipe works

At the base of this bowl is hearty, nutty farro. Farro is traditionally associated with Italy and flavor profiles of the western Mediterranean, but we thought it would stand up well to bold Asian ingredients, so we built a bowl to test that theory. For toppings, we chose crispy seared tofu planks along with simply sautéed mushrooms, shallot, and spinach. We partnered these easy-to-prepare toppings with a potent miso-ginger sauce. The pairing of the farro with the zing of the Asian ingredients turned out to be a match made in grain bowl heaven. We prefer the flavor and texture of whole-grain farro; pearled farro can be used, but the texture may be softer. We found a wide range of cooking times among various brands of farro, so start checking for doneness after 10 minutes. Do not use quick-cooking farro in this recipe.

MISO-GINGER SAUCE
¼ cup mayonnaise

3 tablespoons red miso

2 tablespoons water

1 tablespoon maple syrup

1 tablespoon toasted sesame oil

1½ teaspoons sherry vinegar

1½ teaspoons grated fresh ginger

FARRO BOWLS
1½ cups whole farro

Salt and pepper

2 teaspoons toasted sesame oil

1 teaspoon sherry vinegar

14 ounces firm tofu, sliced crosswise into 8 equal slabs

⅓ cup cornstarch

¼ cup vegetable oil, plus extra as needed

10 ounces cremini mushrooms, trimmed and chopped coarse

1 shallot, minced

2 tablespoons dry sherry

10 ounces (10 cups) baby spinach

2 scallions, sliced thin

1. FOR THE SAUCE Whisk all ingredients in bowl until well combined. Set aside.

2. FOR THE BOWLS Bring 4 quarts water to boil in Dutch oven. Stir in farro and 1 tablespoon salt, return to boil, and cook until grains are tender with slight chew, 15 to 30 minutes. Drain farro and return to now-empty pot. Drizzle with sesame oil and vinegar, toss to coat, and cover to keep warm.

3. While farro cooks, spread tofu on paper towel–lined baking sheet and let drain for 20 minutes. Gently press dry with paper towels and season with salt and pepper.

4. Spread cornstarch in shallow dish. Coat tofu thoroughly in cornstarch, pressing gently to adhere; transfer to plate. Heat 1 tablespoon vegetable oil in 12-inch nonstick skillet over medium-high heat until just smoking. Add tofu and cook until both sides are crisp and browned, about 4 minutes per side, adding more oil as necessary to prevent charring. Transfer to paper towel–lined plate to drain and tent with aluminum foil.

5. In now-empty skillet, heat 2 tablespoons vegetable oil over medium-high heat until shimmering. Stir in mushrooms, shallot, and ⅛ teaspoon salt and cook until vegetables begin to brown, 5 to 8 minutes. Stir in sherry and cook, scraping up any browned bits, until skillet is nearly dry, about 1 minute; transfer to bowl.

6. Heat remaining 1 tablespoon vegetable oil over medium-high heat in now-empty skillet until shimmering. Add spinach, 1 handful at a time, and cook until just wilted, about 1 minute.

7. Divide farro among individual bowls, then top each bowl with tofu, mushrooms, and spinach. Drizzle with miso-ginger sauce, sprinkle with scallions, and serve.

think like a cook

MISO PRIMER

An essential ingredient in the Japanese kitchen, miso paste is made by fermenting soybeans and sometimes grains (such as rice, barley, or rye) with a mold called *koji*. Packed with savory flavor, miso is used to season everything from soups and braises to dressings and sauces. Although countless variations of miso are available, three common types are white *shiro* (despite its name, this miso is light golden in color), red *aka*, and brownish-black *hatcho*. Flavor profiles are altered by changing the type of grain in the mix, adjusting the ratio of grain to soybeans, tweaking the amounts of salt and mold, and extending or decreasing the fermentation time, which can range from a few weeks to a few years.

White miso is mild and sweet, red miso nicely balances salty and sweet, and black miso is strong and complex. Though flavor nuances will vary from brand to brand, if you're looking to keep just one type of miso on hand, moderately salty-sweet red miso (which is called for in the Miso-Ginger Sauce in this recipe) is a good all-purpose choice. Miso will easily keep for up to a year in the refrigerator (some sources say it keeps indefinitely).

Vegetable Bibimbap
Serves 4; Total Time 50 minutes

why this recipe works
A much-beloved staple in Korean cuisine, bibimbap features short-grain rice topped with sautéed vegetables, pickled vegetables, and a fried egg. Sautéed shiitake mushrooms and spinach flavored with soy sauce, garlic, and toasted sesame oil gave our vegetables some heft. We also made a quick pickle of bibimbap toppings: Shredded carrot, bean sprouts, and cucumber steeped in rice vinegar lent bright flavor and crunch. The final step was topping each bowl with a fried egg. Traditionally, the yolk is left runny so it can be broken and stirred throughout the rice and vegetables to provide a built-in sauce that adds richness to this otherwise lean dish. Shred the carrots on the large holes of a box grater. You can use seasoned or unseasoned rice vinegar. You can substitute sushi rice for the short-grain rice. If using medium- or long-grain rice, increase the amount of water to 3 cups and simmer until the grains are tender, 18 to 20 minutes. Serve with Korean Chile Sauce (page 103).

PICKLED VEGETABLES
4 ounces (2 cups) bean sprouts

1 carrot, peeled and shredded

1 cucumber, peeled, halved lengthwise, seeded (see page 29), and sliced ¼ inch thick

1 cup rice vinegar

RICE
2 cups short-grain white rice

2 cups water

2 teaspoons rice vinegar

1 teaspoon salt

VEGETABLES AND EGGS
2 tablespoons vegetable oil

12 ounces shiitake mushrooms, stemmed and sliced ½ inch thick

3 garlic cloves, minced

10 ounces (10 cups) baby spinach

2 tablespoons soy sauce

2 tablespoons toasted sesame oil

1 tablespoon rice vinegar

Salt and pepper

4 large eggs

1. FOR THE PICKLED VEGETABLES Combine all ingredients in bowl, pressing to submerge vegetables in vinegar. Cover and refrigerate for at least 30 minutes or up to 24 hours. Before serving, drain vegetables, discarding liquid.

2. FOR THE RICE Bring rice, water, vinegar, and salt to boil in medium saucepan over high heat. Cover, reduce heat to low, and cook until liquid has been absorbed, 7 to 9 minutes. Remove rice from heat and let sit, covered, until tender, about 15 minutes.

3. FOR THE VEGETABLES AND EGGS Heat 1 tablespoon vegetable oil in 12-inch nonstick skillet over medium-high heat until just smoking. Add mushrooms and cook, stirring occasionally, until they release their liquid, 5 to 7 minutes. Stir in garlic and cook until fragrant, about 30 seconds. Stir in spinach, 1 handful at a time, and cook until leaves are wilted, about 3 minutes. Off heat, stir in soy sauce, toasted sesame oil, and vinegar and season with salt and pepper to taste. Transfer to platter and tent loosely with aluminum foil.

4. Crack eggs into 2 small bowls (2 eggs per bowl) and season with salt and pepper. Wipe out now-empty skillet with paper towels, add remaining 1 tablespoon vegetable oil, and heat over medium heat until shimmering. Working quickly, pour 1 bowl of eggs in 1 side of pan and second bowl of eggs in other side. Cover and cook until whites are set but yolks are still runny, 2 to 3 minutes.

5. To serve, portion rice into bowls, top with vegetables and fried egg, and serve with pickled vegetables.

think like a cook

UMAMI MATTERS

Umami is one of the five primary taste sensations perceived by the human tongue, along with salty, sweet, bitter, and sour. Umami is what we call the quality of meaty savoriness present in not just meat, but a wide variety of foods, from tomato paste to Parmesan cheese. Ingredients with umami are valued for their ability to add tons of deep, complex flavor to a dish.

The compound that gives umami foods their flavor is called glutamate. To amp up the savory, umami elements of a dish, you can simply add ingredients that are high in glutamates, but the real magic happens when ingredients containing glutamates are used in combination with other ingredients containing naturally occurring substances called nucleotides, which are found in meat, seafood, mushrooms, seaweed, and more. When glutamates and nucleotides are both present in your dish, the strength of the umami taste you'll experience is as much as 20 to 30 times greater than if you just use glutamate-heavy ingredients alone. Thus, for the most powerful umami flavor, you have to combine ingredients rich in glutamates (tomatoes, aged cheese, and soy sauce) with ingredients rich in nucleotides (beef, sardines, and mushrooms), as we do in many of our recipes. Using both shiitake mushrooms and soy sauce in our vegetarian bibimbap gives it a serious kick of umami.

sides that go with any meal

Stir-Fried Asparagus with Shiitake Mushrooms

Serves 4; Total Time 15 minutes

SAUCE

2 tablespoons water

1 tablespoon soy sauce

1 tablespoon dry sherry

2 teaspoons packed brown sugar

2 teaspoons grated fresh ginger

1 teaspoon toasted sesame oil

VEGETABLES

1 tablespoon vegetable oil

1 pound asparagus, trimmed and cut on bias into 2-inch lengths

4 ounces shiitake mushrooms, stemmed and sliced thin

2 scallions, green parts only, sliced thin on bias

1. FOR THE SAUCE Whisk all ingredients together in bowl.

2. FOR THE VEGETABLES Heat oil in 12-inch nonstick skillet over high heat until just smoking. Add asparagus and mushrooms and cook, stirring occasionally, until asparagus is spotty brown, 3 to 4 minutes. Add sauce and cook, stirring once or twice, until pan is almost dry and asparagus is crisp-tender, 1 to 2 minutes. Transfer to serving platter, sprinkle with scallions, and serve.

why this recipe works

Stir-frying is a great cooking method for thin spears of asparagus, which can go from raw to overdone in just moments. The intense heat helps caramelize the spears for a flavorful browned exterior that pairs perfectly with a potent stir-fry sauce. To ensure the asparagus cooked evenly, we diluted the sauce with a little water, creating a small amount of steam that cooked the spears through before evaporating and leaving behind a flavorful, clingy glaze. To keep our recipe simple, we used just five bold ingredients in the stir-fry sauce. Thinly sliced shiitake mushrooms added contrasting flavor and texture and cooked in the same amount of time as the asparagus. Look for asparagus spears that are no thicker than ½ inch.

variations

Stir-Fried Asparagus with Red Onion

For the sauce, whisk together 2 tablespoons water, 4 teaspoons fish sauce, 1 tablespoon lime juice, 2 teaspoons packed brown sugar, 2 teaspoons minced lemon grass, and ⅛ teaspoon red pepper flakes. Substitute ½ red onion, sliced through root end into ¼-inch-thick pieces, for mushrooms and 2 tablespoons chopped fresh mint for scallion greens.

Stir-Fried Asparagus with Red Bell Pepper

For the sauce, whisk together 1 tablespoon water, 1 tablespoon orange juice, 1 tablespoon rice vinegar, 1 tablespoon sugar, 1 teaspoon ketchup, and ½ teaspoon salt. Substitute 1 stemmed and seeded red bell pepper, cut into 2-inch-long matchsticks, for mushrooms.

think like a cook

CHOOSING VEGETABLES TO STIR-FRY

Stir-frying is a great technique for a variety of ingredients, including many vegetables. This quick-cooking method is a perfect match for more delicate vegetables that don't stand up well to prolonged heat exposure. It is also a great way to cook hardier vegetables to a perfect crisp-tender (a splash of liquid creates steam to help them cook evenly). The best vegetable stir-fries feature several textures and colors, as in this side dish. To make sure that the vegetables all cook evenly, be sure to cut them into uniform pieces. And cook hardier vegetables separately from more delicate ones, or give them a head start in the pan. We recommend limiting yourself to two or three different vegetables; otherwise, the medley can become cluttered. We also like to mix in some very quick-cooking elements at the end of cooking: chopped fresh herbs such as basil or chives, or scallions (which are actually added off the heat). These combinations create pleasing contrasts in texture and flavor in the dish.

Braised Asparagus, Peas, and Radishes with Tarragon

Serves 4 to 6; Total Time 30 minutes

¼ cup extra-virgin olive oil

1 shallot, sliced into thin rounds

2 garlic cloves, sliced thin

3 sprigs fresh thyme

Pinch red pepper flakes

10 radishes, trimmed and quartered lengthwise

1¼ cups water

2 teaspoons grated lemon zest

2 teaspoons grated orange zest

1 bay leaf

Salt and pepper

1 pound asparagus, trimmed and cut into 2-inch lengths

2 cups frozen peas

4 teaspoons chopped fresh tarragon

why this recipe works

We often associate braising with long cooking, but the technique can bring out the best in even the most delicate ingredients, like these fresh spring vegetables. To build a flavorful braising liquid, we enhanced water with lemon and orange zest and a bay leaf plus a deep flavor base built from sautéed shallot, garlic, thyme, and red pepper flakes. Adding the vegetables in stages ensured each got just the amount of cooking it needed. In no time at all, a simple combination of water and aromatics had turned the vegetables into a radiant dish featuring a deeply flavored broth. Peppery radishes, most commonly associated with salads, turned soft and sweet when cooked, complementing the more vegetal peas and asparagus. A bit of chopped fresh tarragon gave a final nod to spring. Look for asparagus spears that are no thicker than ½ inch.

1. Cook oil, shallot, garlic, thyme sprigs, and pepper flakes in Dutch oven over medium heat until shallot is just softened, about 2 minutes. Stir in radishes, water, lemon zest, orange zest, bay leaf, and 1 teaspoon salt and bring to simmer. Reduce heat to medium-low, cover, and cook until radishes can be easily pierced with tip of paring knife, 3 to 5 minutes. Stir in asparagus, cover, and cook until tender, 3 to 5 minutes.

2. Off heat, stir in peas, cover, and let sit until heated through, about 5 minutes. Discard thyme sprigs and bay leaf. Stir in tarragon and season with salt and pepper to taste. Serve.

think like a cook

COOKING WITH THE SEASONS

Because you can find almost any ingredient year-round, many home cooks are less aware of when particular ingredients would traditionally have been available in their local area. Unless you garden or have a good farmers' market that you frequent, you might be a little out of touch with the seasonality of produce. We're not suggesting that you have to eat only what's in season in order to cook good food, but being tuned in to the yearly food cycles can help you choose the foods that are going to be more delicious and widely available.

It can also help you figure out which ingredients pair best with each other. For thousands of years, cooks mostly relied on the foods that were easily available in their area through the year, and many recipes evolved around ingredients that were in season at the same time. Here, the radishes, asparagus, peas, and fresh herbs are all available in springtime. (Frozen peas are picked at the height of their season and frozen within hours of harvest, so retain more sweetness than almost any fresh peas you'll find.) Since these ingredients tend to be delicate and tender, a gentle cooking method like braising is perfect for them.

Our recipe for Roasted Root Vegetables (page 58) uses roots that would be dug up in fall and kept in a root cellar through the winter. Since these vegetables are hardier, they respond better to a longer, hotter cooking technique: roasting. Even if you're not cooking with farm-fresh produce all the time, you can still use the guidelines of seasonality to help pair ingredients.

Sautéed Snow Peas with Lemon and Parsley

Serves 6; Total Time 15 minutes

1 large shallot, minced

1½ tablespoons vegetable oil

1½ teaspoons grated lemon zest plus 1½ teaspoons juice

Salt and pepper

¼ teaspoon sugar

1¼ pounds snow peas, strings removed

1½ tablespoons minced fresh parsley

1. Combine shallot, 1½ teaspoons oil, and lemon zest in small bowl. Combine ½ teaspoon salt, ¼ teaspoon pepper, and sugar in second small bowl.

2. Heat remaining 1 tablespoon oil in 12-inch nonstick skillet over high heat until just smoking. Add snow peas, sprinkle with salt mixture, and cook, without stirring, for 30 seconds. Stir and continue to cook, without stirring, 30 seconds longer. Continue to cook, stirring constantly, until snow peas are crisp-tender, 1 to 2 minutes longer.

3. Push snow peas to sides of skillet. Add shallot mixture to center and cook, mashing mixture into pan, until fragrant, about 20 seconds. Stir mixture into snow peas. Transfer snow peas to bowl and stir in parsley and lemon juice. Season with salt and pepper to taste, and serve.

why this recipe works

Snow peas are a relatively quick-cooking, delicate vegetable, so most preparations turn them greasy and limp. We tried a traditional stir-fry technique, thinking that this fast, high-heat method might be a winner, but the constant stirring gave us overcooked pods without any browning, which is key to amplifying the delicate flavor of the snow peas. Adding a sprinkle of sugar and cooking the snow peas without stirring for a short time amped up browning and helped to achieve a flavorful sear. We then continued to cook the peas, stirring constantly, until they were just crisp-tender. We paired our perfectly cooked peas with complementary flavors: subtly sweet, fragrant shallot plus acidity and freshness from lemon juice and herbs that drew out the grassy flavors in the snow peas. You can substitute chives or tarragon for the parsley.

variations

Sautéed Snow Peas with Garlic, Cumin, and Cilantro

Substitute 3 minced garlic cloves and ½ teaspoon toasted and lightly crushed cumin seeds for shallot, 1 teaspoon lime zest for lemon zest, cilantro for parsley, and lime juice for lemon juice.

Sautéed Snow Peas with Ginger, Garlic, and Scallions

Substitute 1 tablespoon grated fresh ginger, 3 minced garlic cloves, and 3 minced scallion whites for shallot and lemon zest; red pepper flakes for pepper; 3 sliced scallion greens for parsley; and rice vinegar for lemon juice.

think like a cook

STAGES OF DONENESS FOR VEGETABLES

Perfectly cooked vegetables can be a thing of beauty. Vibrant in color, full of fresh, even juicy, flavor, they can be an awakening for those accustomed to eating over-cooked versions. But nailing doneness can be a challenge if you don't know what to look for.

When we expose vegetables to heat through various cooking methods, what we're really doing is breaking down and dissolving pectin (the glue that holds vegetable cell walls together). The more a vegetable is exposed to heat, the more pectin is dissolved, and the more limp, soft, and mushy a vegetable becomes. One way to know when that perfect crisp-tender texture has been achieved is to pay close attention to the vegetable's appearance. Green vegetables transform from brightly colored to drab and dull as they cook thanks to the way chlorophyll (the molecule that gives green vegetables their hue) reacts to heat. Once a vegetable brightens, it's a sign that heat has penetrated the cell walls and the vegetable is on its way to tenderizing. From there, it's a matter of taste. Like your vegetables on the tender side? Cook them a little longer. As long as you halt cooking before the color turns olive-green, the vegetables will be juicy and bright.

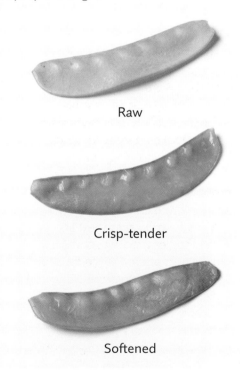

Raw

Crisp-tender

Softened

Roasted Brussels Sprouts
Serves 6 to 8; Total Time 40 minutes

2¼ pounds Brussels sprouts, trimmed and halved
3 tablespoons extra-virgin olive oil
1 tablespoon water
Salt and pepper

1. Adjust oven rack to upper-middle position and heat oven to 500 degrees. Toss Brussels sprouts with oil, water, ¾ teaspoon salt, and ¼ teaspoon pepper in bowl. Transfer sprouts to rimmed baking sheet and arrange cut side down.

2. Cover sheet tightly with aluminum foil and roast for 10 minutes. Remove foil and continue to roast until sprouts are well browned and tender, 10 to 12 minutes. Transfer Brussels sprouts to serving dish and season with salt and pepper to taste. Serve.

variations
Roasted Brussels Sprouts with Bacon and Pecans
While Brussels sprouts roast, cook 4 slices bacon in 12-inch nonstick skillet over medium heat until crisp, 7 to 10 minutes. Transfer bacon to paper towel–lined plate and crumble into small pieces; reserve 1 tablespoon bacon fat. Toss roasted Brussels sprouts with 2 tablespoons extra-virgin olive oil, reserved bacon fat, crumbled bacon, and ½ cup finely chopped toasted pecans before serving.

Roasted Brussels Sprouts with Garlic, Red Pepper Flakes, and Parmesan
While Brussels sprouts roast, cook 3 tablespoons extra-virgin olive oil, 2 minced garlic cloves, and ½ teaspoon red pepper flakes in 8-inch skillet over medium heat until fragrant, 1 to 2 minutes; remove from heat. Toss roasted Brussels sprouts with garlic mixture and sprinkle with ¼ cup grated Parmesan before serving.

why this recipe works
Roasting is a popular way to cook Brussels sprouts, and for good reason: It is one of the simplest and quickest ways to turn these tiny cabbages into perfect little bites that are caramelized on the outside and tender on the inside, which we think is pretty much their ideal state. But simply putting them in the oven can cause the outsides to overcook before the insides become tender. To ensure that the proper balance would be achieved, we started by roasting the sprouts covered with aluminum foil and tossing in a little bit of water to create a steamy environment, which cooked them through. We then removed the foil and roasted them for another 10 minutes to allow the exteriors to dry out and caramelize. If you are buying loose Brussels sprouts, select those that are about 1½ inches long. Quarter (instead of halving) any that are longer than 2½ inches; don't cut sprouts shorter than 1 inch.

think like a cook

WHY DOES OVEN RACK POSITION MATTER?

You may have noticed that recipes often call for placing the oven rack(s) in a specific position—bottom, middle, upper-middle—before heating the oven and placing the food on it. This might seem a little fussy; how important is it to reorganize your oven for every recipe? Pretty important, it turns out. Our many years of experience have taught us that this is one of the easiest ways that a recipe can go wrong. Cooking a dish on the top rack exposes it to much more reflected heat from the top of the oven, while a dish on the bottom rack is getting much more direct exposure to heat on the bottom of the pan. These differences can make or break your recipe. Always try to use the oven rack positions indicated in the recipe. One note: If you have an oven with an even number of racks and the recipe calls for you to use the middle rack position, we recommend opting for the lower-middle rack; this puts food closer to the exact middle of the oven and keeps it from overbrowning.

Carrot, Radish, and Asian Pear Slaw

Serves 4 to 6; Total Time 25 minutes

1½ pounds carrots, peeled and shredded

¼ cup sugar, plus extra for seasoning

Salt and pepper

½ cup extra-virgin olive oil

3 tablespoons rice vinegar, plus extra for seasoning

2 tablespoons Dijon mustard

1 tablespoon toasted sesame oil

2 Asian pears, peeled, halved, cored, and cut into ⅛-inch matchsticks (see page 25)

12 ounces radishes, trimmed, halved, and sliced thin

10 scallions, green parts only, sliced thin on bias

1. Toss carrots, sugar, and 1 teaspoon salt in large bowl and let sit until partially wilted and reduced in volume by one-third, about 15 minutes.

2. Meanwhile, whisk olive oil, vinegar, mustard, sesame oil, ½ teaspoon salt, and ½ teaspoon pepper in large bowl until combined.

3. Transfer carrots to salad spinner and spin until excess water is removed, 10 to 20 seconds. Transfer carrots to bowl with dressing. Add pears, radishes, and scallions and toss to combine. Season with salt, pepper, extra sugar, and/or extra vinegar to taste. Serve immediately.

why this recipe works

Just because cabbage is the traditional choice for a slaw doesn't mean it's the only option, or even the best one. Trading out bland, watery cabbage for vibrant root vegetables adds color and flavor to slaw and makes it a much more versatile side for a variety of mains. We used a box grater (you can also use the food processor's shredding disk) to quickly shred the carrots. To avoid a waterlogged salad, we tossed the shreds with salt and sugar to soften them slightly and draw out their moisture, then spun them dry in a salad spinner. Adding thin slices of radish lightened up the salad's texture; Asian pear and scallion lent additional layers of fresh flavor. A bright Dijon-based vinaigrette brought our slaw together and gave it a gentle acidic bite. To save time, we recommend shredding and treating the carrots before prepping the remaining ingredients.

variations

Celery Root, Celery, and Apple Slaw

Substitute celery root for carrots. Substitute cider vinegar for rice vinegar in dressing and omit sesame oil. Substitute 5 celery ribs, sliced thin on bias, for radishes; Honeycrisp or Fuji apples for Asian pears; and ½ cup coarsely chopped fresh parsley for scallions.

Kohlrabi, Radicchio, and Apple Slaw

Substitute kohlrabi for carrots. Substitute white wine vinegar for rice vinegar and omit sesame oil. Substitute 1 small head radicchio, halved, cored, and sliced ½ inch thick, for radishes; Granny Smith apples for Asian pears; and ½ cup coarsely chopped fresh mint for scallions.

think like a cook

FRUITS AND VEGETABLES THAT BRING THE CRUNCH

There's a group of ingredients that we value for their ability to bring refreshing crunch to a recipe without adding too much obtrusive flavor. These mild but magical fruits and vegetables include Asian pears (which are much crisper than traditional pears), celery root, and kohlrabi (a relative of the turnip, but milder and sweeter). We also count celery, jícama (a bulbous root that tastes like a cross between an apple and a water chestnut), and green papaya (which is simply an unripe papaya) in this group. We most often choose these clean-tasting ingredients for their texture rather than a strong flavor profile. They serve as a neutral base for more assertive flavors and are excellent additions to salads and slaws. We often thinly slice or shred these ingredients or cut them into matchsticks to help disperse the crunch throughout a dish.

Cauliflower Rice
Serves 4; Total Time 30 minutes

1 head cauliflower (2 pounds), cored and cut into 1-inch florets

1 tablespoon extra-virgin olive oil

1 shallot, minced

½ cup chicken broth

Salt and pepper

2 tablespoons minced fresh parsley (optional)

1. Working in batches, pulse cauliflower in food processor until finely ground into ¼- to ⅛-inch pieces, 6 to 8 pulses, scraping down sides of bowl as needed; transfer to bowl.

2. Heat oil in large saucepan over medium-low heat until shimmering. Add shallot and cook until softened, about 3 minutes. Stir in processed cauliflower, broth, and 1½ teaspoons salt. Cover and cook, stirring occasionally, until cauliflower is tender, 12 to 15 minutes.

3. Uncover and continue to cook until cauliflower rice is almost completely dry, about 3 minutes. Off heat, stir in parsley, if using, and season with salt and pepper to taste. Serve.

why this recipe works

You may have seen processed cauliflower "rice" serving as a rice stand-in on health food menus and felt skeptical about this trick, but we're here to tell you that it's a worthy substitution. To make our version of this trend foolproof, we first needed to figure out the best way to chop the florets to the right size. Pulsing in the food processor made quick work of breaking down the florets and created just the right grain-like texture. Next, we needed to give our neutral-tasting cauliflower a boost in flavor; a shallot and a small amount of chicken broth did the trick. To ensure that the cauliflower rice was tender but still maintained a pleasant, rice-like chew, we first steamed it in a covered pot, then finished cooking it uncovered to remove any remaining moisture. This recipe can be doubled; use a Dutch oven and increase the cooking time to about 25 minutes in step 2. This recipe requires a food processor with a capacity of at least 7 cups.

variations
Curried Cauliflower Rice

Add ¼ teaspoon ground cardamom, ¼ teaspoon ground cinnamon, and ¼ teaspoon ground turmeric to saucepan with shallot. Substitute 1 tablespoon minced fresh mint for parsley and stir ¼ cup toasted sliced almonds into cauliflower rice with mint.

Tex-Mex Cauliflower Rice

Add 1 minced garlic clove, 1 teaspoon ground cumin, and 1 teaspoon ground coriander to saucepan with shallot. Substitute cilantro for parsley and stir 1 teaspoon lime juice into cauliflower rice with cilantro.

think like a cook

TAKING THE PULSE OF YOUR FOOD PROCESSOR

To make the most of your food processor, you need to know the difference between processing and pulsing. These two functions are not the same, and if you use one when you're supposed to use the other, you probably won't get the results you're looking for. Recipes call for processing when an ingredient will be pureed. In these cases, hold down the process button for the indicated number of seconds. Pulsing is for when you want to chop or grind ingredients. It offers more control. If you puree when you should pulse, you could end up with nut flour instead of chopped nuts, and if you pulse when you should puree, your hummus will come out chunky instead of silky-smooth.

Recipes using a food processor often call for "one-second pulses." But what does this mean? Should you hold down the button for a full second and then release it? Or just press it for a microsecond, release it, and wait a full second before pressing down again? The answer depends on your machine. Some blades continue to rotate for a second after you lift your finger off the bottom. Others have a quick stop-start motion that we prefer. Test your processor to see exactly what happens when you press the pulse button; the blade should move for about 1 second for a proper pulse.

Whether you're pulsing or pureeing, we recommend scraping down the sides of the workbowl occasionally with a silicone spatula to make sure that any food clinging to the sides gets properly processed (or pulsed).

Mexican Street Corn
Serves 6; Total Time 35 minutes

6 ears corn, husks and silk removed, stalks left intact

1 tablespoon olive oil

½ cup mayonnaise

1 ounce feta cheese, crumbled (¼ cup)

2 tablespoons minced fresh cilantro

1 tablespoon lime juice, plus lime wedges for serving

1 garlic clove, minced

1 teaspoon chili powder

Salt and pepper

1. Adjust oven rack 5 inches from broiler element and heat broiler. Line rimmed baking sheet with aluminum foil. Brush corn all over with oil and transfer to prepared sheet. Broil corn until well browned on 1 side, about 10 minutes. Flip corn and broil until well browned on opposite side, about 10 minutes longer.

2. Meanwhile, whisk mayonnaise, feta, cilantro, lime juice, garlic, chili powder, and ¼ teaspoon salt together in bowl until incorporated.

3. Remove corn from oven and brush evenly on all sides with mayonnaise mixture. (Reserve any extra mayonnaise mixture for serving.) Return corn to oven and broil, rotating frequently, until coating is lightly browned, about 2 minutes. Season with salt and pepper to taste. Serve corn with lime wedges and any extra reserved mayonnaise mixture.

why this recipe works

In Mexico, vendors sell this messy, cheesy, utterly delicious grilled corn from carts. To bring this street food to the home kitchen, we broiled the corn on the cob instead of heading out to the grill, first brushing it with oil to keep it from drying out. Mayonnaise makes a good substitute for Mexican crema, especially when it's dressed up with cilantro, garlic, lime, and chili powder. Hard-to-find traditional Cotija cheese is great, but salty, crumbly feta is just as good. To keep it from crumbling right off the corn, we mixed it in with the mayonnaise before slathering the mixture all over the charred corn and broiling it for another few minutes.

think like a cook

CHAR WITHOUT THE COALS

Traditionally, Mexican street corn is cooked on hot grills over open flames. For our recipe, we've moved the process to the broiler to make this tasty dish more accessible for home cooks. As we discussed earlier (see page 45), there are similarities in the ways broiling and grilling work. Like a grill, the broiler is capable of very high temperatures and, if you're using a gas oven, also exposes the food to an open flame, just like on a grill. This is one of the easiest indoor cooking methods for browning food and encouraging the development of flavor compounds associated with browning and caramelization. Charring also adds a note of bitterness that many people find to be a pleasant contrast to the sweetness of browning. Compared with recipes for boiled corn, our charbroiled corn has way more concentrated, toasty flavor and a crunchier texture. The high sugar content of corn makes it relatively easy to get great browning and charring under the high heat of the broiler, no grill required.

Sautéed Mushrooms with Sesame and Ginger

Serves 4; Total Time 40 minutes

2 tablespoons peanut oil

1½ pounds white mushrooms, trimmed and halved if small or quartered if large

1 tablespoon sesame seeds, toasted (see page 157)

1 tablespoon grated fresh ginger

2 tablespoons mirin

2 tablespoons soy sauce

1 teaspoon toasted sesame oil

2 scallions, sliced thin on bias

1. Heat 1 tablespoon peanut oil in 12-inch skillet over medium-high heat until shimmering. Add mushrooms and cook, stirring occasionally, until mushrooms release liquid, about 5 minutes. Increase heat to high and cook, stirring occasionally, until liquid has completely evaporated, about 8 minutes longer.

2. Add remaining 1 tablespoon peanut oil, reduce heat to medium, and continue to cook, stirring once every minute, until mushrooms are dark brown, about 8 minutes longer.

3. Add sesame seeds and ginger and cook, stirring constantly, until ginger is fragrant, about 30 seconds. Add mirin and soy sauce and cook, stirring constantly, until liquid has evaporated, about 30 seconds. Remove from heat and stir in sesame oil. Transfer to serving dish, sprinkle with scallions, and serve.

why this recipe works

Deeply browned and ultrasavory sautéed mushrooms make a great side dish, but they tend to shrink and shrivel when cooked, leaving you with almost nothing left to serve. We wanted more flavor and less shriveling, and we discovered that overloading the skillet and extending the cooking time helped solve both of these problems. This cooking method allowed the mushrooms to give up just enough liquid to eventually fit in a single layer without shrinking to nothing. They browned nicely after we added a little more oil, and from there it was easy to enhance the dish with a classic Asian flavor profile including ginger, sesame, and soy sauce.

variation
Sautéed Mushrooms with Shallot and Thyme

Substitute vegetable oil for peanut oil. Substitute 1 minced shallot for ginger, 1 tablespoon minced fresh thyme for toasted sesame seeds, and ¼ cup dry Marsala for mirin. Omit soy sauce and toasted sesame oil. Omit scallions. Season with salt and pepper to taste, and serve.

think like a cook

MUSHROOMS: IMPOSSIBLE TO OVERCOOK?

While many foods we cook require precise attention to temperature and time, mushrooms are remarkably forgiving and essentially unique in their ability to maintain a pleasant texture over a range of cooking times.

We ran an experiment using ½-inch-thick planks of portobello mushroom, zucchini, and beef tenderloin, which we steamed in a basket in a Dutch oven for 40 minutes. At 5-minute intervals, we used a piece of equipment called a CT3 Texture Analyzer to determine how much force was required to bite into each piece of food. After 5 minutes of steaming, the tenderloin, portobello, and zucchini required 186, 199, and 239 grams of force, respectively, to compress (or bite) 3 millimeters into the food. Tasters noted that all the samples were tender. Over the course of the next 35 minutes, the tenderloin steadily toughened, eventually turning a whopping 293 percent tougher, while the zucchini decreased in firmness 83 percent and turned mushy and structureless. The portobello, meanwhile, increased in firmness just 57 percent over the same period of time; after a full 40 minutes of cooking, tasters found the mushroom to still be properly tender.

The key to the mushroom's resiliency lies in its cell walls, which are made of a heat-stable polymer called chitin. This unique structure allows us to quickly sauté mushrooms for a few minutes or roast them for the better part of an hour, all the while achieving well-browned, perfectly tender specimens.

Garlic-Parmesan Mashed Potatoes

Serves 4 to 6; Total Time 45 minutes

2 pounds Yukon Gold potatoes, peeled and sliced ½ inch thick

½ teaspoon garlic powder

4 tablespoons unsalted butter, cut into 4 pieces

1¼ teaspoons garlic, minced to paste

1½ ounces Parmesan cheese, grated (¾ cup)

Salt and pepper

⅔ cup warm whole milk

1. Place potatoes in large saucepan and add cold water to cover by 1 inch. Bring water to simmer over medium-high heat. Adjust heat to maintain gentle simmer until paring knife can be slipped into and out of center of potatoes with no resistance, 18 to 22 minutes. Drain potatoes.

2. While potatoes cook, combine garlic powder and ½ teaspoon water in small bowl. Melt butter in 8-inch skillet over medium-low heat. Stir in 1 teaspoon garlic paste and garlic powder mixture; cook, stirring constantly, until fragrant and golden, about 1 minute. Transfer butter mixture to medium bowl and thoroughly stir in Parmesan, 1¼ teaspoons salt, ½ teaspoon pepper, and remaining ¼ teaspoon garlic paste.

3. Place now-empty saucepan over low heat; set ricer or food mill over saucepan. Working in batches, transfer potatoes to hopper and process. Using rubber spatula, stir in butter-Parmesan mixture until incorporated. Stir in warm milk until incorporated. Season with salt and pepper to taste; serve immediately.

why this recipe works

There's more to really great mashed potatoes than just boiling some potatoes and smashing them up, but indiscriminately adding sticks of butter and cups of cream isn't the answer (unfortunately). For the best results, we started with Yukon Gold potatoes: They have the best buttery flavor and supersmooth texture. A modest amount of melted butter and warm whole milk added just enough richness to the mixture. Garlic was the natural choice to take our mashed potatoes to the next level. To get truly complex garlic flavor, we added it in three ways: a tiny bit of raw garlic paste, garlic paste sautéed in butter, and a small amount of rehydrated garlic powder also sautéed in butter. A final savory boost came from grated Parmesan, which stood up to, and complemented, the sweet, sharp, and roasted garlic flavors. If you don't have a ricer (see page 448) or a food mill, you can use a potato masher in this recipe, but the potatoes won't be quite as fluffy.

think like a cook

MINCING GARLIC TO A PASTE

Mincing garlic to a paste goes beyond simply cutting it into very small pieces and actually pulverizes the garlic until it attains a smooth consistency. This helps distribute the garlic evenly throughout a dish. You can use a rasp-style grater or a garlic press to make garlic paste, but if you don't have those tools, there's another easy way that uses a secret ingredient: salt. Sprinkling minced garlic with a little salt and mashing it turns the garlic into a creamy paste. The salt draws moisture out of the garlic cells. As the cells lose moisture, they collapse and soften. Furthermore, salt acts as an abrasive, grinding the garlic particles as you mash. Garlic paste incorporates seamlessly into sauces and vinaigrettes.

To make garlic paste, first finely mince the garlic cloves. Sprinkle the minced garlic with a pinch salt, then scrape the blade of your knife back and forth over the garlic until it forms a fine puree. Continue to mince and drag the knife as necessary until the puree is smooth.

Olive Oil Potato Gratin
Serves 6 to 8; Total Time 2 hours

2 ounces Pecorino Romano cheese, grated (1 cup)

½ cup extra-virgin olive oil

¼ cup panko bread crumbs

Salt and pepper

2 onions, halved and sliced thin

2 garlic cloves, minced

1 teaspoon minced fresh thyme

1 cup chicken broth

3 pounds Yukon Gold potatoes, peeled and sliced ⅛ inch thick

1. Adjust oven rack to upper-middle position and heat oven to 400 degrees. Grease 13 by 9-inch baking dish. Combine Pecorino, 3 tablespoons oil, panko, and ½ teaspoon pepper in bowl; set aside.

2. Heat 2 tablespoons oil in 12-inch skillet over medium heat until shimmering. Add onions, ½ teaspoon salt, and ¼ teaspoon pepper and cook, stirring frequently, until browned, about 15 minutes. Add garlic and ½ teaspoon thyme and cook until fragrant, about 30 seconds. Add ¼ cup broth and cook until nearly evaporated, scraping up any browned bits, about 2 minutes. Remove from heat; set aside.

3. Toss potatoes, remaining 3 tablespoons oil, 1 teaspoon salt, ½ teaspoon pepper, and remaining ½ teaspoon thyme together in bowl. Arrange half of potatoes in prepared dish, spread onion mixture in even layer over potatoes, and distribute remaining potatoes over onions. Pour remaining ¾ cup broth over potatoes. Cover dish tightly with aluminum foil and bake for 1 hour.

4. Remove foil, top gratin with reserved Pecorino mixture, and continue to bake until top is golden brown and potatoes are completely tender, 15 to 20 minutes. Let cool for 15 minutes. Serve.

why this recipe works

Potato gratin is a notoriously heavy side dish, laden with cream and gooey cheese. To shift the focus back to the actual potatoes, we started with rich Yukon Gold potatoes. Their moderate starch content helped them hold their shape. Tossing the potatoes with fruity extra-virgin olive oil heightened their flavor without overpowering them. Sautéed onions, fresh thyme, and garlic added depth. For a crisp, cheesy topping, we mixed more olive oil with panko bread crumbs and a moderate amount of sharp, salty Pecorino Romano. We prefer to use a mandoline to quickly and easily create thin, even slices of potato, but if you don't own one, simply cut a slice from one side of each potato to create a flat, stable surface for thin, even slicing. If you're looking to add a mandoline to your kitchen tool kit, look for one with a large, comfortable hand guard and built-in blades to keep your fingers extra safe. Our favorite is the **Swissmar Börner Original V-Slicer Plus Mandoline** (page 443).

think like a cook

CHOOSING THE RIGHT POTATO

Different varieties of potatoes can have wildly different textures, depending on their starch level. This means you need to choose wisely based on your recipe.

Baking Potatoes (Russet, Idaho)
These dry, floury potatoes contain more total starch than other categories, giving them a dry, mealy texture. They are the best choice when baking and frying. They work well when you want to thicken a stew or soup, but not when you want distinct chunks of potatoes.

Boiling Potatoes (Red Bliss, French Fingerling)
These varieties contain a relatively low amount of total starch, which means they have a firm, smooth, and waxy texture. They are sometimes called new potatoes because they are less-mature potatoes harvested in the late spring and summer. They also have thinner skins than other types of potatoes. Boiling potatoes are perfect when you want a variety that will hold its shape, as with potato salad. They are also a good choice when roasting or (unsurprisingly) boiling.

All-Purpose Potatoes (Yukon Gold, Yellow Finn)
These are considered "in between" potatoes. They contain less starch than dry, floury baking potatoes but more than firm, waxy boiling potatoes. They also have a richer, more buttery flavor than other varieties. All-purpose potatoes can be used pretty successfully in most potato dishes, although there may be another variety that would be a better option.

Twice-Baked Sweet Potatoes with Shallot and Parmesan Topping

Serves 6; Total Time 1 hour 15 minutes

4 small sweet potatoes (8 ounces each), unpeeled, each lightly pricked with fork in 3 places

3 tablespoons unsalted butter, plus 2 tablespoons melted

2 shallots, sliced thin

2 slices hearty white sandwich bread, crusts removed, cut into ⅛- to ¼-inch pieces

1 ounce Parmesan cheese, grated (½ cup)

1 teaspoon minced fresh thyme

Salt and pepper

1 large egg, lightly beaten

1. Place potatoes in shallow baking dish. Microwave until skewer glides easily through flesh and potatoes yield to gentle pressure, 9 to 12 minutes, flipping potatoes every 3 minutes. Let potatoes cool for 10 minutes. Adjust oven rack to middle position and heat oven to 425 degrees.

2. Melt 3 tablespoons butter in 10-inch skillet over medium heat. Add shallots and cook, stirring occasionally, until softened, 2 to 5 minutes. Transfer shallots to bowl. Add bread pieces, ¼ cup Parmesan, thyme, ¼ teaspoon salt, and ¼ teaspoon pepper to bowl with shallots. Toss to combine.

3. Halve each potato lengthwise. Using spoon, scoop flesh from each half into second bowl, leaving about ⅛- to ¼-inch thickness of flesh. Place 6 shells cut side up on wire rack set in rimmed baking sheet (discard remaining 2 shells). Bake shells until dry and slightly crispy, about 10 minutes.

4. Meanwhile, mash potato flesh with ricer, food mill, or potato masher until smooth. Stir in egg, 2 tablespoons melted butter, ½ teaspoon salt, and remaining ¼ cup Parmesan.

5. Remove shells from oven and reduce temperature to 375 degrees. Divide mashed potato mixture evenly among shells. Top each filled shell with bread mixture. Bake until bread mixture is spotty brown, about 20 minutes. Let cool for 5 minutes before serving.

why this recipe works

The process of twice-baking potatoes is relatively simple: You bake them in a hot oven, halve them, and scoop out their flesh, which is then mashed with some combination of butter, spices, and flavorful additions. Then the augmented potato is spooned back into the skins and you bake them again. To apply this technique to sweet potatoes, we made a few adjustments. A microwave start best maintained the integrity of the delicate sweet potato skins. Baking the scooped-out shells in the oven before stuffing transformed them into a stable base. Finishing with a toasted topping of bread crumbs mixed with shallots, Parmesan, and thyme provided a crunchy counterpoint. The skins of the sweet potato are edible and add an earthiness to the dish. When shopping, look for sweet potatoes that are uniform in size, with rounded ends.

Twice-Baked Sweet Potatoes with Bacon Topping

Omit butter and shallots. For step 2, cook 4 slices bacon, cut into ½-inch pieces, in 10-inch skillet over medium heat until crispy, 8 to 10 minutes. Using slotted spoon, transfer bacon to bowl. Add 2 tablespoons fat from skillet, bread pieces, thyme, ¼ teaspoon pepper, and ⅛ teaspoon salt to bowl with bacon. Toss to combine. (Omit Parmesan in topping.)

Twice-Baked Sweet Potatoes with Cinnamon Toast Topping

Omit shallots, Parmesan, and pepper. For step 2, combine 2 tablespoons packed dark brown sugar, ¼ teaspoon ground cinnamon, ⅛ teaspoon cayenne pepper, and pinch salt in medium bowl. Add bread pieces and toss to combine. Melt 5 tablespoons butter in 8-inch skillet over medium heat. Reduce heat to medium-low and continue to cook, swirling pan frequently, until foaming subsides and butter is just beginning to brown, 2 to 4 minutes. Reserve 2 tablespoons browned butter and pour remaining butter over bread pieces. Toss to combine. Substitute reserved browned butter for melted butter in step 4.

think like a cook

SWEET POTATOES 101

In the United States, the terms "sweet potato" and "yam" have become interchangeable, both referring to the orange-skinned, orange-fleshed, sweet-tasting root vegetable traditionally found next to the regular potatoes at the supermarket. However these orange tubers are actually no relation to true yams, which are starchy, fairly bland-tasting root vegetables that can be recognized by their thick, fibrous skin.

Additionally, there is a world of sweet potatoes that extends far beyond the confines of the familiar orange variety. Ninety percent of the world's sweet potatoes are grown in Asia, where they are most often white-fleshed and neither as sweet nor as soft as the traditional orange-fleshed varieties we know in the United States. We prefer the Beauregard variety for traditional orange sweet potatoes and Japanese white for a nontraditional option (note that you should seek out recipes specifically designed for white sweet potatoes rather than using them as a substitute for orange ones).

Sautéed Spinach with Yogurt and Dukkah

Serves 4; Total Time 20 minutes (plus time to make dukkah)

½ cup plain yogurt

1½ teaspoons lemon zest plus 1 teaspoon juice

Salt and pepper

3 tablespoons extra-virgin olive oil

20 ounces curly-leaf spinach, stemmed

2 garlic cloves, minced

¼ cup Dukkah (see right)

1. Combine yogurt and lemon zest and juice in bowl and season with salt and pepper to taste; set aside for serving. Heat 1 tablespoon oil in Dutch oven over high heat until shimmering. Add spinach, 1 handful at a time, and cook, stirring constantly, until wilted, about 1 minute. Transfer spinach to colander and squeeze between tongs to release excess liquid.

2. Wipe pot dry with paper towels. Add remaining 2 tablespoons oil and garlic to now-empty pot and cook over medium heat until fragrant, about 30 seconds. Add spinach and toss to coat, gently separating leaves to evenly coat with garlic oil. Off heat, season with salt and pepper to taste. Transfer spinach to serving platter, drizzle with yogurt sauce, and sprinkle with dukkah. Serve.

why this recipe works

Earthy, tender spinach and creamy, tangy yogurt are a perfect match; think of it as a modern take on Grandma's creamed spinach. Plus, this dish is a perfect showcase for one of our favorite condiments: dukkah, an Egyptian blend of ground chickpeas, nuts, and spices. The dukkah adds great flavor and textural contrast to this simple side. We emphasized the yogurt's tanginess with lemon zest and juice and drizzled it over our garlicky spinach. Two pounds of flat-leaf spinach (about three bunches) can be substituted for the curly-leaf spinach. Don't use baby spinach. We prefer to use our homemade dukkah (see "It's Pronounced DOO-kah"), but you can substitute store-bought dukkah if you wish, or omit it if you don't have time. Check for it at specialty spice stores.

think like a cook

IT'S PRONOUNCED DOO-KAH

Dukkah is a crunchy, addictive blend of nuts, chickpeas, seeds, and spices from the Mediterranean that is traditionally sprinkled over olive oil to use as a dip for bread. We love to have dukkah on hand for those times when we need a last-minute, simpler-than-it-looks appetizer. It also makes a crunchy garnish for soup, salads, and roasted vegetables. You can even add it to plain yogurt or cottage cheese to make a quick dip for crudités or a savory snack. Recipes for dukkah vary. The blend of spices and nuts is often a matter of taste; our recipe reflects the mixture we like best.

Dukkah

Makes 2 cups

Adjust oven rack to middle position and heat oven to 400 degrees. Toss 1 (15-ounce) can rinsed and dried chickpeas with 1 teaspoon extra-virgin olive oil and spread in single layer on rimmed baking sheet. Roast until browned and crisp, 40 to 45 minutes, stirring every 5 to 10 minutes; let cool completely. Process chickpeas in food processor until coarsely ground, about 10 seconds; transfer to bowl. Pulse ½ cup toasted, shelled pistachios and ⅓ cup toasted black sesame seeds in now-empty food processor until coarsely ground, about 15 pulses; transfer to bowl with chickpeas. Process 2½ tablespoons toasted coriander seeds, 2 tablespoons toasted cumin seeds, and 2 teaspoons toasted fennel seeds in again-empty food processor until finely ground, 2 to 3 minutes; transfer to bowl with chickpeas. Add 1½ teaspoons pepper and 1¼ teaspoons salt and toss until well combined. (Dukkah can be refrigerated for up to 1 month.)

Roasted Butternut Squash with Tahini and Feta

Serves 6; Total Time 1 hour

3 pounds butternut squash

3 tablespoons extra-virgin olive oil

Salt and pepper

1 tablespoon tahini

1½ teaspoons lemon juice

1 teaspoon honey

1 ounce feta cheese, crumbled (¼ cup)

¼ cup shelled pistachios, toasted (see page 157) and chopped fine

2 tablespoons chopped fresh mint

1. Adjust oven rack to lowest position and heat oven to 425 degrees. Using sharp vegetable peeler or chef's knife, remove squash skin and fibrous threads just below skin. Trim top and bottom. Cut squash in half where narrow neck and curved bottom meet, then cut both base and neck in half lengthwise to make four quarters. Scrape out seeds from base, then slice each quarter crosswise into ½-inch-thick pieces.

2. Toss squash with 2 tablespoons oil, ½ teaspoon salt, and ½ teaspoon pepper and arrange in single layer in rimmed baking sheet. Roast squash until sides touching sheet toward back of oven are well browned, 25 to 30 minutes. Rotate sheet and continue to roast until sides touching sheet toward back of oven are well browned, 6 to 10 minutes. Use metal spatula to flip each piece and continue to roast until squash is very tender and sides touching sheet are browned, 10 to 15 minutes.

3. Transfer squash to serving platter. Whisk remaining 1 tablespoon oil, tahini, lemon juice, honey, and pinch salt together in bowl. Drizzle squash with tahini dressing and sprinkle with feta, pistachios, and mint. Serve.

why this recipe works

Winter squashes like butternut have a tough skin and dense interior that makes them ideal for slow cooking. They are best roasted until well done, which helps develop the sweetest flavor and smoothest texture. We peel the squash to remove not only the tough outer skin but also the rugged fibrous layer of white flesh just beneath, ensuring supremely tender squash. To encourage the squash slices to caramelize, we used a hot 425-degree oven and placed the squash on the lowest oven rack. Finally, we selected a mix of Greek-inspired toppings that added crunch, creaminess, fresh flavor, and a little sweetness: pistachios, feta, mint, and tahini spiked with honey and lemon juice. This dish can be served warm or at room temperature.

variation

Roasted Butternut Squash with Goat Cheese, Pecans, and Maple

Omit tahini, lemon juice, and honey. Reduce olive oil to 2 tablespoons. Combine 2 tablespoons maple syrup and pinch cayenne pepper and drizzle over cooked squash. Substitute ⅓ cup crumbled goat cheese for feta; ½ cup toasted pecans, coarsely chopped, for pistachios; and 2 teaspoons fresh thyme leaves for mint.

think like a cook

IS SHORTCUT SQUASH WORTH IT?

Sure, it saves prep time to buy precut, prepeeled butter-nut squash, but we had to wonder: How does the flavor and texture of this timesaving squash stand up to a whole squash we cut up at home? Our taste tests confirmed what we suspected; whole squash you peel and cut yourself can't be beat in terms of flavor and texture. That said, when you are trying to make the most of every minute, peeled, halved squash can be an acceptable convenience product, and we found that it performed admirably in most test recipes. However, avoid precut chunks; our tasters all thought that they were dry and stringy, with barely any squash flavor.

Sautéed Summer Squash with Parsley and Garlic

Serves 4; Total Time 25 minutes

1 small garlic clove, minced

1 teaspoon grated lemon zest plus 1 tablespoon juice

4 yellow squashes and/or zucchini (8 ounces each), trimmed

7 teaspoons extra-virgin olive oil

Salt and pepper

1½ tablespoons chopped fresh parsley

1. Combine garlic and lemon juice in large bowl and set aside for at least 10 minutes. Using vegetable peeler, shave each squash lengthwise into ribbons: Peel off 3 ribbons from 1 side, then turn 90 degrees and peel off 3 more ribbons. Continue to turn and peel ribbons until you reach seeds. Discard core.

2. Whisk 2 tablespoons oil, ¼ teaspoon salt, ⅛ teaspoon pepper, and lemon zest into garlic mixture.

3. Heat remaining 1 teaspoon oil in 12-inch nonstick skillet over medium-high heat until just smoking. Add squash and cook, tossing occasionally with tongs, until squash has softened and is translucent, 3 to 4 minutes. Transfer squash to bowl with dressing, add 1 tablespoon parsley, and toss to coat. Season with salt and pepper to taste. Transfer to serving platter and sprinkle with remaining 1½ teaspoons parsley. Serve immediately.

why this recipe works

If you've been burned one too many times by mushy summer squash and zucchini, this recipe is for you; it will prove that these veggies can indeed make a great side dish. To remove excess moisture, many squash recipes call for fussy, time-consuming salting and draining or for shredding and wringing out the squash. We discovered a far simpler approach: Use a vegetable peeler to make thin ribbons of squash and discard the seedy, waterlogged core. The ribbons cooked up to a perfect crisp-tender texture in just a few minutes. A tangy vinaigrette and sprinkle of fresh parsley rounded out the flavors. We like a colorful mix of yellow summer squash and zucchini, but you can use just one or the other. Steeping minced garlic in lemon juice mellows the garlic's bite; do not skip this step. Be sure to start checking for doneness at the lower end of the cooking time.

variations

Sautéed Summer Squash with Mint and Pistachios

Substitute 1½ teaspoons cider vinegar for lemon zest and juice. Omit parsley and toss squash with ⅓ cup chopped fresh mint along with dressing. Sprinkle squash with 2 tablespoons toasted and chopped pistachios before serving.

Sautéed Summer Squash with Oregano and Pepper Flakes

Omit lemon zest and reduce lemon juice to 1 teaspoon. Add ¼ teaspoon red pepper flakes to smoking oil in step 3 and cook, stirring constantly, for 10 seconds before adding squash. Omit parsley and toss squash with 2 teaspoons minced fresh oregano along with dressing.

think like a cook

THE SQUASHES OF SUMMER

Zucchini and yellow squash are the most common varieties of summer squash, in large part because they are well suited to a wide variety of climates and soil conditions. If you've ever tried your hand at gardening or know someone how has, you might be aware of just how easy they are to grow; so easy, in fact, that when midsummer comes around, backyard botanists invariably find themselves faced with a surfeit of these vegetables (and sadly they don't take well to canning or freezing). Because of this natural abundance, quick, easy recipes like the one on this page are an excellent asset to have in your kitchen repertoire. (Although you can also pass along some of the extra produce to your friends and family; August 8th has even been designated National Sneak Some Zucchini onto Your Neighbor's Porch Day by *The Old Farmer's Almanac*.)

Both zucchini and summer squash have thin, edible skins and a high moisture content, so they cook quickly whether steamed, baked, or sautéed. When shopping, choose zucchini and summer squash that are firm and without soft spots. Smaller vegetables are more flavorful and less watery than larger specimens; they also have fewer seeds. While these veggies can definitely grow larger (the Guinness World Record for longest zucchini ever clocked in at 8 feet, 3 inches!), we suggest that you look for zucchini and summer squash no heavier than 8 ounces, and preferably just 6 ounces. Zucchini and summer squash are fairly perishable; store them in the refrigerator in a partially sealed zipper-lock bag for up to five days.

Walk-Away Ratatouille

Serves 6 to 8; Total Time 1 hour 45 minutes

⅓ cup plus 1 tablespoon extra-virgin olive oil

2 large onions, cut into 1-inch pieces

8 large garlic cloves, peeled and smashed

Salt and pepper

1½ teaspoons herbes de Provence

¼ teaspoon red pepper flakes

1 bay leaf

1½ pounds eggplant, peeled and cut into 1-inch pieces

2 pounds plum tomatoes, cored and chopped coarse

2 small zucchini, halved lengthwise and cut into 1-inch pieces

1 red bell pepper, stemmed, seeded, and cut into 1-inch pieces

1 yellow bell pepper, stemmed, seeded, and cut into 1-inch pieces

2 tablespoons chopped fresh basil

1 tablespoon minced fresh parsley

1 tablespoon sherry vinegar

why this recipe works

Ratatouille is a rustic Provençal specialty that transforms late-summer produce into a rich stew. Many ratatouille recipes call for time- and labor-intensive treatments like cooking each vegetable in a separate batch. To create a simplified version, we started by sautéing onions and aromatics with chunks of eggplant and tomato before transferring the uncovered pot to the oven, where the dry heat thoroughly evaporated the vegetables' moisture (preventing the wateriness that can foil many ratatouille recipes) and concentrated their flavors. After 45 minutes, the vegetables became meltingly soft and we mashed them into a thick, silky sauce. Zucchini and bell peppers went into the pot last so that they retained some texture. This dish is best prepared using ripe, in-season tomatoes. If good tomatoes are not available, substitute one 28-ounce can of whole peeled tomatoes that have been drained and chopped coarse. This dish can be served warm, at room temperature, or chilled.

1. Adjust oven rack to middle position and heat oven to 400 degrees. Heat ⅓ cup oil in Dutch oven over medium-high heat until shimmering. Add onions, garlic, 1 teaspoon salt, and ¼ teaspoon pepper and cook, stirring occasionally, until onions are translucent and starting to soften, about 10 minutes. Add herbes de Provence, pepper flakes, and bay leaf and cook, stirring frequently, for 1 minute. Stir in eggplant and tomatoes. Sprinkle with ½ teaspoon salt and ¼ teaspoon pepper and stir to combine. Transfer pot to oven and bake, uncovered, until vegetables are very tender and spotty brown, 40 to 45 minutes.

2. Remove pot from oven and, using potato masher or heavy wooden spoon, smash and stir eggplant mixture until broken down to sauce-like consistency. Stir in zucchini, bell peppers, ¼ teaspoon salt, and ¼ teaspoon pepper and return to oven. Bake, uncovered, until zucchini and bell peppers are just tender, 20 to 25 minutes.

3. Remove pot from oven, cover, and let stand until zucchini is translucent and easily pierced with tip of paring knife, 10 to 15 minutes. Using wooden spoon, scrape any browned bits from sides of pot and stir back into ratatouille. Discard bay leaf. Stir in 1 tablespoon basil, parsley, and vinegar. Season with salt and pepper to taste. Transfer to large platter, drizzle with remaining 1 tablespoon oil, sprinkle with remaining 1 tablespoon basil, and serve.

think like a cook

TURNING A VEGETABLE SIDE DISH INTO A MAIN DISH

Ratatouille is great as an accompaniment to meat or fish, but if you dish out larger servings and serve it with crusty bread or topped with a fried egg, it can also be a satisfying main dish. In fact, many vegetable sides are just a step away from becoming main dishes if you serve them over pasta, lentils, rice, or another hearty grain, perhaps drizzling in a little extra olive oil or adding a handful of grated cheese to tie everything together. This is also a great way to turn the leftovers from last night's side into a quick lunch the next day. Try tossing Roasted Butternut Squash with Tahini and Feta (page 216) with cooked bulgur. Serve Sautéed Mushrooms with Shallot and Thyme (page 206) as a pasta sauce or atop Creamy Parmesan Polenta (page 224). And see Anatomy of a Great Grain Bowl (page 179) for another way to make use of cooked vegetables.

Hasselback Tomatoes

Serves 4 to 6; Total Time 45 minutes

8 ripe plum tomatoes, cored

7 ounces Gruyère cheese, shredded (1¾ cups)

1½ cups fresh basil leaves

6 tablespoons extra-virgin olive oil

¼ cup panko bread crumbs

1 garlic clove, minced

Salt and pepper

1. Line rimmed baking sheet with aluminum foil and set wire rack in sheet. Using serrated knife, cut ¼-inch-thick slice from 1 long side of each tomato to create a flat base. Turn tomatoes onto cut sides so they sit flat, then slice crosswise at ¼-inch intervals, leaving bottom ¼ inch of each tomato intact.

2. Process ¾ cup Gruyère, basil, oil, panko, garlic, ½ teaspoon salt, and ½ teaspoon pepper in food processor until smooth, scraping down sides of bowl with rubber spatula as needed, about 10 seconds.

3. Adjust oven rack 6 inches from broiler element and heat broiler. Combine ¾ teaspoon salt and ¾ teaspoon pepper in bowl. Carefully open tomato slices and sprinkle with salt-pepper mixture. Using small spoon, spread basil mixture evenly between tomato slices (about 2 tablespoons per tomato).

4. Arrange tomatoes on prepared wire rack. Sprinkle remaining 1 cup Gruyère over tomatoes. Broil until cheese is golden brown, about 5 minutes. Serve.

why this recipe works

Named for the hotel where it was invented in Sweden, Hasselbacking is a technique where a vegetable (traditionally potatoes) is partially sliced, accordion style, brushed with butter, sprinkled with bread crumbs, and baked. This approach is also great for tomatoes; think of them as leveled-up stuffed tomatoes featuring tons of crispy edges and great browning. We started with meaty, well-shaped plum tomatoes. We cored them, then cut into them and spread a potent, flavorful homemade basil pesto mixed with some crunchy panko bread crumbs over the interiors. We then topped the tomatoes with shredded Gruyère cheese for added punch and placed the stuffed tomatoes under the broiler for just 5 minutes to melt the cheese and slightly soften the tomatoes without turning them to mush. For the best results, we recommend buying ripe tomatoes of similar weight and size. We developed this recipe with tomatoes that averaged 3 ounces in weight and 2½ inches in length.

think like a cook

TOMATO TIPS

With tomatoes, coring isn't the same as seeding. The core needs to come out because it's tough and can be unpleasant. To remove the core, cut diagonally around it with a paring knife and remove the cone-shaped piece. The seeds, by contrast (and their surrounding jelly) shouldn't be removed unless excess moisture is a concern in your recipe. These tomato "guts" are where most of the tomato's flavor resides, not in the flesh, so try to maintain as much of the seeds and jelly as possible. (That flavor comes from savory glutamates; to learn more about these compounds, see page 189.) In fact, the best-tasting tomatoes tend to have thin walls, which leave more room for the flavorful insides.

Creamy Parmesan Polenta
Serves 4 to 6; Total Time 50 minutes

7½ cups water

Salt and pepper

Pinch baking soda

1½ cups coarse-ground cornmeal

2 ounces Parmesan cheese, grated (1 cup), plus extra for serving

2 tablespoons extra-virgin olive oil

1. Bring water to boil in large saucepan over medium-high heat. Stir in 1½ teaspoons salt and baking soda. Slowly pour cornmeal into water in steady stream while stirring back and forth with wooden spoon or rubber spatula. Bring mixture to boil, stirring constantly, about 1 minute. Reduce heat to lowest setting and cover.

2. After 5 minutes, whisk polenta to smooth out any lumps that may have formed, about 15 seconds. (Make sure to scrape down sides and bottom of saucepan.) Cover and continue to cook, without stirring, until polenta grains are tender but slightly al dente, about 25 minutes longer. (Polenta should be loose and barely hold its shape; it will continue to thicken as it cools.)

3. Off heat, stir in Parmesan and oil and season with pepper to taste. Cover and let sit for 5 minutes. Serve, passing extra Parmesan separately.

variation
Sautéed Cherry Tomato and Fresh Mozzarella Topping

Cook 3 tablespoons extra-virgin olive oil, 2 thinly sliced garlic cloves, pinch red pepper flakes, and pinch sugar in 12-inch nonstick skillet over medium-high heat until fragrant and sizzling, about 1 minute. Stir in 1½ pounds halved cherry tomatoes and cook until just beginning to soften, about 1 minute. Season with salt and pepper to taste. Spoon mixture over individual portions of polenta and top with 1¼ cups shredded fresh mozzarella cheese and 2 tablespoons shredded fresh basil. Serve.

why this recipe works

Polenta is simply cornmeal simmered in water until it softens into a creamy savory pudding. It's a classic Italian side dish and makes an invaluable basic in your arsenal. Use it as a bed for stews, braises, or sautéed vegetables. Traditionally, polenta requires almost constant stirring (for up to an hour!) to avoid intractable lumps. We wanted a less fussy process. The key was adding a pinch of baking soda (a technique borrowed from our chili—see page 259). This helped to soften the cornmeal and reduced the cooking time. It also encouraged the cornmeal to break down, creating a silky, creamy consistency with minimal stirring. Parmesan cheese and olive oil, stirred in at the last minute, ensured a satisfying, rich flavor. To turn this into a meal, try our tomato and mozzarella topping, which can be prepared while the polenta cooks. Or make Sautéed Mushrooms with Shallot and Thyme, page 206. Note: If the polenta bubbles or sputters even slightly after the first 10 minutes, the heat is too high.

think like a cook

JUST A PINCH

In most cases, we're pretty particular about measuring—you should always select the appropriate measuring tool for the type of ingredient and use it properly (see page 38). However, sometimes you need just a tiny amount of an ingredient—a pinch of this, a dash of that, a smidgen of the other thing. While these terms seem vague, recently manufacturers have begun offering measuring spoons labeled with them.

The general consensus is that a dash is ⅛ teaspoon, a pinch is half of a dash or ¹⁄₁₆ teaspoon, and a smidgen is half of a pinch or ¹⁄₃₂ teaspoon. If you're committed to absolute precision, you can use these measurements. However, since measurements that small can be quite difficult to reliably achieve without a set of calibrated measuring tools, and since these terms all refer to very small amounts anyway, you're probably OK estimating in most cases. If we use the word "dash" in a recipe, we usually mean a small splash of a liquid ingredient added to taste, and if we use the word "pinch," we mean the amount of a dry ingredient that you can literally pinch between your thumb and forefinger. We don't use the word "smidgen" in recipes; if you encounter a recipe that does, think of it as about one-half of the amount you can pinch.

Creamy Orzo with Peas and Parmesan

Serves 4; Total Time 40 minutes

2 tablespoons unsalted butter

1 onion, chopped fine

Salt and pepper

2 garlic cloves, minced

1 cup orzo

¼ cup dry white wine

3¾ cups chicken broth

2 ounces Parmesan cheese, grated (1 cup)

½ cup frozen peas, thawed

1. Melt butter in large saucepan over medium-high heat. Add onion and ¼ teaspoon salt and cook until softened, about 5 minutes. Stir in garlic and cook until fragrant, about 30 seconds. Stir in orzo and cook for 1 minute.

2. Stir in wine and cook until evaporated, about 1 minute. Stir in broth and bring to boil; cook, stirring often, until orzo is creamy and tender, about 15 minutes. Off heat, vigorously stir in Parmesan until creamy. Stir in peas and let sit off heat until peas are heated through and sauce has thickened slightly, about 2 minutes. Season with salt and pepper to taste, and serve.

why this recipe works

Orzo is a short, rice-shaped pasta that pairs nicely with vegetables. It can be boiled, but we love its flavor when cooked risotto style to a creamy, hearty texture. We started by toasting the orzo along with onion and garlic, which gave it a deep caramel color and rich, nutty flavor. This also helped create a dish that was tender but not mushy. We then added wine and broth and cooked the orzo until it had absorbed all the liquid. Grated Parmesan stirred in at the end of cooking gave us a rich-tasting dish with a creamy texture, and stirring in delicate peas at the last minute ensured that they kept their freshness. If the finished orzo is too thick, stir in hot water, a few tablespoons at a time, to adjust the consistency.

think like a cook

HOW TO CHOOSE THE BEST PARMESAN

Parmesan is a hard, grainy cheese made from cow's milk. It has a rich, sharp flavor and melt-in-your-mouth texture, and it's one of our go-to ingredients for adding umami punch to all kinds of dishes. We frequently reach for it to sprinkle on top of pasta dishes or to add a rich, salty flavor to sauces, soups, and stews.

There are a lot of Parmesan options available out there, but most are not worth it, especially pregrated versions and, of course, we don't recommend anything that comes in a green shaker can. We recommend buying wedges of authentic Italian Parmigiano-Reggiano, which has a complex flavor and smooth, melting texture that nothing else can match. When shopping, make sure some portion of the words "Parmigiano-Reggiano" is stenciled on the golden rind. We prefer cheese from the edge, near the rind, rather than the interior of the wheel (which measures 18 inches wide); cheese from the outer section is crumblier and more flavorful.

To ensure that you're buying a properly aged cheese, examine the condition of the rind. It should be a few shades darker than the straw-colored interior and penetrate about ½ inch deep (younger or improperly aged cheeses will have a paler, thinner rind). And closely scrutinize the center of the cheese; those small white spots found on many samples are actually good things—they signify the presence of calcium phosphate crystals, which are formed only after the cheese has been aged for the proper amount of time.

Bulgur with Chickpeas, Spinach, and Za'atar

Serves 4 to 6; Total Time 50 minutes

3 tablespoons extra-virgin olive oil

1 onion, chopped fine

Salt and pepper

3 garlic cloves, minced

2 tablespoons za'atar

1 cup medium-grind bulgur, rinsed

1 (15-ounce) can chickpeas, rinsed

¾ cup chicken or vegetable broth

¾ cup water

3 ounces (3 cups) baby spinach, chopped

1 tablespoon lemon juice

why this recipe works

Grains like rice or couscous are pretty familiar as side dishes, but there's a whole wide world of other grains out there to try. This dish combines creamy chickpeas and nutty bulgur, which is made from parcooked ground wheat, with the vegetal punch of fresh spinach. To boost the flavor of this simple side we added the aromatic eastern Mediterranean spice blend *za'atar*. We bloomed half of the za'atar in a base of onion and garlic before adding the bulgur, chickpeas, and cooking liquid and then added the rest of the *za'atar* along with the spinach, off the heat. The residual heat in the bulgur was enough to soften the spinach and highlight the za'atar's more delicate aromas. This dish pairs well with fish or meat entrées. When shopping, don't confuse bulgur with cracked wheat, which has a much longer cooking time and will not work in this recipe.

1. Heat 2 tablespoons oil in large saucepan over medium heat until shimmering. Add onion and ½ teaspoon salt and cook until softened, about 5 minutes. Stir in garlic and 1 tablespoon za'atar and cook until fragrant, about 30 seconds.

2. Stir in bulgur, chickpeas, broth, and water and bring to simmer. Reduce heat to low, cover, and simmer gently until bulgur is tender, 16 to 18 minutes.

3. Off heat, lay clean dish towel underneath lid and let bulgur sit for 10 minutes. Add spinach, lemon juice, remaining 1 tablespoon za'atar, and remaining 1 tablespoon oil and fluff gently with fork to combine. Season with salt and pepper to taste. Serve.

think like a cook

BULGUR FOR BEGINNERS

If you are cooking with bulgur for the first time, it might be helpful to know what it actually is. Bulgur is made from parboiled or steamed wheat kernels that are then dried, partially stripped of their outer bran layer, and coarsely ground. Bulgur is sold in four numbered grind sizes, from #1 (fine) to #4 (extra-coarse), but most recipes using bulgur call for medium grind (#2). We recommend rinsing bulgur before cooking to remove any detritus. While you can certainly simmer it, as we do in this recipe, you can also reconstitute bulgur by simply soaking it in liquid—try water flavored with lemon, lime, or tomato juice—for 60 to 90 minutes (use ⅔ cup liquid for 1 cup bulgur). When it's done, the grains of the bulgur will be somewhat tender but still firm. One of the most well-known uses for bulgur prepared this way is tabbouleh, the traditional Mediterranean grain salad with tomatoes and herbs.

Mujaddara

Serves 4 to 6; Total Time 1 hour 30 minutes

2 pounds onions, halved and sliced ¼ inch thick

Salt and pepper

1⅔ cups vegetable oil

8¾ ounces (1¼ cups) green or brown lentils, picked over and rinsed

1¼ cups basmati rice

3 garlic cloves, minced

1 teaspoon ground coriander

1 teaspoon ground cumin

⅔ teaspoon ground cinnamon

⅔ teaspoon ground allspice

⅛ teaspoon cayenne pepper

1 teaspoon sugar

3 tablespoons minced fresh cilantro

1 recipe Lemon-Yogurt Sauce (page 102)

why this recipe works

This classic Middle Eastern recipe—which can be an accompaniment for meat or a vegetarian main—is a spectacular example of how a few humble ingredients can add up to something satisfying and complex. Tender basmati rice and lentils are seasoned with warm spices and garlic. Deeply flavorful fried onions are stirred into and sprinkled over the dish just before serving. To give the onions the best crispy texture, we microwaved them briefly to remove some liquid, then fried them to a deep golden brown. We used a pilaf method (see page 77) for the rice and lentils, giving the lentils a 15-minute head start to ensure that they finished at the same time as the rice. Served with a garlicky yogurt sauce, this pilaf is global comfort food at its best. Large green or brown lentils both work well in this recipe; do not substitute French green lentils (aka *lentilles du Puy*). It is crucial to thoroughly dry the microwaved onions after rinsing so they won't spatter when you fry them.

1. Toss onions with 2 teaspoons salt in bowl and microwave for 5 minutes. Rinse thoroughly, drain, and pat dry with paper towels. Cook onions and oil in Dutch oven over high heat, stirring often, until golden brown, 25 to 30 minutes. Drain onions in colander set in large bowl, reserving 3 tablespoons oil. Transfer onions to paper towel–lined baking sheet. Do not wash pot.

2. Meanwhile, bring lentils, 4 cups water, and 1 teaspoon salt to boil in medium saucepan over high heat. Reduce heat to low and cook until lentils are tender, 15 to 17 minutes. Drain and set aside.

3. While onions and lentils cook, place rice in medium bowl, add hot tap water to cover by 2 inches, and let stand 15 minutes. Using hands, gently swish grains to release excess starch. Carefully pour off water, leaving rice in bowl. Add cold tap water to rice and pour off water. Repeat adding and pouring off cold water 4 or 5 times, until water runs almost clear. Drain rice in fine-mesh strainer.

4. Heat 3 tablespoons reserved onion oil, garlic, coriander, cumin, cinnamon, allspice, ¼ teaspoon pepper, and cayenne in now-empty Dutch oven over medium heat until fragrant, about 2 minutes. Stir in rice and cook, stirring occasionally, until edges of rice begin to turn translucent, about 3 minutes. Stir in 2¼ cups water, sugar, and 1 teaspoon salt and bring to boil. Stir in lentils, reduce heat to low, cover, and cook until all liquid is absorbed, about 12 minutes.

5. Remove pot from heat, lay clean folded dish towel underneath lid, and let sit for 10 minutes. Fluff rice and lentils with fork and stir in cilantro and half of onions. Transfer to serving platter and top with remaining onions. Serve with yogurt sauce.

think like a cook

GARNISHES: BEYOND PARSLEY SPRIGS

It's easy to discount garnishes, especially if you associate them with parsley sprigs on restaurant plates. But garnishes aren't just for looks! They're your last chance to add flavor and texture (and, yes, color) to a dish. It's a pivotal moment. A burst of acid from a lemon wedge can brighten up a one-dimensional piece of meat. And chopped fresh herbs retain their fullest flavor when sprinkled on at the last minute. A garnish can also be more involved. There's Dukkah (page 215), which adds crunch and a Middle Eastern flavor profile. And then there's these crispy onions that are stirred into and sprinkled over our *mujaddara*. They add sweet-savory depth, richness, and textural interest, turning the pilaf into an incredibly satisfying dish. If you like them, try them in salads and sandwiches or on soups. You can reuse the flavorful onion frying oil—we use 3 tablespoons of it in the dish, but the rest can be refrigerated in an airtight container for up to 4 weeks. Drizzle it on pizza or roasted vegetables, or make a salad dressing.

soups and stews

Chicken Noodle Soup

Serves 8 to 10; Total Time 2 hours

why this recipe works

Chicken noodle soup from a can tastes nothing like soup you make yourself. This version is simple but hearty, with a rich broth and flavorful pieces of meat. Using thighs instead of a whole chicken kept things easier. We first browned them to build up a flavorful fond, then removed the skin to cut down on greasiness before simmering the thighs for a deep, savory broth. Since most people prefer white meat in chicken soup, we also gently poached two boneless chicken breasts in the broth, ensuring tender, juicy meat. Onion, carrot, celery, egg noodles, and herbs rounded out this classic. To keep our soup rich but not greasy, we made sure to remove the fat from the broth before serving. The thighs are used to flavor the broth; once the broth is strained, shred the thigh meat and reserve it for a salad or sandwiches. If you prefer dark meat in your soup, omit the chicken breasts and add the shredded thigh meat to the soup instead.

BROTH

12 (5- to 7-ounce) bone-in chicken thighs, trimmed

Salt and pepper

1 tablespoon vegetable oil

1 onion, chopped

12 cups water

2 bay leaves

2 (8-ounce) boneless, skinless chicken breasts, trimmed

SOUP

1 tablespoon vegetable oil

1 onion, chopped fine

1 carrot, peeled and sliced thin

1 celery rib, halved lengthwise and sliced thin

2 teaspoons minced fresh thyme

6 ounces wide egg noodles

¼ cup minced fresh parsley

Salt and pepper

1. FOR THE BROTH Pat thighs dry with paper towels and season with salt and pepper. Heat oil in Dutch oven over medium-high heat until just smoking. Cook half of thighs skin side down until deep golden brown, about 6 minutes. Turn thighs and lightly brown second side, about 2 minutes. Transfer to strainer set in a large bowl. Repeat with remaining thighs and transfer to strainer; discard fat in bowl. Pour off fat from pot, add onion, and cook over medium heat until just softened, about 3 minutes. Meanwhile, remove and discard skin from thighs. Add thighs, water, bay leaves, and 1 tablespoon salt to pot. Cover and simmer for 30 minutes. Add chicken breasts and continue simmering until broth is rich and flavorful, about 15 minutes.

2. Strain broth into large container, let stand at least 10 minutes, then remove fat from surface (see "Defatting Soup"). Meanwhile, transfer chicken to cutting board to cool. Once cooled, remove thigh meat from bones, shred, and reserve for another use. (The thigh meat can be refrigerated for up to 2 days or frozen for up to 1 month.) Shred breast meat and reserve for soup.

3. FOR THE SOUP Heat oil in now-empty Dutch oven over medium-high heat until shimmering. Add onion, carrot, and celery and cook until onion has softened, 3 to 4 minutes. Stir in thyme and defatted broth and simmer until vegetables are tender, about 15 minutes. Add noodles and shredded breast meat and simmer until noodles are just tender, about 5 minutes. Off heat, stir in parsley and season with salt and pepper to taste. Serve.

think like a cook

DEFATTING SOUP

Defatting a broth or soup is important if you don't want your final dish to look and taste greasy. The simplest method is to let the liquid settle in the pot for 5 to 10 minutes, then skim away the fat with a wide, shallow spoon or ladle. The advantage of this method is that it's very easy; however, some fat will remain in the broth. Straining the broth and pouring it into a tall, narrow container before defatting makes the process easier as it creates a deeper layer of fat that is easier to remove. If you have time, you can refrigerate broth overnight—the fat will collect and solidify on the top as it chills, at which point you can simply scrape the large solid pieces of fat right off the broth before reheating and using.

You can also use a fat separator. This technique works best with broths that don't have much in the way of vegetables taking up space in the pot. There are two types: pitchers and bottom drainers. With both, you pour the liquid into the fat separator and wait a few minutes for the fat to rise to the top. Then you either pour out the broth from a spout set in the base, or you pull a lever set in the handle to release the broth from the bottom of the separator, leaving the fat behind.

Creamy Cauliflower Soup

Serves 4 to 6; Total Time 1 hour

1 head cauliflower (2 pounds)

8 tablespoons unsalted butter, cut into 8 pieces

1 leek, white and light green parts only, halved lengthwise, sliced thin, and washed thoroughly

1 small onion, halved and sliced thin

Salt and pepper

4½–5 cups water

½ teaspoon sherry vinegar

3 tablespoons minced fresh chives

1. Pull off outer leaves of cauliflower and trim stem. Using paring knife, cut around core to remove; slice core thin and reserve. Cut heaping 1 cup of ½-inch florets from head of cauliflower; set aside. Cut remaining cauliflower crosswise into ½-inch-thick slices.

2. Melt 3 tablespoons butter in large saucepan over medium-low heat. Add leek, onion, and 1½ teaspoons salt. Cook, stirring often, until leek and onion are softened but not browned, about 7 minutes.

3. Add 4½ cups water, sliced core, and half of sliced cauliflower. Increase heat to medium-high and bring to simmer. Reduce heat to medium-low and simmer gently for 15 minutes. Add remaining sliced cauliflower and simmer soup until cauliflower is tender and crumbles easily, 15 to 20 minutes.

4. Meanwhile, melt remaining 5 tablespoons butter in 8-inch skillet over medium heat. Add reserved florets and cook, stirring often, until florets are golden brown and butter is browned and has nutty aroma, 6 to 8 minutes. Remove skillet from heat and use slotted spoon to transfer florets to small bowl. Toss florets with vinegar and season with salt to taste. Pour browned butter in skillet into separate bowl and reserve for garnishing.

5. Working in batches, process soup in blender until smooth, about 45 seconds per batch. Return pureed soup to clean pot, bring to brief simmer over medium heat, and adjust consistency with remaining water as needed (soup should have thick, velvety texture but should be thin enough to settle with flat surface after being stirred). Season with salt to taste. Serve, garnishing individual bowls with browned florets, drizzle of browned butter, chives, and pepper.

why this recipe works

This soup highlights the delicate flavor of cauliflower and has all of the comforting depth of a creamy soup without the heaviness of actual cream. Instead it relies on the creaminess of the cauliflower itself; because of the vegetable's low fiber content, it easily breaks down to create a velvety-smooth puree. To emphasize the cauliflower's flavor, we cooked it in water instead of broth, skipped the spice rack entirely, and added the cauliflower to the simmering water in two stages so that we got both the grassy flavor of just-cooked cauliflower and the nuttier flavor of longer-cooked cauliflower. Finally, we browned additional florets in butter and used both the florets and the butter as flavorful and elegant garnishes. White wine vinegar may be substituted for the sherry vinegar. Be sure to thoroughly trim the cauliflower's core of green leaves and leaf stems, which can be fibrous and contribute to a grainy texture in the soup.

variation
Curried Cauliflower Soup

Before adding water to saucepan, stir 1½ tablespoons grated fresh ginger and 1 tablespoon curry powder into vegetables and cook until fragrant, about 30 seconds. Substitute lime juice for sherry vinegar and 2 scallions, sliced thin on bias, for chives. Stir ½ cup canned coconut milk and 1 tablespoon lime juice into pureed soup before serving.

think like a cook

PUREEING SOUP

The texture of a pureed soup should be as smooth and creamy as possible. With this in mind, we tried pureeing several soups with a food processor, a hand-held immersion blender, and a regular countertop blender. We found that the standard blender turned out the smoothest pureed soups. The blade on the blender does an excellent job with soups because it pulls ingredients down from the top of the container. No stray bits go untouched by the blade. And as long as plenty of headroom is left at the top of the blender, there is no leakage.

The immersion blender has appeal because it can be brought to the pot, eliminating the need to ladle hot ingredients from one vessel to another. However, we found that this kind of blender can leave unblended bits of food behind, which is fine if you're aiming for a chunkier puree. The food processor does a decent job of pureeing, but some small bits of vegetables can get trapped under the blade and remain unchopped. Even more troubling is the tendency of a food processor to leak hot liquid. Fill the workbowl more than halfway and you are likely to see liquid running down the side of the food processor base.

Any time you're blending hot soup, follow a couple of precautions: Carefully ladle the soup into the blender to avoid pouring hot liquid directly from a saucepan, and never fill the blender jar more than halfway; otherwise, the soup can explode out the top. Don't expect the lid on a blender to stay in place. Hold the lid securely with a folded dish towel to keep it in place and to protect your hand from hot steam. Finally, pulse several times before blending continuously.

Best French Onion Soup

Serves 6; Total Time 4 hours 45 minutes

why this recipe works

There is no denying the appeal of a great bowl of French onion soup, with its caramelized onions, rich broth, and nutty Gruyère-topped bread. To fully and evenly caramelize 4 whole pounds of onions, we started by cooking them for 2½ hours in the oven, which not only produced golden, soft, sweet onions but also built up plenty of fond on the bottom of the pot. This we deglazed with water—several times, to create additional fond—before adding chicken broth, beef broth, and more water. The soup's crowning glory, the bread and cheese topping, is traditionally broiled directly atop the soup. If your soup bowls can't go under the broiler, sprinkle the toasted bread slices with Gruyère and broil them on the baking sheet until the cheese melts, then float them on top of the soup. The pot of cooked onions in step 2 can be cooled, covered, and refrigerated for up to 3 days before continuing with step 3.

SOUP

4 pounds onions, halved and sliced through root end into ¼-inch-thick pieces

3 tablespoons unsalted butter, cut into 3 pieces

Salt and pepper

2¾–3 cups water, plus extra as needed

½ cup dry sherry

4 cups chicken broth

2 cups beef broth

6 sprigs fresh thyme, tied with kitchen twine

1 bay leaf

CHEESE CROUTONS

1 small baguette, cut into ½-inch slices

8 ounces Gruyère cheese, shredded (2 cups)

1. FOR THE SOUP Adjust oven rack to lower-middle position and heat oven to 400 degrees. Generously spray inside of Dutch oven with vegetable oil spray. Add onions, butter, and 1 teaspoon salt. Cover and cook in oven until onions wilt slightly and look moist, about 1 hour.

2. Stir onions thoroughly, scraping bottom and sides of pot. Partially cover pot and continue to cook in oven until onions are soft and golden brown, 1½ to 1¾ hours longer, stirring onions thoroughly after 1 hour.

3. Carefully remove pot from oven (leave oven on) and place over medium-high heat. Using oven mitts to handle pot, continue to cook onions, stirring and scraping pot often, until liquid evaporates, onions brown, and bottom of pot is coated with dark crust, 20 to 25 minutes. (If onions begin to brown too quickly, reduce heat to medium. Also, be sure to scrape any browned bits that collect on spoon back into onions.)

4. Stir in ¼ cup water, thoroughly scraping up browned crust. Continue to cook until water evaporates and pot bottom has formed another dark crust, 6 to 8 minutes. Repeat deglazing 2 or 3 more times with additional ¼ water each time, until onions are very dark brown.

5. Stir in sherry and cook until evaporated, about 5 minutes. Stir in chicken broth, beef broth, 2 cups water, thyme bundle, bay leaf, and ½ teaspoon salt, scraping up any remaining browned bits. Bring to simmer, cover, and cook for 30 minutes. Discard thyme bundle and bay leaf and season with salt and pepper to taste. (Soup can be refrigerated for up to 3 days; return to simmer before proceeding.)

6. FOR THE CROUTONS While soup simmers, lay baguette slices on rimmed baking sheet and bake until dry, crisp, and lightly golden, about 10 minutes, flipping slices halfway through baking.

7. Position oven rack so rims of crocks will be 4 to 5 inches from broiler element and heat broiler. Set individual broiler-safe crocks on baking sheet and fill each with about 1½ cups soup. Top each bowl with 1 or 2 baguette slices (do not overlap slices) and sprinkle evenly with Gruyère. Broil until cheese is melted and bubbly around edges, 3 to 5 minutes. Let cool for 5 minutes before serving.

think like a cook

ON-HAND CARAMELIZED ONIONS

Our love for caramelized onions goes well beyond this soup: Their deep, earthy richness enhances almost anything. Try them in an omelet, frittata, or scrambled eggs. They taste fantastic on grilled cheese sandwiches, burgers, pizzas, or a potato or green salad. Baked or mashed potatoes? For sure. Or serve them with apples and a good cheese for dessert. To caramelize a relatively small amount of onions, we use a skillet. These onions can be refrigerated in an airtight container for up to 7 days or frozen in a zipper-lock bag for up to 3 months (press out all the air in the bag before freezing).

Small-Batch Caramelized Onions
Makes 1 cup

Trim root end from 2 pounds onions, halve pole to pole, peel, and slice crosswise ¼ inch thick. Heat 1 tablespoon unsalted butter and 1 tablespoon vegetable oil in 12-inch nonstick skillet over high heat; when foam subsides, stir in ½ teaspoon salt and 1 teaspoon packed light brown sugar. Add onions and stir to coat; cook, stirring occasionally, until onions begin to soften and release some moisture, about 5 minutes. Reduce heat to medium and cook, stirring frequently, until deeply browned and slightly sticky, about 40 minutes. (If onions sizzle or scorch, reduce heat. If onions are not browning after 15 minutes, increase heat.) Off heat, stir in 1 tablespoon water; season with pepper to taste.

Red Lentil Soup with North African Spices

Serves 4 to 6; Total Time 45 minutes

4 tablespoons unsalted butter

1 large onion, chopped fine

Salt and pepper

¾ teaspoon ground coriander

½ teaspoon ground cumin

¼ teaspoon ground ginger

⅛ teaspoon ground cinnamon

Pinch cayenne pepper

1 tablespoon tomato paste

1 garlic clove, minced

4 cups chicken broth

2 cups water

10½ ounces (1½ cups) red lentils, picked over and rinsed

2 tablespoons lemon juice, plus extra for seasoning

1½ teaspoons dried mint, crumbled

1 teaspoon paprika

¼ cup chopped fresh cilantro

why this recipe works

Small red lentils break down into a creamy, thick puree—perfect for a satisfying soup—but their mild flavor requires a bit of embellishment (thus the longish ingredient list). To build a flavorful base, we sautéed onion in butter and then added fragrant North African spices to bloom in the warm mixture. Tomato paste and garlic completed the base. Then we added our lentils, along with a mix of chicken broth and water to give the soup a full, rounded character. After only 15 minutes of cooking, the lentils were soft enough to be pureed with a whisk. A generous dose of lemon juice brought the flavors into focus, but to really elevate the flavor, we created a quick spice-infused butter; drizzling this on top, along with a sprinkle of fresh cilantro, completed the transformation of everday ingredients into an exotic yet comforting soup.

1. Melt 2 tablespoons butter in large saucepan over medium heat. Add onion and 1 teaspoon salt and cook, stirring occasionally, until softened but not browned, about 5 minutes. Add coriander, cumin, ginger, cinnamon, cayenne, and ¼ teaspoon pepper and cook until fragrant, about 2 minutes. Stir in tomato paste and garlic and cook for 1 minute. Stir in broth, water, and lentils and bring to simmer. Simmer vigorously, stirring occasionally, until lentils are soft and about half are broken down, about 15 minutes.

2. Whisk soup vigorously until it is coarsely pureed, about 30 seconds. Stir in lemon juice and season with salt and extra lemon juice to taste. Cover and keep warm. (Soup can be refrigerated for up to 3 days. Thin soup with water, if desired, when reheating.)

3. Melt remaining 2 tablespoons butter in small skillet. Remove from heat and stir in mint and paprika. Ladle soup into individual bowls, drizzle each portion with 1 teaspoon spiced butter, sprinkle with cilantro, and serve.

think like a cook

GETTING TO KNOW LENTILS

If you'd like to cook more legumes, lentils are a good place to start. They're quick to prepare, requiring no soaking on account of their thin skins. Rinse lentils before using them and pick through them to remove any pebbles, shriveled lentils, or other debris (a good practice with all dried beans). Lentils come in many sizes and colors, with considerable differences in flavor and texture. Here are the most commonly available types.

Brown and Green Lentils

These larger lentils are what you'll find in every supermarket. They are a uniform brown or green and have a mild, light, earthy flavor and creamy texture. Because they hold their shape well when cooked, they're a good all-purpose option, great in soups and salads or simmered and then tossed with olive oil.

Lentilles du Puy

These dark green French lentils from the city of Le Puy are smaller than the more common brown and green varieties. They are a dark olive green and have a rich, earthy, complex flavor and a firm but tender texture. Use these if you are looking for lentils that will keep their shape and look beautiful on the plate when cooked; they're perfect for salads and dishes where the lentils take center stage.

Red and Yellow Lentils

These Indian lentils are small and orange-red or golden yellow. They come split and skinless, so they completely disintegrate into a uniform consistency when cooked. If you are looking for lentils that will quickly break down into a thick puree, as in our soup recipe, this is the kind to use.

Hearty Minestrone
Serves 6 to 8; Time 1 hour 30 minutes (plus soaking time)

Salt and pepper

8 ounces (1¼ cups) dried cannellini beans, picked over and rinsed

1 tablespoon extra-virgin olive oil, plus extra for serving

3 ounces pancetta, cut into ¼-inch pieces

2 celery ribs, cut into ½-inch pieces

2 small onions, cut into ½-inch pieces

1 carrot, peeled and cut into ½-inch pieces

1 zucchini, cut into ½-inch pieces

½ small head green cabbage, halved, cored, and chopped (2 cups)

2 garlic cloves, minced

⅛–¼ teaspoon red pepper flakes

8 cups water

2 cups chicken broth

1 Parmesan cheese rind, plus grated Parmesan for serving

1 bay leaf

1½ cups V8 juice

½ cup chopped fresh basil

why this recipe works

This Italian classic squeezes every last ounce of flavor out of vegetables and features creamy dried beans and a surprisingly rich broth. Sautéing pancetta and cooking the vegetables in the rendered fat gave our soup layers of flavor, while a Parmesan rind (save a few in the freezer for recipes like this) added richness. V8 juice, though unconventional, added a wallop of vegetable flavor. Starch released from the beans thickened the soup. We prefer to use cannellini beans, but navy or great Northern beans can also be used. We prefer pancetta but bacon can be used. To make this soup vegetarian, substitute 2 teaspoons olive oil for the pancetta and vegetable broth for the chicken broth. The Parmesan rind can be replaced with a 2-inch chunk of the cheese. If you're pressed for time, quick-soak the beans: In step 1, bring the salt, water, and beans to a boil in a Dutch oven over high heat. Remove the pot from the heat, cover, and let stand for 1 hour. Drain and rinse the beans and proceed with the recipe.

1. Dissolve 1½ tablespoons salt in 2 quarts cold water in large bowl or container. Add beans and soak at room temperature for at least 8 hours or up to 24 hours. Drain and rinse well.

2. Heat oil and pancetta in Dutch oven over medium-high heat. Cook, stirring occasionally, until pancetta is lightly browned and fat has rendered, 3 to 5 minutes. Add celery, onions, carrot, and zucchini; cook, stirring frequently, until vegetables are softened and lightly browned, 5 to 9 minutes. Stir in cabbage, garlic, pepper flakes, and ½ teaspoon salt and continue to cook until cabbage starts to wilt, 1 to 2 minutes longer. Transfer vegetables to rimmed baking sheet and set aside.

3. Add drained beans, water, broth, Parmesan rind, and bay leaf to now-empty Dutch oven and bring to boil over high heat. Reduce heat and simmer vigorously, stirring occasionally, until beans are fully tender and liquid begins to thicken, 45 minutes to 1 hour.

4. Add reserved vegetables and V8 juice; cook until vegetables are soft, about 15 minutes. Discard bay leaf and Parmesan rind, stir in basil, and season with salt and pepper. Drizzle with oil and sprinkle with Parmesan. (Soup can be refrigerated for up to 2 days. Add basil just before serving.)

think like a cook

SIX PRINCIPLES OF SOUP MAKING

Soup might seem easy enough to make—but it's hard to hide the mistakes. To make sure every spoonful of soup is richly flavored, with juicy meat and tender vegetables, follow these test kitchen–tested tips.

1. Sauté the Aromatics

Sautéing onions, garlic, and other aromatics softens their texture (preventing unwanted crunch), tames harshness, and develops complexity.

2. Start with a Good Broth

Packaged broth is convenient and can be perfectly acceptable, but the differences among packaged broths are quite significant. Some are pretty flavorful, while others taste like salty dishwater. For our favorite brands, see page 271.

3. Cut the Vegetables to the Right Size

Haphazardly cut vegetables will cook unevenly—some pieces will be underdone and crunchy while others may be mushy. Cutting to the size specified in the recipe ensures that the pieces will all be perfectly cooked.

4. Stagger the Addition of Vegetables

When soups contain a variety of vegetables, the additions must often be staggered to account for their varying cooking times. Hardier vegetables can withstand more cooking time than delicate ones.

5. Simmer, Don't Boil

There is a fine line between the two but it can make a big difference in your soup. Simmering heats food more gently and evenly, while boiling can cause some vegetables to break apart and toughen meat. (We vigorously simmer the beans in our minestrone because we want them to release starch.)

6. Season Just Before Serving

In general, we add salt, pepper, and other seasonings—such as delicate herbs and lemon juice—after cooking, just before serving. The saltiness of the stock and other ingredients, such as canned tomatoes and beans, can vary greatly, so it's always best to taste and adjust the seasoning just before ladling it into bowls for serving.

Sicilian Chickpea and Escarole Soup

Serves 6 to 8; Total Time 2 hours (plus soaking time)

Salt and pepper

1 pound (2¾ cups) dried chickpeas, picked over and rinsed

2 tablespoons extra-virgin olive oil, plus extra for serving

2 fennel bulbs, stalks discarded, bulbs halved, cored, and chopped fine

1 small onion, chopped medium

5 garlic cloves, minced

2 teaspoons minced fresh oregano or ½ teaspoon dried

¼ teaspoon red pepper flakes

7 cups water

5 cups vegetable broth

1 Parmesan cheese rind plus 2 ounces Parmesan, grated (1 cup)

2 bay leaves

1 (3-inch) strip orange zest

1 head escarole (1 pound), trimmed and cut into 1-inch pieces

1 large tomato, cored and chopped medium

why this recipe works

Soup is one place where it's worth using dried beans, since you're already going to be simmering the dish and the beans add tons of flavor and body to the cooking liquid. This soup pairs mild, creamy chickpeas with bitter, leafy escarole. For an aromatic base, we used onion, garlic, oregano, and red pepper flakes. We also included fennel; its mild anise bite complemented the nutty chickpeas. A strip of orange zest added a subtle citrusy note, while a Parmesan rind contributed a nutty richness. Serve with Garlic Toasts (see right). Use a vegetable peeler to remove the zest from the orange. If you're pressed for time, quick-soak the beans: In step 1, bring the salt, water, and beans to a boil in a Dutch oven over high heat. Remove the pot from the heat, cover, and let stand for 1 hour. Drain and rinse the beans and proceed with the recipe.

1. Dissolve 3 tablespoons salt in 4 quarts cold water in large container. Add chickpeas and soak at room temperature for at least 8 hours or up to 24 hours. Drain and rinse well.

2. Heat oil in Dutch oven over medium heat until shimmering. Add fennel, onion, and 1 teaspoon salt and cook until vegetables are softened, 7 to 10 minutes. Stir in garlic, oregano, and pepper flakes and cook until fragrant, about 30 seconds.

3. Stir in water, broth, drained chickpeas, Parmesan rind, bay leaves, and orange zest and bring to boil. Reduce to gentle simmer and cook until chickpeas are tender, 1¼ to 1¾ hours.

4. Stir in escarole and tomato and cook until escarole is wilted, 5 to 10 minutes.

5. Off heat, discard bay leaves, orange zest, and Parmesan rind (scraping off any cheese that has melted and adding it back to pot). Season with salt and pepper to taste. Sprinkle individual portions with grated Parmesan, drizzle with extra oil, and serve.

think like a cook

GARLIC TOASTS ON THE SIDE

Bread has long been a trusty sidekick to soup, whether it's in the form of croutons or oyster crackers scattered over the top of chowder or a warm roll or piece of bread to go alongside it. Here's a quick and easy garlic crouton you can make to accompany this soup or any other in this chapter. The garlic toasts also make a great base for bruschetta—try adding toppings such as a pesto (see page 100) or a salsa (see pages 100–103) for a super simple appetizer. The trick to good garlic toast is to rub raw garlic over the bread after it has been toasted and is still warm. The rough texture of the toasted bread acts like sandpaper on the garlic to release its flavor, while the warmth boosts its fragrance. Be sure to use a high-quality crusty bread, such as a baguette; do not use sliced sandwich bread.

Garlic Toasts

Makes 8 slices

Adjust oven rack 6 inches from broiler element and heat broiler. Spread eight 1-inch-thick slices rustic bread out evenly over rimmed baking sheet and broil, flipping as needed, until well toasted on both sides, about 4 minutes. Briefly rub 1 side of toasts with 1 peeled garlic clove, drizzle with 3 tablespoons extra-virgin olive oil, and season with salt and pepper to taste.

Turkish Tomato, Bulgur, and Red Pepper Soup

Serves 6 to 8; Total Time 1 hour

2 tablespoons extra-virgin olive oil

1 onion, chopped

2 red bell peppers, stemmed, seeded, and chopped

Salt and pepper

3 garlic cloves, minced

1 teaspoon dried mint, crumbled

½ teaspoon smoked paprika

⅛ teaspoon red pepper flakes

1 tablespoon tomato paste

½ cup dry white wine

1 (28-ounce) can diced fire-roasted tomatoes

4 cups chicken or vegetable broth

2 cups water

¾ cup medium-grind bulgur, rinsed

⅓ cup chopped fresh mint

why this recipe works

This Mediterranean-inspired take on tomato soup brings complexity and heartiness to a dish that's often boring and lifeless. We started by softening onion and red bell peppers before building a solid backbone with garlic, tomato paste, white wine, dried mint, smoked paprika, and red pepper flakes. Canned fire-roasted tomatoes contributed even more smokiness and depth. We then added nutty bulgur; stirred into soup, this quick-cooking whole grain absorbs the surrounding flavors and gives off starch that creates a silky texture—no cream needed. We stirred in the bulgur toward the end, giving it just enough time to become tender. A sprinkle of fresh mint gave the soup a final punch of flavor. When shopping, don't confuse bulgur with cracked wheat, which has a much longer cooking time and will not work in this recipe.

1. Heat oil in Dutch oven over medium heat until shimmering. Add onion, bell peppers, ¾ teaspoon salt, and ¼ teaspoon pepper and cook until softened and lightly browned, 6 to 8 minutes. Stir in garlic, dried mint, paprika, and pepper flakes and cook until fragrant, about 30 seconds. Stir in tomato paste and cook for 1 minute.

2. Stir in wine, scraping up any browned bits, and simmer until reduced by half, about 1 minute. Add tomatoes and their juice and cook, stirring occasionally, until tomatoes soften and begin to break apart, about 10 minutes.

3. Stir in broth, water, and bulgur and bring to simmer. Reduce heat to low, cover, and simmer gently until bulgur is tender, about 20 minutes. Season with salt and pepper to taste. Serve, sprinkling individual portions with fresh mint.

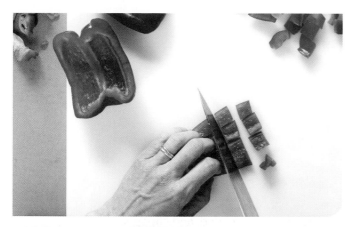

think like a cook

SMOKE WITHOUT FIRE

You've probably had food cooked over a live fire, whether it was grilled, barbecued, spit-roasted, or cooked in a fancy wood-fired oven. So you know that there's a complexity of flavor that you only get when food comes into contact with actual flames and the resulting smoke. That flavor can be hard to access in the average home kitchen; however, there are other ways to get flame-roasted flavor into your food. We have a set of shortcut ingredients that we like to use. These include the smoked paprika and canned fire-roasted tomatoes used in this soup. Both of these ingredients carry deep, smoky flavor from the way they're prepared, and they impart that to any dish to which they're added. Another secret ingredient we'll deploy is liquid smoke, as in our Indoor Barbecued Spare Ribs (page 392). While it may sound like a chemical additive, liquid smoke is made by channeling smoke from smoldering wood chips through a condenser, which quickly cools the vapors, causing them to liquefy (just like the drops that form when you breathe on cold glass). The water-soluble flavor compounds in the smoke are trapped within this liquid, while the insoluble tars and resins are removed by a series of filters, resulting in a clean, smoke-flavored liquid. A good version should contain nothing but smoke and water and will lend pure smoky flavor to any dish.

Gazpacho
Serves 8 to 10; Total Time 25 minutes (plus chilling time)

1½ pounds tomatoes, cored and cut into ¼-inch pieces

2 red bell peppers, stemmed, seeded, and cut into ¼-inch pieces

2 small cucumbers: 1 cucumber peeled, both sliced lengthwise, seeded (see page 29), and cut into ¼-inch pieces

½ small sweet onion, chopped fine, or 2 large shallots, minced

⅓ cup sherry vinegar

2 garlic cloves, minced

Salt and pepper

5 cups tomato juice

8 ice cubes

1 teaspoon hot sauce (optional)

Extra-virgin olive oil

1. Combine tomatoes, bell peppers, cucumbers, onion, vinegar, garlic, and 2 teaspoons salt in large (at least 4-quart) bowl and season with pepper to taste. Let stand until vegetables just begin to release their juices, about 5 minutes.

2. Stir in tomato juice, ice cubes, and hot sauce, if using. Cover and refrigerate to let flavors blend, at least 4 hours or up to 2 days.

3. Discard any unmelted ice cubes and season with salt and pepper to taste. Serve cold, drizzling individual bowls with oil.

why this recipe works

Cold soup! By all rights, it should be a travesty, and yet good gazpacho is ideal warm weather fare that perfectly showcases the brightness of fresh vegetables. We started by chopping the vegetables by hand instead of in a food processor, which ensured they retained their color and firm texture. Letting them sit briefly in a sherry vinegar marinade seasoned them both inside and out, while a combination of tomato juice and ice cubes (which helped chill the soup) provided the right amount of liquid. Chilling for at least 4 hours was critical to allow the flavors to develop and meld. Use a Vidalia, Maui, or Walla Walla (i.e., sweet) onion here. This recipe makes a large quantity because the leftovers are so good, but it can be halved if you prefer. Traditionally, gazpacho is garnished with more of the same diced vegetables that are in the soup, so cut some extra. You can also serve the soup with Homemade Croutons (page 155), chopped pitted black olives, and finely diced avocados. Serve in chilled bowls.

think like a cook

COLD FOOD NEEDS MORE SALT: HOW TEMPERATURE AFFECTS TASTE

Have you ever noticed that food that tasted great right out of the oven can taste incredibly bland when you go back to eat the refrigerated leftovers the next day? It turns out that temperature affects both your ability to taste and the way flavor interacts with your senses.

Our ability to taste is heightened by microscopic receptors on our tastebuds that are extremely sensitive to temperature. These receptors perform better at temperatures close to the temperature inside our mouths than at cooler ones. In fact, studies have shown that when food cooled to 59 degrees or below is consumed, the channels barely open, minimizing flavor perception. However, when food is heated to 98.5 degrees, the channels open up and your flavor sensitivity can be up to 100 times greater. Higher temperatures can also dull flavor perception.

As an experiment, we made a batch of chicken broth, omitting the salt. Then we divided the broth into five batches and seasoned each, using no salt and 1, 2, 3, and 4 teaspoons of salt, respectively. Tasters sampled each broth at three different temperatures—180 degrees, 90 degrees, and 45 degrees. At first, tasters preferred the hot broth seasoned with 3 teaspoons of salt. But as the broth cooled, their preference changed. At 90 degrees, they preferred the broth with 2 teaspoons of salt, and at refrigerator temperature, they preferred the broth with 4 teaspoons salt.

So, dishes meant to be served hot should be reheated before eating, and dishes meant to be served chilled, like this gazpacho, must be aggressively seasoned to make up for the flavor-dulling effects of their cold temperatures. But the next time you make a dish to serve cold, don't jump the gun by oversalting while the food is still hot. Instead, season as you would normally, then, once the food is chilled, taste and add more salt and other seasonings as needed. See page 46 for more information about how to properly adjust seasonings during and after cooking.

Ginger Beef and Ramen Noodle Soup

Serves 4; Total Time 45 minutes

1 (1-pound) flank steak, trimmed

Salt and pepper

1 teaspoon vegetable oil

8 cups chicken broth

1 (2-inch) piece ginger, halved lengthwise and smashed

3 (2½-inch) strips lime zest plus 1 tablespoon juice

4 (3-ounce) packages instant ramen noodles, seasoning packets discarded

5 scallions, sliced thin

¼ cup soy sauce

¼ cup fresh cilantro leaves

1. Pat steak dry with paper towels and season with salt and pepper. Heat oil in 12-inch skillet over medium-high heat until just smoking. Add steak and cook until well browned and thermometer inserted into center registers 120 to 125 degrees for medium-rare, 6 to 8 minutes, flipping once. Transfer to cutting board, tent loosely with aluminum foil, and let rest for 5 minutes. Slice steak in half lengthwise, then slice thin against grain.

2. Meanwhile, bring broth, ginger, and lime zest to boil in Dutch oven over medium-high heat. Reduce heat to medium-low, cover, and simmer for 10 minutes.

3. Remove ginger and lime zest from broth with slotted spoon. Add noodles and cook until tender, about 3 minutes. Stir in scallions, soy sauce, and lime juice. Ladle noodles and broth into 4 serving bowls and divide steak and cilantro evenly among bowls. Serve.

why this recipe works

Ramen noodles: They're not just for completely broke college students anymore. In fact, it's really too bad they ever got that reputation in the first place. In Japan, ramen noodle soup is serious business, with whole restaurants specializing in the dish and countless variations. Although this rich, satisfying soup has been having a moment in the United States, it still feels like restaurant food. But you can make a pretty good approximation at home. Our simplified take uses lime zest and ginger simmered in chicken broth to build a deeply flavored base and then adds thin slices of quick-cooking flank steak on top for a protein boost. Smash the ginger using the flat side of a chef's knife. The familiar supermarket ramen noodles work well here; just discard the dusty flavoring packets. Use a vegetable peeler to remove strips of zest from the lime.

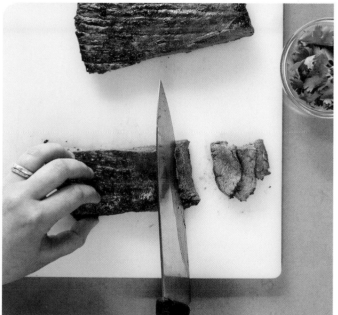

think like a cook

GINGER RULES

We love the pungency of fresh ginger in all kinds of recipes, from soups to stir-fries, but it does come with a few annoyances. First, most recipes that call for fresh ginger require very small amounts, so it's nearly impossible to use up a whole knob at once. Luckily, you can store leftover ginger in the fridge for up to two weeks (just toss it into the refrigerator unwrapped, as wrapping cut ginger in plastic or foil encourages mold). Another issue is that fresh ginger has that thin, papery brown skin that has to be removed before grating it (although it's fine to leave the skin on in this recipe, since the ginger goes into the broth in big pieces that are discarded later). A knife or regular vegetable peeler will remove lots of ginger along with the skin, and these tools are hard to maneuver around the knobs and bumps on the root. Because of this, our favorite way to peel ginger is to use the rounded edge of a small spoon to scrape off the skin (see photo on page 30).

Finally, ginger can be kind of a pain to grate. We like to use a rasp-style grater to do this, and to make it even easier, we sometimes freeze the ginger. The frozen ginger is easier to grate—it doesn't shred or break down like fresh ginger sometimes can with vigorous grating. The tiny teeth of the rasp-style grater are also much easier to clean after grating frozen ginger because the fibers neatly shear crosswise and don't leave frayed bits stuck in the grater. However, frozen ginger does grate up fluffier than unfrozen, so to get accurate volume measurement, you either have to let it thaw after grating or pack it gently into the measuring spoon.

Kimchi Beef and Tofu Soup

Serves 4 to 6; Total Time 1 hour

3 cups kimchi, in brine

1 pound sirloin steak tips, trimmed and cut into ½-inch pieces

Salt and pepper

1 tablespoon vegetable oil

1 tablespoon grated fresh ginger

½ cup mirin

3 cups water

2 cups beef broth

8 ounces firm tofu, cut into ½-inch cubes

4 scallions, sliced thin

1 tablespoon soy sauce

1 tablespoon toasted sesame oil

1. Measure out and reserve 1 cup kimchi brine. Drain kimchi and chop coarse. Pat beef dry with paper towels and season with salt and pepper.

2. Heat vegetable oil in Dutch oven over medium-high heat until just smoking. Add beef and brown on all sides, 8 to 10 minutes.

3. Stir ginger into pot and cook until fragrant, about 30 seconds. Slowly stir in mirin, scraping up any browned bits. Stir in kimchi, reserved kimchi liquid, water, and broth and bring to boil. Reduce heat to low, cover, and simmer until meat is tender, 25 to 30 minutes.

4. Off heat, stir tofu, scallions, soy sauce, and sesame oil into soup. Season with salt and pepper to taste. Serve.

why this recipe works

This simple Korean soup offers a double dose of hearty protein from beef and tofu along with tons of tangy flavor from kimchi, the spicy Korean pickled vegetable condiment. We balanced the kimchi with sweetness from mirin, a Japanese cooking wine that mellows out during cooking. However, this is still a soup with a bit of a bite. Don't discard the kimchi pickling liquid when you measure out the vegetables as it is quite flavorful. We added a cup to our broth for extra zing. You can find kimchi in the refrigerated section of Asian markets and many well-stocked supermarkets. Kimchi varies in heat intensity, flavor, and pungency. If possible, avoid brands with a strong fish or shrimp flavor, which can overpower the beef. For our recipe's supple, tender bites of tofu, we chose firm tofu. Sirloin steak tips, also known as flap meat, are sold as whole steaks, cubes, and strips. To ensure uniform pieces that cook evenly, we prefer to purchase whole steak tips and cut them ourselves.

think like a cook

UNDERSTANDING FERMENTATION

Kimchi is a traditional fermented Korean pickle usually made with napa cabbage (but it can also be made with radish, cucumber, or even watermelon rind). The vegetables are chopped and then salted (to pull out moisture) or packed in a liquid brine and left to ferment. Fermentation is a process in which bacteria and/or yeasts consume the carbohydrates and proteins naturally present in foods, producing alcohols, lactic acid, and/or carbon dioxide as byproducts. Water and salt create a fermentation-friendly environment by preventing bad microbes from forming, giving the good bacteria that cause fermentation a chance to develop. Fermentation's byproducts further inhibit the growth of bacteria and enzymatic activity that create spoilage, so fermentation helps preserve food. It also alters food's flavor, texture, and aroma. Fermented foods are easier to digest, and their bacteria are thought to offer health benefits—which helps explain what makes them so popular.

Foods like pickles (including kimchi), vinegar, and yogurt have the tang that we associate with fermentation. And of course beer and wine are fermented. But everyday foods like chocolate, coffee, olives, bread, vanilla, hot sauce, and cheese also get deep flavor from fermentation. You've probably been enjoying fermented foods your whole life without even realizing it!

Greek Chicken and Rice Soup with Egg and Lemon (Avgolemono)

Serve 4 to 6; Total Time 50 minutes

1½ pounds boneless, skinless chicken breasts, trimmed

Salt and pepper

12 (3-inch) strips lemon zest plus 6 tablespoons juice and extra juice for seasoning (3 lemons)

2 sprigs fresh dill, plus 2 teaspoons chopped

2 teaspoons coriander seeds

1 teaspoon black peppercorns

1 garlic clove, peeled and smashed

8 cups chicken broth

1 cup long-grain rice

2 large eggs plus 2 large yolks

1. Cut each chicken breast in half lengthwise. Toss with 1¾ teaspoons salt and let stand at room temperature for at least 15 minutes or up to 30 minutes. Cut 8-inch square of triple-thickness cheesecloth. Place lemon zest, dill sprigs, coriander seeds, peppercorns, and garlic in center of cheesecloth and tie into bundle with kitchen twine.

2. Bring broth, rice, and spice bundle to boil in large saucepan over high heat. Reduce heat to low, cover, and cook for 5 minutes. Turn off heat, add chicken, cover, and let stand for 15 minutes.

3. Transfer chicken to large plate and discard spice bundle. Using two forks, shred chicken into bite-size pieces. Using ladle, transfer 1 cup cooked rice to blender (leave any liquid in pot). Add lemon juice and eggs and yolks to blender and process until smooth, about 1 minute.

4. Return chicken and any accumulated juices to pot. Return soup to simmer over high heat. Remove pot from heat and stir in egg mixture until fully incorporated. Stir in chopped dill and season with salt, pepper, and extra lemon juice to taste. Serve.

why this recipe works

Like our Creamy Cauliflower Soup (page 236), this recipe is creamy and rich without containing any cream. Instead, this thick, tangy Greek chicken and rice soup gets its texture and flavor from an egg-lemon mixture. For more savory depth and to enhance the lemon flavor, we added an herb and spice bundle (peppercorns, citrusy coriander, lemon zest, garlic, and dill) neatly tied in cheesecloth. Processing eggs, yolks, and a portion of the cooked rice in a blender and then stirring this puree into the hot broth gave our avgolemono a velvety consistency (and helped us avoid scrambled-egg soup). If you have homemade chicken broth (see page 270), we recommend using it in this recipe, as it gives the soup the best flavor and body. Use a vegetable peeler to remove strips of zest from the lemons.

think like a cook

CHOOSING AND JUICING LEMONS

Most of us know that getting as much juice as possible out of a lemon—let alone what is asked for in a recipe—can be a mind- and hand-numbing experience (of course, if you have any tiny cuts on your hand, it is the opposite of numbing—and still not fun). How do you get the most juice from a lemon with the least amount of effort?

First of all, choose your lemons wisely. We've squeezed a lot of lemons in the test kitchen, and still we're amazed at how one lemon can yield two or three times more juice than a seemingly identical one. Wondering if there was a way to tell which lemons contained the most juice, we bought lemons in all shapes and sizes and had a squeezing extravaganza.

We found that certain shapes and sizes can give a hint as to the amount of juice inside. Round lemons were slightly juicier than elliptical ones, and unsurprisingly, bigger lemons yielded more juice than smaller ones. But the best way to find the lemons with the most juice is to squeeze while you shop. Without fail, whole lemons that yielded under pressure contained more juice, even when the lemons were nearly identical in size, shape, and weight.

Cutting into two lemons showed us the reason. The harder lemons had thicker pith (that spongy, bitter white membrane that separates the pulp from the peel), meaning there was less space for juice inside.

As for getting all that juice out, we've tried countless methods and gizmos for juicing lemons and have dismissed most of them. However, we do endorse rolling the lemon vigorously on a hard surface before slicing it open to be juiced. Rolling bruises, breaks up, and softens the rind's tissues while it tears the membranes of the juice vesicles (tear-shaped juice sacs), filling the inside of the lemon with juice even before it is squeezed. Once it's rolled, we recommend using either a wooden reamer, which effectively digs into and tears the lemon to extract as much juice as possible, or a citrus squeezer, which we find is especially easy and fast and equally as effective (see page 447).

New England Clam Chowder
Serves 6; Total Time 1 hour 30 minutes

3 cups water

6 pounds medium hard-shell clams, such as cherrystones

2 slices bacon, chopped fine

2 onions, chopped fine

2 celery ribs, chopped fine

1 teaspoon minced fresh thyme or ¼ teaspoon dried

⅓ cup all-purpose flour

3 (8-ounce) bottles clam juice

1½ pounds Yukon Gold potatoes, peeled and cut into ½-inch pieces

1 bay leaf

1 cup heavy cream

2 tablespoons minced fresh parsley

Salt and pepper

why this recipe works

This New England classic is best when it's packed full of sweet, briny clams and tender potatoes in a rich, creamy broth. For an approachable recipe that didn't skimp on flavor, we started with medium clams that we steamed open instead of laboriously shucking. Mixing 2 cups of the clam steaming liquid with 3 cups of bottled clam juice gave lots of clam taste without being too salty. Yukon Gold potatoes blended seamlessly into our creamy chowder. Thickening the chowder with flour helped to stabilize it; otherwise it can easily separate and curdle. Cream is essential; using a relatively modest amount provided richness without overpowering the flavor of the clams. Finally, we used bacon rather than salt pork, a traditional component of chowder, to enrich the flavor with a subtle smokiness. Serve with oyster crackers.

1. Bring water to boil in Dutch oven over medium-high heat. Scrub clams, add to pot, cover, and cook for 5 minutes. Stir clams thoroughly and continue to cook, covered, until they begin to open, 2 to 7 minutes. Transfer clams to large bowl as they open; let cool slightly. Discard any clams that refuse to open.

2. Measure out and reserve 2 cups of clam steaming liquid, avoiding any gritty sediment that has settled on bottom of pot. Remove clam meat from shells and chop coarse.

3. Clean now-empty Dutch oven, add bacon, and cook over medium heat until crisp, 5 to 7 minutes. Stir in onions and celery and cook until vegetables are softened, 5 to 7 minutes. Stir in thyme and cook until fragrant, about 30 seconds. Stir in flour and cook for 1 minute.

4. Gradually whisk in bottled clam juice and reserved clam steaming liquid, scraping up any browned bits and smoothing out any lumps. Stir in potatoes and bay leaf and bring to boil. Reduce heat to gentle simmer and cook until potatoes are tender, 20 to 25 minutes. (Chopped clams and soup can be refrigerated in separate containers for up to 24 hours; return broth to simmer before proceeding.)

5. Stir in cream and return to brief simmer. Off heat, discard bay leaf, stir in parsley, and season with salt and pepper to taste. Stir in chopped clams, cover, and let warm through, about 1 minute. Serve.

think like a cook

CLAM TIPS

If you're not used to cooking with clams or other shell-fish, they can be a little intimidating, but they're much easier to handle than you might expect. Even though clams are usually sold by the piece at the fish market, we find it more accurate to buy them by weight than by quantity. Just ask your fishmonger to weigh the clams as they count them. For the best flavor and texture, clams should be as fresh as possible. They should smell clean, not sour or sulfurous. The shells should look moist. Look for tightly closed clams—avoid any that are cracked, broken, or sitting in a puddle of water. Some shells may gape slightly, but they should close when they are tapped. Discard any clams that won't close; they may be dead and should not be eaten.

Most clams today are farmed and virtually free of grit. (Soft-shell clams, if you can find them, almost always contain a lot of sand and should be submerged in a large bowl of cold water and drained several times to wash away the sand before cooking.) Clams need to be scrubbed and rinsed; use a brush to remove any sand trapped in the outer shell. The best way to store clams is in the refrigerator in a colander of ice set over a bowl; discard any water that accumulates so that the shellfish are never submerged.

Black Bean Chili

Serves 6 to 8; Total Time 3 hours

1 pound white mushrooms, trimmed and broken into rough pieces

1 tablespoon mustard seeds

2 teaspoons cumin seeds

3 tablespoons vegetable oil

1 onion, chopped fine

9 garlic cloves, minced

1 tablespoon minced canned chipotle chile in adobo sauce

3 tablespoons chili powder

2½ cups vegetable broth

2½ cups water, plus extra as needed

1 pound (2½ cups) dried black beans, picked over and rinsed

1 tablespoon packed light brown sugar

⅛ teaspoon baking soda

2 bay leaves

1 (28-ounce) can crushed tomatoes

2 red bell peppers, stemmed, seeded, and cut into ½-inch pieces

½ cup minced fresh cilantro

Salt and pepper

why this recipe works

Just because your chili doesn't have meat doesn't mean it can't be satisfying. For this vegetarian chili, we used dried beans for their superior texture. However, we didn't bother soaking the beans beforehand; we liked the fact that when we used unsoaked beans, some of them burst during cooking, thickening the chili. White mushrooms, pulsed in a food processor and sautéed with onions, gave the chili meaty texture and flavor. Whole cumin seeds and minced chipotle chile added depth and smokiness, and toasted mustard seeds added complexity. Served with a spritz of lime and a sprinkle of cilantro, this rich chili is so hearty that you won't miss the meat. We prefer the texture and flavor of toasted cumin and mustard seeds here; however, you can substitute ½ teaspoon ground cumin and/or ½ teaspoon dry mustard; add with the chili powder in step 3. Serve with lime wedges, sour cream, shredded cheddar or Monterey Jack cheese, chopped tomatoes, and/or minced onion.

1. Adjust oven rack to lower-middle position and heat oven to 325 degrees. Pulse mushrooms in food processor until uniformly coarsely chopped, about 10 pulses.

2. Toast mustard seeds and cumin seeds in Dutch oven over medium heat, stirring constantly, until fragrant, about 1 minute. Stir in oil, onion, and processed mushrooms, cover, and cook until vegetables have released their liquid, about 5 minutes. Uncover and continue to cook until vegetables are browned, 5 to 10 minutes.

3. Stir in garlic and chipotle and cook until fragrant, about 30 seconds. Stir in chili powder and cook, stirring constantly, until fragrant, about 1 minute. Stir in broth, water, beans, sugar, baking soda, and bay leaves and bring to simmer, skimming as needed. Cover, transfer to oven, and cook for 1 hour.

4. Stir in crushed tomatoes and bell peppers and continue to cook in oven, covered, until beans are fully tender, about 1 hour longer. (If chili begins to stick to bottom of pot or is too thick, add water as needed.)

5. Remove pot from oven and discard bay leaves. Stir in cilantro, season with salt and pepper to taste, and serve. (Chili can be refrigerated for up to 3 days; add water as needed when reheating to adjust consistency.)

think like a cook

UNUSUAL USES FOR BAKING SODA

You're probably familiar with baking soda as a baking staple. In that context it provides leavening and encourages browning in muffins, cakes, and more, but there are other ways you can put this ingredient to work. In this recipe, baking soda's alkaline nature helps break down the cell structure of the beans, resulting in tender beans in less time. This is similar to how it's helping in our Creamy Parmesan Polenta (page 224). It also helps set the color of the black beans. In other recipes, like our Best Ground Beef Chili (page 260), we treat meat with baking soda to help it retain moisture. The increased browning seen in baked goods also applies when we add baking soda to meat: By changing the pH, the meat browns more quickly.

You may have heard that baking soda can also absorb or neutralize odors from the refrigerator or freezer, but our tests putting an open box of baking soda into stinky environments were inconclusive. While it does neutralize acids, the likelihood of gaseous molecules from, say, acidic sour milk coming in contact with the baking soda is slight. However, when this alkaline powder comes into direct contact with smells, it can make a difference. We tested different approaches to removing garlic and onion smells from a cutting board and found scrubbing with a paste of 1 tablespoon baking soda and 1 teaspoon water to be the most effective.

Best Ground Beef Chili

Serves 8 to 10; Total Time 2 hours 45 minutes

why this recipe works

Ground beef chili is way more convenient than chili made with whole chunks of meat, but a truly great version requires a few tricks. To keep the meat moist and tender, we treated it with salt and baking soda (see "Unusual Uses for Baking Soda," page 259). Both ingredients helped the meat hold on to moisture, so it stayed juicy and didn't shed liquid during cooking, which would water down the chili. We also simmered the meat for 90 minutes to fully tenderize it. We made a simple but deeply flavored home-made chili powder, bolstered that with canned chipotles, and cooked both in the fat rendered by the beef to bloom the flavors of the fat-soluble spices throughout the dish. This chili is intensely flavored and should be served with tortilla chips and/or white rice and your favorite chili garnishes, such as lime wedges, chopped cilantro, and minced onion. Diced avocado, sour cream, and shredded Monterey Jack or cheddar cheese are also good options for garnishing.

2 pounds 85 percent lean ground beef

2 tablespoons plus 2 cups water

Salt and pepper

¾ teaspoon baking soda

6 dried ancho chiles, stemmed, seeded, and torn into 1-inch pieces

1 ounce tortilla chips, crushed (¼ cup)

2 tablespoons ground cumin

1 tablespoon paprika

1 tablespoon garlic powder

1 tablespoon ground coriander

2 teaspoons dried oregano

½ teaspoon dried thyme

1 (14.5-ounce) can whole peeled tomatoes

1 tablespoon vegetable oil

1 onion, chopped fine

3 garlic cloves, minced

1–2 teaspoons minced canned chipotle chile in adobo sauce

1 (15-ounce) can pinto beans

2 teaspoons sugar

2 tablespoons cider vinegar

1. Adjust oven rack to lower-middle position and heat oven to 275 degrees. Toss beef with 2 tablespoons water, 1½ teaspoons salt, and baking soda in bowl until thoroughly combined. Set aside for 20 minutes.

2. Meanwhile, toast anchos in Dutch oven over medium-high heat, stirring frequently, until fragrant, 4 to 6 minutes, reducing heat if anchos begin to smoke. Transfer to food processor and let cool.

3. Add tortilla chips, cumin, paprika, garlic powder, coriander, oregano, thyme, and 2 teaspoons pepper to food processor with anchos and process until finely ground, about 2 minutes. Transfer mixture to bowl. Process tomatoes and their juice in now-empty workbowl until smooth, about 30 seconds.

4. Heat oil in now-empty pot over medium-high heat until shimmering. Add onion and cook, stirring occasionally, until softened, 4 to 6 minutes. Add garlic and cook until fragrant, about 1 minute. Add beef and cook, stirring to break meat up into ¼-inch pieces, until beef is browned and fond begins to form on pot bottom, 12 to 14 minutes. Add ancho mixture and chipotle; cook, stirring frequently, until fragrant, 1 to 2 minutes.

5. Add tomato puree, remaining 2 cups water, beans and their liquid, and sugar. Bring to boil, scraping bottom of pot to loosen any browned bits. Cover, transfer to oven, and cook until meat is tender and chili is slightly thickened, 1½ to 2 hours, stirring occasionally to prevent sticking.

6. Remove chili from oven and let stand, uncovered, for 10 minutes. Stir in any fat that has risen to top of chili, then add vinegar and season with salt to taste. Serve. (Chili can be refrigerated for up to 3 days; add water as needed when reheating to adjust consistency.)

think like a cook

DRIED CHILES

Dried chiles offer more than just heat; their flavors vary from earthy and fruity to bright and acidic. While store-bought chili powder (a blend of dried chiles and other spices) and various ground dried chiles work well in many instances, we believe it is worth toasting and grinding or rehydrating dried chiles for superior flavor. Toast chiles in a dry pan over medium-high heat until dry and fragrant, 4 to 6 minutes. (Remove stems and seeds before toasting.) Then either grind in a spice grinder or food processor or soak in warm water until softened but not mushy, about 20 minutes; drain well and use. The commonly available chiles fall into broad flavor categories.

Fruity: Guajillo
These chiles have a mildly hot flavor backed by a subtle natural smokiness.

Earthy: Ancho
Deep, rich flavors that bring to mind chocolate, coffee, raisins, and licorice characterize these chiles.

Smoky: Chipotle
These chiles have charred wood, tobacco, and barbecue flavors balanced by subtle sweetness.

Sweet: New Mexico
This chile has a fresh, sweet flavor reminiscent of roasted red peppers and tomatoes.

Classic Beef Stew

Serves 6 to 8; Total Time 3 hours

1 (3½- to 4-pound) boneless beef chuck-eye roast, pulled apart at seams, trimmed, and cut into 1½-inch pieces

Salt and pepper

2 tablespoons vegetable oil

2 onions, chopped fine

1 tablespoon tomato paste

2 garlic cloves, minced

¼ cup all-purpose flour

3 cups chicken broth

¾ cup dry red wine

1 teaspoon minced fresh thyme

2 bay leaves

1½ pounds Yukon Gold potatoes, unpeeled, cut into 1-inch pieces

1 pound carrots, peeled and cut into 1-inch pieces

2 tablespoons minced fresh parsley

1 cup frozen peas, thawed

why this recipe works

Beef stew is among the all-time best comfort foods. A great version should be rich and satisfying, with tender vegetables and meat draped in gravy. Sadly, many recipes result in dry, tough meat and a watery, bland sauce. To create a foolproof take on this classic, we started with flavorful chuck-eye roast and cut it into pieces ourselves rather than buying chunks of precut "stew beef." Instead of searing the beef before adding it to the stew, we simply cooked the stew uncovered in the oven. This browned the exposed meat and also let some of the sauce evaporate, concentrating its flavor. Along with traditional components like onions, garlic, red wine, and chicken broth, we added tomato paste, which contributed extra savory flavor. Potatoes, carrots, and peas rounded out our classic stew. Use a good-quality, medium-bodied wine, such as a Côtes du Rhône or Pinot Noir, for this stew. Try to find beef that is well marbled with white veins of fat. Meat that is too lean will come out slightly dry.

1. Adjust oven rack to lower-middle position and heat oven to 325 degrees. Pat meat dry with paper towels and season with salt and pepper. Heat oil in Dutch oven over medium-high heat until shimmering. Add onions and cook, stirring often, until well browned, 8 to 10 minutes.

2. Stir in tomato paste and garlic and cook until fragrant, about 2 minutes. Stir in flour and cook for 1 minute. Whisk in broth, wine, thyme, and bay leaves, scraping up any browned bits and smoothing out any lumps. Stir in beef and bring to simmer. Transfer pot to oven and cook, uncovered, for 1½ hours, stirring halfway through cooking.

3. Stir in potatoes and carrots and continue to cook in oven, uncovered, until beef and vegetables are tender, about 1 hour, stirring halfway through cooking.

4. Remove pot from oven. Discard bay leaves. Using large spoon, skim excess fat from surface of stew. Stir in parsley and peas and let peas warm through, about 2 minutes. Season with salt and pepper to taste, and serve. (Stew can be refrigerated for up to 3 days; add water as needed when reheating to adjust consistency.)

think like a cook

CUTTING STEW MEAT

Prepackaged beef stew meat is convenient but not very good. In most markets, the pieces are much too small and are unevenly butchered, so small pieces overcook by the time larger ones are done. Even more problematic is the meat itself. Sometimes it comes from the desired chuck, but often it contains scraps from all over the cow, many of which are not very flavorful. Instead, we recommend buying a single cut and cutting it up yourself. For a beef stew, start with a chuck-eye roast.

To turn the whole roast into stew meat, use your hands to pull apart the roast at its major seams (see how on page 385), which are delineated by lines of fat. Cut away all exposed fat. Then cut the meat into large chunks, usually 1½ to 2 inches. (We think bigger chunks make better stew. They also are less likely to overcook.) Trim any hard knobs of white fat as you work. Don't bother trimming soft, thin lines of fat—they will melt during the stewing process and lubricate the meat.

Best Chicken Stew
Serves 6 to 8; Total Time 2 hours 30 minutes

why this recipe works

Beef stew is great, and it's a classic. But don't limit yourself! Chicken stew can be just as meaty, rich, and satisfying. For ours, we started with two different chicken parts: We seared collagen-rich wings to create a base of rich chicken flavor and plenty of thickening gelatin, then we gently simmered halved boneless chicken thighs so we'd have tender bites throughout the stew. To boost the meatiness of the whole dish, we used an umami-packed combination of bacon, soy sauce, and anchovy paste (for more on umami, see page 189). Finally, we took full advantage of the concentrating effect of reduction by cooking down wine, broth, and aromatics at the start and simmering the stew uncovered during its stay in the oven. Mashed anchovy fillets (rinsed and dried before mashing) can be used instead of anchovy paste. Use small red potatoes measuring 1½ inches in diameter.

2 pounds boneless, skinless chicken thighs, halved crosswise and trimmed

Kosher salt and pepper

3 slices bacon, chopped

1 pound chicken wings, cut at joints

1 onion, chopped fine

1 celery rib, minced

2 garlic cloves, minced

2 teaspoons anchovy paste

1 teaspoon minced fresh thyme

5 cups chicken broth

1 cup dry white wine, plus extra for seasoning

1 tablespoon soy sauce

3 tablespoons unsalted butter, cut into 3 pieces

⅓ cup all-purpose flour

1 pound small red potatoes, unpeeled, quartered

4 carrots, peeled and cut into ½-inch pieces

2 tablespoons chopped fresh parsley

1. Adjust oven rack to lower-middle position and heat oven to 325 degrees. Arrange chicken thighs on baking sheet and lightly season both sides with salt and pepper; cover with plastic wrap and set aside.

2. Cook bacon in Dutch oven over medium-low heat, stirring occasionally, until fat renders and bacon browns, 6 to 8 minutes. Using slotted spoon, transfer bacon to medium bowl. Add chicken wings to pot, increase heat to medium, and cook until well browned on both sides, 10 to 12 minutes; transfer wings to bowl with bacon.

3. Add onion, celery, garlic, anchovy paste, and thyme to fat in pot; cook, stirring occasionally, until dark fond forms on pan bottom, 2 to 4 minutes. Increase heat to high; stir in 1 cup broth, wine, and soy sauce, scraping up any browned bits; and bring to boil. Cook, stirring occasionally, until liquid evaporates and vegetables begin to sizzle again, 12 to 15 minutes. Add butter and stir to melt; sprinkle flour over vegetables and stir to combine. Gradually whisk in remaining 4 cups broth until smooth. Stir in wings and bacon, potatoes, and carrots; bring to simmer. Transfer to oven and cook, uncovered, for 30 minutes, stirring once halfway through cooking.

4. Remove pot from oven. Use wooden spoon to draw gravy up sides of pot and scrape browned fond into stew. Place over high heat, add thighs, and bring to simmer. Return pot to oven, uncovered, and continue to cook, stirring occasionally, until thigh meat offers no resistance when poked with fork and vegetables are tender, about 45 minutes longer. (Stew can be refrigerated for up to 2 days; add water as needed when reheating to adjust consistency.)

5. Discard wings and season stew with up to 2 tablespoons extra wine. Season with salt and pepper to taste, sprinkle with parsley, and serve.

think like a cook

THE MANY USES OF A DUTCH OVEN

In this recipe, as in many of our soups and stews, we use one of our favorite kitchen workhorses, an enameled cast-iron Dutch oven. Thicker and heavier than a traditional stockpot and deeper than a skillet, a Dutch oven (also called a round oven, French oven, or casserole) is pretty high on our list of kitchen essentials. Their thickness and heaviness make them the best choice for braises, pot roasts, and stews, since they can go from the stovetop to the oven. Their tall sides also make them useful for deep frying. If you don't have a large stockpot, Dutch ovens are also very useful for jobs like boiling water for pasta. We even bake bread in it—see our Almost No-Knead Bread (page 434), which uses the steamy environment in a covered Dutch oven to create a homemade loaf with a dramatic open-crumbed structure and shatteringly crisp crust. All in all, while a good Dutch oven probably won't be the cheapest piece of equipment you buy for your kitchen (nor will it be the lightest), we think it's one of the most useful tools you can invest in. (See our shopping guide on page 444.)

African Sweet Potato and Peanut Stew

Serves 6; Total Time 1 hour

1¼ cups dry-roasted peanuts

2 tablespoons unsalted butter

1 onion, chopped fine

1 red bell pepper, stemmed, seeded, and cut into ½-inch pieces

Salt and pepper

3 garlic cloves, minced

½ teaspoon ground coriander

¼ teaspoon cayenne pepper

2 pounds sweet potatoes, peeled and cut into ½-inch pieces

6 cups chicken broth

¼ cup minced fresh cilantro

1. Coarsely chop peanuts. Place peanuts in dry 10-inch skillet and toast over medium heat, shaking pan occasionally, until golden and fragrant, 3 to 5 minutes. Transfer to bowl to cool.

2. Melt butter in Dutch oven over medium heat. Add onion, bell pepper, and ½ teaspoon salt and cook until softened, about 5 minutes. Stir in garlic, coriander, and cayenne and cook until fragrant, about 30 seconds.

3. Stir in sweet potatoes, broth, and 1 cup chopped peanuts and bring to boil. Reduce heat to low and cook, partially covered, until sweet potatoes are tender, 15 to 20 minutes.

4. Measure out 2 cups solids and 1 cup liquid from soup and transfer to blender. Process in blender until completely smooth, about 30 seconds. Return to pot with remaining soup and stir to combine.

5. Stir in cilantro and season with salt and pepper to taste. Serve, sprinkling individual portions with remaining ¼ cup chopped peanuts.

why this recipe works

Sweet potatoes are a highly nutritious vegetable unjustly relegated to side dish status in most American meals. In other parts of the world, however, they are used more widely. This nourishing Senegalese-inspired stew featuring sweet potatoes has an appealing blend of savory and sweet flavors. Dry-roasted peanuts contribute rich, roasted flavor that perfectly complements the earthy sweetness of the sweet potatoes. Pureeing some of the stew gives the broth body while the rest of the dish retains a chunky texture. To make this recipe vegetarian, just substitute vegetable broth for the chicken broth. Although the recipe was developed with standard sweet potatoes (called Beauregards), Jewel and Red Garnet sweet potatoes also work well. But do stick to the orange-fleshed varieties; white- or purple-fleshed sweet potatoes will not work here.

think like a cook

FREEZING AND REHEATING SOUPS

Many soups and stews make a generous number of servings. We recommend stocking your freezer with the leftovers so you can reheat them whenever you like. In general, we recommend freezing broths and soups for no longer than one month. Here's the information you need to properly store and thaw your soups so they are just as flavorful as freshly made.

We like to freeze soup in airtight plastic storage containers; remember to leave a little room at the top of the container(s) to prevent the lid(s) from popping off. Note: Creamy soups and soups that have a pasta component don't freeze very well. The dairy curdles as it freezes and the pasta turns bloated and mushy. Instead, make and freeze the soup without the dairy or pasta component included. After you have thawed the soup and it has been heated through, stir in the uncooked pasta and simmer until just tender, or stir in the dairy and continue to heat gently until hot (do not let it boil).

For safety reasons, we recommend thawing frozen soups and stews in the refrigerator, never at room temperature, for 24 to 48 hours. (That said, if you've forgotten to plan ahead, you can heat frozen soups directly on the stovetop or in the microwave, but the texture of meat and vegetables will suffer a bit.) We prefer to reheat large amounts of soup in a heavy-bottomed pot on the stovetop. Bring the soup to a rolling boil and make sure to stir often to ensure the entire pot reaches the boiling point. If you use the microwave, avoid reheating in the same container used to refrigerate or freeze the soup. Instead, transfer the food to a dish that's somewhat larger than the storage container, and be sure to cover the dish to prevent a mess. Make sure to stop and stir several times to ensure that the soup reheats evenly.

Here's an easy way to freeze convenient single servings of soup: Set out a number of 10- or 12-ounce paper cups for hot beverages and fill each with a portion of cooled soup (but not all the way to the top). Label, wrap well in plastic wrap, and freeze each cup. To reheat one serving, pop the soup into a bowl or mug, cover, and microwave until hot and ready to serve.

Shrimp and Sausage Gumbo
Serves 6 to 8; Total Time 2 hours 20 minutes

why this recipe works

A trademark dish of Louisiana cooking, gumbo is a thick, hearty stew featuring a host of meats, seafood, and vegetables. Its defining ingredient is a dark roux, a slow-cooked combination of fat and flour that adds flavor and thickens the dish. Many recipes say to stir the roux over low heat for up to an hour, watching it carefully the whole time. We make the techniqe more hands-off by toasting the flour on the stovetop, adding the oil, and finishing the roux in the gentle heat of the oven. Convenient chicken broth fortified with fish sauce was an easy substitute for traditional shrimp stock. Gumbos can include seafood, poultry, small game, and sausage. We liked a mix of andouille sausage (a garlicky sausage typical of Cajun cooking), chicken, and shrimp. The chicken broth must be at room temperature to prevent lumps from forming.

¾ cup plus 1 tablespoon all-purpose flour

½ cup vegetable oil

1 onion, chopped fine

1 green bell pepper, stemmed, seeded, and chopped

1 celery rib, chopped fine

5 garlic cloves, minced

1 teaspoon minced fresh thyme

¼ teaspoon cayenne pepper

1 (14.5-ounce) can diced tomatoes, drained

3¾ cups chicken broth, room temperature

¼ cup fish sauce

4 (5- to 7-ounce) bone-in chicken thighs, skin and excess fat removed

Salt and pepper

8 ounces andouille sausage, halved lengthwise and sliced thin

2 cups frozen okra, thawed (optional)

2 pounds extra-large shrimp (21 to 25 per pound), peeled and deveined (see page 99)

1. Adjust oven rack to lowest position and heat oven to 350 degrees. Toast ¾ cup flour in Dutch oven on stovetop over medium heat, stirring constantly, until just beginning to brown, about 5 minutes. Off heat, whisk in oil until smooth. Cover, transfer pot to oven, and cook until mixture is deep brown and fragrant, about 45 minutes. (Roux can be refrigerated in airtight container for 1 week. To use, heat in Dutch oven over medium-high heat, whisking constantly, until just smoking, and continue with step 2.)

2. Transfer Dutch oven to stovetop and whisk cooked roux to combine. Add onion, bell pepper, and celery and cook over medium heat, stirring frequently, until softened, about 10 minutes. Stir in remaining 1 tablespoon flour, garlic, thyme, and cayenne and cook until fragrant, about 1 minute. Add tomatoes and cook until dry, about 1 minute. Slowly whisk in broth and fish sauce until smooth. Season chicken with pepper. Add chicken and bring to boil.

3. Reduce heat to medium-low and simmer, covered, until chicken is tender, about 30 minutes. Skim fat and transfer chicken to plate. When chicken is cool enough to handle, cut into bite-size pieces and return to pot; discard bones.

4. Stir in sausage and okra, if using, and simmer until heated through, about 5 minutes. Add shrimp and simmer until cooked through, about 5 minutes. Season with salt and pepper to taste. Serve. (Gumbo can be refrigerated for up to 24 hours.)

think like a cook

ROUX BASICS

Roux has been used as a go-to thickener in many cuisines for centuries. Even if they didn't know what was happening on the molecular level, cooks understood that adding a cooked mixture of flour and fat to sauces and stews caused key textural and flavor changes in the dish. But there is some pretty interesting chemistry behind these clearly observable reactions. Notably, the flavoring and thickening properties of a roux are interrelated.

Roux are always cooked to a specific shade, which can range from white to blond to peanut butter—and even darker. The darker the color, the more pronounced the roux's flavor. But as a roux darkens, its thickening power lessens. This is because the intense heat from frying the flour in fat causes its starch chains to break down, and the smaller starch chains are less efficient thickeners. So the longer a roux is cooked, the less effective at thickening it will be. Thus it's important to cook a roux to the right color. If you shortchange the cooking time for the roux in a stew recipe like this gumbo, you could end up with a gloppy, overly thickened dish.

In this recipe, we take an unconventional approach to roux that achieves the same results with little need for fussy stirring and a much lower risk of either burning the roux or burning yourself. We achieved this by toasting the flour by itself first before adding the oil, then moving the pot to the oven where the even heat and closed lid provided the perfect no-stir environment for it to brown and thicken. It still takes 45 minutes, but since it's completely hands-off after the pot goes into the oven, you can do all the other ingredient prep while it cooks, which is a definite improvement on the task of centuries past.

Classic Homemade Chicken Broth

Makes about 8 cups; Total Time 5 hours 20 minutes

4 pounds chicken backs and wings

3½ quarts water

1 onion, chopped

2 bay leaves

2 teaspoons salt

1. Combine chicken and water in large stockpot or Dutch oven and heat over medium-high heat until boiling, periodically skimming off any scum that comes to the surface with a slotted spoon. Reduce heat to low and simmer gently for 3 hours.

2. Add onion, bay leaves, and salt and continue to simmer for another 2 hours.

3. Strain broth through fine-mesh strainer into large pot or container, pressing on solids to extract as much liquid as possible. Let broth settle for about 5 minutes, then skim off fat. Cooled broth can be refrigerated for up to 4 days or frozen for up to 1 month.

why this recipe works

Store-bought cans can't compete: Good home-made chicken broth is liquid gold. It will improve anything you cook—not only soup but rice, beans, sauces, and more. Though it takes some time, this broth delivers rich flavor and full body with almost no hands-on work. We chose chicken backs and wings for convenience and because they release plenty of gelatin, which gives the broth a luscious consistency. (If you want a recipe that yields both broth and meat, make Chicken Noodle Soup, page 234.) Minimal additions ensure the broth tastes as chicken-y as possible. Chicken backs are available at super-market butcher counters. For information on how to defat broth, see page 235. If you have a large pot (at least 12 quarts), you can easily double this recipe.

variation
Cheater Chicken Broth

Doctoring store-bought broth with ground chicken, gelatin, and seasonings gives it a flavor and consistency that approaches homemade and comes together much faster.

Heat 1 tablespoon vegetable oil in large saucepan over medium-high heat until shimmering. Add 1 pound ground chicken and 1 chopped onion and cook, stirring frequently, until chicken is no longer pink, 5 to 10 minutes. Add 4 cups water, 4 cups chicken broth, 8 teaspoons unflavored gelatin, 2 bay leaves, and 2 teaspoons salt and bring to simmer. Reduce heat to medium-low, cover, and cook for 30 minutes. Strain broth through fine-mesh strainer into large pot or container, pressing on solids to extract as much liquid as possible. Let broth settle for about 5 minutes, then skim off fat.

think like a cook

WHEN HOMEMADE BROTH IS WORTH IT

There are few—maybe not any—cases where we'd advise against making soup just because you don't have homemade broth. (An exception would be Chicken Noodle Soup, but that recipe makes its own broth.) That said, soup is going to taste like what you put into it. Especially with brothy and minimally seasoned soups, homemade broth is a good idea. Even sauces and risottos will be noticeably improved by the flavor and body of homemade broth. (If you like to make soups, we suggest getting into the habit of making and freezing broths.) With boldly flavored soups, such as Kimchi Beef and Tofu Soup (page 252), the difference between home-made and packaged will be less perceptible—just use a light hand with the salt if you opt for store-bought broth. With many vegetable soups, water is preferable to broth as it allows the vegetable flavor to shine through. The same is true of many bean soups.

Our favorite packaged chicken broth is **Swanson Chicken Stock**. We've had little luck finding a packaged beef broth with true beef flavor, and some taste metallic. Our favorite option, **Better Than Bouillon Roasted Beef Base**, is at least ultrasavory if not very beefy. To boost the flavor of beef broth, we often mix it with chicken broth. Our favorite vegetarian broth is also a powder, **Orrington Farms Vegan Chicken Flavored Broth Base and Seasoning**, which offers plenty of savory depth without the off-flavors (sour, cloyingly sweet, or bitter) that plague many packaged vegetable broths. Better still, make Vegetable Broth Base (page 272) and store it in your freezer to use as needed.

Vegetable Broth Base
Makes about 1¾ cups base, enough for 7 quarts broth;
Total Time 20 minutes

2 leeks, white and light green parts only, chopped and washed thoroughly (2½ cups or 5 ounces)

2 carrots, peeled and cut into ½-inch pieces (⅔ cup or 3 ounces)

½ small celery root, peeled and cut into ½-inch pieces (¾ cup or 3 ounces)

½ cup (½ ounce) parsley leaves and thin stems

3 tablespoons dried minced onion

2 tablespoons kosher salt

1½ tablespoons tomato paste

3 tablespoons soy sauce

1. FOR THE BASE Process leeks, carrots, celery root, parsley, minced onion, and salt in food processor, scraping down sides of bowl frequently, until paste is as fine as possible, 3 to 4 minutes. Add tomato paste and process for 1 minute, scraping down sides of bowl every 20 seconds. Add soy sauce and continue to process 1 minute longer. Transfer mixture to airtight container and tap firmly on counter to remove air bubbles. Press small piece of parchment paper flush against surface of mixture and cover. Freeze for up to 6 months.

2. TO MAKE BROTH For 1 cup of broth, stir 1 tablespoon fresh or frozen broth base into 1 cup boiling water. For particle-free broth, let the broth steep for 5 minutes and then strain it through fine-mesh strainer.

why this recipe works
Vegetable broth is a necessary staple, but commercial offerings don't taste anything like vegetables. Homemade concentrated vegetable broth base is a convenient and economical alternative: Simply mix a small amount of the base with boiling water for instant broth. Our recipe starts with a twist on the classic *mirepoix* of onion, carrots, and celery, with celery root and leeks swapped in for similar but milder flavors. For depth and complexity, we added dried minced onion, tomato paste, and soy sauce. Two tablespoons of kosher salt kept the base from freezing solid, so we could store it in the freezer for months and easily remove a tablespoon at a time. Using kosher salt aids in grinding the vegetables.

think like a cook

THE POWER OF THREE

At the heart of cuisines around the world, you'll find a set of fundamental aromatic ingredients used to build deep flavor. In French cooking, those ingredients are onions, carrots, and celery. Together, they are known as *mirepoix* and they provide the flavor base for all kinds of soups, stews, braises, sauces, stuffings, and more. Between the sweetness from the carrot, the vegetal freshness from the celery, and the savory depth from the onion, these three ingredients contain a balanced foundation upon which to build all kinds of dishes. We use a variation on mirepoix in this recipe with our leek, celery root, and carrot combination.

Depending on the kind of cuisine you're cooking, the three underpinning ingredients will change. In Cuban cooking, a combination of onion, green bell pepper, and garlic called *sofrito* is a key component of many dishes. For Cajun and Creole dishes, cooks rely on what's called the "holy trinity": onion, celery, and green bell pepper. Since Cajun and Creole cuisines reflect a blend of French and Spanish influences, among many others, it is perhaps not surprising that the trinity shares elements with both mirepoix and sofrito.

Beef Bone Broth

Makes about 8 cups; Total Time 24 hours 45 minutes

2 tablespoons extra-virgin olive oil

6 pounds oxtails

1 large onion, chopped

8 ounces white mushrooms, trimmed and chopped

2 tablespoons tomato paste

10 cups water

3 bay leaves

Kosher salt and pepper

1. Heat 1 tablespoon oil in Dutch oven over medium-high heat until just smoking. Pat oxtails dry with paper towels. Sauté half of oxtails until browned all over, 7 to 10 minutes; transfer to large bowl. Repeat with remaining 1 tablespoon oil and remaining oxtails; transfer to bowl.

2. Add onion and mushrooms to fat left in pot and cook until softened and lightly browned, about 5 minutes. Stir in tomato paste and cook until fragrant, about 1 minute. Stir in 2 cups water, bay leaves, 1 teaspoon salt, and ¼ teaspoon pepper, scraping up any browned bits.

3. Adjust oven rack to middle position and heat oven to 200 degrees. Stir remaining 8 cups water into pot, then return browned oxtails and any accumulated juices to pot and bring to simmer. Fit large piece of aluminum foil over pot, pressing to seal, then cover tightly with lid. Transfer pot to oven and cook until broth is rich and flavorful, about 24 hours.

4. Remove oxtails, then strain broth through fine-mesh strainer into large container; discard solids. Let broth settle for 5 to 10 minutes, then defat using wide, shallow spoon or fat separator. Cooled broth can be refrigerated for up to 4 days or frozen for up to 1 month.

why this recipe works

Store-bought beef broths are often tinny and flavorless; homemade can make a world of difference. Our deeply flavorful beef broth can be used in recipes or enjoyed as a drinking broth. We built our broth using convenient, economical oxtails, which are all-in-one bundles of meat, fat, bone marrow, and collagen-rich connective tissue. To extract the most flavor, we browned them before simmering the broth for 24 hours. (See "Cooking with Bones" to learn why this stock is worth the time investment.) A few simple additions enhanced the broth's savory flavor. Oxtails can be found in the freezer section of the grocery store; look for ones that are approximately 2 inches thick and 2 to 4 inches in diameter. (Be sure to thaw completely before using.) For more information on defatting broth, see page 235. For how to store and freeze broth, see page 267.

think like a cook

COOKING WITH BONES

You probably think of bones mostly as the hard, white sticks, but they actually contain a lot of connective tissue and fat in addition to the calcium phosphate that makes them white and rigid. In fact, collagen, which is a protein found in connective tissue, makes up about 40 percent of bone, and when you cook collagen for a long time (say, in a long-simmered broth), that collagen converts into gelatin, which is what makes really good broth so luscious. The fat- and flavor-rich marrow in the bones also leaches into the broth, but this process happens fairly slowly, so the longer the bones are cooked, the more of that flavor you get. We're taking advantage of all of this when we cook the oxtails for 24 whole hours in our Beef Bone Broth.

We also love using bone-in cuts of meat for other preparations. Bone is very porous and thus a relatively poor conductor of heat. This means that the meat located next to the bone doesn't cook as quickly as the rest of the meat—a phenomenon that helps to prevent overcooking and moisture loss and contributes to a noticeably juicier end product. This is why whenever you cut into any bone-in cut of meat, you'll notice that the rarest part is right next to the bone. Bones are also lined with fat, a crucial source of flavor. This is one reason that barbecuing is a popular cooking method for many bone-in cuts. A good number of flavor compounds found in smoke vapor are fat-soluble, and since there is extra fat in the roast or the ribs—courtesy of the bones— the meat is likely to absorb and retain more flavor from the smoke.

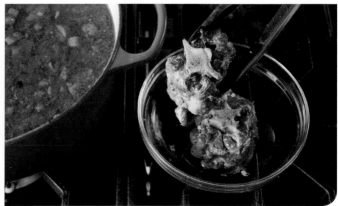

weeknight dinners

Spaghetti with Spring Vegetables
Serves 4 to 6; Total Time 45 minutes

6 ounces cherry tomatoes, halved

6 tablespoons extra-virgin olive oil, plus extra for drizzling

1 small garlic clove, minced, plus 4 cloves, sliced thin

Salt and pepper

1 pound spaghetti

1 zucchini, halved lengthwise and sliced ¼ inch thick

⅛ teaspoon red pepper flakes

1 pound asparagus, trimmed and cut on bias into 1-inch lengths

1 cup frozen peas, thawed

¼ cup minced fresh chives

1 tablespoon lemon juice

¼ cup grated Pecorino Romano cheese, plus extra for serving

2 tablespoons torn fresh mint leaves

1. Toss tomatoes, 1 tablespoon oil, minced garlic, ¼ teaspoon salt, and ¼ teaspoon pepper together in bowl; set aside.

2. Bring 4 quarts water to boil in large pot. Add pasta and 1 tablespoon salt and cook, stirring often, until al dente. Drain pasta and return it to pot.

3. Meanwhile, heat 3 tablespoons oil in 12-inch nonstick skillet over medium-low heat until shimmering. Add zucchini, pepper flakes, sliced garlic, and ½ teaspoon salt and cook, covered, until zucchini softens and breaks down, 10 to 15 minutes, stirring occasionally. Add asparagus, peas, and ¾ cup water and bring to simmer over medium-high heat. Cover and cook until asparagus is crisp-tender, about 2 minutes.

4. Add vegetable mixture, chives, lemon juice, and remaining 2 tablespoons oil to pasta and toss to combine. Transfer to serving bowl, sprinkle with Pecorino, and drizzle with extra oil. Spoon tomatoes and their juices over top and sprinkle with mint. Serve, passing extra Pecorino separately.

why this recipe works

Time was, if you didn't smother your pasta with tomato sauce, it likely received a rich coating of butter, maybe cream. Even the classic *pasta primavera,* or "springtime pasta," amounted to pasta with vegetables in a cream sauce. Nowadays we prefer a pasta primavera that actually highlights the vegetables rather than weighs them down. When properly cooked, some vegetables soften until they turn creamy, providing a lighter base for a pasta sauce. Here, we technically overcooked zucchini, a fairly watery vegetable, until it broke down, developing a silky texture that coated the asparagus, peas, and pasta, tying the dish together. (Don't be alarmed when the zucchini slices turn soft and creamy and lose their shape.) Some olive oil and grated Pecorino brought just enough richness, while lemon juice and fresh mint amplified the vibrancy of this springtime dish. Finally, cherry tomatoes, briefly marinated in garlic and oil, made a bright, juicy topping.

think like a cook

MEASURING PASTA

Many of the pasta recipes in this book (including the one here) call for a full pound of pasta. That's easy enough to measure out, as most packages are sold in this quantity. However, for some recipes you will need less than a pound, and measuring that can be tricky. Obviously, you can weigh out partial amounts of pasta using a scale, or you can judge by how full the box is, but we think it's easiest to measure shaped pasta using a dry measuring cup, and strand pasta by determining the diameter.

Measuring Short Pasta

PASTA TYPE*	8 OUNCES	12 OUNCES
Elbow Macaroni and Small Shells	2 cups	3 cups
Orecchiette	2¼ cups	3⅓ cups
Penne, Ziti, and Campanelle	2½ cups	3¾ cups
Rigatoni, Fusilli, Medium Shells, and Wide Egg Noodles	3 cups	4½ cups
Farfalle	3¼ cups	4¾ cups

* These amounts do not apply to whole-wheat pasta.

Measuring Long Pasta

When 8 ounces of uncooked strand pasta are bunched together into a tight circle, the diameter measures about 1¼ inches. When 12 ounces of uncooked strand pasta are bunched together, the diameter measures about 1¾ inches.

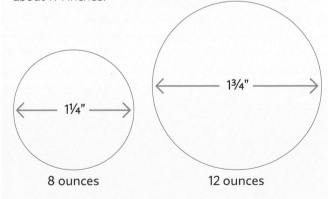

8 ounces   12 ounces

Bucatini with Peas, Kale, and Pancetta

Serves 4 to 6; Total Time: 45 minutes

½ cup panko bread crumbs

1 tablespoon extra-virgin olive oil

Salt and pepper

1½ ounces Parmesan cheese, grated (¾ cup)

1 tablespoon grated lemon zest

2 ounces pancetta, cut into ½-inch pieces

2 garlic cloves, minced

½ cup dry white wine

2½ cups water

2 cups chicken broth

1 pound bucatini or spaghetti

5 ounces (5 cups) baby kale

1 cup frozen peas

1. Combine panko with oil, ¼ teaspoon salt, and ¼ teaspoon pepper in bowl and microwave, stirring often, until crumbs are golden brown, 3 to 5 minutes. Stir in ¼ cup Parmesan and 1 teaspoon lemon zest.

2. Cook pancetta in Dutch oven over medium heat until crisp, 6 to 8 minutes; using slotted spoon, transfer to paper towel–lined plate.

3. Add garlic and remaining 2 teaspoons zest to fat left in pot and cook until fragrant, about 30 seconds. Stir in wine, scraping up any browned bits, and cook until nearly evaporated, about 3 minutes. Stir in water and broth, scraping up any browned bits.

4. Increase heat to high and bring to boil. Stir in pasta, reduce heat to medium, and simmer vigorously, stirring often, until pasta is nearly tender, 8 to 10 minutes.

5. Stir in kale and peas and continue to simmer until pasta and kale are tender, about 4 minutes. Add remaining ½ cup Parmesan and stir vigorously until pasta is creamy and well coated, about 30 seconds. Season with salt and pepper to taste. Serve, sprinkling individual portions with crisp pancetta and panko mixture.

why this recipe works

In a typical pasta-and-sauce dish, you cook the pasta in one pot, the sauce in another, and may even use a third for vegetables or meat. That's a lot of pots for a "simple" dinner. This method streamlines the process by cooking the pasta directly in the sauce. By starting with just the right amount of liquid (a flavorful mix of white wine, chicken broth, and water), we ensured the pasta cooked through just as the liquid had reduced to a sauce, which we thickened with grated Parmesan. To bolster the sauce's flavor, we first crisped chopped pancetta, then used the rendered fat to bloom lemon zest and garlic. Sweet peas and baby kale complemented the meaty pancetta and hollow-stranded bucatini pasta absorbed plenty of sauce. For crunchy contrast, we topped off each serving with the crisped pancetta, along with a mixture of panko, Parmesan, and lemon zest.

think like a cook

FOR A SAVORY BOOST, ADD PANCETTA

Cooks love to talk about how bacon makes nearly any dish taste better. But you know what? It also makes the dish taste *smokier*. And while smokiness is often welcome, it can quickly steal the show and overpower or compete with other flavors. Fortunately, there's pancetta, an ingredient that has all of bacon's rich, meaty savor without the smoke. Pancetta, an Italian pork product made from the belly of the pig, is used to add flavor and meaty depth to many Italian pasta sauces, stews, and braises. Sometimes called Italian bacon, the fatty, succulent cut is also used to make American bacon. However, while American bacon is salted, (usually) sugared, and smoked, pancetta is treated with salt, black pepper, and spices and rolled into a cylinder. It is never smoked. This gives a less obtrusive element of meatiness that's wonderful in everything from tomato sauce to lentil soup.

Pancetta is typically chopped and sautéed to crisp it and render the fat. You the remove the meat (to add back later) and add vegetables or other ingredients to cook in the savory fat. Try that before simmering your next tomato sauce or simply cooking a vegetable such as broccoli or spinach. You may decide you want to keep a chunk of pancetta in the fridge all the time.

Conversely, if you have bacon and the recipe calls for pancetta, you can blanch it to remove some (not all) of its smoky flavor: Put the bacon in boiling water for 2 minutes, then use as you would pancetta. Because blanched bacon has lost some of its fat, you may need to add extra oil to the recipe.

Skillet Lasagna

Serves 4 to 6; Total Time 1 hour

1 (28-ounce) can diced tomatoes

Water

1 tablespoon olive oil

1 onion, chopped fine

Salt and pepper

3 garlic cloves, minced

⅛ teaspoon red pepper flakes

1 pound meatloaf mix

10 curly-edged lasagna noodles, broken into 2-inch lengths

1 (8-ounce) can tomato sauce

1 ounce Parmesan cheese, grated (½ cup), plus 2 tablespoons grated

8 ounces (1 cup) whole-milk ricotta cheese

3 tablespoons chopped fresh basil

why this recipe works

Lasagna is not usually the friendliest dish to tackle on a weeknight. To get our lasagna fix without spending hours making each component and painstakingly arranging them for picture-perfect layers, we made the entire dish in a 12-inch skillet. We added broken-up lasagna noodles and sauce right to the pan of browned meat and aromatics (broken noodles are easier to fit into the skillet). Simmering the noodles in the sauce infused the whole dish with flavor. Meatloaf mix (a blend of ground beef, pork, and veal) contributed deep, complex meatiness. Dollops of ricotta made for a simple but rich and creamy topping. The result was less tightly constructed than traditional lasagna, but no less tasty. A 12-inch nonstick skillet with a tight-fitting lid works best for this recipe. Part-skim ricotta cheese can be substituted if desired. Do not use no-boil lasagna noodles. If meatloaf mix is unavailable, use ground beef—or make the sausage variation.

1. Place tomatoes and their juice in 4-cup liquid measuring cup. Add water until mixture measures 4 cups.

2. Heat oil in 12-inch nonstick skillet over medium heat until shimmering. Add onion and ½ teaspoon salt and cook until onion begins to brown, about 5 minutes. Stir in garlic and pepper flakes and cook until fragrant, about 30 seconds. Add meat and cook, breaking it up into small pieces with wooden spoon, until no longer pink, about 4 minutes.

3. Scatter noodles over meat but do not stir. Pour tomato mixture and tomato sauce over noodles, cover, and bring to simmer. Reduce heat to medium-low and simmer, stirring occasionally, until noodles are tender, about 20 minutes.

4. Off heat, stir in ½ cup Parmesan and season with salt and pepper to taste. Dollop heaping tablespoons of ricotta over top, cover, and let sit for 5 minutes. Sprinkle with basil and remaining 2 tablespoons Parmesan. Serve.

variation

Skillet Lasagna with Italian Sausage and Bell Pepper

Substitute 1 pound Italian sausage, casings removed, for meatloaf mix. Add 1 chopped red bell pepper to skillet with onion.

think like a cook

MAGICAL MEATLOAF MIX

Meatloaf mix is a mixture of ground beef, pork, and veal. The combination of meats makes for a flavorful dish, but there's more to meatloaf mix than just the taste. The beef contributes assertive beefiness, while pork adds dimension with its sweet flavor and fattiness. The veal adds delicacy but also offers up its gelatin, which helps to absorb excess moisture and gives additional body and viscosity when simmered in a sauce, as it is here. Gelatin is formed when collagen, a protein present in connective tissues, breaks down during cooking. The collagen in calves (the source of veal) is more loosely structured and therefore converts more easily and quickly than collagen in adult cows. (This is also why veal stock is used as the base for demiglace, a concentrated liquid that gives body to sauces in classic French cooking.) Many Italian recipes featuring ground meat call for the beef-pork-veal trio (see our Pasta with Classic Bolognese, page 364, for another example), which makes meatloaf mix quite handy.

Pasta alla Norma

Serves 4 to 6; Total Time 1 hour

1½ pounds eggplant, cut into ½-inch pieces

Kosher salt and pepper

¼ cup extra-virgin olive oil

4 garlic cloves, minced

2 anchovy fillets, rinsed and minced

¼–½ teaspoon red pepper flakes

1 (28-ounce) can crushed tomatoes

6 tablespoons chopped fresh basil

1 pound ziti, rigatoni, or penne

3 ounces ricotta salata, shredded (1 cup)

1. Line large plate with double layer of coffee filters and lightly spray with vegetable oil spray. Toss eggplant with 1 teaspoon salt in bowl, then spread evenly over prepared plate. Microwave eggplant, uncovered, until dry to touch and slightly shriveled, about 10 minutes, tossing halfway through cooking. Let eggplant cool slightly, then return to bowl and toss gently with 1 tablespoon oil.

2. Heat 1 tablespoon oil in 12-inch nonstick skillet over medium-high heat until shimmering. Add eggplant and cook, stirring only every 1½ to 2 minutes, until well browned and fully tender, about 10 minutes; transfer to clean plate. Let skillet cool slightly, about 3 minutes.

3. Heat 1 tablespoon oil, garlic, anchovies, and pepper flakes in now-empty skillet over medium heat. Cook, stirring often, until garlic turns golden but not brown, about 3 minutes. Stir in tomatoes, increase heat to medium-high, and simmer, stirring occasionally, until sauce has thickened slightly, 8 to 10 minutes.

4. Stir in eggplant and cook until eggplant is heated through and flavors meld, 3 to 5 minutes. Stir in basil and remaining 1 tablespoon oil, and season with salt to taste.

5. Meanwhile, bring 4 quarts water to boil in large pot. Add pasta and 1 tablespoon salt and cook, stirring often, until al dente. Reserve ½ cup cooking water, then drain pasta and return it to pot. Add sauce and toss to combine. Season with salt and pepper to taste, and add reserved cooking water as needed to adjust consistency. Serve immediately, sprinkled with ricotta salata.

why this recipe works

Pasta alla Norma is a Sicilian classic built on meaty eggplant and a robust tomato sauce. To ensure tender but not watery or greasy eggplant, we salted and microwaved eggplant pieces on a bed of coffee filters (which are safer in the microwave than paper towels), drawing out their moisture much faster than standard salting would. Microwaving also caused the eggplant to collapse, meaning it would soak up less oil during sautéing. A secret ingredient, anchovies, gave our tomato sauce a deep savoriness without any fishiness. Finally, shards of ricotta salata, a slightly aged ricotta, added a salty tang. To prevent the eggplant from breaking into small pieces, do not stir it frequently while sautéing. French feta, Pecorino Romano, or Cotija (a firm, crumbly Mexican cheese) can be substituted for the ricotta salata. We prefer kosher salt because it clings best to the eggplant. If using table salt, reduce all salt amounts by half. To give this dish a little extra kick, add extra red pepper flakes.

think like a cook

TIPS FOR DEALING WITH EGGPLANT

We love eggplant, but cooking the vegetable can be kind of a pain. It contains a lot of moisture, which means it can end up making your dish watery and bland. It's also riddled with air pockets that can make it a magnet for oil. And eggplant can have a bitter taste because of the alkaloids in its seeds. But these issues are fixable! Try to avoid really big eggplants (longer than 12 inches); the bigger and older eggplants are more likely to be bitter. If you're stuck with a large eggplant, slice or cube it, place the pieces in a colander, toss them with salt, and let them drain for 30 minutes. Quickly rinse and thoroughly dry the eggplant before cooking. The salt masks some of the bitterness. Salting is also the answer to watery eggplant; it draws out excess moisture, and you can speed up that step by using the microwave, as we do here. Microwaving first also helps minimize greasiness when sautéing. Another approach is to cook eggplant using dry heat, such as broiling, roasting, or grilling, as they all involve minimal oil (see Broiled Eggplant with Basil and Tahini Sauce, page 60).

When shopping for eggplant, look for one that is firm, with smooth skin and no soft or brown spots. It should feel heavy for its size. There are many varieties of eggplant. They can be anywhere from 2 inches to more than a foot long, round or oblong, and purple, white, and even green. Our favorite all-purpose choice is globe eggplant, with its mild flavor and tender texture. Eggplants are very perishable and will get bitter if they overripen, so aim to use them within a day or two. They can be stored in a cool, dry place for the short term, but for more than one or two days, refrigeration is best.

Classic Macaroni and Cheese
Serves 6 to 8; Total Time 1 hour 10 minutes

3 slices hearty white sandwich bread, torn into quarters

2 tablespoons unsalted butter, cut into 4 pieces and chilled, plus 5 tablespoons unsalted butter

1 pound elbow macaroni

Salt

6 tablespoons all-purpose flour

1½ teaspoons dry mustard

¼ teaspoon cayenne pepper

5 cups whole milk

8 ounces Monterey Jack cheese, shredded (2 cups)

8 ounces sharp cheddar cheese, shredded (2 cups)

1. Adjust oven rack to lower-middle position and heat broiler. Pulse bread and 2 tablespoons chilled butter in food processor until coarsely ground, 7 to 10 pulses; set aside.

2. Bring 4 quarts water to boil in Dutch oven. Add macaroni and 1 tablespoon salt and cook, stirring often, until tender. Drain macaroni and set aside in colander.

3. Melt remaining 5 tablespoons butter in now-empty pot over medium-high heat. Whisk in flour, mustard, cayenne, and 1 teaspoon salt and cook for 1 minute. Slowly add milk, whisking constantly until smooth. Bring mixture to boil, reduce heat to medium, and cook, whisking occasionally, until thickened to consistency of heavy cream, about 5 minutes. Off heat, whisk in cheeses until fully melted. Add macaroni and cook over medium-low heat, stirring constantly, until steaming and heated through, about 6 minutes.

4. Pour mixture into 13 by 9-inch broiler-safe baking dish. Top with bread-crumb mixture and broil until crumbs are deep golden brown, 3 to 5 minutes, rotating dish if necessary for even browning. Let rest for 5 minutes. Serve.

why this recipe works

Put down the boxed macaroni! We have a delicious, foolproof homemade version that's fast enough for a weeknight. For a silky sauce with great cheese flavor, we use two cheeses: Monterey Jack for smooth meltability and sharp cheddar for potent flavor. We melt the cheeses into a béchamel sauce—milk that's thickened with a flour-and-butter roux—and then add cooked pasta and let it heat through on the stovetop. Baking macaroni and cheese can lead to overcooked pasta, curdled cheese, and broken sauce, but since ours is already piping hot when it goes into the baking dish, it needs only a few minutes under the broiler to crisp up the buttery crumb topping. You get all the goodness of a classic macaroni casserole in a fraction of the time. Serve with hot sauce and/or celery salt.

think like a cook

SECRET SAUCE

Ask a classically trained chef about mother sauces and they aren't going to tell you about their mom's legendary Bolognese. "Mother sauces" are the foundational sauces from French cuisine, which include four roux-based sauces (to read about roux, see page 269) that most home cooks have never heard of, plus hollandaise sauce, which you may have had on eggs Benedict. Learning to make the mother sauces has long been a central part of a culinary education, but in modern home cooking they no longer have the status they once did, which is why our sauces section on pages 100–103 focuses on fresher, faster, more flavorful sauce options. However, it's useful to know a little about these grandes dames, and we're still very fond of one in particular: béchamel.

Béchamel is a simple white sauce made from a flour-and-butter roux plus milk. It is the base of a number of creamy dishes, including gratins, creamed spinach, lasagna, and macaroni and cheese, as in this recipe. The steps may seem finicky, but they are there for good reasons. For a proper béchamel, the flour must be adequately cooked to eliminate its raw taste (but not so long that it browns, which would lessen its thickening power) and the milk must be slowly, constantly whisked in to prevent lumps. When it's correctly made, a béchamel is amazingly rich and glossy and adds depth and silky texture to your dish. When you add cheese to a béchamel, as we do here, it becomes a Mornay sauce.

Sesame Noodles with Shredded Chicken

Serves 4 to 6; Total Time 45 minutes

SAUCE
¼ cup sesame seeds

5 tablespoons soy sauce

¼ cup chunky peanut butter

2 tablespoons rice vinegar

2 tablespoons packed light brown sugar

1 tablespoon grated fresh ginger

2 garlic cloves, minced

1 teaspoon hot sauce

5 tablespoons hot water

CHICKEN AND NOODLES
1½ pounds boneless, skinless chicken breasts, trimmed

1 pound fresh Chinese noodles or 12 ounces dried spaghetti

1 tablespoon salt

2 tablespoons toasted sesame oil

4 scallions, sliced thin on bias

1 carrot, peeled and shredded

why this recipe works

Far better than takeout sesame noodles, these avoid the common pitfalls of gummy noodles and bland, pasty sauce. We built our authentic-tasting sauce using pantry staples to deliver the requisite sweet, nutty flavor. Ground together, chunky peanut butter and toasted sesame seeds made the perfect stand-in for hard-to-find Chinese sesame paste. We added fresh garlic and ginger as well as soy sauce, rice vinegar, hot sauce, and brown sugar to the sauce and then thinned it out with water to achieve the best texture. Simple broiled and shredded chicken made this dish a satisfying meal. We prefer the flavor and texture of conventional chunky peanut butter (not natural peanut butter) in the sauce.

1. FOR THE SAUCE Toast sesame seeds in dry nonstick skillet over medium heat until seeds are gold and fragrant, about 4 minutes. Process soy sauce, 3 tablespoons sesame seeds, peanut butter, vinegar, sugar, ginger, garlic, and hot sauce in blender or food processor until smooth, about 30 seconds. With blender running, add hot water, 1 tablespoon at a time, until sauce has consistency of heavy cream.

2. FOR THE CHICKEN AND NOODLES Bring 4 quarts water to boil in large pot. Adjust oven rack 6 inches from broiler element and heat broiler. Line rimmed baking sheet with aluminum foil and spray with vegetable oil spray. Place chicken in baking sheet and broil until lightly browned, 4 to 8 minutes. Flip chicken and continue to broil until thermometer inserted in chicken registers 160 degrees, 6 to 8 minutes. Transfer chicken to cutting board and let rest for 5 minutes. Using 2 forks, shred chicken into bite-size pieces and set aside.

3. Add noodles and salt to boiling water and cook, stirring occasionally, until tender, 4 to 5 minutes for fresh or 10 minutes for dried. Drain noodles, then rinse under cold running water until cool. Drain again, transfer to large bowl, add oil, and toss to coat. Add scallions, carrot, sauce, and shredded chicken and toss to combine. Divide evenly among bowls, sprinkle with remaining 1 tablespoon sesame seeds, and serve.

variation
Sesame Noodles with Sweet Peppers and Cucumbers
Omit chicken. Add 1 red bell pepper, stemmed, seeded, and sliced into ¼-inch-wide strips, and 1 cucumber, peeled, halved lengthwise, seeded, and cut crosswise into ⅛-inch-thick slices, to noodles with sauce. Sprinkle servings with 1 tablespoon chopped fresh cilantro along with sesame seeds.

think like a cook
TURN UP THE HEAT WITH HOT SAUCE
Usually added in small doses, hot sauce can introduce just the touch of heat that a dish might need, whether used in cooking or as a condiment. But the options can be bewildering. While most hot sauces share the same core ingredients—chiles, vinegar, and salt—their heat levels can vary drastically. When you want to avoid a searingly hot bite, we recommend our favorite traditional hot sauce, **Frank's RedHot Original Cayenne Pepper Sauce**, which has mellow heat and deep flavor. It was the base for the original Buffalo sauce recipe.

We also highly recommend **Huy Fong Sriracha Hot Chili Sauce** (with the iconic rooster label). Sriracha is thicker, sweeter, and more garlicky than Mexican- or Cajun-style hot sauces (such as Frank's) but we found it works at least as well in just about any application. A related hot sauce, Asian chili-garlic sauce, is like Sriracha but is coarsely ground rather than a smooth paste. Sambal oelek, the Indonesian hot sauce, is made purely from ground chiles, vinegar, and salt, without garlic or other spices, thus adding a purer chile flavor. We don't recommend Tabasco, the top-selling hot sauce. Its high vinegar content and skimpy amount of salt makes it taste out of balance. Once opened, hot sauces will keep for several months in the refrigerator. Note that some brands of hot sauce are nearly twice as hot as Frank's, so be careful the first time you use one.

Shrimp Pad Thai
Serves 4; Total Time 40 minutes

8 ounces (¼-inch-wide) rice noodles

¼ cup lime juice (2 limes), plus lime wedges for serving

3 tablespoons fish sauce

3 tablespoons packed brown sugar

1 tablespoon rice vinegar

¼ cup vegetable oil

12 ounces medium shrimp (41 to 50 per pound), peeled and deveined (see page 99)

3 garlic cloves, minced

2 large eggs, lightly beaten

¼ teaspoon salt

6 tablespoons unsalted dry-roasted peanuts, chopped

6 ounces (3 cups) bean sprouts

5 scallions, sliced thin on bias

Fresh cilantro leaves

why this recipe works

With its sweet-and-sour, salty-spicy sauce and plump sweet shrimp, pad thai is Thailand's best-known rice noodle dish. But making it can be a chore, thanks to a lengthy ingredient list with hard-to-find items. We found we could achieve just the right balance of flavors in the sauce by using a mixture of fish sauce, lime juice, rice vinegar, and brown sugar. We quickly sautéed our shrimp until just spotty brown, then removed them to finish later. To get the texture of the noodles just right, we soaked them in hot water to soften, then stir-fried them until tender with the shrimp, sauce, scrambled egg, bean sprouts, scallions, and peanuts. No pad thai is complete without garnishes. We finished ours with cilantro and lime wedges. For some heat and brightness, pass around a simple chile vinegar made by combining ⅓ cup distilled white vinegar and 1 sliced serrano chile (let sit for at least 15 minutes). Or serve with Sriracha. Do not substitute other types of noodles for the rice noodles here.

1. Cover noodles with very hot tap water in large bowl and stir to separate. Let noodles soak until softened, pliable, and limp but not fully tender, about 20 minutes; drain. In separate bowl, whisk ⅓ cup water, lime juice, fish sauce, sugar, vinegar, and 2 tablespoons oil together.

2. Pat shrimp dry with paper towels. Heat 1 tablespoon oil in 12-inch nonstick skillet over high heat until just smoking. Add shrimp in single layer and cook, without stirring, until beginning to brown, about 1 minute. Stir shrimp and continue to cook until spotty brown and just pink around edges, about 30 seconds; transfer to bowl.

3. Add remaining 1 tablespoon oil and garlic to skillet and cook over medium heat until fragrant, about 30 seconds. Stir in eggs and salt and cook, stirring vigorously, until eggs are scrambled, about 20 seconds.

4. Add noodles and lime juice mixture. Increase heat to high and cook, tossing gently, until noodles are evenly coated. Add shrimp, ¼ cup peanuts, bean sprouts, and three-quarters of scallions. Cook, tossing constantly, until noodles are tender, about 2 minutes. (If necessary, add 2 tablespoons water to skillet and continue to cook until noodles are tender.) Transfer noodles to serving platter and sprinkle with remaining peanuts, remaining scallions, and cilantro. Serve with lime wedges.

think like a cook

FAKE IT TILL YOU MAKE IT

There's a time and place for strict authenticity, but we often strive to mimic authentic flavors and textures with more widely available ingredients and approachable techniques in order to enjoy the dishes we love, such as pad thai, more often. Truly authentic pad thai as made in Bangkok contains several ingredients that are probably not feasible for the average cook's weeknight dinner, including dried shrimp, preserved daikon radish, palm sugar, and tamarind. How to simplify pad thai while retaining its integrity? Our focus was to re-create the essential flavor profile even if we lost some nuance along the way. The interplay of salty, sweet, and sour tastes is the primary characteristic of pad thai. These flavors typically come from pungent, saline fish sauce; caramel-like palm sugar; and sour, fruity tamarind. Fish sauce is now available in most supermarkets, so it needed no substitute. Brown sugar, with its toffee-like sweetness, stood in well for palm sugar. Tamarind is becoming more available, but for an everyday option we looked to fresh lime juice for fruity sourness. Garnishes play a big role in pad thai, too, bringing texture and layers of flavor. We skipped the preserved daikon and looked to mung bean sprouts and peanuts for crunch and cilantro for herbal freshness. And so, by mixing some authentic ingredients with creative swaps, we worked just the right kind of weeknight alchemy.

Almost Hands-Free Risotto with Parmesan and Herbs

Serves 6; Total Time 50 minutes

5 cups chicken broth

1½ cups water

4 tablespoons unsalted butter

1 large onion, chopped fine

Salt and pepper

1 garlic clove, minced

2 cups Arborio rice

1 cup dry white wine

2 ounces Parmesan cheese, grated (1 cup)

1 teaspoon lemon juice

2 tablespoons chopped fresh parsley

2 tablespoons chopped fresh chives

1. Bring broth and water to boil in large saucepan over high heat. Reduce heat to medium-low to maintain gentle simmer.

2. Melt 2 tablespoons butter in Dutch oven over medium heat. Add onion and ¾ teaspoon salt and cook, stirring frequently, until onion is softened, 5 to 7 minutes. Add garlic and stir until fragrant, about 30 seconds. Add rice and cook, stirring frequently, until grains are translucent around edges, about 3 minutes.

3. Add wine and cook, stirring constantly, until fully absorbed, 2 to 3 minutes. Measure out 5 cups hot broth mixture and stir into rice. Reduce heat to medium-low, cover, and simmer until almost all liquid has been absorbed and rice is just al dente, 16 to 19 minutes, stirring twice during cooking.

4. Add ¾ cup hot broth mixture and stir gently and constantly until risotto becomes creamy, about 3 minutes. Stir in Parmesan. Remove pot from heat, cover, and let stand for 5 minutes. Stir in remaining 2 tablespoons butter, lemon juice, parsley, and chives. To loosen texture of risotto, add remaining broth mixture as needed. Season with salt and pepper to taste, and serve immediately.

why this recipe works

Risotto is Italian comfort food made from a special type of rice called Arborio. Its short grains release a lot of starch as they cook, which combines with the liquid to produce a creamy sauce. Usually risotto recipes require near-constant stirring to release the starch and prevent the rice from burning, making for a very hands-on dish. To reduce stirring to a minimum, we flooded the rice with cooking liquid at the outset, rather than adding it in small increments, and covered the pot. This allowed the natural agitation of the simmering rice to take the place of stirring—save for a few minutes of vigorous stirring at the very end. You end up with perfect risotto. Top servings with shaved Parmesan or dressed greens for an elegant presentation. While this method is pretty hands-off, it does require precise timing, so we recommend using a timer.

variations

Almost Hands-Free Risotto with Fennel and Saffron
Add 1 fennel bulb, cored and chopped fine, to pot with onion and cook until softened, about 12 minutes. Add ¼ teaspoon ground coriander and large pinch saffron threads to pot with garlic.

Almost Hands-Free Risotto with Porcini
Add ¼ ounce rinsed and minced dried porcini mushrooms to pot with garlic. Substitute soy sauce for lemon juice.

think like a cook

"TO THE TOOTH"
You've probably seen the instruction to cook an ingredient until it is "al dente." This Italian term, meaning "to the tooth," indicates the pasta or rice or other grain is fully cooked but still firm when bitten. The texture is a hallmark of risotto. Arborio rice, traditionally used in risotto, actually has a natural defect that helps its grains retain this desirable bite even after simmering. During maturation, the starch structures at the grain's core deform, making for a firm, toothy center when cooked.

What would happen if we attempted risotto with another rice, we wondered? We made a classic Parmesan risotto with four kinds of rice: standard long grain, converted parcooked long grain, regular medium grain, and sushi-style short-grain rice. The two long-grain varieties bombed, turning mushy and lacking creaminess. Medium- and short-grain rice fared much better, turning perfectly creamy, but not toothsome. So if you don't have Arborio, you can substitute another medium- or short-grain rice in your risotto, but you won't get the same characteristic al dente bite.

Pasta Frittata with Sausage and Hot Peppers

Serves 4 to 6; Total Time 1 hour

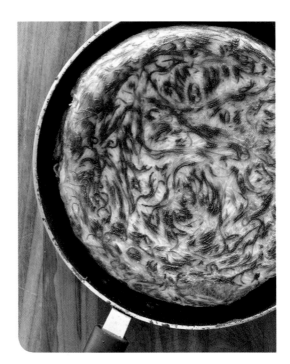

8 large eggs

1 ounce Parmesan cheese, grated (½ cup)

3 tablespoons extra-virgin olive oil

3 tablespoons coarsely chopped jarred hot cherry peppers

2 tablespoons chopped fresh parsley

Salt and pepper

8 ounces sweet Italian sausage, casings removed, crumbled

2 garlic cloves, sliced thin

3 cups water

6 ounces angel hair pasta, broken in half

3 tablespoons vegetable oil

1. Whisk eggs, Parmesan, olive oil, peppers, parsley, ½ teaspoon salt, and ½ teaspoon pepper in large bowl until egg is evenly colored; set aside.

2. Cook sausage in 10-inch nonstick skillet over medium heat, breaking it up with wooden spoon, until fat renders and sausage is about half cooked, 3 to 5 minutes. Stir in garlic and cook for 30 seconds. Remove skillet from heat. Transfer sausage mixture (some sausage will still be raw) to bowl with egg mixture. Wipe out skillet with paper towels.

3. Bring water, pasta, vegetable oil, and ¾ teaspoon salt to boil in now-empty skillet over high heat, stirring occasionally. Cook, stirring occasionally, until pasta is tender, water has evaporated, and pasta starts to sizzle in oil, 8 to 12 minutes. Reduce heat to medium and continue to cook pasta, swirling pan and scraping under edge of pasta with rubber spatula frequently to prevent sticking (do not stir), until bottom turns golden and starts to crisp, 5 to 7 minutes longer (lift up edge of pasta to check progress).

4. Using spatula, push some pasta up sides of skillet so entire pan surface is covered with pasta. Pour egg mixture over pasta. Using tongs, lift up loose strands of pasta to allow egg to flow toward bottom of pan, being careful not to pull up crispy bottom crust. Cover skillet and continue to cook over medium heat until bottom crust turns golden brown and top of frittata is just set (egg below very top will still be raw), 5 to 8 minutes longer.

why this recipe works

Pasta frittatas were invented as a way to turn leftover pasta into a new meal. Since "leftover pasta" is not a concept we're familiar with, we wanted to find a way to make this dish from uncooked dried pasta. After a few tests, it was clear that angel hair was best for the job: The delicate strands brought a satisfying web of pasta to every bite without marring the tender egg texture. In our easy one-skillet method, the angel hair cooks in minimal water and a bit of oil; when the water has evaporated, the pasta starts to fry in the oil, turning crispy. We then added our egg mixture and cooked it gently, ensuring that the exterior didn't overcook while the interior came up to temperature. Sausage and cherry peppers provided richness and a bit of heat. You will need a 10-inch non-stick skillet with a tight-fitting lid. Serve warm or at room temperature, with a salad.

5. Slide frittata onto large plate. Invert frittata onto second large plate and slide it, browned side up, back into skillet. Tuck edges of frittata into skillet with rubber spatula. Continue to cook second side until light brown, 2 to 4 minutes longer.

6. Remove skillet from heat and let stand for 5 minutes. Using your hand or pan lid, invert frittata onto cutting board. Cut into wedges and serve.

think like a cook

WASTE NOT, WANT NOT: PICKLE BRINE

If you pour the liquid in a jar of pickled or preserved vegetables down the sink in your pursuit of the ingredients themselves, we are here to tell you that you are letting liquid gold slip through your fingers. Not only has that brine been carefully seasoned, it has also developed all kinds of complex flavors during the pickling process. In certain recipes, such as Kimchi Beef and Tofu Soup (page 252) or California-Style Fish Tacos (page 372), we call for the brine to deepen the dish's flavors or even repurpose it to pickle other vegetables.

But even when we don't, we still recommend saving the brine, as with the jarred hot cherry peppers used in this dish. You can use leftover brine to make a quick pickle by adding thinly sliced onion or radishes to the juice and letting them marinate for a few days in the refrigerator. Drain the vegetables to use as a topping for sandwiches, salads, or grain bowls. You can also add a splash of brine to mayonnaise to make a tangy spread. The oil that some sun-dried tomatoes or olives comes packed in is similarly flavorful; try brushing it on a pizza crust before adding toppings or incorporating it into a salad dressing.

The Burger Lover's Burger
Serves 4; Total Time 1 hour 10 minutes

1½ pounds sirloin steak tips, trimmed and cut into ½-inch chunks

4 tablespoons unsalted butter, melted and cooled

Salt and pepper

1 teaspoon vegetable oil

4 hamburger buns, toasted if desired

1. Arrange beef chunks on rimmed baking sheet in single layer. Freeze until meat is very firm and starting to harden around edges but still pliable, about 35 minutes.

2. Place one-quarter of meat in food processor and pulse until finely ground into rice-grain-size pieces (about ⅟16 inch), about 20 pulses, stopping and redistributing meat as needed to ensure beef is evenly ground. Transfer meat to baking sheet. Repeat grinding with remaining meat in 3 batches. Spread meat over sheet and inspect carefully, discarding any long strands of gristle or large chunks of hard meat or fat.

3. Adjust oven rack to middle position and heat oven to 300 degrees. Drizzle meat with melted butter, sprinkle with 1 teaspoon pepper, and gently toss with fork to combine. Divide meat into 4 balls. Toss each between your hands until uniformly but lightly packed. Gently flatten into patties ¾ inch thick and about 4½ inches in diameter. Refrigerate patties until ready to cook. (Patties can be refrigerated for up to 1 day.)

4. Season 1 side of patties liberally with salt and pepper. Using spatula, flip patties and season other side. Heat oil in 12-inch skillet over high heat until just smoking. Using spatula, transfer burgers to skillet and cook without moving for 2 minutes. Using spatula, flip burgers and continue to cook for 2 minutes longer. Transfer burgers to clean rimmed baking sheet and bake until until thermometer inserted into center of burger from top edge registers 125 degrees for medium-rare or 130 degrees for medium, 3 to 6 minutes.

5. Transfer burgers to plate and let rest for 5 minutes. Transfer burgers to buns and serve.

why this recipe works

How come restaurant burgers are so much better than the ones you make at home? One big reason is that your favorite restaurants are probably grinding their own meat; and you can too. We started by partially freezing chunks of sirloin steak tips so that they'd grind up relatively coarse in the food processor. Adding melted butter to the meat improved the burgers' flavor and juiciness and boosted browning. To give our burgers a great crust and juicy interior, we seared them in a hot skillet on the stovetop before transferring them to the gentler heat of the oven to cook through evenly. Take care not to overwork the meat or the burgers will be dense. Sirloin steak tips are also sold as flap meat. You can substitute 85 percent lean ground beef for the steak tips; omit butter, skip steps 1 and 2, and proceed with the recipe as directed. For the best flavor, season the burgers aggressively just before cooking. Serve with Pub-Style Burger Sauce (page 102) and your favorite toppings.

think like a cook

BE YOUR OWN BUTCHER

Buying ground meat at the supermarket is a crapshoot; unless your butcher grinds to order, there's no way to know what you're getting. The cut, fat content, and texture can vary widely. Store-bought ground beef is often processed to a pulp, so it cooks up heavy and dense, which is especially apparent in a burger. But when you grind meat yourself in a food processor, you control all the variables. The trick is to pick the right cut and to grind the meat fine enough to ensure tenderness but coarse enough that the patty will stay loose. (Underprocessed meat will be gristly and chunky; overprocessed meat will be pasty.) While chuck is often used for commercial ground beef, it contains connective tissue that must be removed before grinding. So we prefer to use sirloin steak tips for burgers, as they are well marbled and require little trimming. You can also use more than one cut, in order to engineer the right mix of flavor and fat for your burger; boneless short ribs can be a nice addition, and boneless country-style pork ribs and pork tenderloin also grind well.

When grinding meat, we recommend partially freezing it first. That way, the food processor cuts the pieces cleanly instead of pulverizing them. When grinding your own meat, process it in small batches, stopping to redistribute it around the bowl as necessary to ensure a precise, even grind. The exact size of the grind will depend of the type of meat you're using and the type of dish. After grinding, spread the mixture on a rimmed baking sheet and discard any long strands of gristle or large chunks of hard meat or fat.

Pork and Broccoli Rabe Sandwiches

Serves 4; Total Time 1 hour

1 (16-ounce) pork tenderloin, trimmed

6 tablespoons extra-virgin olive oil

Salt and pepper

1 tablespoon minced fresh rosemary

1 tablespoon fennel seeds

1 pound broccoli rabe, trimmed and cut into 1-inch pieces

4 garlic cloves, minced

1 teaspoon red pepper flakes

2 red bell peppers, stemmed, seeded, and sliced thin

4 (6-inch) Italian sub rolls, split lengthwise

6 ounces sliced provolone cheese

2 tablespoons red wine vinegar

1. Adjust oven rack to middle position and heat oven to 450 degrees. Rub tenderloin with 2 tablespoons oil, season with salt and pepper, and sprinkle with rosemary and fennel seeds. Place on 1 side of rimmed baking sheet and roast for 10 minutes.

2. Toss broccoli rabe with 2 tablespoons oil, garlic, and pepper flakes in bowl. In separate bowl, toss bell peppers with 1 tablespoon oil and season with salt and pepper. Remove sheet from oven and flip pork. Spread broccoli rabe and bell peppers on hot sheet next to pork. Continue to roast until thermometer inserted into pork registers 145 degrees and broccoli rabe and bell peppers are browned, about 20 minutes.

3. Remove sheet from oven. Transfer pork to cutting board, tent loosely with aluminum foil, and let rest for 5 minutes. Transfer vegetables to bowl and cover with foil to keep warm. Wipe sheet clean with paper towels, lay split rolls open on sheet, and top with cheese. Bake rolls until bread is lightly toasted and cheese is melted, about 5 minutes.

4. Slice pork as thinly as possible, transfer to clean bowl, and toss with remaining 1 tablespoon oil and vinegar. Nestle pork, broccoli rabe, and bell peppers into warm rolls and serve.

why this recipe works

Sandwiches for dinner doesn't have to be a last resort. A hearty, well-made sandwich is a meal in itself and nothing to be ashamed of on your dinner plate. This rich, complex pork sandwich is a classic from Philadelphia that combines juicy pork, garlicky broccoli rabe, and melty provolone. For a streamlined home version, we roasted the meat and vegetables side by side on a sheet pan. We started with quick-cooking pork tenderloin seasoned heavily with rosemary and fennel seeds. Alongside the tenderloin, we roasted broccoli rabe, tossed with lots of garlic and some pepper flakes for added dimensions of flavor, and sweet red bell pepper, which complemented the bitter greens. While the meat rested, we toasted the rolls; slices of provolone melted over the buns gave us the extra richness we needed to make these sandwiches perfect.

think like a cook

THE BROCCOLI FAMILY

Between the broccoli, broccolini, and broccoli rabe at the supermarket, it's hard to keep them all straight. So what sets them apart? We're all familiar with broccoli, the cruciferous vegetable that's a relative of cabbage. Broccolini is a cross between broccoli and Chinese broccoli (which is itself a bittersweet, leafy relative of ordinary broccoli). It has an elongated stem with tender shoots and a sweet, slightly mineral taste. Broccoli rabe, also known as rapini, has long leafy stems with green buds similar to broccoli flowers, even though it is the same subspecies as a turnip. Raw broccoli rabe has a pungent, bitter flavor, which is tamed by cooking. Its bitterness brings plenty of character to a dish and often tastes best in the presence of something sweet (such as the red peppers in this sandwich) or rich (such as the pork and cheese). Broccoli rabe also perks up milder flavors, such as the white beans and farro in our Farro and Broccoli Rabe Gratin on page 310. And it is excellent in soups, blanched, broiled, or braised.

Grown-Up Grilled Cheese with Cheddar and Shallot

Serves 4; Total Time 30 minutes

7 ounces aged cheddar cheese, cut into 24 equal pieces, room temperature

2 ounces Brie cheese, rind removed

2 tablespoons dry white wine or dry vermouth

4 teaspoons minced shallot

3 tablespoons unsalted butter, softened

1 teaspoon Dijon mustard

8 slices hearty white sandwich bread

1. Adjust oven rack to middle position and heat oven to 200 degrees. Process cheddar, Brie, and wine in food processor until smooth paste forms, 20 to 30 seconds. Add shallot and pulse to combine, 3 to 5 pulses; transfer to bowl. In separate bowl, combine butter and mustard.

2. Brush butter-mustard mixture evenly over 1 side of each slice of bread. Flip 4 slices over and spread cheese mixture evenly over second side. Top with remaining 4 slices bread, buttered side up, and press down gently.

3. Heat 12-inch nonstick skillet over medium heat for 2 minutes. Place 2 sandwiches in skillet, reduce heat to medium-low, and cook until both sides are crisp and golden brown, 6 to 9 minutes per side.

4. Transfer sandwiches to wire rack set in rimmed baking sheet and keep warm in oven. Wipe out skillet with paper towels and cook remaining 2 sandwiches. Serve.

why this recipe works

Grilled cheese has a kids' menu reputation, but just a few tweaks make it a sophisticated dinner option. To create a sandwich with more robust flavor and personality without going overboard on toppings and additions, we focused on the cheese. Our recipe began by mixing flavorful aged cheddar with a small amount of Brie and some wine in a food processor. Those two ingredients helped the cheddar melt evenly without becoming greasy. A little bit of shallot increased the sandwiches' complexity without detracting from the cheese, and a smear of mustard-butter on the bread added a sharp bite. Look for a cheddar aged for about one year (avoid cheddar aged for longer; it won't melt well). To bring the cheddar to room temperature quickly, microwave the pieces until warm, about 30 seconds.

variations

Grown-Up Grilled Cheese with Comté and Cornichon
Substitute Comté for cheddar, minced cornichon for shallot, and rye sandwich bread for white sandwich bread.

Grown-Up Grilled Cheese with Gruyère and Chives
Substitute Gruyère for cheddar, chives for shallot, and rye sandwich bread for white sandwich bread.

Grown-Up Grilled Cheese with Asiago and Dates

Substitute Asiago for cheddar, finely chopped pitted dates for shallot, and oatmeal sandwich bread for white sandwich bread.

Grown-Up Grilled Cheese with Robiola and Chipotle

Substitute Robiola, rind removed, for cheddar; ¼ teaspoon minced canned chipotle chile in adobo sauce for shallot; and oatmeal sandwich bread for white sandwich bread.

think like a cook

HOW CHEESE MELTS

You may have noticed that not all cheese reacts the same way when heated. Some melt into a creamy, cohesive mass, while others just become greasy and grainy. Obviously this is a key subject to understand in order to make the best possible grilled cheese sandwich. First, it helps to know that cheese doesn't melt in the true sense, like an ice cube. Instead, the protein casein, the solid component that gives cheese its structure, breaks down in the presence of heat. The protein molecules then separate and flow, which gives the appearance of melting. Relatively young cheeses, such as fontina and mozzarella, have a high moisture content and a weaker protein structure, allowing the protein to flow at lower temperatures. This higher moisture content means that these cheeses have less of a tendency to "break" and become greasy when they melt.

On the other hand, aged cheeses, such as Gruyère and cheddar, have less moisture and a stronger protein network, which means they melt at higher temperatures. They also contain a lot of fat, which can melt before the proteins begin to flow, leading to breaking and causing greasiness. Once melted, the more developed protein structures in these cheeses break down, leaving behind a gritty texture. (Older definitely isn't better when it comes to cheddar cheeses used for melting; stick with moderately aged cheddars; save the older stuff for eating plain.) To combat this issue in our reengineered grilled cheese, we added a little soft, young Brie and wine to the flavorful aged cheddar that we knew we wanted at the heart of our sandwich and processed everything together. The addition of moisture and a younger, meltier cheese helped the filling melt smoothly and evenly, without any greasiness.

Black Bean Burgers
Serves 6; Total Time 40 minutes (plus 1 to 24 hours chilling)

2 (15-ounce) cans black beans, rinsed

1 ounce tortilla chips, crushed coarse (½ cup)

4 scallions, cut into 1-inch lengths

½ cup fresh cilantro leaves

2 garlic cloves, peeled and smashed

2 large eggs

2 tablespoons all-purpose flour

1 teaspoon ground cumin

1 teaspoon hot sauce

½ teaspoon ground coriander

¼ teaspoon salt

¼ teaspoon pepper

¼ cup vegetable oil

6 hamburger buns

why this recipe works

A veggie burger sounds good in theory. So why do so many taste like hockey pucks, fall apart in the pan, or require a hodgepodge of ingredients? Well, not this burger. Starting with black beans (dried on paper towels to eliminate moisture) gave us a substantial base. To avoid a crumbly burger we minimized starchy binders, finding help in ground tortilla chips, which worked as a binder (along with eggs and a tiny bit of flour) and added toasty corn flavor. Pulsing our beans only coarsely prevented the burgers from becoming gummy. To ensure they held together, we refrigerated the mixture for at least an hour, allowing the starches to absorb additional moisture. (Prepare the patties a day ahead for a faster meal.) To build a Southwestern flavor, we added scallions, cilantro, garlic, cumin, and coriander, plus hot sauce for zip. When forming the patties it is important to pack them firmly together. Serve with Chipotle Mayonnaise (page 102) and your favorite toppings.

1. Line rimmed baking sheet with triple layer of paper towels and spread black beans over towels. Let stand for 15 minutes.

2. Process tortilla chips in food processor until finely ground, about 30 seconds. Add scallions, cilantro, and garlic and pulse until finely chopped, about 15 pulses, scraping down sides of bowl as needed. Add beans and pulse until beans are roughly broken down, about 5 pulses.

3. Whisk eggs, flour, cumin, hot sauce, coriander, salt, and pepper together in large bowl until well combined. Add bean mixture and mix until just combined. Cover and refrigerate for at least 1 hour or up to 24 hours.

4. Adjust oven rack to middle position and heat oven to 200 degrees. Set wire rack in rimmed baking sheet. Divide bean mixture into 6 equal portions. Firmly pack each portion into tight ball, then flatten to 3½-inch-wide burgers.

5. Heat 1 tablespoon oil in 12-inch nonstick skillet over medium heat until shimmering. Carefully place 3 burgers in skillet and cook until bottoms are well browned and crisp, about 5 minutes. Flip burgers, add 1 tablespoon oil, and cook second side until well browned and crisp, 3 to 5 minutes. Transfer burgers to prepared rack and keep warm in oven. Repeat with remaining 3 patties and remaining 2 tablespoons oil. Transfer burgers to buns and serve.

think like a cook

TOPPINGS FOR ANY BURGER

Don't let restaurants have all the fun; take your toppings beyond lettuce, tomato, and onion. Upgrades such as bacon (see page 131) and fried eggs (see page 70) are pretty ubiquitous on pub menus, but there's a world of options. The Pub-Style Burger Sauce (page 102) is classic, as is the Chipotle Mayonnaise used here, but many of the sauces on pages 100–103 would also be great, whether on a bean burger or The Burger Lover's Burger (page 296). Or try the ideas below.

Tex-Mex Burger
Guacamole, sour cream, salsa, and pickled jalapeños

Bistro Burger
Blue cheese, bacon, and caramelized onions (see page 239)

Italian Burger
Either type of pesto (see page 100), fresh mozzarella cheese, tomato, and roasted garlic on focaccia

California Burger
Chipotle Mayonnaise (page 102), sliced avocado, sprouts, and sliced cucumbers on a whole-wheat bun

Aïoli Burger
Garlic Aïoli (page 102), Roasted Red Peppers (page 127), and Bibb lettuce on a brioche roll

Mushroom Burger
Mustard, Gruyère, Sautéed Mushrooms with Shallot and Thyme (page 206), and baby arugula on a pretzel bun

Tofu Banh Mi

Serves 4; Total Time 45 minutes

14 ounces firm tofu

2 carrots, peeled and shredded

⅔ cucumber, peeled, halved lengthwise, seeded (see page 29), and sliced thin

1 teaspoon grated lime zest plus 1 tablespoon juice

1 tablespoon fish sauce

¼ cup mayonnaise

1 tablespoon Sriracha sauce

Salt and pepper

⅓ cup cornstarch

3 tablespoons vegetable oil

4 (8-inch) Italian sub rolls, split lengthwise and toasted

⅓ cup fresh cilantro leaves

1. Slice tofu crosswise into eight ⅔-inch-thick slabs. Arrange tofu on paper towel–lined baking sheet and let sit for 20 minutes. Meanwhile, combine carrots, cucumber, lime juice, and fish sauce in bowl and let sit for 15 minutes. Whisk mayonnaise, Sriracha, and lime zest together in separate bowl.

2. Gently press tofu dry with paper towels and season with salt and pepper. Spread cornstarch in shallow dish. Dredge tofu in cornstarch, pressing gently to adhere, and transfer to plate.

3. Heat oil in 12-inch nonstick skillet over medium-high heat until just smoking. Add tofu and cook until both sides are crisp and browned, about 4 minutes per side. Transfer to paper towel–lined plate.

4. Spread mayonnaise mixture evenly over cut sides of each roll. Assemble 4 sandwiches by layering ingredients as follows in rolls: tofu, pickled vegetables (leaving liquid in bowl), and cilantro. Press gently on sandwiches to set. Serve.

why this recipe works

Banh mi sandwiches inspired by Vietnamese street food have become hugely popular in the United States. For a homemade take that is low fuss but high flavor, we started with a base of crispy tofu. We sliced the tofu into slabs and drained them on paper towels to make it easier to get a crust. Then we dredged the tofu slabs in cornstarch and seared them in a hot skillet until they were nicely browned. Crunchy pickled vegetables are a hallmark of banh mi, so we used a quick-pickling technique to infuse cucumber slices and shredded carrots with tons of flavor in just a little bit of time. Sriracha-spiked mayonnaise gave the sandwich a spicy kick, while a sprinkling of fresh cilantro added an authentic garnish. To make the sandwiches vegetarian, use Bragg Liquid Aminos instead of the fish sauce (see "Vegetarian Substitutes for Fishy Ingredients"). You can use firm or extra-firm tofu in this recipe.

think like a cook

VEGETARIAN SUBSTITUTES FOR FISHY INGREDIENTS

To make our Tofu Banh Mi completely vegetarian and not just pescatarian-friendly, you will need to use a fish sauce substitute that doesn't contain seafood products. Traditional fish sauce is a salty, amber-colored liquid made from fermented fish. It's rich in glutamates, tastebud stimulators that give food the meaty, savory flavor known as umami. Another seafood-based condiment to be aware of is oyster sauce, which indeed contains oysters. Often used in Chinese stir-fries such as our Restaurant-Style Beef Stir-Fry (page 326), it's a thick, salty brown sauce made from a rich, concentrated mixture of oysters, soy sauce, brine, and seasonings. Many recipes in Asian cuisines rely on both of these ingredients.

As a vegetarian substitute for fish sauce, we like **Bragg Liquid Aminos**. Made from 16 amino acids derived from soybeans (amino acids are the structural units that make up proteins), it is advertised as a healthy alternative to soy sauce, but our tasters found it to be surprisingly similar to fish sauce, offering a great saltiness with a bit of fermented flavor. When it comes to oyster sauce, you can find vegetarian options, made from mushrooms, in stores and online.

Spicy Tofu and Basil Lettuce Cups

Serves 4; Total Time 1 hour

28 ounces extra-firm tofu, cut into 2-inch pieces

3 carrots, peeled and shredded

5 tablespoons distilled white vinegar

2 tablespoons plus ¾ teaspoon sugar

4 ounces rice vermicelli

3 tablespoons plus 1 teaspoon vegetable oil

4 cups fresh basil leaves

6 Thai chiles, stemmed

6 garlic cloves, peeled

¼ cup soy sauce

6 shallots, halved and sliced thin

½ cup dry-roasted peanuts, chopped

2 heads Bibb lettuce (1 pound), leaves separated

why this recipe works

This fresh, flavorful dish takes inspiration from Thai cuisine. A filling of mild tofu punched up with basil, garlic, and spicy Thai chiles is served in crisp, cool lettuce cups. Chewy rice vermicelli provides heft to this light meal, and quick pickled carrots make the perfect tangy foil to the spicy tofu. You can use either firm or extra-firm tofu in this dish. You can also use red or green Thai chiles. If fresh Thai chiles are unavailable, substitute two serranos or one jalapeño. For a milder version, remove the seeds and ribs from the chiles.

1. Pulse tofu in food processor until coarsely chopped, about 5 pulses. Spread tofu over paper towel–lined baking sheet and let drain for 20 minutes. Gently press dry with paper towels and set aside.

2. Meanwhile, combine carrots, 3 tablespoons vinegar, and ¾ teaspoon sugar in bowl and toss to combine; set aside.

3. Bring 2 quarts water to boil in medium saucepan. Off heat, add vermicelli to hot water and let stand until tender, about 5 minutes. Drain vermicelli in colander and rinse under cold running water until water runs clear. Drain well then transfer to bowl; toss with 1 tablespoon vinegar and 1 teaspoon oil.

4. Place 2 cups basil, Thai chiles, and garlic in now-empty food processor and pulse until finely chopped, about 15 pulses, scraping down sides of bowl as needed. Transfer 2 tablespoons basil mixture to bowl and stir in soy sauce, remaining 1 tablespoon vinegar, and remaining 2 tablespoons sugar; set aside. Transfer remaining basil mixture to 12-inch nonstick skillet.

5. Stir drained tofu, shallots, and remaining 3 tablespoons oil into skillet with basil mixture. Cook over medium-high heat, stirring occasionally, until mixture starts to brown and tofu appears crumbly, about 15 minutes.

6. Stir reserved basil-soy mixture into skillet and cook, stirring constantly, until well coated, about 1 minute. Add remaining 2 cups basil and cook, stirring constantly, until wilted, 30 to 60 seconds. Off heat, stir in peanuts; transfer mixture to platter. Fill lettuce leaves with noodles and top with tofu mixture and pickled carrots (leaving liquid in bowl). Serve.

think like a cook

PICKLES IN A HURRY

Using a topping of picked vegetables is a great way to add texture and tang to a dish, but traditional pickles take hours, days, or even longer to brine. Of course all kinds of pickles are available at the supermarket but we've also come up with some tips for making faster pickled vegetables to use as high-impact toppings in a fraction of the time (and for much less money than premium premade options). In this recipe, we pickle carrots. See Vegetable Bibimbap (page 188) and Tofu Banh Mi (page 304) for other quick-pickle options, and keep these tricks in mind.

Shredding is Grate

If you shred or thinly slice the veggies you want to pickle, it's easier for the pieces to absorb the brine quickly. We shred carrots here but thinly sliced radishes or cucumbers also work well. We pickle thinly sliced red onions in our California-Style Fish Tacos (page 372).

Let Time Work for You

Make your quick pickle when you start cooking so that it has time to sit and develop flavor while you do everything else. It's the easiest kitchen multitasking you'll ever do.

Cauliflower Steaks with Salsa Verde

Serves 4; Total Time 45 minutes

2 heads cauliflower (2 pounds each)
¼ cup extra-virgin olive oil
Salt and pepper
1 recipe Salsa Verde (page 101)
Lemon wedges

1. Adjust oven rack to lowest position and heat oven to 500 degrees. Working with 1 head cauliflower at a time, discard outer leaves of cauliflower and trim stem flush with bottom florets. Halve cauliflower lengthwise through core. Cut one 1½-inch-thick slab lengthwise from each half, trimming any florets not connected to core. Repeat with remaining cauliflower. (You should have 4 steaks; reserve remaining cauliflower for another use.)

2. Place steaks on rimmed baking sheet and drizzle with 2 tablespoons oil. Sprinkle with ¼ teaspoon salt and ⅛ teaspoon pepper and rub to distribute. Flip steaks and repeat.

3. Cover baking sheet tightly with aluminum foil and roast for 5 minutes. Remove foil and roast until bottoms of steaks are well browned, 8 to 10 minutes. Gently flip and continue to roast until tender and second sides are well browned, 6 to 8 more minutes.

4. Transfer steaks to platter and brush evenly with ¼ cup salsa verde. Serve with lemon wedges and remaining salsa verde.

why this recipe works

With more and more people going meatless at least some of the time, it's useful to rethink what we consider a main ingredient. Dinner doesn't always have to be meat and two vegetables. Case in point: cauliflower steaks. When you cook thick planks of cauliflower, they develop a substantial, meaty texture and become nutty and sweet. First steaming the steaks on a baking sheet covered in foil, then finishing with uncovered high-heat roasting, produced four caramelized seared steaks with tender interiors. A bright green salsa verde elevated them to centerpiece status. Look for fresh, firm, bright white heads of cauliflower that feel heavy for their size and are free of blemishes or soft spots; florets are more likely to separate from older heads of cauliflower. Pair this with a simple grain, such as Quinoa Pilaf with Herbs and Lemon (page 76).

think like a cook

MEATY MEAL-MAKERS

Vegetables have often been relegated to side dishes and salads, but the ones that follow definitely deserve center-of-the-plate status. A variety of different preparation methods can expand their potential, giving them main dish status. Here are a few ingredients that we like for the hearty textures and deep flavors that make them particularly well suited for taking the place of meat in your meals.

Cauliflower Is Everything

A surprising workhorse that takes extremely well to being roasted like meat, cauliflower shines in dishes associated with cuts of meat, as in these cauliflower steaks, and also in hearty roasted vegetable salads such as our North African Cauliflower Salad with Chermoula (page 164). It also helps add heartiness and deep flavor to our vegetarian curry (page 376). (Not to mention that it makes an astonishingly good grain-free substitute for rice—see page 202.)

Exceptional Eggplant

Eggplant is a powerhouse vegetable. It has robust flavor, its texture can range from silky to meaty, and it's filling. This makes it a versatile option, from everyday Pasta alla Norma (page 284), where it gives satisfying meat-like heft to tomato sauce, to a company-worthy Stuffed Eggplant with Bulgur (page 378).

Bean Burgers Can't Be Beat

Black beans make a vegetarian burger that's just as hearty as one made from ground meat. It's also super-easy to add flavor to a bean burger without worries about the integrity of the patty; the texture is much more forgiving than meat. For our Black Bean Burgers (page 302), we opted for a Southwestern profile, using ground tortilla chips, scallions, cilantro, garlic, cumin, coriander, and just a dash of hot sauce. Black beans also made a stellar chili (see page 258), boosted with plenty of umami-rich seasonings.

Farro and Broccoli Rabe Gratin

Serves 6; Total Time 1 hour

2 tablespoons extra-virgin olive oil

1 onion, chopped fine

1½ cups whole farro, rinsed

2 cups vegetable broth

4 ounces Parmesan cheese, grated (2 cups)

Salt and pepper

1 pound broccoli rabe, trimmed and cut into 2-inch lengths

6 garlic cloves, minced

⅛ teaspoon red pepper flakes

1 (15-ounce) can small white beans or navy beans, rinsed

½ cup oil-packed sun-dried tomatoes, chopped

why this recipe works

Casseroles get a bad rap for being stodgy, heavy, and old-fashioned. We set out to create a new kind of vegetarian casserole that was both hearty and healthy. We chose Italian flavors, accenting nutty farro with creamy white beans, bitter broccoli rabe, and salty Parmesan. Toasting the farro gave it some extra nuttiness and jump-started the cooking process. Blanching broccoli rabe in salted water tamed its bitterness. We then sautéed it with garlic and pepper flakes for extra flavor. Sun-dried tomatoes contributed the extra pop of flavor we were after. All that was left was to combine all the ingredients in a baking dish, dust with Parmesan, and stick it under the broiler to brown the cheese. Do not substitute pearled (perlato), quick-cooking, or presteamed farro for the whole farro in this recipe; you may need to read the ingredient list on the package carefully to determine if the farro is presteamed.

1. Heat 1 tablespoon oil in large saucepan over medium heat until shimmering. Add onion and cook until softened and lightly browned, 5 to 7 minutes. Stir in farro and cook until lightly toasted, about 2 minutes. Stir in broth and 1½ cups water and bring to simmer. Reduce heat to low and continue to simmer, stirring often, until farro is just tender and remaining liquid has thickened into creamy sauce, 20 to 25 minutes. Off heat, stir in 1 cup Parmesan and season with salt and pepper to taste.

2. Meanwhile, bring 4 quarts water to boil in Dutch oven. Add broccoli rabe and 1 tablespoon salt and cook until just tender, about 2 minutes. Drain broccoli rabe and transfer to bowl.

3. Wipe now-empty pot dry, add remaining 1 tablespoon oil, garlic, and pepper flakes, and cook over medium heat until fragrant and sizzling, 1 to 2 minutes. Stir in drained broccoli rabe and cook until hot and well coated, about 2 minutes. Off heat, stir in farro mixture, beans, and sun-dried tomatoes. Season with salt and pepper to taste.

4. Adjust oven rack 6 inches from broiler element and heat broiler. Pour bean-farro mixture into 13 by 9-inch broiler-safe baking dish and sprinkle with remaining 1 cup Parmesan. Broil until lightly browned and hot, 3 to 5 minutes. Let cool 5 minutes before serving.

think like a cook

PYREX VS. THE BROILER

For this gratin, you need a broiler-safe baking dish. Not all materials are safe to go under the high heat of the broiler, and that includes our favorite all-purpose casserole dish, the 13 by 9-inch Pyrex tempered glass baking dish. That workhorse has many pluses: It's inexpensive, and the transparent glass makes it easy to track browning. It won't react with acidic foods such as tomatoes (metal pans can) and is safe for use with metal utensils. However, Pyrex does not recommend that its tempered glassware go under the broiler; abrupt temperature changes can cause it to crack or shatter, a condition called thermal shock. Unlike tempered glass (and metal pans with nonstick coatings), many ceramic baking dishes are broiler-safe. (Enameled cast-iron dishes are, too, but we find them to be heavy and challenging to maneuver.) So when it comes to dishes that spend time under the broiler's intense heat, we like to use the lightweight **HIC Porcelain Lasagna Baking Dish**. See our shopping guide on page 445 for more information.

Artichoke, Pepper, and Chickpea Tagine

Serves 4 to 6; Total Time 1 hour

why this recipe works

Tagines are complexly spiced North African stews. Many feature long-braised meats, but they can also highlight boldly flavored vegetables, as in this filling tagine that is packed with chunks of artichokes, peppers, and tender chickpeas and spiked with pungent garlic, lots of warm spices, briny olives, and tangy lemon. For the aromatic lemon flavor that distinguishes tagines, we used lemon zest two ways—first as strips that we cooked with the vegetables, then as grated zest, which we stirred in at the end for a fresh hit of lemon. To thaw the artichokes quickly, microwave them, covered, for 3 to 5 minutes. Plain whole-milk yogurt can be substituted for Greek, but the sauce will be thinner. A rasp-style grater makes quick work of turning the garlic into a paste. Serve with couscous.

18 ounces frozen artichokes, thawed

¼ cup extra-virgin olive oil, plus extra for drizzling

2 yellow or red bell peppers, stemmed, seeded, and sliced

1 onion, halved and sliced ¼ inch thick

4 (2-inch) strips lemon zest plus 1 teaspoon grated zest (2 lemons)

8 garlic cloves (6 minced, 2 minced to paste)

1 tablespoon paprika

½ teaspoon ground cumin

¼ teaspoon ground ginger

¼ teaspoon ground coriander

¼ teaspoon ground cinnamon

⅛ teaspoon cayenne pepper

2 tablespoons all-purpose flour

3 cups vegetable broth

2 (15-ounce) cans chickpeas, rinsed

½ cup pitted kalamata olives, halved

½ cup golden raisins

2 tablespoons honey

½ cup plain whole-milk Greek yogurt

½ cup minced fresh cilantro

Salt and pepper

1. Part artichokes dry and cut into quarters if they aren't already. Heat 1 tablespoon oil in Dutch oven over medium heat until shimmering. Add artichokes and cook until golden brown, 5 to 7 minutes; transfer to bowl.

2. Add 1 tablespoon oil to now-empty pot and heat over medium heat until shimmering. Stir in bell peppers, onion, and lemon zest strips and cook until vegetables are softened and lightly browned, 5 to 7 minutes. Stir in minced garlic, paprika, cumin, ginger, coriander, cinnamon, and cayenne and cook until fragrant, about 30 seconds. Stir in flour and cook for 1 minute.

3. Gradually whisk in broth, scraping up any browned bits and smoothing out any lumps. Stir in browned artichokes, chickpeas, olives, raisins, and honey and bring to simmer. Cover, reduce to gentle simmer, and cook until vegetables are tender, about 15 minutes.

4. Off heat, discard lemon zest strips. Stir ¼ cup of hot liquid into yogurt to temper, then stir yogurt mixture into pot. Stir in remaining 2 tablespoons oil, grated lemon zest, garlic paste, and cilantro. Season with salt and pepper to taste. Serve, drizzling individual portions lightly with additional olive oil.

think like a cook

THE BEST ZEST

Citrus zest is the outermost part of the citrus peel—the colorful part of the rind. This is where most of the volatile oils that give citrus its flavor reside, so it's a valuable part of the fruit, especially when you want citrus presence without the acidity of the juice. But the term "zest" can be very confusing because there are various ways to extract zest and each yields a different-size piece. In most instances, we want finely grated zest that can easily incorporate into a recipe. Our favorite tool for this job is a rasp-style grater. When we want a larger strip of zest (like you might see in a cocktail), which can handle longer simmering, we use a vegetable peeler to cut off a swath of peel. You might think the gadget called a zester, which pushes strings of zest through narrow holes, would be preferred for its namesake task, but we actually turn to that tool the least. When zesting, try to avoid removing the bitter white pith under the peel by grating over the same area only once or twice. Use a paring knife to scrape any pith from larger strips of zest.

Chicken Piccata
Serves 4; Total Time 45 minutes

4 (6- to 8-ounce) boneless, skinless chicken breasts, trimmed

Kosher salt and pepper

2 large lemons

¾ cup all-purpose flour

¼ cup plus 1 teaspoon vegetable oil

1 shallot, minced

1 garlic clove, minced

1 cup chicken broth

3 tablespoons unsalted butter, cut into 6 pieces

2 tablespoons capers, rinsed

1 tablespoon minced fresh parsley

why this recipe works

Chicken piccata is one of those Italian dishes that tastes complex but is actually easy to prepare. Tender seared chicken cutlets are bathed in a rich lemon-butter pan sauce cut with the briny bite of capers. But this recipe carries lessons in flavoring the dish: Don't muck it up with extra ingredients (as many versions do) and don't use so little lemon and capers that you end up with boring, bland chicken. To give our piccata multidimensional flavor, we used plenty of fresh lemon juice and also simmered lemon slices in our sauce, imbuing it with fruity aroma from the zest and a subtle bitterness from the pith. A full 2 tablespoons of capers went in toward the end to retain their flavor and structural integrity. Simmering the browned cutlets briefly avoided any gumminess from residual uncooked flour; the flour simply sloughed off into the sauce, thickening it nicely. Serve with buttered noodles, rice, or crusty bread.

1. Cut each chicken breast in half crosswise, then cut each thick piece horizontally in half, creating 3 cutlets of similar thickness from each breast. Place cutlets between sheets of plastic wrap and gently pound to even ½-inch thickness. Place cutlets in bowl and toss with 2 teaspoons salt and ½ teaspoon pepper. Set aside for 15 minutes.

2. Halve 1 lemon lengthwise. Trim ends from 1 half, halve lengthwise again, then cut crosswise ¼-inch-thick slices; set aside. Juice remaining half and whole lemon and set aside 3 tablespoons juice.

3. Spread flour in shallow dish. Dredge 1 cutlet at a time in flour, shaking gently to remove excess, and place on wire rack set in rimmed baking sheet. Heat 2 tablespoons oil in 12-inch skillet over medium-high heat until just smoking. Place 6 cutlets in skillet, reduce heat to medium, and cook until golden brown on 1 side, 2 to 3 minutes. Flip and cook until golden brown on second side, 2 to 3 minutes. Return cutlets to wire rack. Repeat with 2 tablespoons oil and remaining 6 cutlets.

4. Add remaining 1 teaspoon oil and shallot to skillet and cook until softened, about 1 minute. Add garlic and cook until fragrant, about 30 seconds. Add broth, reserved lemon juice, and reserved lemon slices and bring to simmer, scraping up any browned bits.

5. Add cutlets to sauce and simmer for 4 minutes, flipping halfway through simmering. Transfer cutlets to platter. Sauce should be thickened to consistency of heavy cream; if not, simmer 1 minute longer. Off heat, whisk in butter. Stir in capers and parsley. Season with salt and pepper to taste. Spoon sauce over chicken and serve.

think like a cook

WHICH CUT IS A CUTLET?

A cutlet is simply a thin piece of meat, which in past decades was frequently veal, but nowadays is more often chicken. Unlike a boneless chicken breast, a cutlet has been flattened—through slicing and/or pounding—so it cooks quickly; a boon for weeknight dinners. But supermarket options can be ragged and uneven (which defeats the purpose), so we recommend preparing your own. You could pound a whole chicken breast flat but that tends to tear the sides. The classic method involves cutting a breast in half horizontally, but since breasts have a thicker and thinner end, you still have to carefully pound them. When an elongated cutlet shape doesn't matter, a simpler method is to halve the breast crosswise, then split the thick side horizontally to create three similar-size pieces that require minimal pounding. A meat pounder is the ideal tool for that task, but the side of a rolling pin works in a pinch. The medallion-size cutlets cook like a breeze, and are ideal for a skillet chicken dinner prepared on the fly.

Rustic Braised Chicken with Mushrooms

Serves 4; Total Time 45 minutes

4 slices bacon, chopped coarse

4 (12-ounce) bone-in split chicken breasts, trimmed

Kosher salt and pepper

8 ounces cremini mushrooms, trimmed and sliced thin

1 onion, chopped

¼ cup tomato paste

¾ ounce dried porcini mushrooms, rinsed and minced

3 garlic cloves, minced

2 teaspoons minced fresh thyme or ½ teaspoon dried

1 cup water

¼ cup minced fresh parsley

1 tablespoon red wine vinegar

1. Cook bacon in Dutch oven over medium heat until crisp, 5 to 7 minutes. Using slotted spoon, transfer bacon to paper towel–lined plate; set aside. Pour off all but 1 tablespoon fat from pot.

2. Pat chicken dry with paper towels and season with salt and pepper. Heat fat left in pot over medium-high heat until just smoking. Brown chicken well, about 5 minutes per side; transfer to plate. Remove and discard chicken skin.

3. Add cremini mushrooms and onion to fat left in pot and cook over medium heat until softened and lightly browned, about 8 minutes. Stir in tomato paste, porcini mushrooms, garlic, and thyme and cook until fragrant, about 1 minute. Stir in water, scraping up any browned bits, and bring to simmer.

4. Nestle chicken into pot along with any accumulated juices. Reduce heat to medium-low, cover, and simmer gently until thermometer inserted into chicken registers 160 degrees, 10 to 15 minutes. Transfer chicken to serving platter. Stir crisp bacon, parsley, and vinegar into sauce and season with salt and pepper to taste. Spoon sauce over chicken and serve.

why this recipe works

Sometimes you want a cozy, comforting meal, but it's a Tuesday night and you just need to get dinner on the table. This satisfying dish is the answer. It delivers deep flavor in the time it takes bone-in chicken breasts to cook through. To build a savory base, we crisped up some bacon, then browned skin-on chicken breasts in the fat to create a fond before removing the skin so it didn't get soggy in the braise. Sautéing cremini mushrooms and aromatics in the bacon fat (with a savory lift from tomato paste) deepened their flavors. We also added a hefty amount of minced dried porcini mushrooms. This served two purposes: It added a punch of bold mushroom flavor and thickened the sauce so that it clung perfectly to the chicken even without a long simmer. Serve with potatoes, rice (see page 74), or buttered noodles.

think like a cook

FLAVOR BOOSTER: DRIED MUSHROOMS

Incorporating dried mushrooms into a dish is an easy way to add a concentrated dose of earthy umami. Porcini and shiitake mushrooms are both good options. As with fresh vegetables, quality can vary dramatically, so always inspect dried mushrooms closely before buying. Avoid packages filled with small, dusty pieces or pieces full of small holes (which can indicate worms) and those labeled "wild mushroom mix"—which are often older and of lesser quality. Dried mushrooms should have an earthy (not musty) aroma. Store dried mushrooms in an airtight container in a cool, dry place for up to one year.

Dried mushrooms should be rinsed thoroughly to remove any dirt and grit. If you aren't cooking them in liquid (as in this recipe), you can simply mince them and add them. Otherwise, you typically want to rehydrate them before using. An easy way to do this is to micro-wave the mushrooms, covered, with at least twice the volume of water or broth for about 30 seconds, then let them stand for 5 minutes until they become pliable. (Alternatively, pour boiling water over them and soak for about 5 minutes.) Don't throw out the soaking liquid; once strained, it adds even more flavor to soups, stews, and rice dishes. We use a fine-mesh strainer lined with a single paper towel or paper coffee filter.

An even more convenient way to add mushroomy flavor to a dish is to process dried porcini into a powder with a spice grinder (or mortar and pestle). This potent powder can be sprinkled anywhere you want a hit of flavor, or used as a dry rub for chicken and meat.

Chicken and Cauliflower Tikka Masala with Basmati Rice

Serves 4; Total Time 1 hour

1½ cups basmati rice

2¼ cups water

Salt and pepper

1 tablespoon garam masala

4 (6- to 8-ounce) boneless, skinless chicken breasts, trimmed and cut into 1-inch cubes

2 tablespoons vegetable oil

½ head cauliflower (1 pound), cored and cut into ½-inch pieces

1 onion, chopped fine

2 tablespoons grated fresh ginger

3 garlic cloves, minced

1 (28-ounce) can crushed tomatoes

¼ cup heavy cream

¼ cup fresh cilantro leaves

why this recipe works

With its fragrant, deeply spiced tomato sauce and tender meat, chicken tikka masala is one of the most popular takeout dishes in the world. But it's also completely approachable for weeknight home cooking—with the right combination of ingredients and time-saving tricks. For our version, we saved time (and dishes) by poaching cubes of boneless chicken breast directly in the flavorful sauce. A combination of garlic, ginger, and garam masala brought depth of flavor to our sauce without the usual laundry list of spices. Adding cauliflower made this a heartier dinner option; we started it in the pot at the beginning of the cooking process to ensure it was tender by the time the chicken cooked through. Long-grain white, jasmine, or Texmati rice can be substituted for the basmati.

1. Rinse rice in fine-mesh strainer until water runs clear. Bring rice, water, and ¼ teaspoon salt to simmer in large saucepan over medium heat. Reduce heat to low, cover, and simmer until rice is tender and liquid is absorbed, 16 to 18 minutes. Remove pot from heat, lay clean folded dish towel underneath lid, and let sit for 10 minutes.

2. While rice cooks, combine garam masala, ¾ teaspoon salt, and ½ teaspoon pepper in small bowl. In medium bowl, toss chicken with 1 tablespoon oil and 1 tablespoon spice mixture.

3. Heat remaining 1 tablespoon oil in Dutch oven over medium-high heat until shimmering. Add cauliflower and onion and cook until onion is softened, about 5 minutes. Stir in ginger, garlic, and remaining spice mixture and cook until fragrant, about 30 seconds.

4. Add chicken and tomatoes to pot, bring to simmer, and cook until chicken is cooked through and cauliflower is tender, 10 to 12 minutes.

5. Off heat, stir in cream. Season with salt and pepper to taste, and sprinkle with cilantro. Serve with rice.

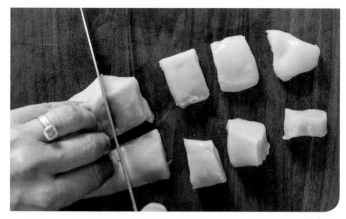

think like a cook

ALL ABOUT CANNED TOMATOES

Since canned tomatoes are processed at the height of freshness, they deliver more flavor than off-season fresh tomatoes. We tested a variety of canned tomato products to determine the best uses for each.

Whole Tomatoes

Whole peeled tomatoes are best when fresh tomato flavor is a must. Whole tomatoes are quite soft and break down quickly when cooked. Those packed in juice rather than puree have a livelier, fresher flavor.

Diced Tomatoes

Machine-diced tomatoes often contain calcium chloride, which helps the chunks maintain their shape. We use them in sauces and long-cooked stews and soups where distinct pieces of tomato are desired. We favor diced tomatoes packed in juice rather than in puree.

Crushed Tomatoes

Crushed tomatoes are whole tomatoes ground very finely, then enriched with tomato puree. Their thicker consistency makes them ideal when you want to make a sauce quickly, as we do here. You can make your own by crushing canned diced tomatoes in a food processor.

Tomato Puree and Tomato Sauce

These are both cooked and strained to remove the seeds. They're much smoother and thicker than other products, but lack a fresh tomato flavor. This makes them more suited to long-cooked dishes (think braised meat sauces), where their thick, even texture is important and bright tomato flavor is not.

Lime-Ginger Chicken and Rice with Edamame and Shiitakes

Serves 4; Total Time 1 hour

4 (6- to 8-ounce) boneless, skinless chicken breasts, trimmed

Salt and pepper

2 tablespoons vegetable oil

1 onion, chopped fine

8 ounces shiitake mushrooms, stemmed and sliced thin

2 tablespoons grated fresh ginger

4 garlic cloves, minced

½ teaspoon grated lime zest plus 2 tablespoons juice

3½ cups chicken broth

1½ cups long-grain white rice

4 carrots, peeled and sliced on bias ½ inch thick

1 cup frozen shelled edamame

⅓ cup dry-roasted peanuts, chopped

2 tablespoons soy sauce

1 tablespoon toasted sesame oil

2 scallions, sliced thin on bias

why this recipe works

Chicken and rice for dinner; nothing more basic, right? Well, it doesn't have to be that way. This version tastes like a cross between chicken with rice and chicken fried rice, with a bright flavor profile that's anything but boring. We started with ginger, garlic, and lime zest, which we bloomed in the skillet to deepen their flavors. Cooking the chicken, rice, vegetables, and aromatics in a single pan infused the whole dish with tons of flavor. Be sure to use chicken breasts that are roughly the same size for even cooking. You will need a 12-inch skillet with a tight-fitting lid for this recipe. Once you add the browned chicken in step 2, the skillet will be fairly full, so you may want to use a straight-sided skillet or sauté pan if you have one. Serve with lime wedges and Sriracha.

1. Pat chicken dry with paper towels and season with salt and pepper. Heat 1 tablespoon vegetable oil in 12-inch skillet over medium-high heat until just smoking. Add chicken and cook until golden brown on 1 side, 4 to 6 minutes; transfer to plate.

2. Add remaining 1 tablespoon vegetable oil to now-empty skillet and heat over medium heat until shimmering. Add onion, mushrooms, and ½ teaspoon salt and cook until vegetables are softened and mushrooms have released their liquid, about 5 minutes. Stir in ginger, garlic, and lime zest and cook until fragrant, about 30 seconds. Stir in broth, rice, and carrots, scraping up any browned bits. Nestle chicken, browned side up, into skillet along with any accumulated juices. Bring to simmer, then reduce heat to medium-low, cover, and simmer gently until thermometer inserted into chicken registers 160 degrees, about 10 minutes.

3. Transfer chicken to cutting board, tent loosely with aluminum foil, and let rest while finishing rice. Stir edamame into rice mixture in skillet, cover, and cook until liquid is absorbed and rice is tender, 5 to 10 minutes.

4. Off heat, stir peanuts, lime juice, soy sauce, and sesame oil into rice mixture, then season with salt and pepper to taste and gently fluff with fork. Slice chicken into ½-inch-thick slices and arrange on top of rice. Sprinkle with scallions and serve.

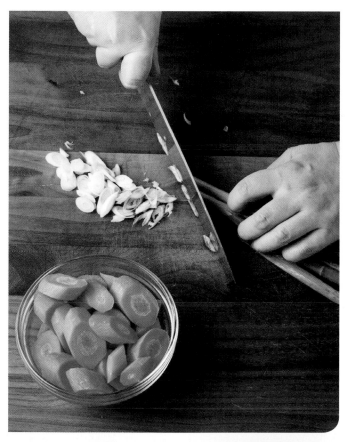

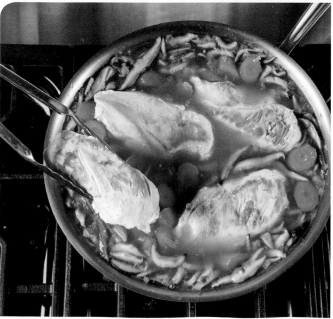

think like a cook

MAKING THE MOST OF CHICKEN PARTS

Chicken parts are quick and easy to cook and take well to many preparations. However, it pays to know the differences among the cuts. All have their advantages.

Bone-In Parts

Perhaps the most versatile choice, bone-in breasts can be cooked by any method. The bones protect the meat from drying out during searing or roasting and help flavor soups and stews. And the skin, when prepared right, can be delightfully crisp. Just be sure to avoid overcooking, as breasts will turn tough and dry.

Bone-in thighs also take well to any cooking method. Richer and less mild than breasts, they lend great flavor when braised and leave a great fond when seared—the perfect base for a sauce. Unlike breasts, thighs are nearly impossible to overcook (see page 323) and are even better when cooked to a higher temperature.

Boneless Parts

Boneless breasts are the hero of weeknight dinners for their convenience. But stick to fast preparations like stir-frying or searing, as they quickly turn from moist to dry and stringy. In the recipe here, the rice insulates the chicken, helping to prevent overcooking.

Boneless thighs do well in strongly flavored dishes and dishes with longer cooking times so the meat breaks down into tender pieces. This is a good cut to use whenever you'll be shredding the chicken (think tacos, chili, or pulled chicken) as there are no skin and bones to work around.

Drumsticks

Because of their shape, drumsticks don't sear well, but otherwise can be treated similar to bone-in thighs. Braised or stewed, they can become tender and silky. Roasted, the skin can turn out shatteringly crisp.

One-Pan Lemon-Braised Chicken Thighs with Chickpeas and Fennel

Serves 4; Total Time 1 hour 10 minutes

2 (15-ounce) cans chickpeas, rinsed

6 (5- to 7-ounce) bone-in chicken thighs, trimmed

Salt and pepper

1 tablespoon olive oil

1 large fennel bulb, stalks discarded, bulb halved and cut into ½-inch-thick wedges through core

4 garlic cloves, minced

2 teaspoons grated lemon zest plus 1½ tablespoons juice

1 teaspoon ground coriander

½ teaspoon red pepper flakes

½ cup dry white wine

1 cup pitted large brine-cured green olives, halved

¾ cup chicken broth

1 tablespoon honey

2 tablespoons chopped fresh parsley

why this recipe works

People think of braises as all-day affairs, but with bone-in chicken thighs, a hearty braise can be a relatively quick meal. When braising chicken, we often remove the skin as it can turn flabby, but there is a way to maintain crispiness. We first browned bone-in thighs and removed them to build a hefty sauce of chickpeas (mashing some to thicken the sauce), fennel, and olives. We then nestled the chicken back in the pan: Elevated just enough, the chicken's skin remained crispy even as the meat braised away in the liquid below. "Overcooking" the chicken to a temperature of 185 degrees rendered fat and melted the tough connective tissues for a rich dish with ultratender meat. We prefer briny green olives such as Manzanilla, Picholine, or Cerignola in this recipe; look for them at your grocery store's salad bar or in the pickle aisle.

1. Adjust oven rack to upper-middle position and heat oven to 350 degrees. Place ½ cup chickpeas in bowl and mash to coarse puree with potato masher; set aside. Pat chicken dry with paper towels and season with salt and pepper.

2. Heat oil in ovensafe 12-inch skillet over medium-high heat until just smoking. Cook chicken, skin side down, until skin is crisped and well browned, 8 to 10 minutes. Transfer chicken to plate, skin side up.

3. Pour off all but 2 tablespoons fat from skillet. Heat fat left in skillet over medium heat until shimmering. Add fennel, cut side down; sprinkle with ¼ teaspoon salt. Cook, covered, until lightly browned, 3 to 5 minutes per side. Add garlic, lemon zest, coriander, and pepper flakes and cook, uncovered, until fragrant, about 30 seconds. Stir in wine, scraping up any browned bits, and cook until almost evaporated, about 2 minutes.

4. Stir in olives, broth, lemon juice, honey, mashed chickpeas, and remaining whole chickpeas and bring to simmer. Nestle chicken into liquid, keeping skin above surface. Transfer skillet to oven and bake, uncovered, until fennel is tender and thermometer inserted into chicken registers 185 degrees, 35 to 40 minutes. Sprinkle with parsley and serve.

think like a cook

OVERCOOK YOUR CHICKEN THIGHS: JUST TRUST US

Unlike white chicken meat, which dries out and toughens when overcooked, dark meat benefits from being cooked beyond the temperature at which it's technically done (175 degrees). That's because dark meat contains twice as much collagen as white meat. The longer the meat cooks, the more that collagen breaks down into gelatin, which coats the muscle fibers and makes the meat juicy and tender. (Dark meat also contains roughly twice as much fat, which coats the meat's proteins, and has a higher pH, which helps it retain moisture more effectively.) But it's important to cook thighs low and slow: The more time the meat spends between 140 degrees (the temperature at which collagen begins to break down) and its final temperature, the more collagen will be converted into gelatin and the more tender and juicy the meat will be. We proved the point by cooking two batches of chicken thighs to the high temperature of 195 degrees, one on the stovetop and one in a 300-degree oven. Whereas the stovetop-cooked thighs reached 195 degrees in about 25 minutes and were moderately tender, the oven-cooked thighs lingered for nearly twice as long and were much more tender and pleasant to eat. The final oven-braising step does the same for the chicken thighs in this one-pan dinner.

Italian Sausage with White Beans and Kale

Serves 4; Total Time 1 hour

2 (15-ounce) cans cannellini beans, rinsed

1 (28-ounce) can diced tomatoes, drained with juice reserved

1 cup chicken broth

2 tablespoons extra-virgin olive oil

1 pound sweet or hot Italian sausage, pricked all over with fork

1 onion, chopped fine

3 garlic cloves, minced

1 pound kale, stemmed and chopped

Salt and pepper

1. Puree ½ cup beans, ½ cup tomatoes, reserved tomato juice, and chicken broth in food processor until smooth, about 30 seconds.

2. Heat oil in Dutch oven over medium heat until shimmering. Add sausages and brown on all sides, about 5 minutes; transfer to plate.

3. Add onion to fat left in pot and cook until softened, 5 to 7 minutes. Stir in garlic and cook until fragrant, about 30 seconds. Stir in bean puree mixture, remaining drained tomatoes, kale, and ¼ teaspoon salt, scraping up any browned bits. Cover and simmer, stirring occasionally, until kale is wilted and tender, about 15 minutes.

4. Stir in remaining whole beans, then nestle browned sausages and any accumulated juices into pot. Cover and simmer until thermometer inserted into sausages registers 160 degrees and sauce is thickened slightly, about 10 minutes. Season with salt and pepper to taste, and serve.

why this recipe works

This dish of sausage, beans, and greens is the ideal back-pocket dinner. Few combinations are as delicious, as hearty, or as simple. We browned sausages in a Dutch oven and then removed them and sautéed chopped onion and garlic in the rendered fat. Next, we added diced tomatoes and chopped kale to simmer until tender. Finally, we added back the sausage along with drained canned cannellini beans and simmered them just to cook the sausage through and allow the beans to absorb some of the sauce. Since the resulting sauce was a bit thin, we decided to puree a portion of the tomatoes and white beans with some chicken broth for additional flavor and stir this into the pot along with the tomatoes and kale. Serve with crusty bread.

think like a cook

SAUSAGE PRIMER

Sausages can be made from almost any type of meat (or combination of meats), although in the test kitchen we tend to favor highly seasoned pork sausages. They can add meaty, spicy depth to soups, stews, stuffings, casseroles, and pasta, or even take center stage for a simple dinner as in the recipe here. These are the four types we use most.

Andouille

Born in France, this very spicy smoked and cured sausage emigrated to Louisiana, finding wide acceptance in its new home. You can't make a gumbo (see page 268) or jambalaya without andouille. It is seasoned with garlic, dried hot pepper, and herbs. It doesn't need to be cooked (although cooking augments its flavor).

Chorizo

The most common chorizo in American markets is sold fully cooked and is seasoned with garlic and chili powder. We use it to lend kick to casseroles, potatoes, eggs, and any dishes with Latin origins. Less common in this country are Spanish- and Mexican-style chorizos. The former is a hard, smoky cured sausage with the texture of pepperoni; it is often served as an appetizer with cheese. The latter is made from fresh pork seasoned with garlic, paprika, and chili powder and must be cooked.

Italian

Italian sausages are either hot or sweet. Both are made with coarsely ground fresh (not cured or smoked) pork flavored with garlic and fennel seeds. The hot variety is also seasoned with red pepper flakes. Both need to be cooked. Grill or sauté whole sausages or remove the casing and crumble the meat into pastas or stews.

Kielbasa

This smoked sausage hails from Poland. Although its main seasoning is garlic, it's neither hot nor assertive. Kielbasa is sold fully cooked, but a good sear improves both flavor and texture. Some brands are much saltier than others, so always taste for seasoning when you cook with kielbasa.

Restaurant-Style Beef Stir-Fry

Serves 4; Total Time 1 hour

why this recipe works

We covered our simple stir-fry rules earlier (on page 67). This slightly more complex recipe is designed to re-create restaurant-style beef stir-fry, characterized by its velvety, tender beef. We adapted a Chinese restaurant technique called velveting, which uses a marinade of egg whites, cornstarch, water, and salt to tenderize the meat and give it a plush, silky coating. To simplify the multistep process, we applied an easier tenderizing trick by soaking sliced flank steak in a baking soda solution, then added it to a soy sauce–cornstarch marinade for perfectly tender beef. The Cantonese dish, black pepper beef (*hei hu jiao niu liu*), inspired the vegetables and salty-sweet-spicy pepper sauce that completed the stir-fry. Prepare the vegetables and aromatics while the beef is marinating. Serve with rice (see page 74).

1 tablespoon plus ¼ cup water

¼ teaspoon baking soda

1 pound flank steak, trimmed, cut lengthwise into 2- to 2½-inch strips, then cut crosswise against grain into ¼-inch-thick slices

3 tablespoons soy sauce

3 tablespoons Chinese rice wine or dry sherry

1 tablespoon cornstarch

2½ teaspoons packed light brown sugar

1 tablespoon oyster sauce

2 teaspoons rice vinegar

1½ teaspoons toasted sesame oil

2 teaspoons coarsely ground pepper

3 tablespoons plus 1 teaspoon vegetable oil

1 red bell pepper, stemmed, seeded, and cut into ¼-inch strips

1 green bell pepper, stemmed, seeded, and cut into ¼-inch strips

6 scallions, white parts sliced thin on bias, green parts cut into 2-inch pieces

3 garlic cloves, minced

1 tablespoon grated fresh ginger

1. Combine 1 tablespoon water and baking soda in medium bowl. Add beef and toss to coat. Let sit at room temperature for 5 minutes.

2. Whisk 1 tablespoon soy sauce, 1 tablespoon rice wine, 1½ teaspoons cornstarch, and ½ teaspoon sugar together in small bowl. Add mixture to beef, stir to coat, and let sit at room temperature for 15 to 30 minutes.

3. Whisk remaining ¼ cup water, 2 tablespoons soy sauce, 2 tablespoons rice wine, 1½ teaspoons cornstarch, 2 teaspoons sugar, oyster sauce, vinegar, sesame oil, and pepper in second bowl and set sauce aside.

4. Heat 2 teaspoons vegetable oil in 12-inch nonstick skillet over high heat until just smoking. Add half of beef in single layer. Cook without stirring for 1 minute. Continue to cook, stirring occasionally, until spotty brown on both sides, about 1 minute longer. Transfer to bowl. Repeat with 2 teaspoons vegetable oil and remaining beef.

5. Return skillet to high heat, add 2 teaspoons vegetable oil, and heat until just smoking. Add bell peppers and scallion greens and cook, stirring occasionally, until vegetables are spotty brown and crisp-tender, about 4 minutes. Transfer vegetables to bowl with beef.

6. Return now-empty skillet to medium-high heat and add remaining 4 teaspoons vegetable oil, scallion whites, garlic, and ginger. Cook, stirring frequently, until lightly browned, about 2 minutes. Return beef and vegetables to skillet and stir to combine. Whisk sauce to recombine. Add to skillet and cook, stirring constantly, until sauce has thickened, about 30 seconds. Serve immediately.

think like a cook

GOING AGAINST THE GRAIN

To get small, tender pieces of beef in this stir-fry, you first cut flank steak along the grain of the meat into long strips, and then slice these against the grain into pieces. If that sounds confusing, let's start with the fact that meat has a grain. The grain is determined by the direction in which the muscle fibers run. The grain of flank steak is pretty easy to see; all the fibers run parallel to one another. Those wide muscle fibers are also what makes flank steak chewier than some other cuts.

Cutting the meat perpendicular to its muscle striations, or against the grain, breaks them up, making the meat more tender. This applies to both cooked meat that you're slicing to serve and raw meat that you're cutting before cooking, as in this stir-fry. We've actually tested flank steak cut both with and against the grain using a texture analyzer, which tests how much force is needed to "bite" into the slices. We found that steak cut with the grain required four times more force to "chew" it to the same degree, so proper slicing can make a huge difference in the meat's tenderness. If you're ever unable to tell the direction of the grain in meat, make a test slice. If you see that you've cut parallel to the grain, turn the meat 90 degrees before cutting again.

Easy Steak Frites

Serves 4; Total Time 1 hour

4 tablespoons unsalted butter, softened

1 shallot, minced

1 tablespoon minced fresh parsley

1 garlic clove, minced

Kosher salt and pepper

2½ pounds large Yukon Gold potatoes, unpeeled

6 cups plus 1 tablespoon peanut or vegetable oil

2 (1-pound) boneless strip steaks, 1¼ to 1½ inches thick, trimmed and halved crosswise

1. Mash butter, shallot, parsley, garlic, ½ teaspoon salt, and ¼ teaspoon pepper together in bowl; set compound butter aside.

2. Square off potatoes by cutting ¼-inch-thick slice from each of their 4 long sides; discard slices. Cut potatoes lengthwise into ¼-inch-thick planks. Stack 3 or 4 planks and cut into ¼-inch-thick fries. Repeat with remaining potatoes. (Do not place sliced potatoes in water.)

3. Line rimmed baking sheet with triple layer of paper towels. Combine potatoes and 6 cups oil in Dutch oven. Cook over high heat until oil is vigorously bubbling, about 5 minutes. Continue to cook, without stirring, until potatoes are limp but exteriors are beginning to firm, about 15 minutes. Using tongs, stir potatoes, gently scraping up any that stick, and continue to cook, stirring occasionally, until golden and crispy, 7 to 10 minutes longer.

4. Meanwhile, pat steaks dry with paper towels and season with salt and pepper. Heat remaining 1 tablespoon oil in 12-inch skillet over medium-high heat until just smoking. Add steaks and cook, turning once, until well browned and thermometer inserted into center registers 120 to 125 degrees (for medium-rare), 4 to 7 minutes per side. Transfer steaks to platter, top each with compound butter, tent with aluminum foil, and let rest for 10 minutes.

5. Using spider skimmer or slotted spoon, transfer fries to prepared sheet and season with salt. Serve fries with steaks.

why this recipe works

Steak frites (aka steak with French fries) is an absolute classic and a French bistro staple. To bring this restaurant regular home without the benefit of a commercial deep-fryer or a sous chef, we streamlined the usual frying process. An unusual frying technique—starting the potatoes in cold oil—resulted in crispy exteriors and creamy interiors for our fries without the usual fuss of monitoring the oil temperature and frying the potatoes twice, as is traditionally done. For the steaks, thick-cut boneless strip steaks gave us time to get a nice crust on the exteriors. A quick compound butter dolloped on top of the steaks while they rested made the world's simplest sauce. For the best French fries, we recommend using large Yukon Gold potatoes (10 to 12 ounces each) that are similar in size. We prefer peanut oil for frying for its high smoke point and clean taste, but you can use vegetable oil, if desired. Use a Dutch oven that holds 6 quarts or more for this recipe.

think like a cook

BUTTER IT UP

Compound butters—butters mixed with fresh herbs or other potent ingredients—are an easy way to add flavor to meat, fish, and vegetables, as well as baked goods like biscuits and muffins. They can be savory, as in the herb and garlic butter we put on our Easy Steak Frites, or sweet. Here are a few combinations we like—simply combine these ingredients with 4 tablespoons of softened unsalted butter and season to taste with salt and pepper. The compound butter can then either be shaped into a log and rechilled, or simply used as is.

Rosemary-Parmesan Butter

3 tablespoons grated Parmesan + 2 teaspoons minced fresh rosemary + 1 minced garlic clove + 1 pinch red pepper flakes

Tarragon-Lime Butter

1 tablespoon minced fresh tarragon + 2 teaspoons lime juice + 2 tablespoons minced scallions

Sweet Orange Butter

½ teaspoon grated orange zest + 1 teaspoon sugar + dash vanilla extract (season with salt only; omit pepper)

Honey Butter

2 tablespoons honey (season with salt only; omit pepper)

Crunchy Pork Chops with Winter Squash and Cranberry Sauce

Serves 4; Total Time 1 hour

¼ cup all-purpose flour

2 large eggs

3 tablespoons Dijon mustard

2 cups panko bread crumbs

2 ounces Parmesan cheese, grated (1 cup)

¼ cup minced fresh parsley

3 tablespoons extra-virgin olive oil

Salt and pepper

4 (6- to 8-ounce) boneless pork chops, ¾ to 1 inch thick, trimmed

1 large acorn squash (2 pounds), sliced into ½-inch-thick rings and seeded

1 cup plus 1 tablespoon sugar

12 ounces (3 cups) fresh or thawed frozen cranberries

¼ cup water

¼ teaspoon five-spice powder

why this recipe works

One-pan meals are a weeknight cook's best friend. Here, a wire rack in a sheet pan is the setting for a full menu of fall flavors (with a little help from the microwave). We used a combination of panko bread crumbs—toasted in the microwave—and grated Parmesan to give our pork chops a supercrunchy crust. Elevating the chops on a wire rack ensured they stayed crunchy as they cooked. For a complementary side dish, we sliced acorn squash into rings and then softened them in the microwave before adding them to the sheet pan with the pork, so they would finish cooking at the same time as the meat. A sweet-tart cranberry sauce rounded out our menu. The microwave helped a third time here; it easily cooked the cranberries, producing the perfect sauce for our hearty roasted dinner.

1. Adjust oven rack to middle position and heat oven to 425 degrees. Spray wire rack with vegetable oil spray, then set in rimmed baking sheet lined with aluminum foil. Spread flour in shallow dish. Whisk eggs and mustard together in second shallow dish. Toast panko in bowl in microwave, stirring often, until deep golden brown, 3 to 5 minutes; let cool briefly. Toss toasted panko, Parmesan, parsley, and 2 tablespoons oil together in third shallow dish and season with salt and pepper.

2. Pat pork dry with paper towels and cut 2 slits, about 2 inches apart, through fat on edges of each chop. Season with salt and pepper. Working with 1 chop at a time, dredge in flour, dip in egg mixture, then coat with toasted panko mixture, pressing gently to adhere. Lay breaded chops on 1 side of prepared wire rack, spaced at least ¼ inch apart.

3. Place squash on large plate, brush with remaining 1 tablespoon oil, and season with salt and pepper. Microwave squash until it begins to soften but still holds its shape, 8 to 10 minutes.

4. Place squash on prepared wire rack opposite pork, slightly overlapping if needed, and sprinkle with 1 tablespoon sugar. Bake pork chops and squash until thermometer inserted in center of chops registers 145 degrees and squash is slightly tender, 20 to 30 minutes. Remove sheet from oven and let rest for 5 minutes.

5. While chops bake, combine remaining 1 cup sugar, cranberries, water, five-spice powder, and ¼ teaspoon salt in bowl and microwave, stirring occasionally, until cranberries are broken down and juicy, about 10 minutes. Coarsely mash cranberries with fork and serve with pork chops and squash.

think like a cook

SHEET PAN + WIRE RACK = DINNER MAGIC

One of the busiest pans in the test kitchen is the rimmed baking sheet (aka the sheet pan). The pan has many uses beyond baking, but our favorite is this: If you stick a wire grid-style cooling rack inside one, you have a nifty way to elevate food for better air circulation and to catch drips, and this becomes your go-to setup for roasting and broiling meat and holding foods after frying. Cooked this way, our breaded pork chops crisp evenly above and below; we also use the setup to roast beef (see page 82) and chicken parts (see page 88), among other things. To do this properly, you need a pan that won't warp under high heat and will accommodate a wire rack; one with straight, smooth sides best contains pan juices. An 18 by 13-inch pan does the job. Our winner is **Nordic Ware Baker's Half Sheet**. Our winning wire rack, which can withstand a hot broiler, cleans up without warping, and fits snugly in a standard rimming baking sheet, is **Libertyware Half Size Sheet Pan Cooling Rack**. See pages 444 and 450 for more information.

Maple-Glazed Pork Chops

Serves 4; Total Time 25 minutes

GLAZE
½ cup maple syrup
2 teaspoons Dijon mustard
¼ cup cider vinegar
1 teaspoon minced fresh thyme

CHOPS
4 (6- to 8-ounce) boneless pork chops, ¾ to 1 inch thick, trimmed
Salt and pepper
1 tablespoon vegetable oil

1. FOR THE GLAZE Combine all ingredients in bowl.

2. FOR THE CHOPS Cut 2 slits, about 2 inches apart, through fat on edges of each pork chop. Pat chops dry with paper towels and season with salt and pepper. Heat oil in 12-inch skillet over medium-high heat until just smoking. Add chops and cook until well browned on first side, about 5 minutes.

3. Turn chops and add glaze to pan. Reduce heat to medium-low and cook until thermometer inserted into center of chops registers 145 degrees, 5 to 8 minutes.

4. Transfer chops to plate and tent with aluminum foil. Increase heat to medium and continue to simmer glaze until thick and glossy, 2 to 6 minutes, adding any accumulated pork juices to pan. Pour glaze over chops and serve.

why this recipe works

Throwing a few boneless pork chops into a skillet sounds like a promising route to a week-night meal. But the lean chops quickly dry out. A simple solution that also adds flavor is to give them a glaze. We started by cutting slits in the pork's fat and silverskin to prevent the chops from contracting and curling up in the hot pan. We seared the chops on just one side to impart browning without overcooking and then flipped them, added our glaze, and lowered the heat to cook them gently. A glaze of maple syrup, mustard, and cider vinegar walked the line between sweet and savory. When the chops finished, we removed them to rest and reduced the glaze until thick and glossy, but not overly syrupy, adding in the juices from the rested meat. Be careful not to overreduce the glaze in step 4. If the glaze thickens to the correct consistency before the chops reach 145 degrees, add a few table-spoons of water to the pan. Serve with Pan-Roasted Potatoes (page 56).

variations

Orange-Chipotle-Glazed Pork Chops
Substitute following mixture for maple glaze: ⅔ cup orange juice (2 oranges), 1 teaspoon lime juice, 1 teaspoon minced canned chipotle chile in adobo sauce, and 1½ tablespoons sugar. Simmer glaze as directed, adding ½ teaspoon grated lime zest to glaze with accumulated pork juices.

Pineapple-Soy-Glazed Pork Chops
Substitute following mixture for maple glaze: ⅔ cup pineapple juice, 1 tablespoon soy sauce, ¼ cup rice vinegar, 1 teaspoon grated fresh ginger, and 2 tablespoons packed brown sugar. Simmer glaze as directed, adding ½ teaspoon toasted sesame oil with accumulated pork juices.

think like a cook

GLAZING OVER

Unlike rubs and marinades, which are added before cooking, and unlike sauces, which are typically added after cooking, a glaze is applied during cooking, usually towards the end, so that it has time to build flavor and even caramelize in the pan but not enough time to burn (since most glazes are high in sugar, they tend to burn easily). Applying the glaze toward the end of cooking also gives the meat time to develop a sear or for the skin to crisp up if you're cooking poultry. In this pork chop recipe, we use a two-step approach, first simmering the chops in a maple syrup mixture that then gets reduced down to a glaze, which is poured over the meat for a double dose of flavor. In longer-cooked recipes where the glaze isn't the cooking medium, such as when we are grilling or baking, we sometimes brush on layers of glaze in stages, letting each coat dry so the next has something to cling to. This builds additional flavor without the danger of the outermost layer getting overcooked.

Thai-Style Pork Burgers with Sesame Green Beans

Serves 4; Total Time 1 hour

1 pound green beans, trimmed

Salt and pepper

¼ cup mayonnaise

4 teaspoons Sriracha sauce

1½ teaspoons grated lime zest plus 1 tablespoon juice

1 tablespoon toasted sesame oil

1 tablespoon sesame seeds

3 tablespoons milk

1 teaspoon fish sauce

3 tablespoons minced fresh cilantro plus ½ cup leaves

1 slice hearty white sandwich bread, torn into 1-inch pieces

1½ pounds ground pork

1 tablespoon vegetable oil

4 hamburger buns

1. Bring 2 quarts water to boil in large saucepan. Fill large bowl halfway with ice and water. Add green beans and 1 tablespoon salt to boiling water and cook until crisp-tender, about 6 minutes. Drain green beans and place in ice bath to cool. Drain again, transfer to salad spinner, and spin dry.

2. Meanwhile, whisk mayonnaise, 2 teaspoons Sriracha, and ½ teaspoon lime zest together in small bowl. Season with salt to taste; set aside. Transfer drained beans to serving bowl and toss with lime juice, sesame oil, and sesame seeds. Season with salt and pepper to taste; set aside.

3. Combine remaining 2 teaspoons Sriracha, remaining 1 teaspoon lime zest, milk, fish sauce, minced cilantro, bread, and 1 teaspoon pepper in large bowl. Mash to paste with fork. Using your hands, add pork and mix until well combined.

4. Divide pork mixture into 4 equal balls, then flatten each into ¾-inch-thick patties, about 4 inches wide.

why this recipe works

Meaty burgers don't always have to be about the beef. Ground pork is just as convenient and quick, and it lends itself to a different profile of flavors. However, burgers made from ground pork are notoriously dry and crumbly, so we added a panade (a mixture of bread and milk) to keep the patties moist and cohesive. The panade also provided an opportunity to pack in the flavor; we added cilantro, lime zest, Sriracha, and a single teaspoon of salty, potent fish sauce to the bread and milk to give the mild pork a Thai-style flavor boost. A simple green bean salad with complementary flavors paired perfectly with the burgers. Shocking the cooked beans in ice water—a classic technique used when blanching vegetables—halted their cooking abruptly, ensuring they maintained their vibrant color and crisp bite.

5. Heat vegetable oil in 12-inch nonstick skillet over medium-low heat until shimmering. Add patties and cook until well browned on first side, 6 to 8 minutes. Flip burgers and continue to cook until second side is well browned and thermometer inserted into center of burger from top edge registers 150 degrees, 7 to 9 minutes, flipping as needed to ensure even browning. Transfer burgers to wire rack set in rimmed baking sheet and let rest for 5 to 10 minutes.

6. To serve, spread Sriracha mayo onto bun bottoms. Top with burgers, cilantro leaves, and bun tops. Serve with green beans.

think like a cook

AN ICE COLD BATH

Though it's often overlooked for the sake of convience, giving vegetables a dunk in boiling salted water before plunging them into ice water (aka blanching and shocking) is a trick with many uses. A veggie platter is more pleasant when tougher items like broccoli, green beans, and asparagus have been brought to a gentle crunch, and the salt water enhances their flavor. Tomatoes and peaches can be easily peeled after a 30- to 60-second blanch before shocking (skip the salt; score an X into the base of each with a paring knife before blanching).

The method is also ideal when you want a side dish that you don't have to fuss with at the last minute. When a vegetable is cooked until crisp-tender, it can be simply dressed and served as a salad at room temperature, as it is here. Vegetables can also be blanched (and even refrigerated) in advance, then warmed through in a little butter or olive oil in just a few minutes. Add salt and pepper, maybe a chopped herb, and you're done.

Lemon-Herb Cod Fillets with Crispy Garlic Potatoes

Serves 4; Total Time 1 hour 15 minutes

why this recipe works

This simple but elegant recipe streamlines the classic pairing of cod and roasted potatoes into one dish while bringing some needed character to the rather mild fish and starchy root vegetable. After tossing potato slices with butter, garlic, and thyme for plenty of flavor, we assembled them into four individual beds and roasted them until just tender and slightly browned. Placing the cod fillets on top (along with more butter, thyme, and fresh lemon slices) not only insulated the fish from the direct heat of the pan, helping to keep it moist, but also permitted the cod's juices to baste the potatoes as it cooked, tying together the whole dish. Serving it was as easy as transferring each portion to a plate. Halibut and haddock are good substitutes for the cod.

1½ pounds russet potatoes, unpeeled, sliced into ¼-inch-thick rounds

2 tablespoons unsalted butter, melted, plus 3 tablespoons cut into ¼-inch pieces

3 garlic cloves, minced

1 teaspoon minced fresh thyme, plus 4 sprigs

Salt and pepper

4 (6- to 8-ounce) skinless cod fillets, 1 to 1½ inches thick

1 lemon, thinly sliced

1. Adjust oven rack to lower-middle position and heat oven to 425 degrees. Toss potatoes with melted butter, garlic, minced thyme, ½ teaspoon salt, and ¼ teaspoon pepper in bowl. Shingle potatoes into four 6 by 4-inch rectangular piles on rimmed baking sheet.

2. Roast potatoes until spotty brown and just tender, 30 to 35 minutes, rotating sheet halfway through roasting.

3. Pat cod dry with paper towels and season with salt and pepper. Lay 1 cod fillet, skinned side down, on top of each potato pile and top with butter pieces, thyme sprigs, and lemon slices. Bake until cod flakes apart when gently prodded with paring knife and thermometer inserted into flesh registers 140 degrees, about 15 minutes.

4. Remove sheet from oven. Slide spatula underneath potatoes and cod and gently transfer to individual plates. Serve.

think like a cook

BUYING AND STORING FISH

With so many varieties available and freshness of paramount importance, the fish counter can be intimidating. But that's not a reason to avoid fish! Follow these tips.

What to Look For

Always buy fish from a trusted source (preferably one with high volume to help ensure freshness). The store, and the fish in it, should smell like the sea, not fishy or sour. And all the fish should be on ice or properly refrigerated. Fillets and steaks should look bright, shiny, and firm, not dull or mushy. Whole fish should have moist, taut skin, clear eyes, and bright red gills.

What to Ask For

It is always better to have your fishmonger slice steaks and fillets to order rather than buying precut pieces that may have been sitting around. Don't be afraid to be picky at the seafood counter; a ragged piece of cod or a tail end of salmon will be difficult to cook properly. It is important to keep your fish cold, so if you have a long ride home, ask for a bag of ice.

How to Store It

Because fish is so perishable, it's best to buy it the day it will be cooked. If that's not possible, it's important to store it properly. When you get home, unwrap the fish, pat it dry, put it in a zipper-lock bag, press out the air, and seal the bag. Then set the fish on a bed of ice in a bowl or other container (that can hold the water once the ice melts), and place it in the back of the fridge, where it is coldest. If the ice melts before you use the fish, replenish it. The fish should keep for one day.

Salmon Cakes with Asparagus and Lemon-Herb Sauce

Serves 4; Total Time 45 minutes

LEMON-HERB SAUCE

¼ cup mayonnaise

1 tablespoon lemon juice

1 scallion, minced

2 teaspoons minced fresh parsley

Salt and pepper

SALMON CAKES AND ASPARAGUS

1 slice hearty white sandwich bread, torn into 1-inch pieces

1 pound skinless salmon, cut into 1-inch pieces

2 tablespoons mayonnaise

2 tablespoons minced fresh parsley

1 tablespoon Dijon mustard

2 teaspoons capers, rinsed and minced

1 shallot, minced

Salt and pepper

1 pound asparagus, trimmed

1 teaspoon extra-virgin olive oil

1. FOR THE SAUCE Combine all ingredients in bowl and season with salt and pepper to taste. Cover and refrigerate until serving.

2. FOR THE SALMON CAKES AND ASPARAGUS Adjust oven rack 3 inches from broiler element and heat broiler. Pulse bread in food processor to coarse crumbs, about 8 pulses, then transfer to large bowl; you should have about ¾ cup crumbs. Working in 2 batches, pulse salmon in food processor until coarsely ground, about 4 pulses; transfer to bowl with bread crumbs and toss to combine.

3. Whisk mayonnaise, parsley, mustard, capers, shallot, ½ teaspoon salt, and ⅛ teaspoon pepper together in small bowl, then gently fold into salmon mixture until well combined. Divide salmon mixture into 4 equal portions and gently pack into 1-inch-thick patties.

why this recipe works

Salmon cakes are a fresh and simple way to have fish for dinner. The most important rule is to avoid too many flavor-muting binders or you'll end up with bread patties instead of clean fish flavor. We used a food processor to coarsely chop the salmon so our cakes had a meaty texture. A single slice of bread and 2 tablespoons of mayonnaise provided enough binding. Broiling the patties made them easy to flip and kept them from overcooking. We arranged them on one end of a baking sheet, leaving plenty of room for a broiler-friendly vegetable—asparagus—to cook simultaneously. A quick lemon and parsley sauce rounded out the meal. Don't overprocess the salmon in step 2, or the cakes will have a pasty texture. Lay the salmon cakes on one side of the baking sheet so that the asparagus has space for browning.

4. Place salmon cakes on 1 side of rimmed baking sheet. Toss asparagus with oil, ½ teaspoon salt, and ¼ teaspoon pepper and spread in single layer on empty side of sheet. Broil until cakes are lightly browned on both sides, barely translucent at center, and thermometer inserted into center from top edge registers 125 degrees (for medium-rare) and asparagus is lightly browned and tender, 8 to 12 minutes. Halfway through broiling, flip cakes and turn asparagus.

5. Remove sheet from oven, transfer salmon and asparagus to platter, and let rest for 5 minutes. Serve with lemon-herb sauce.

think like a cook

PANADE TO THE RESCUE

A panade is a mixture of a starch and liquid. It can be simple, such as bread mixed with milk, or it can be complex, incorporating panko or saltines plus buttermilk or yogurt or even gelatin. But a panade always has the same goals: to help a ground protein dish hold its shape and to keep it moist and tender. Panades are frequently used in meatballs, meatloaf, and burgers. But how exactly does mashed up bread and milk help? Here's what's happening: Starches from the bread or crackers absorb moisture from the milk or other liquid to form a gel that coats and lubricates the protein molecules in the meat, much in the same way as fat does, keeping them moist and preventing them from linking together and shrinking into a tough matrix. This keeps the food from becoming dense and dried out. We're always careful to keep the panade-to-meat ratio just right in our recipes to make sure the flavor of the dish doesn't get washed out by the addition of the panade.

Oven-Steamed Mussels
Serves 2 to 4; Total Time 40 minutes

4 pounds mussels, scrubbed

1 tablespoon extra-virgin olive oil

3 garlic cloves, minced

Pinch red pepper flakes

1 cup dry white wine

3 sprigs fresh thyme

2 bay leaves

¼ teaspoon salt

2 tablespoons unsalted butter, cut into 4 pieces

2 tablespoons minced fresh parsley

why this recipe works

Don't be intimidated by mussels. These tender bivalves are inexpensive and quick to prepare. And they create their own briny-sweet broth when steamed in a pan of liquid—the flavor of which can be easily varied with just a few tweaks to the additions. However, mussels come in all different sizes, so they cook at different rates, especially when piled up in a pot. To help them cook evenly, we took the unconventional approach of cooking the mussels in a wide roasting pan in the oven so the heat surrounded the mussels on all sides, leading to more even (and gentle) cooking than was possible on the stove. With wine, thyme, and bay leaves as a base, the mussels' liquid made a tasty broth. Discard any mussel with an unpleasant odor or with a cracked shell or a shell that won't close. Serve with crusty bread.

1. Adjust oven rack to lowest position and heat oven to 500 degrees. Debeard mussels, if necessary: Holding 1 mussel at a time in your hand, remove weedy piece protruding from between shells, tugging and using flat surface of paring knife as leverage (see page 369).

2. Heat oil, garlic, and pepper flakes in large roasting pan over medium heat and cook, stirring constantly, until fragrant, about 30 seconds. Stir in wine, thyme sprigs, and bay leaves and boil until wine is slightly reduced, about 1 minute.

3. Stir in mussels and salt. Cover pan tightly with aluminum foil and transfer to oven. Cook until most mussels have opened (a few may remain closed), 15 to 18 minutes.

4. Remove pan from oven. Push mussels to sides of pan. Add butter to center and whisk until melted. Discard thyme sprigs and bay leaves. Stir in parsley and serve.

variations
Oven-Steamed Mussels with Hard Cider and Bacon
Substitute 4 slices thick-cut bacon, cut into ½-inch pieces, for garlic and pepper flakes; cook until bacon has rendered and is starting to crisp, about 5 minutes. Substitute dry hard cider for wine and ¼ cup heavy cream for butter.

Oven-Steamed Mussels with Tomatoes and Chorizo

Omit red pepper flakes and increase oil to 3 tablespoons. Heat oil and 12 ounces Spanish-style chorizo sausage, cut into ½-inch pieces, in roasting pan until chorizo starts to brown, about 5 minutes. Add garlic and cook until fragrant, about 30 seconds. Proceed with recipe as directed, adding 1 (28-ounce) can crushed tomatoes to roasting pan before adding mussels and increasing butter to 3 tablespoons.

think like a cook

SIX GOOD THINGS TO KNOW ABOUT MUSSELS

1. They're Safe to Eat
Mussels are routinely tested by state and local agencies for the presence of algae-derived toxins. The Monterey Bay Aquarium's Seafood Watch program calls them a "Best Choice" for environmental sustainability.

2. They Need Almost No Cleaning
Most mussels are cultivated on long ropes suspended from rafts, which leaves them free of sand and grit—and for the most part, beards. In general, all they need is a quick scrub under the tap.

3. It's Easy to Tell When They're Fresh
A live mussel will smell pleasantly briny. If open, its shell should close up when lightly tapped (but give it a moment; some mussels take longer than others to clam up).

4. It's Equally Easy to Tell When They're Not
A dead mussel deteriorates rapidly and will smell almost immediately. Also discard any mussel with a cracked or broken shell or a shell that won't close.

5. You Can Store Mussels for up to Three Days
As soon as you bring them home, place them in a bowl, cover it with a wet paper towel, and store it in the fridge.

6. Unopened Cooked Mussels Needn't Be Discarded
A mussel that's closed after cooking isn't unfit to eat. It's a sign that the mussel needs more cooking. To open a reluctant mussel, microwave it briefly (30 seconds or so).

Tequila-Lime Shrimp Quesadillas

Serves 4; Total Time 1 hour

3 tablespoons vegetable oil

12 ounces Monterey Jack cheese, shredded (3 cups)

¼ cup minced fresh cilantro

2 scallions, white and green parts separated and sliced thin

1½ pounds medium-large shrimp (31 to 40 per pound), peeled, deveined (see page 99), tails removed, and halved lengthwise

Salt and pepper

2 garlic cloves, minced

1 teaspoon minced canned chipotle chile in adobo sauce

⅓ cup tequila

1 teaspoon grated lime zest

4 (10-inch) flour tortillas

1. Adjust oven rack to middle position and heat oven to 450 degrees. Line rimmed baking sheet with aluminum foil and brush with 1 tablespoon oil. Toss Monterey Jack with cilantro and scallion greens.

2. Pat shrimp dry with paper towels and season with salt and pepper. Heat 1 tablespoon oil in 12-inch nonstick skillet over medium heat until shimmering. Add scallion whites, garlic, chipotle, and ¼ teaspoon salt and cook until softened, about 2 minutes. Add tequila and simmer until tequila has evaporated and pan is dry, about 5 minutes.

3. Add shrimp and cook, stirring often, until cooked through and opaque throughout, about 3 minutes. Transfer to bowl, stir in zest, and let cool for 5 minutes; drain well.

4. Lay tortillas on counter. Sprinkle half of cheese mixture over half of each tortilla, leaving ½-inch border around edge. Arrange shrimp on top in single layer, then sprinkle with remaining cheese mixture. Fold other half of each tortilla over top and press firmly to compact.

5. Arrange quesadillas in single layer on prepared sheet with rounded edges facing center of sheet. Brush with remaining 1 tablespoon oil. Bake until quesadillas begin to brown, about 10 minutes. Flip quesadillas over and press gently with spatula to compact. Continue to bake until crisp and golden brown on second side, about 5 minutes. Let quesadillas cool on wire rack for 5 minutes, then slice each into 4 wedges and serve.

why this recipe works

We love a simple cheese quesadilla, but add a filling of succulent shrimp spiked with tequila and lime zest and you turn Mexico's griddled cheese sandwich into a party. To make them substantial enough for a meal, we started with 10-inch flour tortillas. To make four at once, we turned to the oven. By placing the quesadillas on an oiled baking sheet and then brushing their tops with oil, we were able to brown and crisp them on both sides without having to cook each individually. To keep the quesadillas from getting soggy while ensuring juicy shrimp, we parcooked the shrimp slightly on the stovetop with aromatics and tequila; this gave them a head start while evaporating most of the liquid. It was essential to cut the shrimp in half so that they released most of their moisture into the pan. Cilantro, scallion greens, and lime zest provided welcome freshness, and Monterey Jack cheese offered melty richness.

think like a cook

DIY TORTILLA CHIPS

Tortillas may be the ideal wrapper for all manner of handheld meals. But when they're sliced into wedges and fried, tortillas (typically corn) become the ideal munchable snack. If you've ever had a basket of fresh-made tortilla chips at a restaurant, you know that even the best store-bought chips can't compare with the fresh corn flavor and ultracrispy texture of homemade. Whether you choose to buy corn tortillas or make them yourself (see page 432), frying your own tortilla chips is a great way to level up your Mexican cuisine game. A frying temperature of 350 degrees browns the chips quickly without burning them, and frying in two batches ensures that the oil's temperature doesn't drop too much when adding the tortilla wedges. As soon as they come out of the oil, sprinkle them with kosher salt, which is easier to distribute evenly than table salt. We prefer peanut oil for deep frying because of its high smoke point, but vegetable or corn oil will also work. Cooled chips can be stored in a zipper-lock bag at room temperature for up to 4 days. (For more about deep frying, see "Fearless Frying," page 373.)

Homemade Tortilla Chips
Serves 4

Cut eight 6-inch corn tortillas into 6 wedges each. Line 2 baking sheets with several layers of paper towels. Heat 5 cups peanut oil in Dutch oven over medium-high heat to 350 degrees. Add half of tortilla wedges and fry until golden and crispy around edges, 2 to 4 minutes. Transfer chips to prepared sheets, sprinkle lightly with salt, and let cool. Repeat with remaining tortillas. Serve.

Skillet Pizza

Makes two 11-inch pizzas; Serves 4; Total Time 2¾ hours
(1¼ hours with premade dough)

DOUGH
2 cups (11 ounces) plus 2 tablespoons bread flour

1⅛ teaspoons instant or rapid-rise yeast

¾ teaspoon salt

1 tablespoon extra-virgin olive oil

¾ cup ice water

SAUCE AND TOPPINGS
1 (28-ounce) can whole peeled tomatoes,
drained with juice reserved

5 tablespoons extra-virgin olive oil

2 garlic cloves, minced

1 teaspoon red wine vinegar

1 teaspoon dried oregano

½ teaspoon salt

¼ teaspoon pepper

8 ounces fresh mozzarella cheese, sliced ¼ inch thick
and patted dry with paper towels

2 tablespoons chopped fresh basil

why this recipe works

Making pizza can be a big project requiring a baking stone, or it can be as approachable as this version, which is especially convenient if you make the dough ahead (see "Freezing Pizza Dough"). Baking the pizza in a skillet eliminated the nerve-racking step of sliding a topped pie onto a baking stone in the oven. Yet, when preheated on the stovetop and transferred to a 500-degree oven, the skillet functioned like a pizza stone, crisping the crust in minutes. The dough came together easily in the food processor. If you'd like more substantial toppings, sprinkle them on before baking; but keep the additions light enough for the thin crust. The sauce will yield more than is needed; extra sauce can be refrigerated for up to one week or frozen for up to one month. If you don't have time to make dough, you can also use 1 pound of store-bought pizza dough. For more on how to knead, see page 437.

1. **FOR THE DOUGH** Pulse flour, yeast, and salt in food processor until combined, about 5 pulses. With processor running, add oil, then ice water, and process until rough ball forms, 30 to 40 seconds. Let dough rest for 2 minutes, then process for 30 seconds longer.

2. Sprinkle counter lightly with flour, then transfer dough to counter. Knead by hand to form smooth ball, 30 seconds. Place dough seam side down in lightly greased large bowl or container, cover tightly with plastic wrap, and let rise until doubled in size, 1½ to 2 hours. (Unrisen dough can be refrigerated for at least 8 hours or up to 16 hours; let sit at room temperature for 30 minutes before shaping in step 5.)

3. **FOR THE SAUCE AND TOPPINGS** Clean and dry food processor. Process tomatoes, 1 tablespoon oil, garlic, vinegar, oregano, salt, and pepper until smooth, about 30 seconds. Transfer mixture to 2-cup liquid measuring cup and add reserved tomato juice until sauce measures 2 cups. Reserve 1 cup sauce; set aside remaining sauce for another use.

4. Adjust oven rack to upper-middle position. Heat oven to 500 degrees.

5. Place dough on lightly floured counter; divide in half. Cover 1 piece loosely with greased plastic. Using your fingertips, gently press other piece into 8-inch disk, then use rolling pin to roll into 11-inch round.

6. Grease 12-inch ovensafe skillet with 2 tablespoons oil. Transfer dough to skillet and reshape as needed. Spread ½ cup sauce over dough, leaving ½-inch border around edge. Top with half of mozzarella.

7. Set skillet over high heat and cook until outside edge of dough is set, pizza is lightly puffed, and bottom of crust looks spotty brown when gently lifted with spatula, about 3 minutes.

8. Transfer skillet to oven and bake pizza until edges are brown and cheese is melted and spotty brown, 7 to 10 minutes. Using potholders, remove skillet from oven and slide pizza onto wire rack; let cool slightly. Sprinkle with 1 tablespoon basil, cut into wedges, and serve. Being careful of hot skillet, repeat with remaining oil, dough, ½ cup sauce, remaining mozzarella, and basil.

think like a cook

FREEZING PIZZA DOUGH

To make from-scratch pizza more convenient for weeknight dinners, keep a stash of homemade pizza dough in your freezer. Once the dough has fully risen and doubled in size, shape it into a ball, wrap it in plastic wrap coated in vegetable oil spray, place it in a zipper-lock bag, and freeze it for up to 2 weeks. The best way to defrost dough is to let it sit on the counter for a couple of hours or overnight in the refrigerator. (Thawing pizza dough in a microwave or low oven isn't recommended as it will dry the dough out.)

Cheesy Stuffed Poblanos

Serves 4 to 6; Total Time 1 hour 15 minutes

2 (15-ounce) cans pinto beans, rinsed

1 cup water

1 tablespoon vegetable oil

1 onion, chopped fine

4 garlic cloves, minced

1 tablespoon ground cumin

1 tablespoon minced fresh oregano or 1 teaspoon dried

1 teaspoon chili powder

1 teaspoon grated lime zest plus 1 tablespoon juice

Salt and pepper

⅛ teaspoon cayenne pepper

2 cups frozen corn

4 ounces Monterey Jack cheese, shredded (1 cup)

4 ounces sharp cheddar cheese, shredded (1 cup)

¼ cup minced fresh cilantro

8 poblano chiles

1 recipe Cherry Tomato Salsa (page 102)

why this recipe works

Stuffed peppers are a great way to make a hearty, simple vegetarian dinner. Poblanos are perfect for stuffing; their relatively large size makes them easy to fill, and their grassy, vegetal flavor pairs well with bold ingredients. We set out to create a simple recipe for poblanos stuffed with a cheesy filling. To make the peppers pliable enough to fill, we microwaved them briefly. To improve our filling's flavor and to anchor the cheese in the peppers, we added a couple of cans of pinto beans (half of which we mashed for a more cohesive filling), corn, garlic, onion, and spices to a combination of Monterey Jack and cheddar cheeses. Roasting the stuffed peppers tenderized them and deepened their flavor. Fresh cherry tomato salsa nicely balanced the rich, cheesy peppers.

1. Adjust oven racks to upper-middle and lower-middle positions and heat oven to 425 degrees. Line 2 rimmed baking sheets with aluminum foil and set wire rack in each. Using potato masher, mash half of beans and water together in bowl until mostly smooth.

2. Heat oil in 12-inch nonstick skillet over medium heat until shimmering. Add onion and cook until softened, about 5 minutes. Stir in garlic, cumin, oregano, chili powder, lime zest, ½ teaspoon salt, and cayenne and cook until fragrant, about 30 seconds. Stir in mashed bean mixture and cook, stirring constantly, until nearly all liquid has evaporated, 3 to 5 minutes. Stir in remaining beans and corn and cook until warmed through, about 2 minutes. Off heat, stir in Monterey Jack, cheddar, cilantro, and lime juice. Season with salt and pepper to taste.

3. Leaving stem intact, cut slit lengthwise down 1 side of each poblano. Microwave poblanos in covered bowl until just pliable, about 2½ minutes. Gently pry open poblanos, remove seeds, and stuff evenly with bean-cheese mixture. Lay poblanos, stuffed side up, on prepared sheets. Bake until tender, 30 to 40 minutes, switching and rotating sheets halfway through baking. Serve with salsa.

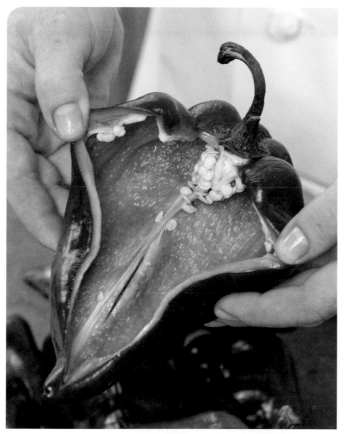

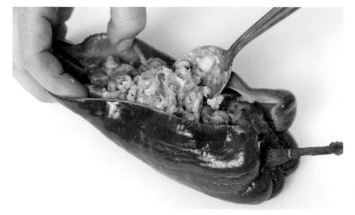

think like a cook

A FIELD GUIDE TO FRESH CHILES

Chiles are the backbone of Mexican cuisine. Some chiles are used for their heat, while others are used to provide flavor to sauces, stews, and more. Fresh chiles often have vegetal or grassy flavors, with clean, punchy heat, while dried chiles tend to have deeper, fruitier flavors, with nutty or even smoky undertones (see more about dried chiles on page 261). We've rated the ones below on a scale of 1 to 4, with 1 being barely any heat and 4 being very hot, but keep in mind that even among chiles of the same variety, heat levels can vary. When shopping for fresh chiles, look for those with bright color and tight, unblemished skin. Be aware that the same chiles can go by different names in different parts of the country and can even vary in color.

Poblano
Large, triangular, green to red-brown; crisp, vegetal; substitutions: bell pepper, Anaheim
Heat: 1.0

Anaheim
Large, long, skinny, yellow-green to red; mildly tangy, vegetal; substitution: poblano
Heat: 2.0

Jalapeño
Small, smooth, shiny, green or red; bright, grassy; substitution: serrano
Heat: 2.5

Serrano
Small, dark green; bright, citrusy; substitution: jalapeño
Heat: 3.0

Thai
Narrow and petite; bright red or green, flavor similar to black peppercorns; substitution: half-dose habanero
Heat: 3.5

Habanero
Bulbous, bright orange to red; deeply floral, fruity; substitution: double-dose Thai
Heat: 4.0

sunday suppers

Chicken with 40 Cloves of Garlic

Serves 4; Total Time 1 hour

40 garlic cloves (3–4 heads), peeled

2 teaspoons vegetable oil

½ teaspoon sugar

8 (5- to 7-ounce) bone-in chicken thighs, trimmed

Salt and pepper

½ cup dry sherry

¾ cup chicken broth

½ cup heavy cream

2 sprigs fresh thyme

1 bay leaf

2 teaspoons cornstarch mixed with 1 tablespoon water

1 tablespoons chopped fresh parsley leaves

why this recipe works

Yes, you read it right: This classic French dish has 40 whole cloves of garlic in it, but instead of being overwhelming, the garlic is mellow and sweet, part of a sauce that transforms a few simple ingredients into a transcendent braise. We started by microwaving the garlic to remove its harsh edge. A bit of sugar helped mimic the sweetness of long-roasted garlic and encouraged the cloves to brown. After searing bone-in chicken thighs to crisp their skin, we added our garlic to the pan to brown, then built a sauce before nestling the chicken back in the skillet, skin side up so it would stay crispy during the oven braise. When everything was cooked, we mashed half of the garlic to ensure its flavor would permeate every bite. You can substitute four bone-in, skin-on chicken breasts (halved crosswise) for the thighs; bake them until they register 160 degrees, 15 to 20 minutes. You will need a 12-inch ovensafe skillet for this recipe. Serve with crusty bread.

1. Adjust oven rack to upper-middle position and heat oven to 450 degrees. Toss garlic, 1 teaspoon oil, and sugar together in bowl. Microwave garlic mixture until garlic is slightly softened and lightly spotted, about 4 minutes, stirring halfway through microwaving.

2. Pat chicken dry with paper towels and season with salt and pepper. Heat remaining 1 teaspoon oil in 12-inch ovensafe skillet over medium-high heat until just smoking. Brown chicken well on skin side only, 7 to 10 minutes; transfer to plate.

3. Pour off all but 1 tablespoon fat left in skillet. Add microwaved garlic mixture and cook over medium-low heat until evenly browned, about 1 minute. Stir in sherry, scraping up any browned bits. Increase heat to medium and simmer until sherry has nearly evaporated, about 4 minutes. Add broth, cream, thyme sprigs, and bay leaf. Whisk in cornstarch mixture and simmer until slightly thickened, about 3 minutes.

4. Return chicken to skillet, skin side up, with any accumulated juices. Transfer skillet to oven and bake until thermometer inserted into chicken registers 175 degrees, 18 to 22 minutes.

5. Transfer chicken and half of garlic to serving dish. Discard thyme sprigs and bay leaf. Using potato masher, mash remaining garlic into sauce. Season with salt and pepper to taste and pour some of sauce around chicken. Sprinkle with parsley and serve with remaining sauce.

think like a cook

DO I HAVE TO PEEL 40 GARLIC CLOVES?

Forty cloves is a lot of garlic—that's the point of this recipe. But don't fret. Our testing has shown that prepeeled supermarket garlic works fine in this recipe (and others), as long as you use it pretty quickly—the shelf life of prepeeled garlic in a jar, which must be refrigerated, is only about two weeks, compared with three weeks or more for a whole head of garlic stored in a cool, dry place. If you prefer the shortcut product, just make sure the cloves look firm and white with a matte finish when you purchase them.

If you prefer to buy whole heads of garlic, here's a short-cut we came up with for peeling a lot in one go. Break the heads of garlic into individual cloves and place them in a heavy-duty zipper-lock bag. Squeeze out most of the air, seal the bag, and gently pound the garlic with a rolling pin. Then just remove the peeled cloves from the bag, zip the bag back up (with the skins still inside), and discard. Microwaving the cloves for 10 to 20 seconds can also help the skins come off more easily.

Chicken Saltimbocca
Serves 4; Total Time 50 minutes

4 (6- to 8-ounce) boneless, skinless chicken breasts, trimmed

½ cup all-purpose flour

Salt and pepper

1 tablespoon minced fresh sage, plus 8 large leaves (optional)

8 thin slices prosciutto (4 ounces)

¼ cup olive oil

1¼ cups dry vermouth or dry white wine

2 teaspoons lemon juice

4 tablespoons unsalted butter, cut into 4 pieces and chilled

1 tablespoon minced fresh parsley

1. Remove tenderloin (small strip of meat loosely attached to underside of breast) from chicken; discard or save for another use. Place each breast flat on cutting board, resting one hand on top of chicken, and use chef's knife to carefully slice chicken in half horizontally. Cover chicken halves with plastic wrap and pound to even ¼-inch thickness with meat pounder. Combine flour and 1 teaspoon pepper in shallow dish.

2. Pat chicken dry with paper towels. Working with 1 cutlet at a time, dredge in flour mixture, shaking off excess. Sprinkle cutlets evenly with minced sage. Place 1 prosciutto slice on top of each cutlet, covering sage, and press lightly to help it adhere.

3. Heat 2 tablespoons oil in 12-inch skillet over medium-high heat until shimmering. Add sage leaves, if using, and cook until leaves begin to change color and are fragrant, 15 to 20 seconds. Remove sage leaves with slotted spoon or tongs and transfer to paper towel–lined plate.

4. Place 4 cutlets in skillet, prosciutto side down, and cook over medium-high heat until golden brown on first side, about 3 minutes. Flip cutlets, reduce heat to medium, and cook until no longer pink and lightly browned on second side, about 2 minutes longer. Transfer cutlets to platter. Wipe out skillet. Repeat with remaining 2 tablespoons oil and remaining 4 cutlets. Tent loosely with aluminum foil and set aside.

5. Pour off all fat left in skillet. Add vermouth, scraping up any browned bits. Bring to simmer and cook until reduced to ⅓ cup, 5 to 7 minutes. Stir in lemon juice. Reduce heat to low and whisk in butter, 1 tablespoon at a time. Off heat, stir in parsley and season with salt and pepper to taste. Pour sauce over chicken, place sage leaf on top of each cutlet, if using, and serve immediately.

why this recipe works
Chicken saltimbocca ("jump in the mouth" in Italian) is ideal when you want an impressive dish without spending too much time in the kitchen. It features a pretty package of chicken, prosciutto, and sage, which is sautéed and given a tasty sauce. Many recipes secure the trio with a toothpick, but we found the prosciutto stuck quite well to our chicken, which we had sliced ourselves in long, flat cutlets. We fried sage leaves separately; they looked beautiful and their piney flavor turned delicate and nutty. We also sprinkled the cutlets with more minced sage to ensure its flavor in every bite. A pan sauce of vermouth, lemon, and butter made a simple but sophisticated finish. Make sure to buy prosciutto that is thinly sliced, not shaved, and large enough to cover one side of each cutlet; avoid slices that are too thick, as they won't stick to the chicken. To make slicing the chicken easier, freeze it for 15 minutes. Although whole sage leaves make a nice presentation, they can be omitted.

think like a cook

WINE FOR COOKING

Over the years, the test kitchen has developed hundreds of recipes with wine. We've learned that you should not cook with anything you would not drink. This includes the supersalty "cooking wines" sold in many supermarkets. That said, there's no need to spend a fortune on wine destined for sauces or stews. We've tested good $10 bottles versus better-tasting $30 wines and while we can tell the difference in the glass, it's not appreciable in a cooked application.

White Wine

Medium-bodied, unoaked varieties that aren't terribly sweet are the best white wines for cooking. We prefer clean, dry Sauvignon Blancs to sweet Rieslings or heavily oaked Chardonnays, which can dominate subtle flavors.

Vermouth

Dry vermouth makes a good substitute for white wine in many sauces and other savory recipes, and because it has a shelf life of several months, it's easy to keep a bottle on hand. Vermouth adds herbaceous notes to any dish and is a bit more alcoholic than white wine. Replace white wine with an equal amount of vermouth.

Red Wine

The best red wines for cooking are medium-bodied, unoaked varieties that aren't terribly tannic. Go with blended (nonvarietal) American or Australian wines, or choose a Pinot Noir, Merlot, or a Côtes du Rhône. Avoid heavy Cabernets, which turn bitter when cooked.

Nonalcoholic Substitutes for Wine

Broth can work as an equal replacement in sauces and stews that call for small amounts of wine. The dish won't taste exactly the same, but at least the recipe will work. For every ½ cup broth used, you should also stir in ½ teaspoon red or white wine vinegar or lemon juice before serving, which will mimic some of the acidity otherwise provided by the wine.

Peruvian Roast Chicken with Swiss Chard and Sweet Potatoes

Serves 6; Total Time 1 hour 45 minutes (plus 1 hour for marinating)

¼ cup fresh mint leaves

10 garlic cloves (5 chopped, 5 sliced thin)

¼ cup extra-virgin olive oil

1 tablespoon ground cumin

1 tablespoon honey

2 teaspoons smoked paprika

2 teaspoons dried oregano

2 teaspoons grated lime zest plus ¼ cup juice (2 limes), plus lime wedges for serving

Salt and pepper

1 teaspoon minced habanero chile

6 (10-ounce) chicken leg quarters, trimmed

3 pounds sweet potatoes, peeled, ends trimmed, and sliced into 1-inch-thick rounds

4 pounds Swiss chard, stemmed and cut into 1-inch pieces

2 tablespoons minced fresh cilantro

why this recipe works

While we love plain roast chicken, some meals call for a special treatment. One of the best roast chickens we've come across, Peruvian *pollo a la brasa,* derives robust flavor from a paste of garlic, spices, salt, limes, chile, and mint. It's spit-roasted whole, but for our rotisserie-less home kitchen, we used chicken leg quarters. This underutilized cut has lots of surface area for smearing with paste—and we did, over and under the skin, before resting the chicken to meld flavors. To take full advantage of our roasting pan, we first used it to brown a side of sweet potatoes before arranging the chicken on top and roasting both together. In the resulting juices we sautéed Swiss chard for a glorious one-pan meal. Some leg quarters come with the backbone attached; removing it (with a chef's knife or kitchen scissors) before cooking makes the chicken easier to serve.

1. Adjust oven rack to middle position and heat oven to 425 degrees. Process mint, chopped garlic, 1 tablespoon oil, cumin, honey, paprika, oregano, lime zest and juice, 2 teaspoons pepper, 1 teaspoon salt, and habanero in blender until smooth, 20 seconds.

2. Using your fingers, gently loosen skin covering thighs and drumsticks and spread half of paste directly on meat. Spread remaining half of paste over exterior of chicken. Place chicken in 1-gallon zipper-lock bag, seal, and refrigerate for at least 1 hour or up to 24 hours.

3. Toss potatoes with 1 tablespoon oil and ½ teaspoon salt in bowl. Heat remaining 2 tablespoons oil in 16 by 12-inch roasting pan over medium-high heat (over 2 burners, if possible) until shimmering. Add potatoes, cut side down, and cook until well browned on bottom, 6 to 8 minutes.

4. Off heat, flip potatoes. Lay chicken, skin side up, on top. Roast in oven until thermometer inserted into thighs and drumsticks registers 175 degrees and potatoes are tender, 40 to 50 minutes, rotating pan halfway through roasting.

5. Transfer potatoes and chicken to platter, tent loosely with aluminum foil, and let rest for 10 minutes. Being careful of hot pan handles, pour off all but ¼ cup liquid left in pan. Add sliced garlic to pan and cook over high heat (over 2 burners, if possible) until fragrant, about 30 seconds. Add chard and ¼ teaspoon salt and cook, stirring constantly, until chard is wilted and tender, about 8 minutes; transfer to serving bowl.

6. Sprinkle cilantro over chicken and potatoes and serve with chard and lime wedges.

think like a cook

THE POWER OF THE PASTE

A paste is a mixture of robustly flavored seasonings, such as spices, herbs, chiles, or garlic, mixed with fat and rubbed on proteins (or even vegetables) before cooking. Pastes offer a boost of complex flavor and, as they brown in the oven, a nice crust that brings textural contrast and visual appeal. What they don't do, we've learned, is penetrate very deeply into the meat, no matter how long you wait—at least not the flavors from the garlic, spices, and acids. Only sodium compounds like salt travel farther into the meat the longer it sits. So our pastes provide a mostly superficial flavoring. But we still let our chicken rest for an hour or up to 24 (any longer and the acids would start to break down the meat) so that the salt in the paste can ramp up the chicken's flavor from skin to bone. We make sure to season under the skin for best results, while rubbing more of the paste over the skin for nice browning. The best way to apply the paste is to simply use your fingers. Carefully slide your fingers under the skin to loosen it, and then gently rub the paste underneath.

Really Good Turkey Meatloaf

Serves 4 to 6; Total Time 2 hours 10 minutes

why this recipe works

Don't overlook the benefits of a good meatloaf; though humble, it can be just the thing for a comforting meal, and leftovers make great sand- wiches. Turkey meatloaf offers a lighter take on the classic, but because store-bought ground turkey is fine and pasty, it often comes out dense and mushy. To fix this, we exchanged the usual bread panade for quick oats, which added some chew and opened up the loaf's texture. Cornstarch, Parmesan, butter, and egg yolks enriched the turkey's thin juices and added more body. Because turkey's mild flavor is easily overwhelmed, we kept the other add-ins modest. Instead, we gave our meatloaf a double coat of glaze, letting the first dry in the oven so the second would adhere. Baking our loaf free-form permitted more space for glazing. Do not use 99 percent lean ground turkey. The pinch of baking soda helps the onions soften quickly. Three tablespoons of rolled oats, chopped fine, can be substituted for the quick oats; do not use steel-cut oats.

MEATLOAF

3 tablespoons unsalted butter

Pinch baking soda

½ onion, chopped fine

Salt and pepper

1 garlic clove, minced

1 teaspoon minced fresh thyme

2 tablespoons Worcestershire sauce

3 tablespoons quick oats

2 teaspoons cornstarch

2 large egg yolks

2 tablespoons Dijon mustard

2 pounds 85 or 93 percent lean ground turkey

1 ounce Parmesan cheese, grated (½ cup)

⅓ cup chopped fresh parsley

GLAZE

1 cup ketchup

¼ cup packed brown sugar

2½ teaspoons cider vinegar

½ teaspoon hot sauce

1. FOR THE MEATLOAF Adjust oven rack to upper-middle position and heat oven to 350 degrees. Line wire rack with aluminum foil and set in rimmed baking sheet. Melt butter in 10-inch skillet over low heat. Stir baking soda into melted butter. Add onion and ¼ teaspoon salt, increase heat to medium, and cook, stirring frequently, until onion is softened and beginning to brown, 3 to 4 minutes. Add garlic and thyme and cook until fragrant, about 1 minute. Stir in Worcestershire and continue to cook until slightly reduced, about 1 minute longer. Transfer onion mixture to large bowl and set aside. Combine oats, cornstarch, ¾ teaspoon salt, and ½ teaspoon pepper in second bowl.

2. FOR THE GLAZE Whisk all ingredients in small saucepan until sugar dissolves. Bring mixture to simmer over medium heat and cook until slightly thickened, about 5 minutes; set aside.

3. Stir egg yolks and mustard into cooled onion mixture until well combined. Add turkey, Parmesan, parsley, and oat mixture and, using your hands, mix until well combined. Transfer turkey mixture to center of prepared rack. Using your wet hands, shape into 9 by 5-inch loaf. Using pastry brush, spread half of glaze evenly over top and sides of meatloaf. Bake meatloaf for 40 minutes.

4. Brush remaining glaze onto top and sides of meatloaf and continue to bake until thermometer inserted into meatloaf registers 160 degrees, 35 to 40 minutes longer. Let meatloaf cool for 20 minutes before slicing and serving.

think like a cook

LEAN, BUT NOT TOO LEAN
Using ground turkey in place of beef has become common as many of us strive to eat less red meat. But turkey is, literally, a different beast. Despite containing more moisture than beef or pork, turkey lacks the fat and gelatin of those meats and has a harder time holding onto its moisture, so it dries out easily. For that reason we recommend avoiding 99 percent lean commercial ground turkey and choosing either 93 or 85 percent lean, whichever you can find. (Packages usually state the percentage; another tip-off is that, typically, the darker the meat, the higher the fat content.)

Buy Store-Ground If You Can
We developed our turkey meatloaf using commercial ground turkey, which tends to have a very fine texture. If your supermarket or butcher grinds turkey in-house, buy that instead. Store-ground turkey is typically more coarsely ground and will produce meatloaf with a slightly less compacted texture.

Meatballs and Marinara
Serves 8; Total Time 1 hour 40 minutes

why this recipe works

Meatballs and marinara sauce are the epitome of comfort food, and we think this recipe should always be in your freezer so you have comfort at the ready whenever you need it. For an easier approach to this classic, we turned to the oven and roasted our meatballs at a high temperature, which ensured they developed a nice, browned crust. To keep our meatballs moist and tender, we added a panade (a paste of milk and bread). In addition to ground beef, using Italian sausage for the pork gave the meatballs a flavor boost, as did simmering them in the sauce after baking. To keep the recipe easy and streamlined, the meatballs and sauce incorporate the same onion mixture for aromatic flavor. This recipe makes enough for 2 pounds of pasta, and the meatballs and sauce are also good in a sandwich or served over Creamy Parmesan Polenta (page 224).

ONION MIXTURE
¼ cup olive oil

3 onions, chopped fine

8 garlic cloves, minced

1 tablespoon dried oregano

¾ teaspoon red pepper flakes

EASY MARINARA
1 (6-ounce) can tomato paste

1 cup dry red wine

1 cup water

4 (28-ounce) cans crushed tomatoes

1 ounce Parmesan cheese, grated (½ cup)

¼ cup fresh basil leaves

Salt

1–2 teaspoons sugar, as needed

MEATBALLS
4 slices hearty white sandwich bread

¾ cup milk

8 ounces sweet Italian sausage, casings removed

2 ounces Parmesan cheese, grated (1 cup)

½ cup chopped fresh parsley

2 large eggs

2 garlic cloves, minced

1½ teaspoons salt

2½ pounds 85 percent lean ground beef

1. FOR THE ONION MIXTURE Heat oil in Dutch oven over medium-high heat until shimmering. Cook onions until golden, 10 to 15 minutes. Add garlic, oregano, and pepper flakes and cook until fragrant, about 30 seconds. Transfer half of onion mixture to large bowl and set aside for the meatballs.

2. FOR THE MARINARA Add tomato paste to remaining onion mixture in pot and cook until fragrant, about 1 minute. Add wine and cook until slightly thickened, about 2 minutes. Stir in water and tomatoes and simmer over low heat until sauce is no longer watery, 45 to 60 minutes. Stir in Parmesan and basil. Season with salt and sugar to taste.

3. FOR THE MEATBALLS Meanwhile, adjust oven rack to upper-middle position and heat oven to 475 degrees. Mash bread and milk in bowl with reserved onion mixture until smooth. Add sausage, Parmesan, parsley, eggs, garlic, and salt to bowl and mash to combine. Add beef and knead with hands until well combined. Gently roll mixture into 2½-inch meatballs (you should have about 16 meatballs), place on rimmed baking sheet, and bake until well browned, about 20 minutes.

4. Transfer meatballs to pot with sauce. Simmer for 15 minutes. Serve. (Meatballs and marinara can be frozen for up to 1 month.)

think like a cook

GROUND BEEF DOS AND DON'TS

Supermarkets label ground beef either by fat content, by cut, or—preferably—both. Some tips when shopping:

» DO buy ground chuck (80 to 85 percent lean) for meatballs, burgers, or whenever you want rich beefy flavor as well as moisture from the fat.

» DO buy ground sirloin (90 to 93 percent lean) when a recipe has additional sources of fat and moisture.

» DON'T buy packages labeled "ground round," a lean, tough cut, or "ground beef," which can be from any part of the cow and might be liver-y or tough.

» DON'T buy beef that looks brown or has leached juices into the package—signs that it may not be freshly ground and that it may have been previously frozen, respectively.

Unstuffed Shells with Butternut Squash and Leeks

Serves 4 to 6; Total Time 1 hour 15 minutes

8 ounces (1 cup) whole-milk ricotta cheese

2 ounces Parmesan cheese, grated (1 cup)

1 teaspoon grated lemon zest

Salt and pepper

1 tablespoon extra-virgin olive oil

1½ pounds butternut squash, peeled, seeded, and cut into ½-inch pieces (5 cups)

1 pound leeks, white and light green parts only, halved lengthwise, sliced thin, and washed thoroughly

2 garlic cloves, minced

Pinch cayenne pepper

¼ cup dry white wine

4 cups water

1 cup heavy cream

12 ounces jumbo pasta shells

2 tablespoons chopped fresh basil

why this recipe works

For a bubbling, cheesy pan of shells and sauce without the tedium of preboiling and filling individual shells, we deconstructed it—and we updated the sauce, too, with butternut squash and leeks, for a hearty vegetarian meal. Cooking all of this in one skillet required perfect timing. We gave the leeks and squash a head start so they would finish just as our pasta became tender. Instead of stuffing the shells, we simply added grated Parmesan and dollops of lemony ricotta before sliding the pan into the oven to brown and melt the cheesy topping. You can substitute large or medium shells, ziti, farfalle, campanelle, or orecchiette. The skillet will be very full when you add the shells (stir gently to start), but will become more manageable as the pasta becomes malleable. You will need a 12-inch ovensafe nonstick skillet here.

1. Adjust oven rack to middle position and heat oven to 375 degrees. Combine ricotta, ½ cup Parmesan, lemon zest, ¼ teaspoon salt, and ¼ teaspoon pepper in bowl; cover and refrigerate until needed.

2. Heat oil in 12-inch ovensafe nonstick skillet over medium heat until shimmering. Add squash, leeks, and ½ teaspoon salt and cook until leeks are softened, about 5 minutes. Stir in garlic and cayenne and cook until fragrant, about 30 seconds. Add wine and cook until almost completely evaporated, about 1 minute.

3. Stir in water and cream, then add pasta. Increase heat to medium-high and cook at vigorous simmer, stirring gently and often, until pasta is tender and liquid has thickened, about 15 minutes.

4. Season with salt and pepper to taste. Sprinkle remaining ½ cup Parmesan over top, then dollop evenly with ricotta mixture. Transfer skillet to oven and bake until Parmesan is melted and spotty brown, about 5 minutes. Remove skillet from oven (skillet handle will be hot). Let cool for 10 minutes, then sprinkle with basil and serve.

think like a cook

BUYING RICOTTA

Good ricotta cheese should be both creamy and dense, with a fresh dairy flavor, perfect for filling or dolloping on pasta or slathering on toast. The word *ricotta* means "recooked" in Italian, a reference to its traditional preparation method of heating whey, a byproduct of cheese making, with acid to coagulate it and form curds.

In the United States, as you might expect, manufacturers are not held to the standards of Italian ricotta makers, and not all even use whey, which is partially why the ricottas we find can be so variable. Some are wet with visible curds (like cottage cheese); some can be tangy. But we prefer ricottas that taste mildly sweet, with a creamy, pleasantly dense consistency. **BelGioioso Ricotta con Latte Whole Milk Ricotta Cheese,** our favorite, has a rich, dense consistency that tasters described as "luscious." Whatever you buy, we suggest sticking with whole-milk ricotta, as part-skim options inspired descriptions ranging from "grainy" and "soggy" to "rancid." If you do go that route, opt for a brand made without gums and stabilizers, such as **Calabro**.

A good ricotta's shelf life may only be a matter of days, but one spoonful should be enough to guarantee its quick disappearance from your fridge.

Roasted Zucchini and Eggplant Lasagna

Serves 8; Total Time 2 hours

why this recipe works

Vegetable lasagna recipes are often filled with watery, tasteless vegetables and weighed down by excess cheese. We wanted a flavorful vegetable lasagna that didn't fall into any of the usual traps. Eggplant and zucchini are easy to prep, making them excellent choices. Roasting the vegetables not only drove off excess liquid that would otherwise water down the sauce, but it also caramelized the vegetables, adding savory depth. Ricotta cheese is traditional in lasagna, but we found that it muted the roasted vegetable flavor, so we layered our lasagna with only mozzarella and Parmesan, which lent plenty of rich cheese flavor and gooey texture. No-boil noodles made quick work of the assembly. Be sure to grease the baking sheets before spreading the vegetables so they don't stick during roasting.

SAUCE
1½ pounds zucchini, cut into ½-inch pieces

1½ pounds eggplant, cut into ½-inch pieces

5 tablespoons extra-virgin olive oil

9 garlic cloves, minced

Salt and pepper

1 onion, chopped fine

1 (28-ounce) can crushed tomatoes

1 (28-ounce) can diced tomatoes

2 tablespoons chopped fresh basil

LASAGNA
12 no-boil lasagna noodles

12 ounces whole-milk mozzarella cheese, shredded (3 cups)

4 ounces Parmesan cheese, grated (2 cups)

1. FOR THE SAUCE Adjust oven racks to upper-middle and lower-middle positions and heat oven to 400 degrees. Toss zucchini and eggplant with 3 tablespoons oil, two-thirds of garlic, 1 teaspoon salt, and 1 teaspoon pepper. Spread vegetables in single layer on 2 greased rimmed baking sheets and roast, stirring occasionally, until softened and golden brown, 35 to 45 minutes; set aside.

2. Heat remaining 2 tablespoons oil in large saucepan over medium heat until shimmering. Add onion and cook until softened, about 5 minutes. Stir in remaining garlic and cook until fragrant, about 30 seconds. Stir in crushed tomatoes and diced tomatoes and their juice, bring to simmer, and cook until flavors meld, about 5 minutes. Off heat, stir in basil and season with salt and pepper to taste. (You should have 7 cups sauce. Add water as needed to reach 7 cups.)

3. FOR THE LASAGNA Spread 1 cup sauce over bottom of 13 by 9-inch baking dish. Lay 3 noodles in dish, spread one-quarter of vegetables over noodles, then top with 1 cup sauce, ⅔ cup mozzarella, and ½ cup Parmesan (in that order). Repeat layering process 2 more times. Top with remaining 3 noodles, remaining vegetables, remaining 3 cups sauce, remaining 1 cup mozzarella, and remaining ½ cup Parmesan.

4. Cover dish tightly with greased aluminum foil, place on foil-lined rimmed baking sheet, and bake for 15 minutes. Uncover, and continue to bake until spotty brown and bubbling around edges, 25 to 35 minutes. Let casserole cool for 10 minutes before serving.

think like a cook

NO-BOIL KNOW-HOW

We love no-boil (also called oven-ready) noodles for their convenience, saving the cook from having to first boil and then drain noodles before making lasagna. No-boil noodles are precooked and dehydrated at the factory. During baking, the moisture from the sauce rehydrates and softens them, especially when the pan is covered as the lasagna bakes. The most common no-boil noodle measures 7 inches long and 3½ inches wide; 3 noodles fit perfectly in a 13 by 9-inch dish. (Note that traditional noodles are not interchangeable with no-boil, even if you precook them.) Our favorite is **Barilla Oven-Ready Lasagne**; we found these delicate, flat noodles closely resembled fresh pasta in texture.

Pasta with Classic Bolognese
Serves 4 to 6; Total Time 3 hours 45 minutes

5 tablespoons unsalted butter

2 tablespoons finely chopped onion

2 tablespoons finely chopped carrot

2 tablespoons finely chopped celery

12 ounces meatloaf mix

Salt

1 cup whole milk

1 cup dry white wine

1 (28-ounce) can whole peeled tomatoes, drained with juice reserved, chopped fine

1 pound fresh or dried linguine, fettuccine, or tagliatelle

Grated Parmesan cheese

why this recipe works

If you have never tasted a true Bolognese, the first mouthful is a revelation. The deep, rust-colored, slow-simmered meat sauce transforms a bowl of pasta into a dish that stacks up against anything you'll find in a restaurant. Although it takes time, Bolognese requires almost no work. We used a mix of beef, pork, and veal (often sold as meatloaf mix); the veal added delicacy while the pork made it sweet. Bathing the meat with milk, wine, and tomato juices turned it tender and built deep flavor. The finished sauce is thick, so be sure to reserve some of the pasta cooking water to add to the sauce when tossing with the pasta, if needed. Fresh egg pasta (see page 366) is traditional, but just about any pasta will work. If you can't find meatloaf mix, use equal amounts of 85 percent lean ground beef, veal, and pork; you can also substitute ground beef for veal. To double the recipe, simmer the milk and wine for 30 minutes each, and simmer the sauce for 4 hours after adding the tomatoes.

1. Melt 3 tablespoons butter in Dutch oven over medium heat. Add onion, carrot, and celery and cook until softened, 5 to 7 minutes. Stir in meatloaf mix and ½ teaspoon salt and cook, breaking up any large pieces with wooden spoon, until no longer pink, about 3 minutes.

2. Stir in milk, bring to simmer, and cook until milk evaporates and only rendered fat remains, 10 to 15 minutes. Stir in wine, bring to simmer, and cook until wine evaporates, 10 to 15 minutes. Stir in tomatoes and reserved juice and bring to simmer. Reduce heat to low so that sauce continues to just barely simmer, with occasional bubble or two at surface, until liquid has evaporated, about 3 hours. Season with salt to taste. (Sauce can be refrigerated for up to 2 days or frozen for up to 1 month.)

3. Bring 4 quarts water to boil in large pot. Add pasta and 1 tablespoon salt and cook, stirring often, until al dente. Reserve ½ cup cooking water, then drain pasta and return it to pot. Add sauce and remaining 2 tablespoons butter to pasta and toss to combine. Adjust consistency with reserved cooking water as needed. Serve, passing Parmesan separately.

think like a cook

DON'T JUST DUMP AND STIR!

There are times in cooking when it's perfectly acceptable to throw all your ingredients into the pot and let the flavors develop as they bubble away. But try that with Bolognese and the proverbial Italian grandmother would flinch. Why? One secret to ragu's depth and velvety texture is the sequential cooking off of liquids that flavor and tenderize the meat before adding more liquid. Here is a breakdown of the process.

The Milk

When meat is sautéed it toughens. To avoid pebbly results, we added milk first, before the meat has become crusty or tough; this way, it penetrated the meat easily, tenderizing it and making it sweeter.

The Wine

Wine gets added next; it's cooked down to remove any alcoholic taste, while leaving behind its aromatic complexity. We preferred the delicacy of white wine to the robustness of red in our sauce, but either will work.

The Cooking Medium

Homemade stock typically contributes velvetiness from gelatin, but making Bolognese is time-consuming enough, and store-bought broth tasted off when heavily reduced. So we relied on the juice from canned tomatoes, which added brightness to offset the rich meat.

The Final Hour

Long, slow simmering properly tenderizes the meat and melds flavors. A few bubbles may rise to the surface but the pot should not be simmering all over. Even after 2 hours the meat will still be firm, but after 3 it achieves its melt-in-the-mouth consistency.

Taming the Flame

Having trouble maintaining your pot at a bare simmer? Place a flame tamer over your burner; it adds a layer of metal between the pot and heating element. You can buy one, but it's easy enough rig your own: Shape a sheet of heavy-duty aluminum foil into a 1-inch-thick ring that fits on your burner, making sure the ring is of even thickness. Place it on your burner and place the pot on top to cook.

Fresh Pasta Without a Machine

Makes 1 pound; Serves 4 to 6; Total Time 1 hour (plus resting time)

2 cups (10 ounces) all-purpose flour, plus extra as needed

2 large eggs plus 6 large yolks

2 tablespoons olive oil

1 tablespoon salt

1. Process flour, eggs and yolks, and oil in food processor until mixture forms cohesive dough that feels soft and is barely tacky to touch, about 45 seconds. (If dough sticks to fingers, add up to ¼ cup flour, 1 tablespoon at a time, until barely tacky. If dough doesn't become cohesive, add up to 1 tablespoon water, 1 teaspoon at a time, until it just comes together; process 30 seconds longer.)

2. Turn dough ball onto dry counter and knead until smooth, 1 to 2 minutes. Shape dough into 6-inch-long cylinder. Wrap with plastic wrap and set aside at room temperature to rest for at least 1 hour or up to 4 hours.

3. Cut cylinder crosswise into 6 equal pieces. Working with 1 piece of dough at a time (rewrap remaining dough), dust both sides with flour, place cut side down on clean counter, and press into 3-inch square. Using heavy rolling pin, roll into 6-inch square. Dust both sides of dough lightly with flour. Starting at center of square, roll dough away from you in 1 motion. Return rolling pin to center of dough and roll toward you in 1 motion. Repeat steps of rolling until dough sticks to counter and measures roughly 12 inches long. Lightly dust both sides of dough with flour and continue rolling dough until it measures roughly 20 inches long and 6 inches wide, frequently lifting dough to release it from counter. (You should be able to easily see outline of your fingers through dough.) If dough firmly sticks to counter and wrinkles when rolled out, dust dough lightly with flour.

4. Transfer pasta sheet to dish towel and let stand, uncovered, until firm around edges, about 15 minutes; meanwhile, roll out remaining dough. Starting with 1 short end, gently fold pasta sheet at 2-inch intervals until sheet has been folded into flat, rectangular roll. With sharp chef's knife, slice crosswise to desired width (¼ inch for fettuccine, ⅜ inch for tagliatelle, ¾ inch for pappardelle). Use fingers to unfurl pasta and transfer to baking sheet. Repeat folding and cutting remaining sheets of dough. Set pasta aside while making sauce; pasta should be cooked within 1 hour of cutting. (Nests of pasta can be frozen on baking sheet until firm, then transferred to zipper-lock bag and stored in freezer for up to 2 weeks; cook as directed in step 5.)

why this recipe works

Dried pasta may be convenient, but it can't compare with the texture and chew of homemade fresh pasta. It's a bit of a project, it's true: You need time, patience, and counter space. What you don't need is a pasta maker, because we've made a dough that's a cinch to roll out by hand. For a very pliable dough, we added more fat than traditional pasta dough in the form of olive oil and extra egg yolks, which softened the dough without building up gluten. Resting the dough made it even more malleable; all we needed was a rolling pin and chef's knife to get perfect strands. Note that if you're using a high-protein flour like King Arthur brand, you should increase the number of egg yolks to 7. The longer the dough rests in step 2, the easier it will be to roll. Avoid adding too much extra flour when rolling the dough, which will make it tougher. Serve with Classic Bolognese (page 364), Quick Tomato Sauce (page 102), or your favorite sauce.

5. Bring 4 quarts water to boil in large pot. Add pasta and salt and cook, stirring often, until tender but still al dente, about 3 minutes. Reserve 1 cup pasta cooking water. Drain pasta and serve immediately with sauce.

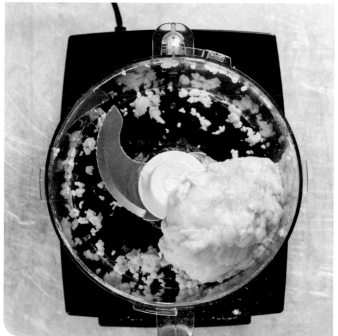

think like a cook

PASTA DOUGH DOS AND DON'TS

Our fresh pasta dough is designed to be tacky enough to stick lightly to the counter, giving it traction to be stretched ultrathin, but not so sticky that it wrinkles when rolled out. Variables such as flour brand, measuring technique, and size of the eggs may lead to slight differences in consistency. Here are tips on how to work with this particular dough and how to roll out doughs in general.

» DO start with rested dough; resting gives the gluten time to relax for more pliable dough. For other types of dough, you might also need to chill the dough before rolling it out.

» DO dust the dough and/or counter with flour; otherwise the dough will stick to the counter and tear.

» DON'T just roll in one direction; rolling both toward and away from yourself helps stretch the dough evenly rather than overworking some areas and ignoring others.

» DON'T lose the shape; the dough for this pasta should be rolled into a roughly rectangular shape. Don't let it get too round. (Pie dough, on the other hand, should usually be rolled into a circle.)

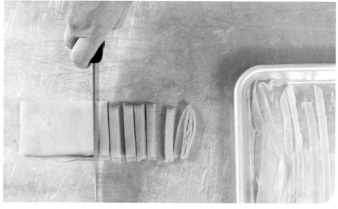

Paella

Serves 6; Total Time 1 hour 30 minutes

why this recipe works

With its bright colors and flavors, Spain's famous rice dish is a guaranteed party hit. But since versions can contain everything from rabbit to snails, it can feel overwhelming. This version gets at the heart of what paella is—a saffron-infused, something-and-rice, one-dish meal—without letting the process get out of hand. We love a paella that mixes briny seafood with smoky Spanish chorizo, so we started with chorizo, shrimp, and mussels, and then added chicken for heartiness; none of these required much prep work. Sautéed bell pepper and thawed frozen peas added color and sweetness. Fresh chorizo or linguiça sausage can be substituted for dry-cured Spanish chorizo. To debeard the mussels, simply tug off the weedy black fibers, using the flat surface of a paring knife as leverage.

1 pound extra-large shrimp (21 to 25 per pound), peeled and deveined (see page 99)

Salt and pepper

2 tablespoons olive oil, plus extra as needed

8 garlic cloves, minced

1 pound boneless, skinless chicken thighs, trimmed and halved crosswise

1 red bell pepper, stemmed, seeded, and cut into ½-inch-wide strips

8 ounces Spanish-style chorizo sausage, sliced ½ inch thick on bias

1 onion, chopped fine

1 (14.5-ounce) can diced tomatoes, drained, minced, and drained again

2 cups Valencia or Arborio rice

3 cups chicken broth

⅓ cup dry white wine

½ teaspoon saffron threads, crumbled

1 bay leaf

12 mussels, scrubbed and debearded

½ cup frozen peas, thawed

2 teaspoons chopped fresh parsley

Lemon wedges

1. Adjust oven rack to lower-middle position and heat oven to 350 degrees. Toss shrimp, ¼ teaspoon salt, ¼ teaspoon pepper, 1 tablespoon oil, and 1 teaspoon garlic in medium bowl. Cover and refrigerate until needed. Season chicken thighs with salt and pepper and set aside.

2. Heat 2 teaspoons oil in Dutch oven over medium-high heat until shimmering. Add bell pepper and cook, stirring occasionally, until skin begins to blister and turn spotty black, 3 to 4 minutes. Transfer bell pepper to small plate and set aside.

3. Heat remaining 1 teaspoon oil in now-empty pot until shimmering. Add chicken pieces in single layer and cook, without moving, until browned, about 3 minutes. Turn pieces and continue to cook until browned on second side, about 3 minutes longer. Transfer chicken to medium bowl. Reduce heat to medium and add chorizo to pot. Cook, stirring frequently, until deeply browned and fat begins to render, 4 to 5 minutes. Transfer chorizo to bowl with chicken and set aside.

4. Add enough oil to fat in pot to equal 2 tablespoons and heat over medium heat until shimmering. Add onion and cook, stirring frequently, until softened, about 3 minutes. Stir in remaining garlic and cook until fragrant, about 1 minute. Stir in tomatoes and cook until mixture begins to darken and thicken slightly, about 3 minutes. Stir in rice and cook until grains are well coated with tomato mixture, 1 to 2 minutes. Stir in broth, wine, saffron, bay leaf, and ½ teaspoon salt. Return chicken and chorizo to pot, increase heat to medium-high, and bring to boil, stirring occasionally. Cover pot, transfer to oven, and cook until rice absorbs almost all liquid, about 15 minutes. Remove pot from oven. Uncover pot, scatter shrimp over rice, insert mussels, hinged side down, into rice (so they stand upright), arrange bell pepper strips in pinwheel pattern, and scatter peas over top. Cover, return to oven, and cook until shrimp are opaque and mussels have opened, 10 to 12 minutes.

5. Let paella stand, covered, for 5 minutes. Discard any mussels that have not opened and bay leaf, if it can be easily removed. Sprinkle with parsley and serve, passing lemon wedges separately.

think like a cook

THE WORLD'S MOST EXPENSIVE SPICE

Sometimes called "red gold," saffron is the world's most expensive spice. It's made from the dried stigmas of *Crocus sativus* flowers, which are so delicate they must be painstakingly harvested by hand. Luckily, a little saffron goes a long way, adding a distinct reddish-gold color, notes of honey and grass, and a hint of bitterness to dishes like paella and risotto. The saffron you find in the supermarket is usually Spanish. When shopping for saffron, look for dark red threads (left) from the top of the stigma with no spots of yellow or orange. We found that broths infused with the reddest threads yielded the most intensely flavorful, heady, perfumed broths. Or, to save money, a good-quality powdered saffron (right) can be just as flavorful and fragrant.

Miso-Marinated Salmon with Sesame Sushi Rice

Serves 4; Total Time 40 minutes (plus 6 to 24 hours for marinating)

MISO-MARINATED SALMON

½ cup white miso

¼ cup sugar

3 tablespoons sake

3 tablespoons mirin

4 (6- to 8-ounce) skin-on salmon fillets

Lemon wedges

SESAME SUSHI RICE

2½ cups water

2 cups sushi rice or other short-grain white rice

2 teaspoons seasoned rice vinegar

1 teaspoon salt

2 scallions, sliced thin

2 tablespoons toasted sesame oil

1 tablespoon sesame seeds, toasted (see page 157)

why this recipe works

Marinating in miso uses just a few bold ingredients but produces salmon with a deeply caramelized, almost candy-like exterior and a salty, sweet, rich flavor. Some recipes marinate the fish in miso, sugar, and sake for 3 days. We found that 6 hours was plenty of time to season the fish and draw out moisture, giving the flesh an appealing dense texture. To caramelize the crust, we broiled the fish a good 8 inches from the heat to prevent the glaze from burning. The fillets became tender just as the glaze turned a deep bronze. For a simple side, we flavored sushi rice with sweet-tangy seasoned rice vinegar and sesame oil. Use salmon fillets of similar thickness. The best way to ensure this is to buy a 1½-pound whole center-cut fillet and cut it into 4 pieces. We prefer white miso here but earthier yellow or red will also work; do not use light or low-sodium miso.

1. FOR THE SALMON Whisk miso, sugar, sake, and mirin together in medium bowl until sugar and miso are dissolved (mixture will be thick). Dip each fillet into miso mixture to coat all flesh sides. Place fish skin side down in baking dish and pour remaining mixture over top. Cover with plastic wrap and refrigerate for at least 6 hours or up to 24 hours.

2. FOR THE RICE Bring water, rice, vinegar, and salt to boil in medium saucepan over high heat. Cover, reduce heat to low, and simmer until liquid is absorbed, 14 to 16 minutes. Remove rice from heat and let sit, covered, until tender, about 15 minutes. Fluff rice with fork, stir in scallions, oil, and sesame seeds; set aside.

3. Adjust oven rack 8 inches from broiler element and heat broiler. Place wire rack in rimmed baking sheet and cover with aluminum foil. Using your fingers, scrape miso mixture from fillets (do not rinse) and place fish skin side down on foil, leaving at least 1 inch between fillets.

4. Broil salmon until deeply browned and thermometer inserted into centers of fillets registers 125 degrees (for medium-rare), 8 to 12 minutes, rotating sheet halfway through broiling and shielding edges of fillets with foil if necessary. Transfer to platter. Serve with rice and lemon wedges.

think like a cook

REMOVING PINBONES FROM SALMON

When a fish is filleted, the flesh is removed from the backbone and ribs, but the relatively soft, thin, needle-like pinbones, also known as intermuscular bones, are not attached to the main skeleton and thus must be removed in a second step. While most fish are sold with the pinbones removed, they are difficult to see and are sometimes missed by the fishmonger. It's always a good idea to check for bones before cooking. The easiest way to do this is to drape the fillet over an inverted mixing bowl to help any pinbones protrude. (This will work with any size fillet.) Then, working from the head end to the tail end, locate the pinbones by running your fingers along the length of the fillet. When you find one, use tweezers or small pliers to grasp the tip of the bone. To avoid tearing the flesh, pull slowly but firmly at a slight angle in the direction the bone is naturally pointing rather than straight up. Repeat until all the pinbones are removed.

California-Style Fish Tacos

Serves 6; Total Time 1 hour

why this recipe works

A surfside treat, California fish tacos feature battered and fried crispy white fish and sprightly pickled vegetables. When done right, they are light and fresh, with a lively mix of textures and flavors. This recipe may look involved, but the components come together quickly, so invite your friends to help. The frying uses a mere ¾-inch layer of oil (no splattering vats). We made an ultrathin batter by adding two sources of carbonation, beer and baking powder; they provided lift and their slight acidity limited gluten development. Frying in batches helped maintain the oil's temperature. For toppings, we quick-pickled onion and jalapeños and then used the brine to brighten shredded cabbage (never throw out brine—see page 295). If you can't find crema, you can make your own; see page 102. Slice fish on the bias if your fillets are not 4 inches wide. Serve with green salsa if desired.

PICKLED ONION AND CABBAGE

1 small red onion, halved and sliced thin

2 jalapeño chiles, stemmed and sliced into thin rings

1 cup white wine vinegar

2 tablespoons lime juice

1 tablespoon sugar

Salt and pepper

3 cups shredded green cabbage

TACOS

2 pounds skinless white fish fillets, such as cod, haddock, or halibut

Salt and pepper

¾ cup all-purpose flour

¼ cup cornstarch

1 teaspoon baking powder

1 cup beer

1 quart peanut or vegetable oil

18 (6-inch) corn tortillas, warmed (see page 433)

1 cup fresh cilantro leaves

1 cup crema

1. FOR THE PICKLED ONION AND CABBAGE Combine onion and jalapeños in medium bowl. Bring vinegar, lime juice, sugar, and 1 teaspoon salt to boil in small saucepan. Pour vinegar mixture over onion mixture and let sit for at least 30 minutes, or refrigerate for up to 2 days. Transfer ¼ cup pickling liquid to second medium bowl, add cabbage, ½ teaspoon salt, and ½ teaspoon pepper and toss to combine.

2. FOR THE TACOS Adjust oven rack to middle position and heat oven to 200 degrees. Set wire rack in rimmed baking sheet. Cut fish crosswise into 4 by 1-inch strips. Pat dry with paper towels; season with salt and pepper. Whisk flour, cornstarch, baking powder, and 1 teaspoon salt together in large bowl. Add beer and whisk until smooth. Add fish and toss to coat evenly.

3. Add oil to large Dutch oven until ¾ inch deep. Heat over medium-high heat to 350 degrees.

4. Remove 5 or 6 pieces of fish from batter, allowing excess to drip back into bowl, and add to hot oil, briefly dragging fish along surface of oil to prevent sticking. Adjust burner, if necessary, to maintain oil temperature between 325 and 350 degrees. Fry fish, stirring gently to prevent pieces from sticking together and turning as needed, until golden brown and crisp, about 8 minutes.

5. Using slotted spoon or spider skimmer, transfer fish to prepared wire rack and place in oven to keep warm. Return oil to 350 degrees and repeat with remaining fish. Serve fish and pickled onions and cabbage with tortillas, cilantro, and crema.

think like a cook

FEARLESS FRYING

Every frying recipe is different, but most require a wide, deep pot; hot oil at the right temperature; a place to drain the food; and your full attention. Even with the relatively small amount of oil used here, expect splattering: Wear an apron to protect yourself from any oil that escapes the pot. Use tongs, a slotted spoon, or spider skimmer to add and remove food.

Maintaining oil temperature is key for even frying (food will fry up limp and soggy if oil is too cold, and brown too quickly if it is too hot). Use a clip-on deep-fry thermometer to monitor temperature (our favorite is the **ThermoWorks ChefAlarm**). The oil temperature will drop a little when you first add the food, so we usually increase the heat right after that to minimize the change. And we allow time for the oil to return to temperature between batches. Drain foods on a wire rack set in a rimmed baking sheet (some recipes use paper towels). If you're salting fried food, do it immediately; salt clings better to hot food.

Seared Scallops with Squash Puree and Sage Butter

Serves 4; Total Time 45 minutes

2 pounds butternut squash, peeled, seeded, and cut into 1-inch pieces (5 cups)

4 tablespoons unsalted butter

1 tablespoon half-and-half

Salt and pepper

⅛ teaspoon cayenne pepper

1½ pounds large sea scallops, tendons removed

2 tablespoons vegetable oil

1 shallot, minced

2 teaspoons minced fresh sage, plus 8 leaves

1 tablespoon lemon juice

1. Place squash in bowl, cover, and microwave until tender, 8 to 12 minutes, stirring halfway through microwaving. Drain, then transfer to food processor. Add 1 tablespoon butter, half-and-half, ½ teaspoon salt, and cayenne and process until smooth, about 20 seconds. Return to bowl and cover to keep warm.

2. Pat scallops dry with paper towels and season with salt and pepper. Heat 1 tablespoon oil in 12-inch nonstick skillet over high heat until just smoking. Add half of scallops and cook, without moving, until well browned, 1½ to 2 minutes. Flip scallops and cook until sides are firm and centers are opaque, 30 to 90 seconds. Transfer to plate and tent with aluminum foil. Wipe out skillet with paper towels and repeat with remaining 1 tablespoon oil and remaining scallops. Transfer to plate with first batch.

3. Melt remaining 3 tablespoons butter in now-empty skillet over medium heat. Continue to cook, swirling skillet constantly, until butter is starting to brown and has nutty aroma, 1 to 2 minutes. Add shallot, minced sage, and sage leaves and cook until fragrant, about 1 minute. Off heat, stir in lemon juice and season with salt and pepper to taste. Pour sauce over scallops and serve with butternut squash.

why this recipe works

Elegant yet casual, restaurant-worthy caramelized scallops served alongside a homey squash puree will make guests feel spoiled. In order to brown properly, scallops need to be totally dry when they hit the pan, so pat them well with paper towels. And get that pan smoking hot; this ensures they'll caramelize before the interiors overcook. A quick browned butter pan sauce provided an elegant finish. For a silky smooth squash puree to accompany the scallops, we simply microwaved butternut squash before pureeing it in the food processor with half-and-half, butter, and seasonings. To keep your kitchen time to a minimum, you can make the squash puree in advance. We recommend buying "dry" scallops for this recipe (see "Funny, My Scallops Don't Look Dry").

think like a cook

FUNNY, MY SCALLOPS DON'T LOOK DRY

When it comes to buying scallops, there is only one type worth buying: sea scallops. The other varieties, bay and calico, are much smaller and either too rare and expensive or very cheap and rubbery. Plump sea scallops are ideal for searing, grilling, and frying.

Distinguishing Dry from Wet

Many scallops are dipped in preservatives to extend their shelf life; these are "wet" scallops. Unfortunately, the preservatives can ruin a scallop's flavor and texture. Unprocessed, or "dry," scallops have much more flavor and a creamy texture, plus they brown nicely. Dry scallops look ivory or pinkish; wet scallops are bright white. If you are still unsure, try this test: Place one scallop on a paper towel–lined plate and microwave for 15 seconds. A dry scallop will exude very little water, but a wet scallop will leave a sizable ring of moisture. (The microwaved scallop can be cooked as is.)

Treating Wet Scallops

What if you can find only wet scallops? You can improve the taste by soaking them in a solution of 1 quart cold water, ¼ cup lemon juice, and 2 tablespoons salt for 30 minutes. Be sure to pat the scallops very dry afterward. These will be harder to brown than untreated dry scallops.

Preparing Scallops

Scallops require little preparation, just a rinse, but you should remove the crescent-shaped tendon that is often attached to the side, as it becomes incredibly tough once cooked. Simply pull it off with your fingers.

Cauliflower and Potato Curry

Serves 4 to 6; Total Time 1 hour

1 (14.5-ounce) can diced tomatoes

3 tablespoons vegetable oil

4 teaspoons curry powder

1½ teaspoons garam masala

2 onions, chopped fine

12 ounces red potatoes, unpeeled, cut into ½-inch chunks

Salt and pepper

3 garlic cloves, minced

1 serrano chile, stemmed, seeded, and minced

1 tablespoon grated fresh ginger

1 tablespoon tomato paste

½ head cauliflower (1 pound), cored and cut into 1-inch florets

1½ cups water

1 (15-ounce) can chickpeas, rinsed

1½ cups frozen peas

½ cup canned coconut milk

¼ cup minced fresh cilantro

why this recipe works

There's something very satisfying about taking a pile of unassuming vegetables and aromatics and turning them into a fragrant, flavorful curry. A curry starts with blooming spices, the selection of which is traditionally a matter of the cook's palate. We used two spice blends, curry powder and garam masala, to create dimensions of flavor with ease. Generous amounts of onion, garlic, ginger, and fresh chile, plus tomato paste for sweetness, completed our base. Potatoes, cauliflower, peas, and canned chickpeas gave us a hearty curry, and canned tomatoes and a splash of coconut milk added plenty of flavor. For more heat, include the chile seeds and ribs when mincing. We prefer the richer flavor of regular coconut milk here; however, light coconut milk can be substituted. Serve over rice with Cilantro-Mint Chutney (page 103).

1. Pulse diced tomatoes and their juice in food processor until nearly smooth, with some ¼-inch pieces visible, about 3 pulses.

2. Heat oil in Dutch oven over medium-high heat until shimmering. Add curry powder and garam masala and cook until fragrant, about 10 seconds. Stir in onions, potatoes, and ¼ teaspoon salt and cook, stirring occasionally, until onions are browned and potatoes are golden brown at edges, about 10 minutes.

3. Reduce heat to medium. Stir in garlic, serrano, ginger, and tomato paste and cook until fragrant, about 30 seconds. Add cauliflower and cook, stirring constantly, until coated with spices, about 2 minutes.

4. Gradually stir in water, scraping up any browned bits. Stir in chickpeas and processed tomatoes and bring to simmer. Cover, reduce to gentle simmer, and cook until vegetables are tender, 20 to 25 minutes.

5. Uncover, stir in peas and coconut milk and continue to cook until peas are heated through, 1 to 2 minutes. Off heat, stir in cilantro, season with salt and pepper to taste, and serve.

think like a cook

SPICES IN BLOOM

The technique of cooking whole or ground spices in hot butter or oil for a few seconds is called blooming and is used at the start of many curries, soups, and other spice-infused dishes. Blooming spices extracts far more flavor than simmering spices in water. Why? The main flavor compounds in many spices (and herbs such as thyme, rosemary, lavender, sage, savory, and bay leaves) are largely fat-soluble. Blooming not only deepens spices' flavors, but it also flavors the fat in which the remaining ingredients will be cooked.

To bloom spices, heat oil in a nonstick skillet (to prevent sticking and burning) over medium-high heat until shimmering (if using butter, heat until the foaming subsides) and add all the spices together. Cook the spices until they become fragrant and their color turns a shade darker—which happens quickly, in as little as 10 seconds. (Whole spices do not get ground after blooming, so they should be discarded—particularly large ones such as cardamom, cinnamon sticks, and cloves—if not being served whole in the finished dish.)

Stuffed Eggplant with Bulgur

Serves 4; Total Time 1 hour 30 minutes

4 (10-ounce) Italian eggplants, halved lengthwise

2 tablespoons extra-virgin olive oil

Salt and pepper

½ cup fine- or medium-grind bulgur, rinsed

¼ cup water

1 onion, chopped fine

3 garlic cloves, minced

2 teaspoons minced fresh oregano or ½ teaspoon dried

¼ teaspoon ground cinnamon

Pinch cayenne pepper

1 pound plum tomatoes, cored, seeded, and chopped

2 ounces Pecorino Romano cheese, grated (1 cup)

2 tablespoons pine nuts, toasted (see page 157)

2 teaspoons red wine vinegar

2 tablespoons minced fresh parsley

why this recipe works

For a hearty, showstopping vegetarian dinner, we turned to stuffed eggplant. Stuffing eggplant is popular in many Mediterranean cuisines; cooks in that part of the world have figured out that, when baked, eggplant loses its bitterness and becomes a rich, creamy vessel for a fragrant filling. Italian eggplants (smaller than the ubiquitous globe variety) are the perfect size. Scoring and roasting the eggplant halves before stuffing prevented them from turning watery and deepened their flavor. Nutty bulgur made a perfect filling base, which we enriched with Pecorino cheese and toasted pine nuts; tomatoes added bright flavor. Be sure to use fine- or medium-grind bulgur; do not use coarse-grind or cracked-wheat bulgur. Do not skip rinsing the bulgur before soaking. The time it takes for the bulgur to become tender will depend on the age and type of bulgur used. To seed plum tomatoes, halve them lengthwise, then scoop out the seeds and gelatinous material with your finger.

1. Adjust oven racks to upper-middle and lowest positions, place rimmed baking sheet lined with parchment paper on lower rack, and heat oven to 400 degrees.

2. Score flesh of each eggplant half in 1-inch diamond pattern, about 1 inch deep (do not cut through skin). Brush scored sides of eggplant with 1 tablespoon oil and season with salt and pepper. Lay eggplant, cut side down, on hot baking sheet and roast until flesh is tender, 40 to 50 minutes. Transfer eggplant, cut side down, to paper towel–lined baking sheet and let drain.

3. Meanwhile, toss bulgur with water in large bowl and let sit until grains are tender and fluffy, 20 to 40 minutes.

4. Heat remaining 1 tablespoon oil in 12-inch skillet over medium heat until shimmering. Add onion and cook until softened, 5 to 7 minutes. Stir in garlic, oregano, cinnamon, cayenne, and ½ teaspoon salt and cook until fragrant, about 30 seconds. Stir in soaked bulgur, tomatoes, ¾ cup Pecorino, pine nuts, and vinegar and let warm through, about 1 minute. Season with salt and pepper to taste.

5. Return eggplant, cut side up, to parchment-lined baking sheet. Using two forks, gently push eggplant flesh to sides to make room for filling. Mound bulgur mixture into eggplant shells, pack lightly with back of spoon, and sprinkle with remaining ¼ cup Pecorino. (Stuffed eggplant can be held at room temperature for 2 hours before baking.)

6. Bake on upper rack until cheese is melted, 5 to 10 minutes. Sprinkle with parsley and serve.

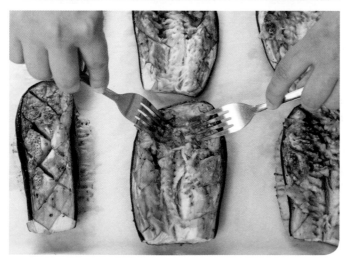

think like a cook

GET STUFFED (VEGETABLES)

Stuffing vegetables is a great way turn them into a hearty main dish, and you can adapt the method to almost any cuisine. Beyond eggplant, we also like to stuff tomatoes, peppers (see Cheesy Stuffed Poblanos, page 346), mushrooms, and squash of all kinds. While precise instructions will vary depending on your choice of vegetable and filling, we do have a few general tips.

Parcook the Vegetable

Since you want to be able to eat the vessel as well as the filling, you have to make sure that the vegetable you're stuffing is fully cooked and tender when the filling is done. Often this will mean that the vegetable has to be parcooked, either by roasting, as we do with the eggplant in this recipe, or microwaving for some smaller, quicker-cooking vegetables, such as peppers.

Eliminate Excess Moisture

Parcooking not only jump-starts cooking, it also drives off unwanted moisture that can wash out a stuffed vegetable dish. But often this isn't sufficient. In this recipe, we drain the eggplant after roasting it; for other vegetables we'll scoop out the watery seeds, gills, or flesh before parcooking, and sometimes even treat the vegetables with salt (this is useful for stuffed tomatoes).

Balance the Stuffing

A stuffing that's too wet will sog out the dish while one that's too dry won't hold together, so we like to combine heartier ingredients like bulgur and rice with juicier ones like spinach and tomatoes. A small amount of cheese can go a long way toward making a cohesive stuffing. Precooking the stuffing often helps meld the ingredients together.

Tex-Mex Cheese Enchiladas

Serves 6; Total Time 1 hour 10 minutes

why this recipe works

When all you want is to tuck into a cheesy pan of enchiladas, the labor demanded by most recipes can seem unfathomable. That's why these Texas-style cheese enchiladas, lovely in their simplicity, are right up our alley. A bright red ancho chile gravy smothers corn tortillas rolled around melty, gooey cheese. That's it. Toasting and grinding the chiles and cumin seeds gave our quick-cooking sauce deep flavor: smoky, slightly fruity, with an edge of bitterness. To achieve ooziness without resorting to processed cheese, we mixed sharp cheddar with highly meltable Monterey Jack. Oiling and microwaving the tortillas made them pliable without the typical frying. Since dried chiles vary in size and weight, seed and tear them before measuring; you need about ½ cup. And although you'll lose some flavor, you can substitute 2 tablespoons of ancho chile powder and 1 tablespoon of ground cumin for the whole chiles and cumin seeds, decreasing the toasting time to 1 minute.

GRAVY

2 dried ancho chiles, stemmed, seeded, and torn into ½-inch pieces (½ cup)

1 tablespoon cumin seeds

1 tablespoon garlic powder

2 teaspoons dried oregano

3 tablespoons vegetable oil

3 tablespoons all-purpose flour

Salt and pepper

2 cups chicken broth

2 teaspoons distilled white vinegar

ENCHILADAS

12 (6-inch) corn tortillas

1½ tablespoons vegetable oil

8 ounces Monterey Jack cheese, shredded (2 cups)

6 ounces sharp cheddar cheese, shredded (1½ cups)

1 onion, chopped fine

1. FOR THE GRAVY Toast anchos and cumin in 12-inch skillet over medium-low heat, stirring frequently, until fragrant, about 2 minutes. Transfer to spice grinder and let cool for 5 minutes. Add garlic powder and oregano and grind to fine powder.

2. Heat oil in now-empty skillet over medium-high heat until shimmering. Whisk in flour, ½ teaspoon salt, ½ teaspoon pepper, and spice mixture and cook until fragrant and slightly deepened in color, about 1 minute. Slowly whisk in broth and bring to simmer. Reduce heat to medium-low and cook, whisking frequently, until gravy has thickened and reduced to 1½ cups, about 5 minutes. Whisk in vinegar and season with salt and pepper to taste. Remove from heat, cover, and keep warm. (Gravy can be made up to 24 hours in advance. To reheat, add 2 tablespoons water and microwave until loose, 1 to 2 minutes, stirring halfway through microwaving.)

3. FOR THE ENCHILADAS Adjust oven rack to middle position and heat oven to 450 degrees. Brush both sides of tortillas with oil. Stack tortillas, then wrap in damp dish towel. Place tortillas on plate and microwave until warm and pliable, about 1 minute.

4. Spread ½ cup gravy in bottom of 13 by 9-inch baking dish. Combine Monterey Jack and cheddar in bowl; set aside ½ cup cheese mixture for topping enchiladas. Place ¼ cup cheese mixture across center of each tortilla, then sprinkle each with 1 tablespoon onion. Tightly roll tortillas around filling and lay them seam side down in dish (2 columns of 6 tortillas will fit neatly across width of dish). Pour remaining 1 cup gravy over enchiladas, then sprinkle with reserved cheese mixture.

5. Cover dish with aluminum foil and bake until sauce is bubbling and cheese is melted, about 15 minutes. Let enchiladas cool for 10 minutes, then sprinkle with remaining onion. Serve.

think like a cook

WHY YOU WANT A SPICE GRINDER

In a perfect world, spices would be bought whole and ground before using. Freshly ground spices have more potent flavor than preground, since grinding releases their flavorful oils, which then immediately begin to degrade. For that reason, whole spices have a longer shelf life than ground, which lose their punch after a year. Of course, the reality is that most cooks, including us, rely on the convenience of ground spices most of the time. But when a spice's flavor is paramount, we'll reach for our spice grinder. We use a small coffee grinder, reserved for this purpose (see page 451 for recommendations).

There are other advantages. A spice grinder can pulverize dried chiles, which you can't always find in powdered form. And we use it to grind dried porcini mushrooms for an umami-boosting powder. Overall, being able to grind what you like gives you more control over your cooking.

Spinach Pie for a Crowd

Serves 10 to 12; Total Time 2 hours

why this recipe works

A buttery, flaky spinach pie can come in handy. It's a satisfying vegetarian main dish as well as the ideal party food. This Albanian-style version, creamier and more subtle than Greek spanakopita, might appear easy (and it is!), but it is sure to impress. For a crisp, layered crust, we didn't mess around with preparing our own dough; store-bought puff pastry came to our rescue. The filling was as simple as stirring frozen spinach and Parmesan into a béchamel sauce (for more on béchamel, see page 287). We assembled our pie on a rimmed baking sheet, crimped the edges, and scored the top crust with a knife before baking. To thaw frozen puff pastry, let it sit in the refrigerator for 24 hours or on the counter for 30 minutes to 1 hour. Make sure the filling has cooled completely before assembling the pie.

2 tablespoons unsalted butter

2 shallots, minced

4 garlic cloves, minced

¼ cup all-purpose flour

1½ cups whole milk

3 ounces Parmesan cheese, grated (1½ cups)

20 ounces frozen whole-leaf spinach, thawed and squeezed dry

1 teaspoon salt

½ teaspoon pepper

2 (9½ by 9-inch) sheets puff pastry, thawed

1 large egg, lightly beaten

1. Melt butter in medium saucepan over medium heat. Add shallots and garlic and cook until softened, about 2 minutes. Stir in flour and cook until golden, about 30 seconds. Slowly whisk in milk and bring to simmer. Cook, stirring constantly, until thickened, about 3 minutes.

2. Off heat, stir in Parmesan until melted. Stir in spinach, salt, and pepper until combined. Transfer spinach mixture to bowl and let cool completely.

3. Adjust oven rack to lower-middle position and heat oven to 400 degrees. Grease rimmed baking sheet. Sprinkle counter lightly with flour. Place 1 puff pastry sheet on counter and roll into 14 by 10-inch rectangle. Loosely roll dough around rolling pin and unroll it onto prepared sheet. Spread spinach mixture evenly over dough, leaving ½-inch border. Brush border with egg.

4. Roll remaining puff pastry sheet into 14 by 10-inch inch rectangle on lightly floured counter. Loosely roll dough around rolling pin and unroll it over filling. Press edges of top and bottom sheets together to seal. Roll edge inward and use your fingers to crimp edge. Using sharp knife, cut top dough into 24 squares. Brush top dough evenly with egg.

5. Bake until crust is golden brown, 30 to 35 minutes. Transfer sheet to wire rack and let pie cool completely, about 30 minutes. Slide pie onto cutting board and cut along lines. Serve.

think like a cook

ENTERTAINING MVP: FROZEN PUFF PASTRY

Puff pastry is a superflaky dough characterized by dozens of buttery layers. It is made by wrapping a simple pastry dough around a square of cold butter, rolling out the dough, and folding the dough numerous times (chilling it between folds) in order to create dozens of layers—a process called lamination. When the dough is baked, the water in the butter creates steam, which prompts the dough to puff into flaky, delicate layers.

A dough this laborious taxes even our patience. Making it would be unthinkable for most occasions. Thankfully, **Pepperidge Farm Puff Pastry Sheets** are available in virtually every supermarket and work well. Each 1-pound package contains two 9½ by 9-inch sheets.

Because the dough is frozen, however, it must be defrosted before it can be worked; otherwise it can crack and break apart. We have found that thawing the dough in the refrigerator overnight is the best method as the dough can't overheat that way, but it takes some forethought. Countertop defrosting works fine, but don't rush it. Depending upon the ambient temperature, it may take between 30 and 60 minutes. The dough should unfold easily, but feel firm. If the seams crack, rejoin them by rolling them smooth with a rolling pin. When rolling or cutting the pastry on the counter, do so quickly. If the dough becomes too soft, return it to the refrigerator for 5 minutes or so to firm up.

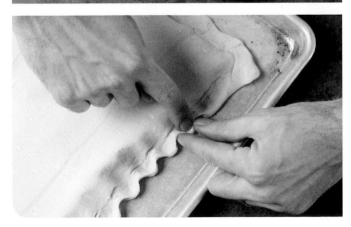

Classic Pot Roast

Serves 6 to 8; Total Time 5 hours

1 (3½- to 4-pound) boneless beef chuck-eye roast

Kosher salt and pepper

2 tablespoons unsalted butter

2 onions, halved and sliced thin

1 large carrot, peeled and chopped

1 celery rib, chopped

2 garlic cloves, minced

2–3 cups beef broth

¾ cup dry red wine

1 tablespoon tomato paste

1 bay leaf

1 sprig fresh thyme, plus ¼ teaspoon chopped

1 tablespoon balsamic vinegar

why this recipe works

Pot roast has a reputation as a boring, flavorless way to prepare mediocre cuts of meat for an uninspired, old-school American meal. But if done correctly, this is a no-frills, low-fuss way to produce a meltingly tender roast with a full-bodied gravy for your dinner table. We started by choosing well-marbled chuck-eye roast, which is full of collagen and well suited for low-and-slow braising. Cutting the meat into two smaller roasts shaved cooking time and allowed the salt we used to season the lobes to penetrate even further. Many pot roast recipes submerge the meat in broth and wine. But we cut back on the liquid so the meat could actually brown in the covered pot, and we added an aluminum foil cover on the pot (under the lid) to create a tight seal and trap all the moisture inside. If you're planning ahead for a big meal, note that this recipe actually improves when made in advance; chilling the whole cooked pot roast overnight enriches its flavor and makes it moister and easier to slice.

1. Pull apart roast at its major seam to yield two smaller pieces. Cut away all large knobs of fat from each piece. Sprinkle pieces of meat with 1 tablespoon salt (1½ teaspoons if using table salt), place on wire rack set in rimmed baking sheet, and let stand at room temperature for 1 hour.

2. Adjust oven rack to lower-middle position and heat oven to 300 degrees. Melt butter in Dutch oven over medium heat. Add onions and cook, stirring occasionally, until softened and beginning to brown, 8 to 10 minutes. Add carrot and celery; continue to cook, stirring occasionally, about 5 minutes. Add garlic and cook until fragrant, about 30 seconds. Stir in 1 cup broth, ½ cup wine, tomato paste, bay leaf, and thyme sprig; bring to simmer.

3. Pat beef dry with paper towels and season generously with pepper. Using 3 pieces of kitchen twine, tie each piece of meat into loaf shape for even cooking.

4. Nestle meat on top of vegetables. Cover pot tightly with large piece of aluminum foil and cover with lid; transfer pot to oven. Cook beef until fully tender and sharp knife easily slips in and out of meat, 3½ to 4 hours, turning halfway through cooking.

5. Transfer roasts to carving board and tent loosely with foil. Strain liquid through fine-mesh strainer into 4-cup liquid measuring cup. Discard bay leaf and thyme sprig. Transfer vegetables to blender jar. Allow liquid to settle 5 minutes, then skim any fat from surface. Add 1 to 2 cups beef broth as necessary to bring liquid amount to 3 cups. Place liquid in blender with vegetables and blend until smooth, about 2 minutes. Transfer sauce to medium saucepan and bring to simmer over medium heat.

6. While sauce heats, remove twine from roasts and slice against grain into ½-inch-thick slices. Transfer meat to large serving platter. Stir chopped thyme, remaining ¼ cup wine, and vinegar into sauce and season with salt and pepper to taste. Spoon half of sauce over meat and serve, passing remaining sauce separately.

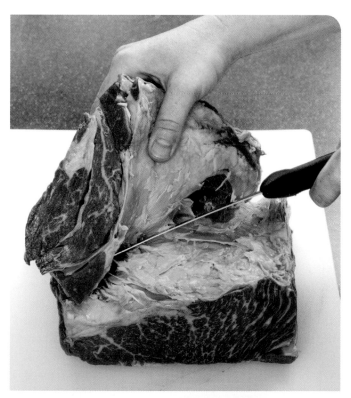

think like a cook

TURNING TOUGH TO TENDER

When it comes to buying and cooking large roasts, you don't have to opt for the high-end tenderloin or prime rib. Less expensive cuts can yield tons of flavor, but they often need special attention in order to get the best results. The less expensive cuts tend to be tougher cuts, generally from the more heavily exercised parts of the animal, such as the shoulder or rump. When a muscle gets a lot of exercise, it needs more connective tissue, which is predominantly collagen, a protein so tough it's nearly impossible to chew when raw.

Cooking changes that, melting the collagen into much softer gelatin, which lubricates and tenderizes meat and thickens cooking liquid, giving it a silky, unctuous texture. This transformation can take several hours; the longer food cooks, the more collagen breaks down. But while extended cooking destroys lean cuts with little collagen (think pork tenderloin) because the muscle fibers give up their juices, it actually improves the texture of collagen-rich cuts like beef chuck roast. That's because gelatin can hold up to 10 times its weight in moisture: As the abundant collagen softens into gelatin, the gelatin helps the meat to stay moist as it cooks. Cooking at a low temperature helps meat stay moist, too, since proteins shrink less and express less liquid at lower temperatures. So be patient! Don't rush this pot roast. You'll be rewarded with meltingly tender, richly flavored meat napped in a succulent sauce.

Chinese Braised Beef
Serves 6; Total Time 3 hours

1½ tablespoons unflavored gelatin

2½ cups plus 1 tablespoon water

½ cup dry sherry

⅓ cup soy sauce

2 tablespoons hoisin sauce

2 tablespoons molasses

3 scallions, white and green parts separated, green parts sliced thin on bias

1 (2-inch) piece ginger, peeled, halved lengthwise, and crushed

4 garlic cloves, peeled and smashed

1½ teaspoons five-spice powder

1 teaspoon red pepper flakes

3 pounds boneless beef short ribs, trimmed and cut into 4-inch lengths

1 teaspoon cornstarch

why this recipe works

Every culture has its slow-cooked comfort foods. One of our favorites is Chinese red-cooked beef, featuring ultratender meat cloaked in a thick, fragrant sauce. It's complexity typically comes from braising beef shanks in a sweet-salty sauce deepened by caramelized sugar. We used more readily available beef short ribs, which became fork-tender in half the time. Some molasses replicated the bitter sweetness of caramelized sugar, while five-spice powder added complexity without the bother of multiple whole spices. Red pepper flakes brought heat. Two thickeners—gelatin and cornstarch—gave our sauce a velvety texture. If you can find beef shanks and have some extra time, they're a great and economical cut. Use cross-cut shanks and cook for 4 hours in step 2; decrease gelatin to 2¼ teaspoons. Serve with white rice (see page 74) and steamed bok choy or Sautéed Snow Peas with Ginger, Garlic, and Scallions (page 196).

1. Sprinkle gelatin over 2½ cups water in Dutch oven and let sit until gelatin softens, about 5 minutes. Adjust oven rack to middle position and heat oven to 300 degrees.

2. Heat softened gelatin over medium-high heat, stirring occasionally, until gelatin dissolves, 2 to 3 minutes. Stir in sherry, soy sauce, hoisin, molasses, scallion whites, ginger, garlic, five-spice powder, and pepper flakes. Stir in beef and bring to simmer. Remove pot from heat. Place large sheet of aluminum foil over pot and press to seal, then cover tightly with lid. Transfer to oven and cook until beef is tender, 2 to 2½ hours, stirring halfway through cooking.

3. Using slotted spoon, transfer beef to cutting board. Strain sauce through fine-mesh strainer into fat separator, discarding solids. Wipe out pot with paper towels. Allow liquid to settle for 5 minutes, then return defatted liquid to pot. Cook liquid over medium-high heat, stirring occasionally, until thickened and reduced to 1 cup, 20 to 25 minutes.

4. While sauce reduces, use 2 forks to break beef into 1½-inch pieces. Whisk cornstarch and remaining 1 tablespoon water together in small bowl.

5. Reduce heat to medium-low, whisk cornstarch mixture into reduced sauce, and cook until sauce is slightly thickened, about 1 minute. Return beef to sauce and stir to coat. Cover and cook, stirring occasionally, until beef is heated through, about 5 minutes. Sprinkle scallion greens over top. Serve.

think like a cook

SECRET INGREDIENT: GELATIN

When we call for gelatin in a recipe like our Chinese Braised Beef, we're not telling you to add lime Jell-O to your dinner. Gelatin is a flavorless, nearly colorless substance derived from the collagen in animals' connective tissue and bones, as we discuss on page 385. We use it many ways: to stabilize whipped cream, to shore up fruit pies with loose fillings, and to thicken soups and braises. Here we use it to bolster the natural gelatin in the short ribs to create a silky, clingy sauce that approximates the original dish made with collagen-rich beef shanks. Even cross-cut beef shanks lack the collagen of an uncut shank and benefit from a bit of gelatin.

Beef en Cocotte with Creamy Mushroom Barley and Salsa Verde

Serves 6; Total Time 2 hours

BEEF

1 (3- to 4-pound) boneless top sirloin roast, trimmed

Salt and pepper

3 tablespoons vegetable oil

8 ounces white mushrooms, trimmed and sliced thin

1¼ cups pearl barley, rinsed

1 onion, chopped

½ ounce dried porcini mushrooms, rinsed and minced

3 garlic cloves, minced

1 tablespoon tomato paste

1 teaspoon minced fresh thyme or ¼ teaspoon dried

3 tablespoons cognac

2 cups beef broth

1 cup chicken broth

1 cup water

1 ounce Parmesan cheese, grated (½ cup)

SALSA VERDE

5 tablespoons extra-virgin olive oil

¼ cup minced fresh parsley

2 teaspoons sherry vinegar

1 garlic clove, minced

Salt and pepper

why this recipe works

Special occasions needn't require investing in an expensive roast and worrying about not overcooking it while you juggle the sides. In this earthy yet elegant meal, beef sirloin (flavorful but moderately priced) turns succulent as it cooks slowly in a covered pot. The low-heat, high-moisture method guards against overcooking. Adding barley and mushrooms turns the dish into a one-pot meal. Better still, the barley insulates the beef, helping it to cook gently and helping both grain and meat to finish together. Such a dinner warranted luxurious flavors, so we incorporated porcini mushrooms for depth, cognac for deglazing, and Parmesan for creaminesss, and accented it all with a bright herb sauce. To keep the barley from becoming greasy, trim the beef well. You will need a Dutch oven with a tight-fitting lid.

1. FOR THE BEEF Adjust oven rack to lowest position and heat oven to 250 degrees. Pat beef dry with paper towels. To help beef fit in pot, tie around center with kitchen twine. Season with salt and pepper. Heat 2 tablespoons oil in Dutch oven over medium-high heat until just smoking. Add beef and brown on all sides, 7 to 10 minutes; transfer to plate.

2. Add remaining 1 tablespoon oil, white mushrooms, barley, onion, and porcini mushrooms to now-empty pot and cook over medium heat until onion is softened, 5 to 7 minutes. Stir in garlic, tomato paste, and thyme and cook until fragrant, about 30 seconds. Stir in cognac, scraping up any browned bits, and cook until almost completely evaporated, about 30 seconds. Stir in broths and water and bring to simmer.

3. Off heat, add browned beef and any accumulated juices. Place large sheet of aluminum foil over pot and press to seal, then cover tightly with lid. Transfer pot to oven and cook until thermometer inserted into roast registers 120 to 125 degrees (for medium-rare), 60 to 80 minutes.

4. Remove pot from oven. Transfer beef to carving board, tent loosely with foil, and let rest for 20 minutes. (If barley is underdone, continue to cook over medium heat, adding additional water as needed, until tender.) Stir Parmesan into barley mixture and cook over medium heat until creamy, 1 to 2 minutes. Season with salt and pepper to taste, and cover to keep warm.

5. FOR THE SALSA VERDE Whisk all ingredients together in bowl and season with salt and pepper to taste. Remove twine from beef and slice against grain into ¼-inch-thick slices. Serve beef with barley and salsa.

think like a cook

COOKING IN A COVERED POT

The method used in this recipe is derived from a French technique known as casserole roasting, or cooking *en cocotte*. It's typically used for chicken and lamb, though it works well for beef, pork, and even fish. The meat is seasoned and placed in a pot with a small handful of chopped vegetables, covered, and baked slowly at very low temperature. Though similar to braising, cooking en cocotte uses no liquid. Instead, juices are drawn from the meat into the pot. These eventually create a moist-heat environment, so that the meat cooks gently—in effect, braising in its own juices. The result is unbelievably tender and succulent meat.

Most casserole-roasted meats fly solo, but we took the method a step further by adding a hearty portion of barley and mushrooms, enlisting the same moist environment to cook protein, grains, and vegetables together. Since the barley requires some liquid to cook, our method might be considered a cross between braising and true en cocotte. But the enclosed pot and very low heat create results similar to the real deal. Unlike with braising, where tough, fatty cuts of meat simmer until falling off the bone, cooking en cocotte gives you control over the meat's doneness. Here, even after a long cooking time (which encourages muscle fibers to break down, turning the meat tender), lean beef sirloin can be left at a juicy medium-rare.

Bacon-Wrapped Pork Loin with Potatoes and Peach Sauce

Serves 8; Total Time 2 hours 15 minutes (plus 1 to 24 hours for salting)

1 (3½-pound) boneless center-cut pork loin roast, trimmed

3 tablespoons sugar

2 teaspoons minced fresh thyme or ¾ teaspoon dried

Salt and pepper

3 pounds small red potatoes (1 to 2 inches in diameter), unpeeled, halved

1 small shallot, minced

1 tablespoon extra-virgin olive oil

12 ounces bacon

10 ounces frozen peaches, thawed and cut into 1-inch pieces

¼ cup dry white wine

1 tablespoon cider vinegar

2 teaspoons whole-grain mustard

1. Rub pork with 1 tablespoon sugar and half of thyme and season with salt and pepper. Wrap in plastic wrap and refrigerate for at least 1 hour or up to 24 hours.

2. Adjust oven rack to middle position and heat oven to 250 degrees. Combine potatoes, shallot, oil, remaining thyme, ½ teaspoon salt, and ¼ teaspoon pepper in 16 by 12-inch roasting pan.

3. Arrange bacon slices parallel to counter's edge on cutting board, overlapping them slightly to match length of roast. Unwrap roast and place in center of bacon, with longer side of roast perpendicular to counter's edge. Bring ends of bacon up and around sides of roast, overlapping ends of slices as needed. Place bacon-wrapped roast, seam side down, on top of potatoes. Roast pork and potatoes until thermometer inserted into center of pork registers 90 degrees, 50 minutes to 1 hour.

4. Remove pan from oven and increase oven temperature to 475 degrees. Continue to roast pork and potatoes until bacon is crisp and browned and meat registers 140 degrees, 30 to 40 minutes.

5. Transfer pork to carving board, tent loosely with aluminum foil, and let rest for 15 minutes. Toss potatoes with pan juices, season with salt and pepper to taste, and transfer to platter; cover with foil to keep warm.

why this recipe works

What's the best part of a bacon-wrapped pork loin roasted over potatoes? Is it how the bacon bastes and flavors the lean cut of meat, or how it infuses the potatoes with smoky, bacony taste? Hard to say, but it's easy to call this one of our favorite dinner-party recipes. To add extra flavor and juiciness, we rubbed the pork with sugar and thyme, then chilled it for an hour or more. Wrapping overlapping bacon slices around the meat encased it perfectly—and made for a beautiful presentation. We started the roast in a low oven to render some of the fat, then cranked up the heat to crisp the bacon. Below, the potatoes cooked in the drippings until tender and crisp. A simple peach sauce contrasted with the savory meat. A ¼-inch-thick layer of fat on top of the roast is ideal; if your roast has a thicker fat cap, trim it accordingly.

6. While pork rests, combine peaches, wine, vinegar, mustard, and remaining 2 tablespoons sugar in bowl and microwave, stirring occasionally, until thickened, 8 to 10 minutes. Slice pork into ½-inch-thick pieces and serve with potatoes and peach sauce.

think like a cook

HOW TO BUY AND COOK PORK

The majority of pork sold in today's supermarkets bears little resemblance to the pork our grandparents consumed. New breeding techniques and feeding systems have slimmed down the modern pig, which contains much less fat than it did 30 years ago. This means that many cuts, including tenderloins and center-cut loins and chops, are quite lean and prone to drying out without special attention. Wrapping a loin in bacon, as we do here, obviously helps keep the meat moist. But the real key is paying attention to the final temperature. For juicy pork that retains a slight tinge of pink you want the final temperature to be about 150 degrees. (Even 10 degrees higher, as recommended by many older books, yields tough, dry meat.) Since meat continues to cook off heat as it rests, that means removing chops and tenderloins when they are 145 degrees, and larger roasts when they reach 140.

We also suggest avoiding any pork labeled "enhanced." This refers to pork that has been injected with a sodium solution to remedy its leanness. While enhanced pork does cook up juicy (it has been pumped full of water!), we find its texture almost spongy and its flavor unpleasantly salty. We prefer to brine or salt pork ourselves, as we do here.

Indoor Barbecued Spare Ribs

Serves 4 to 6; Total Time 6 hours 30 minutes (or up to overnight)

why this recipe works

Even if you have access to a grill, authentic-tasting barbecue is hard to achieve without a smoker and pit setup. But while "indoor barbecue" is usually code for mushy meat drowned in cloying sauce, this recipe is different. By layering on flavors (first with a spice rub, then with sauce) over the course of multiple hours, we allow time for flavor to develop slowly—a hallmark of great barbecue. We started with St. Louis–cut spareribs, which are meatier than baby backs but more manageable than regular spareribs. After rubbing on a sweet-smoky spice mixture, we roasted the ribs in a moderate oven for 5 hours. The first 2 hours allowed the spice rub to cook into the meat. After that, we built up layers of "bark" by painting the ribs with barbecue sauce. Espresso powder, mustard, and liquid smoke added to a traditional barbecue sauce base of vinegar, ketchup, and molasses offered deep flavor and even smokiness. Look for liquid smoke that contains no salt or additional flavorings.

RUB AND RIBS

3 tablespoons smoked paprika

2 tablespoons packed brown sugar

1 tablespoon salt

1 teaspoon pepper

¼ teaspoon cayenne pepper

2 (2½- to 3-pound) racks St. Louis–style spareribs

BARBECUE SAUCE

1 tablespoon vegetable oil

1 onion, chopped fine

Salt and pepper

1 tablespoon smoked paprika

1½ cups chicken broth

¾ cup cider vinegar

¾ cup dark corn syrup

¾ cup ketchup

½ cup molasses

2 tablespoons spicy brown mustard

1 tablespoon hot sauce

1 tablespoon instant espresso powder

½ teaspoon liquid smoke

1. FOR THE RUB AND RIBS Combine paprika, sugar, salt, pepper, and cayenne in bowl. Trim ribs of any excess surface fat and remove thin membrane lining concave side of rib rack, if present. Pat ribs dry with paper towels. Rub evenly with spice mixture, wrap in plastic wrap, and refrigerate for at least 1 hour or up to 24 hours.

2. FOR THE SAUCE Heat oil in large saucepan over medium heat until shimmering. Add onion and ¼ teaspoon salt and cook until softened, about 5 minutes. Stir in paprika and cook until fragrant, about 30 seconds. Whisk in broth, vinegar, corn syrup, ketchup, molasses, mustard, hot sauce, and espresso powder and bring to simmer. Reduce heat to medium-low and simmer, stirring occasionally, until thickened and reduced to 2 cups, 50 minutes to 1 hour. Off heat, stir in liquid smoke and season with salt and pepper to taste. Measure out ½ cup sauce and set aside for serving. (Sauce can be refrigerated for up to 1 week; bring to room temperature before serving.)

3. TO COOK THE RIBS Adjust oven rack to middle position and heat oven to 275 degrees. Set wire rack in aluminum foil–lined rimmed baking sheet. Place ribs, meat side up, on rack and bake for 2 hours.

4. Remove ribs from oven and brush top of each rack with ¼ cup barbecue sauce. Return ribs to oven and bake until tender and fork inserted into meat meets no resistance, 2½ to 3 hours longer, brushing with additional barbecue sauce every hour. (Ribs can be refrigerated for up to 3 days. To reheat, place ribs on wire rack set in foil-lined rimmed baking sheet and let sit at room temperature for 30 minutes, then cover with foil and reheat in 400-degree oven for 15 minutes, uncover, and continue to cook until edges of meat begin to sizzle, 5 to 10 minutes; then proceed with step 5.)

5. Remove ribs from oven, tent with foil, and let rest for 20 minutes. Slice meat between bones to separate ribs, and serve with reserved sauce.

think like a cook

KNOW YOUR RIBS
They may all let you indulge your inner cave person, but various ribs cook and eat quite differently. A primer: Baby back ribs come from a pig's rib cage closest to the backbone; they are relatively lean and can be pricey. Spareribs are cut closer to the belly and are fattier. A full rack (5 pounds or more) can be unwieldy, so we prefer St. Louis–style spareribs (3 pounds or so), which have had the brisket bone removed for a narrower rack. Country-style ribs, cut from the upper rib cage, are boneless and meaty. Short ribs come from cows. We prefer English-style short ribs (cut between the bones) when cooking them bone-in. More frequently, however, we turn to boneless short ribs. Those aren't actually short ribs at all, however, but strips cut from the chuck.

Braised Lamb Shanks with Bell Peppers and Harissa

Serves 4; Total Time 3 hours

why this recipe works

Lamb has a rich flavor unmatched by beef or pork, which enables it to stand up to intense seasonings. Here, we took inspiration from the robust, fragrant flavors of North African cuisine by braising lamb shanks with harissa—a potent blend of ground chiles, garlic, and spices. We balanced the harissa with sweet bell peppers that we cooked until soft and then blended with the braising liquid into a rich, complex sauce. To keep the sauce clean and light, we trimmed our shanks of all visible fat before cooking, and strained and defatted the cooking liquid after braising. To finish the sauce, we sprinkled on fresh mint. We prefer to use our homemade harissa, but you can substitute store-bought if you wish, though spiciness can vary greatly by brand. Serve with couscous.

4 (10- to 12-ounce) lamb shanks

Salt and pepper

1 tablespoon extra-virgin olive oil

1 onion, chopped fine

4 bell peppers (red, orange, and/or yellow), stemmed, seeded, and cut into 1-inch pieces

¼ cup Harissa (page 101)

2 tablespoons tomato paste

4 garlic cloves, minced

2½ cups chicken broth

2 bay leaves

1 tablespoon red wine vinegar

2 tablespoons minced fresh mint

1. Adjust oven rack to lower-middle position and heat oven to 350 degrees. Trim shanks of all visible fat; pat dry with paper towels and season with salt and pepper. Heat oil in Dutch oven over medium-high heat until just smoking. Brown shanks on all sides, 8 to 10 minutes; transfer to bowl.

2. Add onion, peppers, and ½ teaspoon salt to fat left in pot and cook over medium heat until softened, about 5 minutes. Stir in 3 tablespoons harissa, tomato paste, and garlic and cook until fragrant, about 30 seconds. Stir in broth and bay leaves, scraping up any browned bits, and bring to simmer.

3. Nestle shanks into pot and return to simmer. Cover, transfer pot to oven, and cook until lamb is tender and fork slips easily in and out of meat and peppers begin to break down, 2 to 2½ hours, turning shanks halfway through cooking. Transfer shanks to bowl, tent loosely with aluminum foil, and let rest while finishing sauce.

4. Strain braising liquid through fine-mesh strainer into fat separator; discard bay leaves and transfer solids to blender. Let braising liquid settle for 5 minutes, then pour defatted liquid into blender with solids and process until smooth, about 1 minute.

5. Transfer sauce to now-empty pot and stir in vinegar and remaining 1 tablespoon harissa. Return shanks and any accumulated juices to pot, bring to gentle simmer over medium heat, and cook, spooning sauce over shanks occasionally, until heated through, about 5 minutes. Season with salt and pepper to taste. Transfer shanks to serving platter, spoon 1 cup sauce over top, and sprinkle with mint. Serve, passing remaining sauce separately.

think like a cook

BUYING A LITTLE LAMB

Lamb, which has traditionally been less popular than beef and pork, has been staging somewhat of a comeback—and for good reason. Lamb can be relatively inexpensive; it takes well to a variety of cooking methods, such as roasting, stewing, and grilling; and its rich flavor can't be beat. While almost all the beef and pork sold in American markets is raised domestically, you can purchase imported as well as domestic lamb. Domestic lamb is distinguished by its larger size and milder flavor, while lamb imported from Australia or New Zealand features a gamier taste. Imported lamb is pasture-fed on mixed grasses, while lamb raised in the United States begins on a diet of grass but finishes with grain. The switch to grain has a direct impact on the composition of the animal's fat, reducing the concentration of the medium-length branched fatty-acid chains that give lamb its characteristic "lamby" flavor—and ultimately leading to sweeter-tasting meat. Note that most markets contain just a few cuts, and you may need to special-order lamb. Generally, younger lamb has a milder flavor that most people prefer. The only indication of slaughter age at the supermarket is size.

back-pocket baking

Brown Sugar Cookies
Makes 24 cookies; Total Time 1 hour (plus cooling time)

14 tablespoons unsalted butter

2 cups plus 2 tablespoons (10½ ounces) all-purpose flour

½ teaspoon baking soda

¼ teaspoon baking powder

1¾ cups packed (12¼ ounces) dark brown sugar, plus ¼ cup for rolling

½ teaspoon salt

1 large egg plus 1 large yolk

1 tablespoon vanilla extract

¼ cup (1¾ ounces) granulated sugar

why this recipe works

This dead-easy sugar cookie has bold notes of butterscotch and toffee. Who could resist? We can't, which is why this has become one of our favorite cookies for everyday baking. Turning up the volume on a plain sugar cookie was as easy as swapping out granulated sugar for brown (for its deep toffee notes) and browning the butter, which gave it a nutty flavor and aroma. Adding a full tablespoon of vanilla underscored the caramel notes, which we balanced with a dash of salt. For the signature crystalline sugar-cookie coating, we stuck with brown sugar but added a little white sugar to prevent clumping. Resist the temptation to bake both sheets at once, and pull the cookies from the oven when slightly soft; a light touch should produce a slight indentation in the cookie's surface. Use fresh, moist brown sugar for cookies with the best texture.

1. Melt 10 tablespoons butter in 10-inch skillet over medium-high heat. Continue to cook, swirling skillet constantly, until butter is dark golden brown and has nutty aroma, 1 to 3 minutes. Transfer browned butter to large bowl and stir in remaining 4 tablespoons butter until melted; let cool for 15 minutes.

2. Meanwhile, adjust oven rack to middle position and heat oven to 350 degrees. Line 2 rimmed baking sheets with parchment paper. Whisk flour, baking soda, and baking powder together in bowl.

3. Whisk 1¾ cups brown sugar and salt into cooled browned butter until smooth and no lumps remain, about 30 seconds. Whisk in egg and yolk and vanilla until incorporated, another 30 seconds. Using rubber spatula, stir in flour mixture until just combined, about 1 minute.

4. Combine remaining ¼ cup brown sugar and granulated sugar in shallow dish. Working with 2 tablespoons dough at a time, roll into balls, then roll in sugar to coat; space dough balls 2 inches apart on prepared sheets. (Dough balls can be frozen for up to 1 month; bake frozen dough balls on 1 baking sheet set inside second sheet in 325-degree oven for 20 to 25 minutes.)

5. Bake cookies, 1 sheet at a time, until edges have begun to set but centers are still soft, puffy, and cracked (cookies will look raw between cracks and seem underdone), 12 to 14 minutes, rotating sheet halfway through baking. Let cookies cool on sheet for 5 minutes, then transfer to wire rack. Let cookies cool completely before serving.

think like a cook

6 STEPS TO PERFECTLY BAKED COOKIES

Cookies may be more forgiving than some other baked goods, but small changes can still have big effects on the results, from too-tightly arranged cookies that fuse in the oven to cookies that brown unevenly. For an end-to-end sheet of well-baked cookies, follow these pointers.

1. Use the Right Pan

We use sturdy rimmed baking sheets. Rimless "cookie sheets" will work, but cookies may finish several minutes early because hot air flows more quickly over the dough. Flimsy sheets of either type will result in overbaked cookies. For our recommendation, see page 444. Don't forget to line your sheet with parchment, which minimizes sticking.

2. Use the Right Oven Rack

The middle of the oven is always a safe bet; the closer to the bottom of the oven, the browner the bottoms of your cookies will be relative to the tops. We nearly always bake individual sheets on the middle rack. When baking two sheets, we use the upper-middle and lower-middle racks.

3. Allow Adequate Space Between Cookies

Proper spacing ensures cookies don't spread into each other during baking.

4. Rotate Your Pans

Even the best ovens have hot and cold spots, so rotating the sheet halfway through baking is essential (so the cookies that were in front are now in the back). If baking two trays of cookies at once, swap the positions when you rotate to avoid the cookies on the upper rack browning faster around the edges.

5. Check for Doneness at the Time Range's Low End

You can always bake a cookie longer, but there's no going back once it's overbaked.

6. Cool Pans Between Batches

A hot pan will start the dough cooking too early, so run the pans under cold water, dry them off, and line with fresh parchment before reusing.

Chocolate Chunk Oatmeal Cookies with Pecans and Cherries

Makes 16 cookies; Total Time 1 hour (plus cooling time)

1¼ cups (6¼ ounces) all-purpose flour

¾ teaspoon baking powder

½ teaspoon baking soda

½ teaspoon salt

1¼ cups (3¾ ounces) old-fashioned rolled oats

1 cup pecans, toasted (see page 157) and chopped

1 cup dried sour cherries, chopped coarse

4 ounces bittersweet chocolate, chopped into chunks about size of chocolate chips

12 tablespoons unsalted butter, softened

1½ cups packed (10½ ounces) dark brown sugar

1 large egg

1 teaspoon vanilla extract

why this recipe works

Bake these cookies and you don't have to choose between oatmeal and chocolate chip. We incorporated appealing chunks of bittersweet chocolate into an oatmeal dough, balancing them with toasted pecans and tart dried cherries. If you associate oatmeal cookies with being dry and cakey, these will change your mind: They are superlatively chewy. Using all dark brown sugar brought deep molasses flavor and a chewy texture. Making big cookies and baking them until slightly underdone further ensured chewiness. You can substitute walnuts or skinned hazelnuts for the pecans and dried cranberries for the cherries. Regular old-fashioned oats work best in this recipe.

1. Adjust oven racks to upper-middle and lower-middle positions and heat oven to 350 degrees. Line 2 rimmed baking sheets with parchment paper. Whisk flour, baking powder, baking soda, and salt together in bowl. Stir oats, pecans, cherries, and chocolate together in second bowl.

2. Using electric mixer on medium speed, beat butter and sugar in large bowl until no sugar lumps remain, about 1 minute, scraping down bowl as needed. Reduce speed to medium-low, add egg and vanilla, and beat until fully incorporated, about 30 seconds, scraping down bowl as needed. Reduce speed to low, add flour mixture, and mix until just combined, about 30 seconds. Gradually add oat mixture until just incorporated. Give dough final stir by hand to ensure that no flour pockets remain and ingredients are evenly distributed.

3. Working with ¼ cup dough at a time, roll into balls and space them 2½ inches apart on prepared sheets. Using bottom of greased dry measuring cup, press each ball to 1-inch thickness.

4. Bake cookies until medium brown and edges have begun to set but centers are still soft (cookies will look raw between cracks and seem underdone), 20 to 22 minutes, switching and rotating sheets halfway through baking. Let cookies cool on sheets for 5 minutes, then transfer to wire rack. Let cookies cool completely before serving.

think like a cook

CHEWY VS. CAKEY: A DEBATE FOR THE AGES

Cookie texture is polarizing. Some prefer cookies that are chewy, with crisp edges and a yielding center. The milk dunkers like things crispy. Others enjoy a cookie that is cake-like, with a more open, tender crumb. We think there is a place for all kinds in the cookie jar, but it helps to know the science behind the textures.

A big determining factor is aeration from beating softened butter with sugar; this builds structure for a cookie with a more cakey texture. For chewier cookies, we'll add vegetable oil or use melted butter (see Brown Sugar Cookies, page 398), which doesn't aerate as well and interacts more freely with flour to develop gluten, increasing chew. Brown sugar also creates chewiness. The molasses in it is hygroscopic: It holds onto moisture during and even after baking. Of course, leaveners play a role. Baking powder provides lift that can make cookies more cakey. Baking soda, by contrast, weakens a cookie's structure since it acts before the dough can set, helping it to spread out and even collapse a bit—ideal for a chewy cookie. Other chewy influencers include egg yolks, while using additional eggs or liquid creates structure and steam that increases cakiness. You can imagine the amount of testing required to explore all the variables for a perfectly textured cookie!

Fudgy Brownies

Makes 36 brownies; Total Time 1 hour (plus cooling time)

5 ounces bittersweet or semisweet chocolate, chopped

2 ounces unsweetened chocolate, chopped

8 tablespoons unsalted butter, cut into 4 pieces

3 tablespoons unsweetened cocoa powder

1¼ cups (8¾ ounces) sugar

3 large eggs

2 teaspoons vanilla extract

½ teaspoon salt

1 cup (5 ounces) all-purpose flour

1. Adjust oven rack to middle position and heat oven to 350 degrees. Make foil sling for 8-inch square baking pan by folding 2 long sheets of aluminum foil so each is 8 inches wide. Lay sheets of foil in pan perpendicular to each other, with extra foil hanging over edges. Push foil into corners and up sides of pan, smoothing foil flush to pan. Grease foil.

2. Microwave bittersweet and unsweetened chocolates in bowl at 50 percent power for 2 minutes. Stir in butter and continue to microwave, stirring often, until melted. Whisk in cocoa and let mixture cool slightly.

3. Whisk sugar, eggs, vanilla, and salt in large bowl until combined. Whisk chocolate mixture into sugar mixture until smooth. Using rubber spatula, stir in flour until no dry streaks remain. Transfer batter to prepared pan and smooth top. Bake until toothpick inserted in center comes out with few moist crumbs attached, 35 to 40 minutes, rotating pan halfway through baking.

4. Let brownies cool completely in pan on wire rack, about 2 hours. Using foil overhang, remove brownies from pan. (Uncut brownies can be refrigerated for up to 3 days.) Cut into 36 squares before serving.

why this recipe works

We all know the feeling; it's getting late and you remember that you're supposed to bring a treat to work or school the next day. In these desperate moments, boxed brownie mix looks pretty good. But while convenient, mixes leave much to be desired in terms of flavor and texture. For decadent, fudgy brownies that take only a little more effort than a mix, we used three forms of chocolate: unsweetened chocolate for intensity, cocoa powder for complexity, and bittersweet or semisweet chocolate for moisture and well-rounded flavor. Melting the butter was key to getting fudgy texture, as was limiting the flour to just a cup. Granulated sugar gave the brownies a delicate, shiny, crackly crust. You can use 5 ounces of bittersweet or semisweet chocolate chips in place of the bar chocolate. If you use a glass baking dish, let the brownies cool for 10 minutes and then remove them from the dish. (The superior heat retention of glass can lead to overbaking.)

variation

Fudgy Triple-Chocolate Espresso Brownies

Whisk in 1½ tablespoons instant espresso powder or instant coffee powder along with cocoa in step 2.

think like a cook

THE DEEPEST CHOCOLATE FLAVOR

If you like baking with chocolate (and who doesn't?), you'll start to notice that different recipes call for different kinds of chocolate—unsweetened, bittersweet, cocoa, and so on. Some, like our Fudgy Brownies, use several. While that sounds wonderfully decadent, it raises the question of why go to the fuss. And which kind of chocolate brings the most intense flavor?

Based on taste, you might be tempted to think bittersweet. In fact, the amount of flavor a chocolate variety can provide depends on the amount of cocoa solids it contains. That's why nearly all brownie recipes calling for bar chocolate include unsweetened chocolate, which contains just cocoa butter and chocolate solids. Many brownie recipes also use bittersweet chocolate; it contains more fat and sugar, so while it contributes less chocolate flavor it can help deliver a moist texture.

But when we want to pack a brownie with the most chocolate punch, we turn to cocoa powder: Ounce for ounce, cocoa powder has more cocoa solids—and thus more chocolate flavor—than any other type of chocolate. In order to equal the amount of chocolate solids in 1 ounce of cocoa powder, we had to use 1.63 ounces of unsweetened bar chocolate or 3.8 ounces of bittersweet chocolate.

The takeaway: While we never use just cocoa powder in our brownies (with all the starch and none of the fat of cocoa butter, it can make dry brownies), adding some can give brownies a big chocolate boost without weighing them down.

Molten Mocha Microwave Mug Cakes

Makes 2; Total Time 10 minutes

4 tablespoons unsalted butter

1 ounce bittersweet chocolate, chopped, plus 1 ounce broken into 4 equal pieces

¼ cup (1¾ ounces) sugar

2 large eggs

2 tablespoons unsweetened cocoa powder

1 tablespoon instant espresso powder

1 teaspoon vanilla extract

¼ teaspoon salt

¼ cup (1¼ ounces) all-purpose flour

½ teaspoon baking powder

1. Microwave butter and chopped chocolate in large bowl at 50 percent power, stirring often, until melted, about 1 minute. Whisk sugar, eggs, cocoa, espresso powder, vanilla, and salt into chocolate mixture until smooth. In separate bowl, combine flour and baking powder. Whisk flour mixture into chocolate mixture until combined. Divide batter evenly between 2 (12-ounce) coffee mugs.

2. Place mugs on opposite sides of microwave turntable. Microwave at 50 percent power for 45 seconds. Stir batter and microwave at 50 percent power for 45 seconds (batter will rise to just below rim of mug).

3. Press 2 chocolate pieces into center of each cake until chocolate is flush with top of cake. Microwave at 50 percent power for 30 seconds to 1 minute (chocolate pieces should be melted and cake should be slightly wet around edges of mug and somewhat drier toward center). Let cakes sit for 2 minutes before serving.

why this recipe works

The craving for fudgy cake and warm chocolate can strike at any moment. Why wait? This recipe produces two molten chocolate cakes (with a boost of espresso) in the microwave in 10 minutes. And it's good, unlike many mug cake recipes, which can be rubbery, chalky, or even explode over the brim. To avoid overflow, we incorporated cocoa powder: It has less fat than chocolate, so produces less steam. For a tender crumb, we microwaved the cakes gently at 50 percent power. Dropping pieces of bittersweet chocolate into each cake gave them a molten center. We developed this recipe in a full-size, 1200-watt microwave. If you're using a compact microwave with 800 watts or fewer, increase the cooking time to 90 seconds for each interval. Set to 50 percent power at each stage of cooking. Use mugs that hold at least 12 ounces.

think like a cook

BEST SUPPORTING INGREDIENT: ESPRESSO POWDER

There's your average joe, and then there's freshly brewed espresso. The same gulf separates regular instant coffee from instant espresso; its more concentrated flavor adds dimension and depth in convenient form. When you use enough of it, the fine-textured powder can give a big shot of flavor to baked goods, as it does here. But we also use smaller amounts in all kinds of chocolate recipes where we don't want a coffee flavor to stand out. Why? Instant espresso powder can sharpen and amplify the flavor of the chocolate from behind the scenes, making it taste deeper, richer, fruitier, and more complex without delivering discernible coffee notes. Some flavor scientists believe that when foods complement each other well, it's because they contain related flavor compounds. Coffee and chocolate are prime examples. They share some of the same flavor compounds (pyrazines) because they are both made from fermented beans.

Lemoniest Lemon Bars
Makes 12 bars; Total Time 45 minutes (plus cooling time)

CRUST
1 cup (5 ounces) all-purpose flour

¼ cup (1¾ ounces) granulated sugar

½ teaspoon salt

8 tablespoons unsalted butter, melted

FILLING
1 cup (7 ounces) granulated sugar

2 tablespoons all-purpose flour

2 teaspoons cream of tartar

¼ teaspoon salt

3 large eggs plus 3 large yolks

2 teaspoons grated lemon zest plus ⅔ cup juice (4 lemons)

4 tablespoons unsalted butter, cut into 8 pieces

Confectioners' sugar (optional)

why this recipe works
Have you ever met anyone who didn't love a lemon bar? The sunny, sweet-tart treats can brighten any day, and the lemon flavor in these bars shines right through. The secret was not relying solely on lemon juice, since the more juice you use, the more flavor-dulling eggs and starch are needed to thicken and stabilize the wobbly top layer. So in addition to using a full ⅔ cup of lemon juice, we added 2 teaspoons of lemon zest (straining it out before cooking). But we wanted more tartness, too, without adding more juice, which would require increasing the thickeners. Here we turned to a pantry staple: cream of tartar. Typically used when whipping egg whites, the white powder tastes plenty sour, and 2 teaspoons of it brought our lemon bars' flavor into sharp focus. Precooking the lemon filling on the stove ensured it wouldn't curdle or brown in the oven. Do not substitute bottled lemon juice for fresh here.

1. **FOR THE CRUST** Adjust oven rack to middle position and heat oven to 350 degrees. Make foil sling for 8-inch square baking pan by folding 2 long sheets of foil so each is 8 inches wide. Lay sheets of foil in pan perpendicular to each other, with extra foil hanging over edges of pan. Push foil into corners and up sides of pan, smoothing foil flush to pan.

2. Whisk flour, sugar, and salt together in bowl. Add melted butter and stir until combined. Transfer to prepared pan and press into even layer over entire bottom of pan (do not wash bowl). Bake crust until dark golden brown, 19 to 24 minutes, rotating pan halfway through baking.

3. **FOR THE FILLING** While crust bakes, whisk granulated sugar, flour, cream of tartar, and salt together in now-empty bowl. Whisk in eggs and yolks until no streaks of egg remain. Whisk in lemon zest and juice. Transfer to saucepan and cook over medium-low heat, stirring constantly, until mixture thickens and registers 160 degrees, 5 to 8 minutes. Off heat, stir in butter until melted. Strain through fine-mesh strainer set over bowl.

4. Pour filling over hot crust and tilt pan to spread evenly. Bake until filling is set and barely jiggles when pan is shaken, 8 to 12 minutes. (Filling around perimeter of pan may be slightly raised.) Let bars cool completely in pan on wire rack, at least 1½ hours. Using foil overhang, lift bars out of pan and transfer to cutting board. Cut into bars, wiping knife clean between cuts as necessary. Before serving, dust bars with confectioners' sugar, if using.

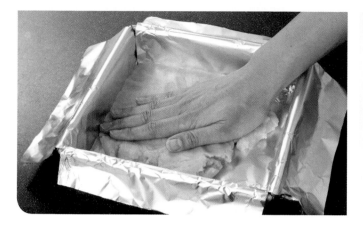

think like a cook

LEMON FLAVOR THAT LINGERS

In considering how to make our lemon bars more lemony, we took a step back and considered how flavor in lemon juice (and all foods) works: When you take a bite of food, you encounter taste with your tongue and aroma through a channel in the back of your mouth that leads directly to your nose. In fact, our brains register the five tastes (sweet, sour, salty, bitter, and umami) on the tongue, but potentially register a trillion aromas through the pathway in the back of the mouth that leads to the nasal passages. The dominant taste chemical in lemon juice, citric acid, is nonvolatile and registers only on the tongue. But lemon juice also contains a small amount of volatile compounds that give it subtle fruity-floral flavors as well. With that in mind, we looked to lemon zest, which is full of the aromatic oils limonene, pinene, citral, neral, geranial, and linalool and would enhance the experience of lemon flavor in the nose. For a tangy boost from a nonliquid ingredient that would register on the tongue, we flirted with the idea of adding pure citric acid powder until we realized we had a sour-tasting powder in our pantry already: cream of tartar, aka tartaric acid.

Skillet Apple Crisp

Serves 6 to 8; Total Time 1 hour 25 minutes

TOPPING
¾ cup (3¾ ounces) all-purpose flour

¾ cup pecans, chopped fine

¾ cup (2¼ ounces) old-fashioned rolled oats

½ cup packed (3½ ounces) light brown sugar

¼ cup (1¾ ounces) granulated sugar

½ teaspoon ground cinnamon

½ teaspoon salt

8 tablespoons unsalted butter, melted

FILLING
3 pounds Golden Delicious apples, peeled, cored, halved, and cut into ½-inch wedges

¼ cup (1¾ ounces) granulated sugar

¼ teaspoon ground cinnamon

1 cup apple cider

2 teaspoons lemon juice

2 tablespoons unsalted butter

why this recipe works

Warm spices, toasty oats, and not-too-sweet apples are a combination made in autumnal heaven. We love the unfussiness of this fall dessert (it also makes a respectable breakfast), but wanted a method that guaranteed tender apples: no rock-hard slices or mushy sauce. We first switched from a baking dish to a skillet. This way we could start the apples over direct heat for better caramelization and stir them for more even results. To improve the flavor, we added apple cider to the filling. We then sprinkled on our topping and finished the crisp in the oven. If your skillet is not ovensafe, prepare the recipe through step 3 and then transfer the filling to a 13 by 9-inch baking dish; top as directed and bake for 5 minutes longer than the times given in the recipe. You can substitute Honeycrisp or Braeburn apples for the Golden Delicious; do not use Granny Smith. While old-fashioned rolled oats are preferable, you may substitute quick oats; do not use instant oats. Serve with vanilla ice cream.

1. FOR THE TOPPING Adjust oven rack to middle position and heat oven to 450 degrees. Line rimmed baking sheet with aluminum foil. Combine flour, pecans, oats, brown sugar, granulated sugar, cinnamon, and salt in bowl. Stir in melted butter until mixture is thoroughly moistened and crumbly.

2. FOR THE FILLING Toss apples, sugar, and cinnamon together in large bowl. Bring cider to simmer in 12-inch ovensafe skillet over medium heat and cook until reduced to ½ cup, about 5 minutes. Transfer reduced cider to liquid measuring cup and stir in lemon juice.

3. Melt butter in now-empty skillet over medium heat. Add apple mixture and cook, stirring frequently, until apples begin to soften and become translucent, 12 to 14 minutes. (Do not fully cook apples.) Off heat, gently stir in cider mixture until apples are coated.

4. Sprinkle topping evenly over fruit, breaking up any large chunks. Place skillet on prepared baking sheet and bake until fruit is tender and topping is deep golden brown, 15 to 20 minutes, rotating baking sheet halfway through baking. Transfer to wire rack and let cool for 15 minutes. Serve warm.

variations

Skillet Apple Crisp with Raspberries and Almonds

Substitute slivered almonds for pecans. Add ⅛ teaspoon almond extract to reduced cider with lemon juice. Stir 1 cup raspberries into apple mixture with reduced cider.

Skillet Apple Crisp with Vanilla, Cardamom, and Pistachios

Substitute ½ cup shelled pistachios and ¼ cup walnuts for pecans. Substitute ½ teaspoon ground cardamom for cinnamon in filling and add seeds from 1 vanilla bean to apple, sugar, and cardamom mixture.

think like a cook

HOW DO YOU LIKE THEM APPLES?

The fact that an apple tastes great eaten raw does not mean that it will taste good in a recipe. Choosing the right apple varieties for different cooked applications is key. Apart from flavor differences, you also have to think about texture: Some apples turn mushy in the oven while others hold their shape. In general, more tart apples—Cortland, Empire, Granny Smith—hold their shape. Meanwhile, Golden Delicious, Braeburn, and Jonagold varieties are all sweeter and will break down when cooked or baked. (There are exceptions: McIntosh apples are tart, but they also fall apart and become very watery when you bake them.) We often use a mix of sweet and tart apples in a recipe for balanced flavor and texture. In our Skillet Apple Crisp, where the apples are precooked before a very short baking time, we prefer Golden Delicious for their mellow, honeyed flavor. Our precooking technique allows that to shine through without the apples becoming too mushy during baking.

Texas-Style Blueberry Cobbler

Serves 8 to 10; Total Time 1 hour 20 minutes (plus cooling time)

4 tablespoons unsalted butter, cut into 4 pieces, plus 8 tablespoons melted and cooled

1½ cups (10½ ounces) sugar

1½ teaspoons grated lemon zest

15 ounces (3 cups) blueberries (thawed if frozen)

1½ cups (7½ ounces) all-purpose flour

2½ teaspoons baking powder

¾ teaspoon salt

1½ cups milk

1. Adjust oven rack to upper-middle position and heat oven to 350 degrees. Place 4 tablespoons cut-up butter in 13 by 9-inch baking dish and transfer to oven. Heat until butter is melted, 8 to 10 minutes.

2. Meanwhile, pulse ¼ cup sugar and lemon zest in food processor until combined, about 5 pulses; set aside. Using potato masher, mash blueberries and 1 tablespoon lemon sugar together in bowl until berries are coarsely mashed.

3. Combine flour, remaining 1¼ cups sugar, baking powder, and salt in large bowl. Whisk in milk and 8 tablespoons melted butter until smooth. Remove baking dish from oven, transfer to wire rack, and pour batter into prepared dish.

4. Dollop mashed blueberry mixture evenly over batter and sprinkle with remaining lemon sugar. Bake cobbler until golden brown and edges are crisp, 45 to 50 minutes, rotating dish halfway through baking. Let cobbler cool on wire rack for 30 minutes. Serve warm.

why this recipes works

In much of America, cobblers have a biscuit topping. But in Texas Hill Country, it's a wholly different dessert: Melt lots of butter in a baking dish, add a simple batter and some sugar, then scatter on fruit. The fruit sinks during baking and forms juicy pockets underneath a craggy top. But versions we tried were thin and a little bland. We scaled it up and shifted most of the butter into our batter to enrich it while avoiding a greasy base. Swapping out Texas peaches for blueberries transported the cobbler to New England in summer. A potato masher broke them up, producing a more cohesive filling. Finally, a hit of lemon sugar, both sprinkled on top and mixed with the berries, brightened the cobbler and gave it a crisp top. Keep a close eye on the butter as it melts in the oven so that it doesn't scorch. Place the hot baking dish with butter on a wire rack after removing it from the oven. Avoid untreated aluminum pans here. Serve with vanilla ice cream.

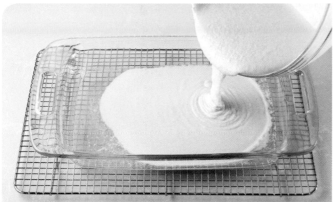

think like a cook

COBBLER, BUCKLE, OR SLUMP?
Rustic fruit dessert terminology is a sticky matter: One region's cobbler is another's buckle. Here is a short list of our favorites and the names we use for them.

Betty (Also Known As Brown Betty)
Sweetened fruit, usually apples, rhubarb, or bananas, layered with bread crumbs and butter and baked.

Buckle
Cake batter poured over fruit, often berries, and baked. Some resemble a streusel-topped coffee cake.

Cobbler
The most controversial moniker; it's often fruit topped with biscuit dough and baked to resemble cobblestones, but can also be a rectangular pie or like a buckle. And then there's Texas-style cobbler.

Crisp and Crumble
Fruit, often apples or peaches, baked under a crunchy, streusel-like topping, which often contains oats.

Grunt and Slump
Fruit cooked underneath dollops of dumpling dough on the stovetop. Dumplings "grunt" under heat.

Pandowdy
Fruit baked under pie dough or sliced stale bread; topping is pressed into fruit while it cooks.

Sonker
Syrupy cooked fruit baked under a pancake-like batter.

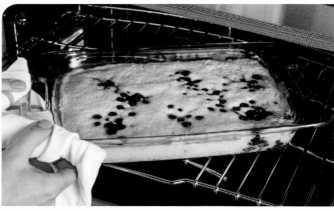

Free-Form Summer Fruit Tart
Serves 6; Total Time 2 hours 30 minutes (plus cooling time)

1½ cups (7½ ounces) all-purpose flour

½ teaspoon salt

10 tablespoons unsalted butter, cut into ½-inch pieces and chilled

6–7 tablespoons ice water, plus 1 tablespoon water

1 pound peaches, halved, pitted, and cut into ½-inch-thick wedges

5 ounces (1 cup) blackberries

6 tablespoons sugar

1. Process flour and salt in food processor until combined, about 3 seconds. Scatter butter over top and pulse until mixture resembles coarse crumbs, about 10 pulses. Transfer to bowl. Sprinkle 6 tablespoons ice water over mixture. Using rubber spatula, stir and press dough until it sticks together, adding up to 1 tablespoon more ice water if it will not come together.

2. Turn dough onto lightly floured counter, form into 4-inch disk, wrap tightly in plastic wrap, and refrigerate for 1 hour. (Wrapped dough can be refrigerated for up to 2 days or frozen for up to 1 month.)

3. Adjust oven rack to lower-middle position and heat oven to 375 degrees. Line rimmed baking sheet with parchment paper. Let chilled dough sit on counter to soften slightly, about 10 minutes, before rolling. Roll dough into 12-inch circle on lightly floured counter, then transfer to prepared sheet.

4. Gently toss peaches, blackberries, and 5 tablespoons sugar together in bowl. Mound fruit in center of dough, leaving 2-inch border around edge. Carefully grasp 1 edge of dough and fold up 2 inches over fruit. Repeat around circumference of tart, overlapping dough every 2 inches; gently pinch pleated dough to secure, but do not press dough into fruit.

5. Brush dough with remaining 1 tablespoon water and sprinkle remaining 1 tablespoon sugar evenly over dough and fruit. Bake until crust is deep golden brown and fruit is bubbling, 45 to 50 minutes, rotating sheet halfway through baking. Transfer sheet to wire rack and let tart cool for 10 minutes. Using metal spatula, loosen tart from parchment and slide onto wire rack; let cool until warm, about 30 minutes. Cut into wedges and serve.

why this recipe works

A free-form tart offers the irresistible elements of fruit pie—crisp, flaky crust and a just-sweet-enough filling—with far less effort. To make a free-form tart, a single crust is folded around a fruit filling, leaving the center exposed. Don't aim for perfection: The tart's rustic nature is part of its appeal. A mix of peaches and black-berries offers a nice contrast in flavors and textures and requires little preparation. Taste your fruit before adding any sugar; use less sugar if the fruit is very sweet, more if it is tart. Do not add the sugar to the fruit until you are ready to fill and form the tart. Serve with vanilla ice cream or with All-Purpose Whipped Cream (page 420).

think like a cook

ON A ROLL

Watching an experienced baker roll out pie and tart doughs can appear magical, but don't be frustrated if your attempts turn out more amorphous. This recipe is especially forgiving, and you can always use a knife to trim the result. Make sure the dough is in the shape of a flat disk before you roll it. Then follow these pointers.

Bring Your Dough to the Right Temperature

We often chill dough for about 1 hour and then let it sit for 10 minutes to ensure that the butter is just cold enough to work with. Overly cold dough will crack when rolled; warm dough can tear or stick to the counter. If dough softens too much when rolling, slide it onto a baking sheet and chill it for a bit.

Roll from the Center Outward and Rotate as You Go

This avoids overworking the same section of dough and helps maintain a nice, round shape. Use even, gentle pressure and give the dough a quarter turn after every few rolls.

Dust the Surface with Flour (Not Too Much)

A dusting of flour minimizes sticking without working too much flour into the dough. Sprinkle flour loosely from a foot above the surface for even coating. Toss additional flour underneath the dough as needed to keep it from sticking to the counter.

Roll Fragile Dough Between Floured Parchment

All-butter doughs are especially fragile. Using parchment is easier and helps keep the dough from breaking. Sturdier doughs can be rolled on the counter.

Olive Oil–Yogurt Bundt Cake

Serves 12; Total Time 1 hour 10 minutes (plus cooling time)

why this recipe works

Cake doesn't have to be an elaborately frosted affair, or reserved for special occasions. This simple, lightly sweet Mediterranean cake is one of our favorite everyday cakes, perfect with tea, at breakfast, or anytime. Extra-virgin olive oil and yogurt contribute to a moist, delicate cake with a slightly coarse crumb and a subtly tangy, mildly fruity flavor profile. The simplicity of the cake allows the subtle aroma of the olive oil to shine through. We tested a range of yogurts and found that plain whole-milk yogurt yielded the best results; cakes made with Greek yogurt were too thick and dense, while cakes made with low-fat yogurts were dry and crumbly. An easy-to-make lemon glaze (with a touch of tangy yogurt) added an elegant finishing touch. For the best flavor, be sure to use high-quality extra-virgin olive oil.

CAKE
3 cups (15 ounces) all-purpose flour

1 tablespoon baking powder

1 teaspoon salt

1¼ cups (8¾ ounces) granulated sugar

4 large eggs

1¼ cups extra-virgin olive oil

1 cup plain whole-milk yogurt

LEMON GLAZE
2–3 tablespoons lemon juice

1 tablespoon plain whole-milk yogurt

2 cups (8 ounces) confectioners' sugar

1. FOR THE CAKE Adjust oven rack to lower-middle position and heat oven to 350 degrees. Grease 12-cup nonstick Bundt pan using baking spray with flour. Whisk flour, baking powder, and salt together in bowl. In separate large bowl, whisk sugar and eggs together until sugar is mostly dissolved and mixture is pale and frothy, about 1 minute. Whisk in oil and yogurt until combined. Using rubber spatula, stir in flour mixture until combined and no dry flour remains.

2. Pour batter into prepared pan, smooth top, and gently tap pan on counter to settle batter. Bake until cake is golden brown and wooden skewer inserted into center comes out clean, 40 to 45 minutes, rotating pan halfway through baking.

3. FOR THE GLAZE Whisk 2 tablespoons lemon juice, yogurt, and confectioners' sugar together in bowl until smooth, adding more lemon juice gradually as needed until glaze is thick but still pourable (mixture should leave faint trail across bottom of mixing bowl when drizzled from whisk).

4. Let cake cool in pan for 10 minutes, then gently turn cake out onto wire rack. Drizzle half of glaze over warm cake and let cool for 1 hour. Drizzle remaining glaze over cake and let cool completely, about 2 hours. Serve.

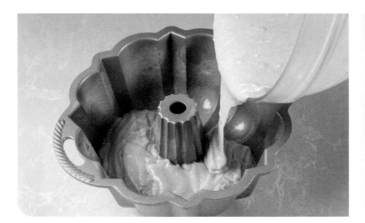

think like a cook

PREPARING CAKE PANS

A Bundt pan produces an attractive cake—if you can get it out in one piece. Properly preparing a pan at the start ensures a clean release.

We often line pans with parchment paper to facilitate removal but that's not possible with Bundt pans. Instead, a generous spray of baking spray with flour does the job for properly baked cakes (underbaked cakes will stick).

For layer cakes, cut out a parchment circle using the cake pan as a guide. Grease the bottom and sides of the pan with vegetable oil spray or butter. Fit the parchment into the pan, grease the parchment, and then sprinkle with flour. Shake and rotate the pan to coat it evenly and tap out the excess.

For loaf cakes or if you're serving the cake right out of the pan, you can simply grease and flour the pan.

Pear-Walnut Upside-Down Cake
Serves 8 to 10; Total Time 2 hours (plus cooling time)

TOPPING
4 tablespoons unsalted butter, melted
½ cup packed (3½ ounces) dark brown sugar
2 teaspoons cornstarch
⅛ teaspoon salt
3 ripe but firm Bosc pears (8 ounces each)

CAKE
1 cup walnuts, toasted (see page 157)
½ cup (2½ ounces) all-purpose flour
½ teaspoon salt
¼ teaspoon baking powder
⅛ teaspoon baking soda
3 large eggs
1 cup (7 ounces) granulated sugar
4 tablespoons unsalted butter, melted
¼ cup vegetable oil

why this recipe works

The star of an upside-down cake is the rich
_____ it cooks on the
bottom of the pan, which becomes an irresistible topping when the cake is inverted. This
version features fresh pears and a rich walnut
cake—but it's surprisingly easy to make. Slicing
the pears into wedges meant we didn't have to
precook them. To simplify the batter, we used
the food processor two ways: first grinding the
walnuts with the dry ingredients, then whipping the eggs and sugar, which gave the cake
structure without making it dense. Letting
the baked cake sit for just 15 minutes before
unmolding allowed the fruit top to set while
preventing the bottom from turning soggy. We
recommend baking this cake in a light-colored
cake pan with sides that are at least 2 inches
tall. If using a dark-colored pan, start checking
for doneness at 1 hour; note that the cake may
dome in the center and the topping may be too
sticky. Serve with vanilla ice cream or All-Purpose
Whipped Cream (page 420).

1. FOR THE TOPPING Adjust oven rack to middle position and heat
oven to 300 degrees. Grease 9-inch round cake pan and line bottom
with parchment paper. Pour melted butter over bottom of pan and swirl
to evenly coat. Combine sugar, cornstarch, and salt in small bowl and
sprinkle evenly over melted butter.

2. Peel, halve, and core pears. Set aside 1 pear half and reserve for other
use. Cut remaining 5 pear halves into 4 wedges each. Arrange pears in
circular pattern around cake pan with tapered ends pointing inward.
Arrange two smallest pear wedges in center.

3. FOR THE CAKE Place walnuts, flour, salt, baking powder, and baking
soda in food processor and pulse until walnuts are finely ground, 8 to
10 pulses. Transfer walnut mixture to bowl.

4. Process eggs and sugar in now-empty processor until very pale yellow,
about 2 minutes. With processor running, add melted butter and oil in
steady stream until incorporated. Add walnut mixture and pulse to combine, 4 to 5 pulses. Pour batter evenly over pears (some pear may show
through; cake will bake up over fruit).

5. Bake until center of cake is set and bounces back when gently pressed and toothpick inserted in center comes out clean, 1 hour 10 minutes to 1 hour 15 minutes, rotating pan after 40 minutes. Let cake cool in pan on wire rack for 15 minutes. Carefully run paring knife or offset spatula around sides of pan. Set wire rack on top of pan; flip cake onto rack and set rack in rimmed baking sheet. Discard parchment and let cake cool completely, about 2 hours. Transfer to serving plate and serve.

think like a cook

PICK THE RIGHT PEAR

While we love their sweet, floral flavor, pears have long been a distant second to apples from a baking standpoint, perhaps because there's a lack of good information about them. Recipes often don't name a variety, simply suggesting pears be "ripe but firm," but what exactly does that mean?

Bosc—the Baking Pear

Bosc pears are ideal for baking and poaching, especially when a visual presentation matters, as with our upside-down cake. That's not only because of their elongated necks but also because, unlike other varieties, they develop sweetness before they fully soften, so can be used when firmer. This means there is a wider window in which they will taste sweet but hold their shape. Bartletts are also good baking pears, but can turn mushy more quickly; save them for pies and crisps. Anjou pears are very juicy and too soft for baking.

Check the Neck

Pears ripen from the inside out, so the fruit's narrowest point—the neck—will be the earliest indication that the pear has started to ripen. For baking, you're looking for the neck to give only slightly when pressed and feel a bit softer than a russet potato—that's the meaning of "ripe but firm." For eating, the pear should yield slightly more, like a ripe avocado, when pressed at the neck. Pears that are soft at the base are overripe.

Storage

Pears ripen best off the tree so may be underripe when purchased. Keep them at cool room temperature and let them ripen slowly. (In a pinch, speed up ripening by storing them in a paper bag.) Once pears are ripe, move them to the refrigerator.

Buttery Yellow Layer Cake with Foolproof Chocolate Frosting

Serves 8 to 10; Total Time 1 hour 30 minutes (plus cooling time)

½ cup whole milk, room temperature

4 large eggs, room temperature

2 teaspoons vanilla extract

1¾ cups (7 ounces) cake flour

1½ cups (10½ ounces) sugar

2 teaspoons baking powder

¾ teaspoon salt

16 tablespoons unsalted butter, cut into 16 pieces and softened

1 recipe Foolproof Chocolate Frosting (page 420)

1. Adjust oven rack to middle position. Heat oven to 350 degrees. Grease two 9-inch round cake pans, line with parchment paper, grease parchment, and flour pans, tapping sides to remove excess flour. Whisk milk, eggs, and vanilla together in small bowl.

2. In large bowl, whisk flour, sugar, baking powder, and salt together. Using electric mixer on medium-low speed, beat butter into flour mixture, one piece at a time, about 30 seconds. Continue to beat mixture until it resembles moist crumbs, 1 to 3 minutes.

3. Beat in all but ½ cup of milk mixture, then increase mixer speed to medium and beat batter until smooth, light, and fluffy, 1 to 3 minutes. Reduce mixer speed to low and slowly beat in remaining ½ cup milk until batter looks slightly curdled, about 15 seconds.

4. Give batter final stir with rubber spatula to make sure it is thoroughly combined. Scrape batter into prepared pans, dividing batter as evenly as possible; smooth tops and gently tap pans on counter to release air bubbles. Bake until toothpick inserted into center comes out with few moist crumbs attached, 20 to 25 minutes, rotating pans halfway through.

5. Let cakes cool in pans on wire rack for 10 minutes. One at a time, set wire rack on cake pan and flip cake out onto rack. Discard parchment. Flip cake right-side up on second rack. Let cool completely, 2 hours.

6. Frost cake following instructions on page 421. Use 1½ cups frosting to fill the cake and remainder for top and sides. (Assembled cake can be refrigerated for up to 24 hours. Bring to room temperature before serving.)

why this recipe works

Everyone needs a really good classic yellow birthday cake recipe in their back pocket. This one is picture-perfect. It produces a sturdy yet velvety cake with rich flavor. For a truly tender cake, we used cake flour. We also employed the reverse-creaming method (see "Getting Even Layers"), which produced a light, flat-topped cake with a delicate crumb and just enough heft, ideal for layering and slathering with frosting. Bring all the ingredients to room temperature before beginning this recipe. Be sure to use cake pans with at least 2-inch-tall sides (see page 449 for our recommendation). Do not substitute all-purpose flour for cake flour in this recipe. We prefer to use a stand mixer for this recipe but a handheld mixer will also work.

think like a cook

GETTING EVEN LAYERS

Ever wonder how bakeries achieve such even-looking layer cakes? It starts with level cake layers. This is often achieved by sawing off a cake's domed top. But our recipe for buttery yellow cake avoids the domes in the first place. Doming is the result of creaming butter and sugar, which beats air into the batter. The step may be common in the world of baking, but we don't follow it all that much for layer cakes. Instead, when we want a level cake that's ready to be stacked and frosted, we turn to reverse creaming (the same method we use in our Make-Ahead Coffee Cake, page 146). Rather than beat butter with sugar, we mix it into the dry ingredients. Less air is incorporated this way, and the butter coats the flour particles, which minimizes gluten development for a cake with an ultrafine, downy crumb.

A second key to getting even cake layers is to divide the batter as evenly as possible between the pans. Then, you typically want to smooth the top of the batter with a rubber spatula for a level result; this is particularly important with thick batters. Finally, if a batter isn't too delicate, tap it on the counter to further settle it or to release any air bubbles that could leave holes in the finished cake.

FROSTING AND WHIPPED CREAM

All-Purpose Whipped Cream

Makes about 1 cup

The lightly sweetened flavor and creamy texture of whipped cream make it the ideal partner to numerous desserts, but perfect whipped cream can be hard to achieve. The cream can go from watery to properly whipped to curdled and stiff in a matter of seconds. For more foolproof fluffy mounds, we begin whipping on medium-low, then increase the speed and continue just until the mixture is thick and billowy. If the cream becomes granular, you've beaten it too long. If you accidentally overwhip, add unwhipped cream to the overwhipped mixture 1 tablespoon at a time. Gently fold it in, adding more unwhipped cream until the desired consistency is reached. Look for regular heavy cream,
which has a slightly higher fat content than "whipping cream." The fat helps it stay whipped for longer without losing stability. We like pasteurized (not ultra-pasteurized) heavy cream with 40 percent fat and no added ingredients like emulsifiers or stabilizing agents.

½ cup heavy cream

2 teaspoons sugar

½ teaspoon vanilla extract

Pinch salt

Using handheld electric mixer or stand mixer fitted with whisk attachment, whip ingredients on medium-low speed until foamy, about 1 minute. Increase speed to high and whip until stiff peaks form, 1 to 3 minutes.

Foolproof Chocolate Frosting

Makes 5 cups

A combination of melted chocolate and cocoa powder gives this frosting deep chocolate flavor, while confectioners' sugar and corn syrup turns it smooth and glossy. Mixing the frosting in a food processor eliminates the risk of incorporating too much air. The result is a thick, fluffy chocolate frosting that spreads like a dream. This recipe may be made with milk, semisweet, or bittersweet chocolate. Cool the chocolate to between 85 and 100 degrees before adding it to the butter mixture.

20 tablespoons (2½ sticks) unsalted butter, softened

1 cup (4 ounces) confectioners' sugar

¾ cup (2¼ ounces) Dutch-processed cocoa powder

Pinch salt

¾ cup light corn syrup

1 teaspoon vanilla extract

8 ounces chocolate, melted and cooled

In food processor, process butter, sugar, cocoa, and salt until smooth, about 30 seconds, scraping sides of bowl as needed. Add corn syrup and vanilla and process until just combined, 5 to 10 seconds. Scrape sides of bowl, then add chocolate and pulse until smooth and creamy, 10 to 15 seconds. (Frosting can be kept at room temperature for up to 3 hours before frosting cake, or refrigerated for up to 3 days. If refrigerated, let stand at room temperature for 1 hour before using.)

FROSTING A CAKE

1. KEEP THE CAKE PLATTER CLEAN Cover the edges of the platter with strips of parchment paper to ensure that extra frosting doesn't end up on the platter. Place one layer on the platter.

2. FROST THE FIRST LAYER Dollop a portion of frosting in the center of the cake layer. Using an offset spatula, spread the frosting in an even layer from the center right to the edge of the cake.

3. FROST THE SECOND LAYER Place the second layer on top, pressing gently and making sure it's aligned with the first layer. Finish by dolloping more frosting in the center and spread evenly across the top layer, pushing it slightly over the edge of the cake.

4. GATHER UP FROSTING FOR THE SIDES A narrow, flexible offset spatula is ideal for spreading frosting on vertical surfaces. Mound a few tablespoons of frosting on the spatula's tip and press it against the side of the cake to adhere.

5. FROST THE SIDES Gently smear the frosting onto the sides of the cake. Repeat until the sides are covered. Use gentle motions and don't press too hard or you will wind up with crumbs in the frosting. Clean off the spatula as needed.

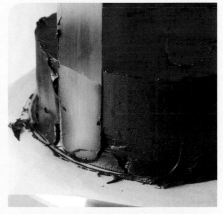

6. SMOOTH OUT THE ROUGH SPOTS Gently run the edge of the spatula around the sides to smooth out any bumps and tidy the area where the frosting from the top and sides merges. You can run the edge of the spatula over the top of the cake to give it a smooth look too. Remove the strips of parchment before serving.

Easiest-Ever Cheesecake

Serves 12 to 16; Total Time 3 hours (plus cooling and chilling time)

why this recipe works

To many people, homemade cheesecake seems like too much work. Better to leave this to the pros. But after many rounds of experimentation, we have to disagree. Producing a perfect cheesecake is merely a matter of paying close attention to the temperature of the oven and the temperature of the cheesecake itself. Aside from that, the ingredient list is short and the method is easy. Our food processor took care of both the graham cracker crust and the filling. We relied on our oven thermometer to make sure thaature was correct and an instaeter to ensure the cheesecake's temperature didn't rise too high. With this level of precision, a water bath was unnecessary. Reduce the oven temperature as soon as the crust is finished baking and be sure it has dropped to 250 degrees before you begin baking the cheesecake. Make sure to thoroughly scrape the processor bowl as you make the filling to eliminate lumps.

CRUST
6 whole graham crackers, broken into pieces
⅓ cup (2⅓ ounces) sugar
½ cup (2½ ounces) all-purpose flour
¼ teaspoon salt
6 tablespoons unsalted butter, melted

CHEESECAKE
2 pounds cream cheese
1¼ cups (8¾ ounces) sugar
4 large eggs
¼ cup heavy cream
¼ cup sour cream
2 teaspoons vanilla extract

1. FOR THE CRUST Adjust oven rack to middle position and heat oven to 325 degrees. Spray 9-inch springform pan with vegetable oil spray. Process cracker pieces and sugar in food processor until finely ground, about 30 seconds. Add flour and salt and pulse to combine, about 2 pulses. Add melted butter and pulse until crumbs are evenly moistened, about 10 pulses.

2. Using your hands, press crumb mixture evenly into pan bottom. Using bottom of dry measuring cup, firmly pack crust into pan. Bake until fragrant and beginning to brown around edges, about 13 minutes. Let cool completely.

3. FOR THE CHEESECAKE Reduce oven temperature to 250 degrees. In clean, dry processor bowl, process cream cheese and sugar until smooth, about 3 minutes, scraping down bowl as needed. With processor running, add eggs, one at a time, until just incorporated, about 30 seconds total. Scrape down sides of bowl. Add heavy cream, sour cream, and vanilla and process to combine, about 30 seconds.

4. Pour cheesecake mixture onto cooled crust. Gently tap pan on counter to release air bubbles. Gently draw tines of fork across surface of cake to pop any bubbles that have risen to surface.

5. Once oven temperature has reached 250 degrees, bake cheesecake until edges are set, center jiggles slightly when shaken, and thermometer inserted into center registers 155 degrees, 1 hour 20 minutes to 1½ hours.

Transfer pan to wire rack and let cool completely, about 2 hours. Refrigerate cheesecake, uncovered, until cold, about 6 hours. (Cake can be covered and refrigerated for up to 4 days.)

6. To unmold cheesecake, run tip of sharp paring knife between cake and side of pan and remove side. Slide thin metal spatula between crust and pan bottom to loosen, then slide cake onto serving platter. Let cheesecake stand at room temperature for 30 minutes. To serve, dip a sharp knife in very hot water and wipe dry before and after each cut.

think like a cook

DON'T TRUST YOUR OVEN

Ovens are inaccurate. Since all ovens cycle on and off to maintain temperature, even the best periodically deviate by a couple of degrees and some can be off by as much as 50 degrees unless they're recalibrated regularly. An oven's internal thermometer only gauges the temperature of the location where it's installed, which is necessarily in an out-of-the-way spot. But ovens can be subject to hot spots or drafts. Only a good freestanding thermometer can tell you what's going on right in the middle, where most food cooks. A good oven thermometer should be easy to read and easy to mount securely and safely out of the way in your oven. It should also be durable. Our favorite model, the **CDN ProAccurate Oven Thermometer,** costs less than $10 and can save you a lot of grief in the kitchen.

Flourless Chocolate Cake
Serves 12; Total Time 1 hour 30 minutes (plus cooling and chilling)

12 ounces bittersweet chocolate,
broken into 1-inch pieces

16 tablespoons unsalted butter

6 large eggs

1 cup (7 ounces) sugar

½ cup water

1 tablespoon cornstarch

1 tablespoon vanilla extract

1 teaspoon instant espresso powder

½ teaspoon salt

1. Adjust oven rack to middle position and heat oven to 275 degrees. Spray 9-inch springform pan with vegetable oil spray. Microwave chocolate and butter in bowl at 50 percent power, stirring occasionally with rubber spatula, until melted, about 4 minutes. Let chocolate mixture cool for 5 minutes.

2. Whisk eggs, sugar, water, cornstarch, vanilla, espresso powder, and salt together in large bowl until thoroughly combined, about 30 seconds. Whisk in chocolate mixture until smooth and slightly thickened, about 45 seconds. Strain batter through fine-mesh strainer into prepared pan, pressing against strainer with rubber spatula or back of ladle to help batter pass through.

3. Gently tap pan on counter to release air bubbles; let sit on counter for 10 minutes to allow air bubbles to rise to top. Use tines of fork to gently pop any air bubbles that have risen to surface. Bake cake until edges are set and center jiggles slightly when cake is shaken gently, 45 to 50 minutes. Let cake cool for 5 minutes, then run paring knife between cake and sides of pan. Let cake cool in pan on wire rack until barely warm, about 30 minutes.

4. Cover cake tightly with plastic wrap, poke small hole in top, and refrigerate until cold and firmly set, at least 6 hours.

5. To unmold cake, remove sides of pan and slide thin metal spatula between cake bottom and pan bottom to loosen, then slide cake onto serving platter. Let cake stand at room temperature for 30 minutes. To serve, dip a sharp knife in very hot water and wipe dry before and after each cut.

why this recipe works
Dense and decadent, flourless chocolate cake is an ideal back-pocket dessert for dinner parties or whenever you want to impress. It looks sophisticate⸺⸺⸺⸺urious but requires very little w⸺⸺⸺⸺⸺tored in the fridge until you nc⸺⸺⸺⸺e microwave to gently melt chocolate and butter, then whisked in all the other ingredients. To ensure a perfectly smooth, crack-free cake, we strained the batter into the pan, rested it, and then carefully popped any bubbles that rose to the surface. To avoid the trouble of baking the cake in a water bath, which helps prevent it from cooking too quickly and developing cracks, we found gentle heat by way of a low 275-degree oven. Plan ahead: This cake needs to chill for at least 6 hours, so we recommend making it a day ahead of time. Dollop with All-Purpose Whipped Cream (page 420) before serving.

think like a cook

A CLEAN SLICE

In the life of any cake, there comes the final step—serving it. At this point, if it's for a special occasion, guests will often exchange nervous glances. Who's going to cut into it? Often, people will feign incompetence and suggest the cake's baker do the honors. The expectation to produce clean, professional slices can feel great. This burden is not lightened by the number of cake cutting gadgets available, from wagon wheel–shaped contraptions that cut the entire thing in one go to scary-looking pieces of wire. Of course, the cake will be just as delicious if it smudges or topples, but don't just reach for any old knife or server.

It may seem obvious, but you want a knife that will reach into the center of the cake so that you can make slices of the same depth all the way around. We use a chef's knife. The next step is key: Dip the knife in very hot water and wipe it dry before the first and after each cut. Wiping the knife ensures that crumbs, frosting, and anything else won't mar successive slices. Heating the knife causes it to very slightly melt what it's cutting, preventing the surface from cracking and allowing for a clean separation of each piece. This is critical with our Flourless Chocolate Cake and Easiest-Ever Cheesecake (page 422), as the custardy centers are so soft.

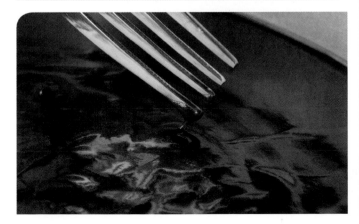

Buttermilk Drop Biscuits

Makes 12 biscuits; Total Time 35 minutes

2 cups (10 ounces) all-purpose flour

2 teaspoons baking powder

½ teaspoon baking soda

1 teaspoon sugar

¾ teaspoon salt

1 cup buttermilk, chilled

8 tablespoons unsalted butter, melted, plus 2 tablespoons unsalted butter

1. Adjust oven rack to middle position and heat oven to 475 degrees. Line rimmed baking sheet with parchment paper. Whisk flour, baking powder, baking soda, sugar, and salt together in large bowl. Stir buttermilk and melted butter together in 2-cup liquid measuring cup until butter forms clumps.

2. Add buttermilk mixture to flour mixture and stir with rubber spatula until just incorporated. Using greased ¼-cup dry measuring cup, drop level scoops of batter 1½ inches apart on prepared sheet. Bake until tops are golden brown, rotating sheet halfway through baking, 12 to 14 minutes.

3. Melt remaining 2 tablespoons butter and brush on biscuit tops. Transfer biscuits to wire rack and let cool for 5 minutes before serving.

why this recipe works

Maybe you think baking a loaf of actual bread is beyond your abilities in the kitchen. First of all, that's probably not true—see our foolproof recipes on page 434 and 436. But if you are intimidated, or even if you just need something to fill the bread basket within the next hour, a solid biscuit recipe is your best bet. Drop biscuits are easy. Unlike traditional biscuits, which need to be rolled and cut out with a biscuit cutter, drop biscuits are simply dropped onto the baking sheet. Still, to get flaky layers, the butter typically has to be cut into flour, which can be a hassle. This recipe gets around that: We devised a method of combining hot melted butter and cold buttermilk. When the butter hits the milk, it clumps into pieces just the right size. *Voilà*—light, fluffy, and easy stir-and-drop biscuits in plenty of time for dinner. To refresh day-old biscuits, heat them in a 300-degree oven for 10 minutes.

variations

Cheddar and Pimento Drop Biscuits

In step 1, add ¾ cup shredded extra-sharp cheddar cheese and ¼ cup finely chopped jarred pimentos to flour mixture.

Mixed Herb Drop Biscuits

In step 1, add 2 tablespoons chopped fresh basil, 2 tablespoons minced fresh parsley, and 2 teaspoons minced fresh oregano to flour mixture.

Mustard and Dill Drop Biscuits

In step 1, add 1 tablespoon minced fresh dill to flour mixture and 2 table-spoons whole-grain mustard to buttermilk mixture.

Rosemary and Olive Drop Biscuits

In step 1, add ¼ cup finely chopped pitted kalamata olives and 1½ tea-spoons minced fresh rosemary to flour mixture.

think like a cook

DELICIOUS SCIENCE: LAYERS OF BUTTER MAKE FLAKY PASTRY

Butter is the key to many great biscuits and pie crusts because when it's heated, the water in it turns into steam, which lifts the dough and creates a flaky texture. For the steam to have a significant effect, the butter must be evenly dispersed in layers throughout the dough. This way, when the butter layers melt, the steam helps separate the superthin layers of dough into striated flakes. The challenge is getting the butter evenly dispersed throughout the dough while leaving it in distinct layers. If the butter becomes fully incorporated (as when making a cake, for instance), the flakes won't form. In traditional rolled biscuits, this is accomplished by incorporating tiny pea-size chunks of cold butter in the dough. In our drop biscuit recipe, the clumps of butter created when the hot butter mixes with cold buttermilk helps distribute the butter in pockets for results that are almost as light and fluffy as rolled biscuits, without any of the fussiness or extra steps.

Southern-Style Cornbread
Makes 1 loaf; Total Time 1 hour

2¼ cups (11¼ ounces) stone-ground cornmeal

1½ cups sour cream

½ cup whole milk

¼ cup vegetable oil

5 tablespoons unsalted butter

2 tablespoons sugar

1 teaspoon baking powder

1 teaspoon baking soda

¾ teaspoon salt

2 large eggs

1. Adjust oven rack to middle position and heat oven to 450 degrees. Toast cornmeal in 10-inch cast-iron skillet over medium heat, stirring frequently, until fragrant, about 3 minutes. Transfer cornmeal to large bowl, whisk in sour cream and milk, and set aside.

2. Wipe skillet clean with paper towels. Add oil to now-empty skillet, place skillet in oven, and heat until oil is shimmering, about 10 minutes. Using potholders, remove skillet from oven, carefully add butter, and gently swirl to incorporate. Being careful of hot skillet handle, pour all but 1 tablespoon oil-butter mixture into cornmeal mixture and whisk to incorporate. Whisk sugar, baking powder, baking soda, and salt into cornmeal mixture until combined, then whisk in eggs.

3. Quickly scrape batter into skillet with remaining fat and smooth top. Transfer skillet to oven and bake until top begins to crack and sides are golden brown, 12 to 15 minutes, rotating skillet halfway through baking.

4. Let bread cool in skillet for 15 minutes. Remove bread from skillet and transfer to wire rack. Serve warm or at room temperature.

why this recipe works

Of all the quick breads out there, cornbread is probably our favorite. And of all the ways to make cornbread, using a cast-iron skillet is definitely the best. The greased, preheated skillet gives the bread a seriously crunchy, golden crust. Using a combination of oil and butter to grease the skillet (as well as to enrich the batter) struck the perfect balance in the flavor and structure of the bread—the butter added richness, and the oil raised the smoke point so the butter wouldn't burn. We also used the skillet to toast the cornmeal before adding it to the batter for superpotent corn flavor. We added a small amount of sugar to the mix in order to enhance the natural sweetness of the cornmeal. A cornmeal mush created by moistening the toasted cornmeal with sour cream and milk produced bread with a fine, moist crumb. You can use any type of fine- or medium-ground cornmeal here, but do not use coarse-ground.

variation

Spicy Southern-Style Cornbread

Whisk 2 minced jalapeño chiles and 2 teaspoons grated lime zest into cornmeal mixture with eggs in step 2.

think like a cook

THE MAGIC OF CAST IRON

There are a host of practical and culinary reasons why we love cast iron. One of its greatest advantages is that a cast-iron pan is possibly the only piece of kitchen gear you can buy that noticeably improves after years of heavy use. As you cook in it, a cast-iron pan gradually develops a natural, slick patina, called seasoning, which releases food easily. A well-seasoned cast-iron skillet can be just as nonstick as an aluminum or stainless-steel pan and will definitely outlast them.

Cast iron doesn't heat very evenly because its thermal conductivity, or ability to transfer heat from one part of the metal to another, is very low. What cast iron does do well is hold onto heat: Once a cast-iron pan is hot, it will stay that way much more effectively than stainless steel. This makes cast iron the ideal material for high-heat applications, such as searing steak, and browning, in recipes like our cornbread.

Cast iron's durability is legendary—many people are still cooking on cast-iron pans handed down through their family for generations. Cast iron is virtually indestructible and easily restored if mistreated. Cast iron's ability to develop a nonstick coating also makes it incredibly versatile. This is a boon for minimalist cooks but also for gourmet cooks who appreciate the particular benefits cast iron offers for specific dishes and techniques.

Brown Irish Soda Bread
Makes 1 loaf; Total Time 1 hour (plus cooling time)

2 cups (10 ounces) all-purpose flour

1½ cups (8¼ ounces) whole-wheat flour

½ cup (1½ ounces) toasted wheat germ

1½ teaspoons salt

1 teaspoon baking powder

1 teaspoon baking soda

1¾ cups buttermilk

3 tablespoons sugar

3 tablespoons unsalted butter, melted

1. Adjust oven rack to lower-middle position and heat oven to 400 degrees. Line rimmed baking sheet with parchment paper. Whisk all-purpose flour, whole-wheat flour, wheat germ, salt, baking powder, and baking soda together in large bowl. Whisk buttermilk, sugar, and 2 tablespoons melted butter in second bowl until sugar has dissolved.

2. Using rubber spatula, gently fold buttermilk mixture into flour mixture, scraping up dry flour from bottom of bowl, until dough starts to form and no dry flour remains. Transfer dough to lightly floured counter and knead by hand until cohesive mass forms, about 30 seconds. Pat dough into 7-inch round and transfer to prepared sheet.

3. Using sharp paring knife or single-edge razor blade, make two 5-inch-long, ¼-inch-deep slashes with swift, fluid motion along top of loaf to form cross. Bake loaf until golden brown and skewer inserted in center comes out clean, 45 to 50 minutes, rotating sheet halfway through baking.

4. Transfer loaf to wire rack and brush with remaining 1 tablespoon melted butter. Let cool completely, about 3 hours, before serving.

why this recipe works
Probably the easiest whole-grain bread you'll ever bake, brown Irish soda bread requires barely 15 minutes of work. Being a quick bread, it requires no yeast or long rise. But while most quick breads are rather sweet, this hearty bread has a robust, wheaty flavor with only slight sweetness, making it as suitable for the dinner table as it is at breakfast, slathered with butter and jam. In Ireland, coarse whole-meal flour is responsible for the bread's deeply flavored crumb; we used easier-to-find whole-wheat flour along with toasted wheat germ to achieve a similar nutty flavor. Just a touch of sugar and a few tablespoons of butter added a hint of sweet richness. The dough required only a brief knead, and shaping it was a cinch—we simply patted it into a round. Finally, brushing melted butter on the hot loaf gave this authentic soda bread a rich crust.

variation
Brown Irish Soda Bread with Currants and Caraway
Add 1 cup dried currants and 1 tablespoon caraway seeds to dry ingredients in step 1.

think like a cook

SLICING INTO WARM BREAD: JUST SAY NO

The hard work is over, and your reward is a beautifully browned, lofty loaf of bread with an appetite-inducing aroma. But there is one more difficult step: resisting the urge to slice into the warm bread! The interior of a loaf needs to cool to room temperature from the 190 to 210 degrees it was when it emerged from the oven. During this time, the starches in the loaf continue to gelatinize, or absorb water and set into a solid mass; excess moisture evaporates; and the true flavor of the loaf comes to the fore. We've found that this takes about 3 hours for most large loaves. For perfect cooking, take your bread or rolls off their cooking surface or out of the pan and transfer them (after a brief wait, in some cases) to a wire rack so that air can circulate, preventing the escaping moisture from softening the crust. Once this wait period is complete, you can finally slice your homemade creation. The tool you use is of utmost importance. A chef's knife may be sharp, but it will squash your loaf's crumb as you press down on it. A serrated knife, in contrast, relies on a slicing motion in which the blade is dragged across the bread's surface as it moves down through it, so it preserves the bread's crust and interior holes.

Homemade Corn Tortillas

Makes about 12 (6-inch) tortillas; Total Time 1 hour

2 cups (8 ounces) masa harina
2 teaspoons vegetable oil
¼ teaspoon salt
1¼ cups warm water, plus extra as needed

1. Cut sides of sandwich-size zipper-lock bag but leave bottom seam intact so that bag unfolds completely. Place open bag on counter and line large plate with 2 damp dish towels.

2. Mix masa, 1 teaspoon oil, and salt together in medium bowl. Using rubber spatula, stir in warm water to form soft dough. Using your hands, knead dough in bowl, adding extra warm water, 1 tablespoon at a time, until dough is soft and tacky but not sticky (texture is like Play-Doh). Cover dough and set aside for 5 minutes.

3. Meanwhile, heat remaining 1 teaspoon oil in 8-inch nonstick skillet over medium-high heat until shimmering. Using paper towel, wipe out skillet, leaving thin film of oil on bottom. Pinch off 1-ounce piece of dough (about 2 tablespoons) and roll into smooth 1¼-inch ball. Cover remaining dough with damp paper towel. Place ball in center of open bag and fold other side of bag over ball. Using clear pie plate, press down on plastic to flatten ball into 5-inch disk, rotating plastic during pressing to ensure even thickness. Working quickly, gently peel plastic away from tortilla.

4. Carefully place tortilla in skillet and cook, without moving it, until tortilla moves freely when pan is shaken, about 30 seconds. Flip tortilla and cook until edges curl and bottom surface is spotty brown, about 1 minute. Flip tortilla again and continue to cook until bottom surface is spotty brown and puffs up in center, 30 to 60 seconds. Place toasted tortilla between the 2 damp dish towels. Repeat shaping and cooking with remaining dough. (Cooled tortillas can be transferred to zipper-lock bag and refrigerated for up to 5 days. Reheat before serving.)

why this recipe works

For most uses, supermarket bagged tortillas are fine, especially if you buy the freshest you can find. But if you have a little extra time, tortillas aren't actually that hard to make. Fresh corn tortillas have a lightly sweet flavor and a soft, springy texture unmatched by store-bought. Our recipe features a short ingredient list, a very forgiving dough, and no need for a tortilla press. We tested a few variables, including whether to add salt (yes) and how long to rest the dough before pressing (5 minutes so the masa is fully hydrated). Vegetable oil, although nontraditional, made the dough soft, pliable, and easy to work with. Pressing the dough between a cut-open zipper-lock bag prevented sticking, and a pie plate pressed out even rounds. Using a clear pie plate makes it easy to see the tortilla. Distribute your weight evenly over the dough when pressing. You can find masa harina in the supermarket's international aisle or near the flour.

think like a cook

WARMING TORTILLAS

Whether you are making your own tortillas or buying them, for many dishes you probably want to warm the tortillas before serving. Warming tortillas not only makes them more pliable but can also add flavorful toasty char, depending on the method. Here are three methods we like. Whichever method you use, once the tortillas are warm, wrap them in foil or clean dish towels to keep them warm until serving.

If you have a gas stove, turn one burner to medium and use tongs to place the tortillas one at a time directly over the flame of the burner until lightly charred, about 30 seconds per side.

If playing with an open flame makes you nervous or you don't have a gas stove, you can use a dry nonstick skillet over medium-high heat; toast the tortillas one at a time until softened and spotty brown, 20 to 30 seconds per side.

If you'd rather avoid the stove altogether, you can also use the microwave. Wrap up to 6 tortillas in a damp, clean dish towel and microwave until warm, 30 to 45 seconds.

Almost No-Knead Bread
Makes 1 loaf; Total Time 11 hours (plus cooling time)

3 cups (15 ounces) all-purpose flour

1½ teaspoons salt

¼ teaspoon instant or rapid-rise yeast

¾ cup water, room temperature

½ cup mild lager, room temperature

1 tablespoon distilled white vinegar

1. Whisk flour, salt, and yeast together in large bowl. Whisk water, beer, and vinegar together in 4-cup liquid measuring cup. Using rubber spatula, gently fold water mixture into flour mixture, scraping up dry flour from bottom of bowl, until dough starts to form and no dry flour remains. Cover bowl tightly with plastic wrap and let sit at room temperature for at least 8 hours or up to 18 hours.

2. Lay 18 by 12-inch sheet of parchment paper on counter and lightly spray with vegetable oil spray. Transfer dough to lightly floured counter and knead by hand until smooth and elastic, about 1 minute.

3. Shape dough into ball by pulling edges into middle, then transfer seam side down to center of prepared parchment.

4. Using parchment as sling, gently lower loaf into Dutch oven (let any excess parchment hang over pot edge). Cover tightly with plastic and let rise until loaf has doubled in size and dough springs back minimally when poked gently with your knuckle, 1½ to 2 hours.

5. Adjust oven rack to middle position. Using sharp paring knife or single-edge razor blade, make two 5-inch-long, ½-inch-deep slashes with swift, fluid motion along top of loaf to form cross. Cover pot and place in oven. Turn oven to 425 degrees and bake loaf for 30 minutes while oven heats.

6. Remove lid and continue to bake until loaf is deep golden brown and thermometer inserted into bread registers 205 to 210 degrees, 25 to 30 minutes. Using parchment sling, remove loaf from pot and transfer to wire rack; discard parchment. Let cool completely, about 3 hours, before serving. (Bread is best eaten the day it is baked, but can be wrapped in aluminum foil and stored in a cool, dry place for up to 2 days.)

why this recipe works

Artisan-style loaves—with a thick, crisp crust that breaks open to a chewy, open interior—take professional skills, right? Wrong. Not only is it possible to make a rustic loaf for your table, it's easy with the no-knead method. This technique replaces the kneading (which develops gluten to give bread structure) with a long (but hands-off) resting period, or *autolyse*. During autolyse, enzymes break up proteins so the dough requires only a brief turn to develop its gluten. The dough is then baked in a covered Dutch oven; the humid environment gives the loaf a dramatic open crumb and a crust. But the breads we tasted needed more structure and flavor. So we added vinegar for tang and beer for yeastiness; just a minute of kneading strengthened up the dough. Use a mild-flavored lager, such as Budweiser (nonalcoholic lager also works). In step 5, start the 30-minute timer as soon as you put the bread in the cold oven. Do not wait until the oven has preheated or the bread will burn.

think like a cook

WHAT IS GLUTEN, ANYWAY?

Gluten is the protein developed in bread making that gives bread its chew. This elastic protein is formed when two partial proteins present in wheat flour, glutenin and gliadin, come into contact with water during mixing, in a process called hydration, and then bond. Glutenin provides dough with strength; gliadin provides stretch. Hydrating the proteins allows them to unwind and become flexible. Then, through mixing, they begin to link up with one another to form long, elastic chains of gluten. Finally, typically through prolonged kneading, the proteins align and continue to cross-link until the chains combine to form a gluten network. Here's an easy way to look at it: Imagine these proteins as bundled-up balls of yarn that need to be unwound and tied together into one longer piece that's then sewn into a wider sheet. In their balled-up state they can't be tied together; first you have to untangle and straighten them. Liquid does the untangling, mixing ties the proteins together, and kneading sews them into a sheet.

In this recipe, however, gluten develops through a long rest called *autolyse*: With an extremely wet dough such as this one, enzymes naturally present in the dough are able to act like scissors, cutting the balled-up proteins into pieces that are easily straightened with just a minute of kneading, or even no kneading with enough time and a sufficiently hydrated dough. We found just a minute of kneading and slightly less hydration than a totally hands-off bread would require reaped substantial improvements: a loaf with superior structure and an 8-hour minimum resting time instead of 12.

How does gluten work? A strong gluten network provides dough with structure to expand. Starch granules in the flour swell when hydrated, while yeast creates gas bubbles; both of these stretch the gluten network, and it traps the air—much like a balloon—so that the bread develops an airy crumb. Different types of baked goods benefit from more or less gluten formation—a rustic bread or pizza dough needs a lot of gluten for structure and chew, while a cake or quick bread needs much less in order to maintain its tender texture.

American Sandwich Bread

Makes 1 loaf; Total Time 4 hours (plus cooling time)

2 tablespoons unsalted butter, melted

2 tablespoons honey

¾ cup whole milk, chilled

⅓ cup ice water

2½ cups (13¾ ounces) bread flour

2 teaspoons instant or rapid-rise yeast

1½ teaspoons salt

1. Whisk melted butter and honey together in 4-cup liquid measuring cup until honey has dissolved. Whisk in milk and ice water until combined.

2. Pulse flour, yeast, and salt in food processor until combined, about 5 pulses. With processor running, add milk mixture and process until dough forms rough, elastic ball that begins to clear sides of bowl, 30 seconds to 1 minute.

3. Transfer dough to lightly floured counter. Using your lightly floured hands, knead dough to form smooth, round ball, about 30 seconds. Place dough seam side down in lightly greased large bowl or container, cover tightly with plastic wrap, and let rise until doubled in size, 1½ to 2 hours.

4. Grease 8½ by 4½-inch loaf pan. Press down gently on dough to deflate. Turn dough out onto lightly floured counter (side of dough that was against bowl should now be facing up). Press and stretch dough into 8 by 6-inch rectangle, with long side parallel to counter edge.

5. Roll dough away from you into firm cylinder, keeping roll taut by tucking it under itself as you go. Pinch seam closed and place loaf seam side down in prepared pan, pressing dough gently into corners. Cover loosely with greased plastic and let rise until loaf reaches 1 inch above lip of pan and dough springs back minimally when poked gently with your knuckle, 1 to 1½ hours.

6. Adjust oven rack to lower-middle position and heat oven to 350 degrees. Mist loaf with water and bake until deep golden brown and thermometer inserted into loaf registers 205 to 210 degrees, 35 to 40 minutes, rotating pan halfway through baking. Let loaf cool in pan for 15 minutes. Remove loaf from pan and let cool completely on wire rack, about 3 hours, before serving.

why this recipe works

Tall and domed, with a fine crumb and a light brown crust, this bread is a far cry from bouncy plastic-wrapped supermarket loaves. And it's simple to make with the food processor, which handles most of the kneading. Sandwich loaves take the form of their pan, obviously, but they still need to be shaped. Rolling the dough into a tight cylinder enforced the gluten structure and prevented the loaf from being misshapen. To preserve air from the first rise, we worked the dough gently. We lightly floured our hands as well as the counter to keep the dough from sticking. Placing the loaf in the pan seam side down ensured that it didn't split open as it rose. The test kitchen's preferred loaf pan measures 8½ by 4½ inches; if you use a 9 by 5-inch loaf pan, increase the shaped rising time by 20 to 30 minutes and, when baking, start checking for doneness 10 minutes earlier than advised. Be sure to use chilled milk and ice water in the dough to prevent the food processor from overheating.

Whole-Wheat American Sandwich Bread

Increase honey to 3 tablespoons. Reduce bread flour to 1½ cups (8¼ ounces) and add 1 cup (5½ ounces) whole-wheat flour and 3 tablespoons toasted wheat germ in step 2.

think like a cook

IF YOU WANT TO KNEAD BY HAND

We prefer to mix and knead most bread doughs with either a stand mixer or food processor depending on the dough, because these methods are almost effortless and produce great bread. But you can still make most breads by hand, the exception being doughs that are simply too wet or enriched for hand kneading.

Whisk the liquid ingredients together in a medium bowl and whisk the dry ingredients together in a large bowl. Using a rubber spatula, stir the liquid mixture into the dry mixture until the dough comes together and looks shaggy. Turn the dough onto a clean counter. To knead, start each stroke by gently pressing the dough down and away from you with the heel of your hand. Lift the edge of the dough that's farthest away and fold the dough in half toward you. Repeat pressing and folding until the dough is smooth and elastic and forms a ball, 15 to 25 minutes, adding flour as needed to prevent the dough from sticking to the counter.

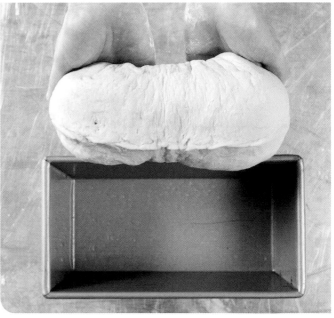

appendix

TALK LIKE A COOK

Following a recipe successfully requires understanding what it is telling you to do. That may sound obvious, but translating what happens in the kitchen to the printed page can be anything but. We cover basic terms in "A Walk Through Your Kitchen." Here are some additional terms worth knowing; most are covered in greater detail in individual recipes.

Al Dente
A doneness indication usually used with pasta, rice, and other grains. From the Italian for "to the tooth," it describes food that is fully cooked but still firm when bitten into.

Baste
To moisten food regularly with a liquid (usually butter or pan drippings) during cooking.

Beat
To stir into a froth or foam, usually with a whisk, fork, or electric mixer.

Blanch
To briefly submerge fruits or vegetables in boiling water to set their color, flavor, and texture. It is often followed by immediately transferring the food to an ice bath to halt cooking.

Bloom
To cook ground spices or dried herbs in fat to intensify their flavor.

Brine
To soak food in a water and salt solution to season and tenderize it before cooking.

Butterfly
To remove the backbone from a whole chicken or turkey (or other poultry) in order to flatten the bird for fast, even cooking. Also known as spatchcocking. You can also butterfly other large cuts, such as pork roasts, and shrimp.

Caramelization
The chemical reactions that take place when any sugar is heated to the point that its molecules begin to break apart and generate hundreds of new flavor, color, and aroma compounds.

Carryover Cooking
The cooking that continues even after food has been removed from a heat source.

Cream
To combine sugar and a fat into a homogeneous mixture.

Crimp
To seal and embellish the edge of a pie crust or other pastry.

Deglaze
To use liquid (usually wine or broth) to loosen the brown bits known as fond that develop and stick to a pan during sautéing or searing.

Dredge
To coat food with flour, cornmeal, sugar, or some other dry ingredient.

Emulsion
A mixture of two liquids—such as oil and water—that would not ordinarily stay combined. In an emulsion, one liquid (often the fat) is broken into very small droplets that are suspended in the other liquid (often water).

En Papillote
A cooking method of enclosing food in a parchment paper packet. The food steams in its own juices so that the flavors are pure and clean. Although parchment is the traditional choice in this classic French technique, aluminum foil can also be used.

Fermentation
A process in which bacteria and/or yeasts consume the carbohydrates and proteins that are naturally present in foods, producing alcohols, acetic acid, and/or carbon dioxide as byproducts. Fermentation helps preserve food and alters its texture, scent, and flavor. Fermented foods are also easy to digest, and their bacteria are thought to offer health benefits.

Flambé
To ignite the alcohol vapor above a pan of food in order to create a set of high-temperature reactions for flavor development.

Flute
To create a scalloped pattern around the edge of a pie crust or other pastry.

Foil Sling
A baking-pan lining made from two folded sheets of aluminum foil that prevents the food from sticking to the pan and makes it easier to lift out after baking.

Fold
To mix delicate batters and incorporate fragile ingredients using a gentle under-and-over motion that minimizes deflation.

Fond
The caramelized browned bits that remain on the bottom of the pan after food has been sautéed or pan-seared.

Glaze
To coat food with a glossy syrup or paste (frequently sugar-based).

Grate
To shred a food into small, uniform pieces using a tool like a box grater or rasp-style grater.

Knead
To work and press bread dough to develop gluten and create a strong network of cross-linked proteins.

Macerate
To toss an ingredient (often fruit) with sugar and leave it to sit to draw out moisture.

decoding package labels

ORGANIC
According to the U. S. Department of Agriculture's (USDA) definition, organic food is produced by farmers who emphasize the use of renewable resources and the conservation of soil and water to enhance environmental quality for future generations. Organic meat, poultry, eggs, and dairy come from animals that are given no antibiotics or growth hormones. Organic food is produced without using: most conventional pesticides, fertilizers made with synthetic ingredients or sewage sludge, bioengineering, and ionizing radiation.

NATURAL
Unlike organic, the term "natural" is not heavily regulated by the USDA. "Natural" simply means that the meat was minimally processed and contains no artificial ingredients. The USDA defines minimally processed meat as meat "processed in a manner that does not fundamentally alter the product." However, it doesn't cover how the animal was raised. So a producer can tack the label on a package of chicken even if the animal was fed an unnatural diet, pumped with antibiotics, and/ or injected with broth or brine during processing.

ENHANCED
More than half of the fresh pork sold in supermarkets is now "enhanced"—injected with a salt solution to make lean cuts, such as center-cut roasts and chops, seem moister. Poultry can also be enhanced. But we think natural, unenhanced meat has a better flavor and texture. Unsure whether what you're buying is enhanced? Check for an ingredient list: If it has one, it's enhanced.

AIR-CHILLED
During processing, some chickens are soaked in a water bath (or "water-chilled") in which they absorb up to 14 percent of their weight in water—which you pay for since chicken is sold by the pound. Chickens labeled "air-chilled" hang from a conveyor belt and circulate around a cold room. Lacking excess water weight, they will be less spongy in texture (but still plenty juicy) and have more chicken flavor.

Marinate

To let food sit in a seasoned mixture of oil, liquid, herbs, spices, and other flavorings before cooking to increase flavor and improve texture.

Mise en Place

The preparation and measuring of ingredients for a dish before cooking; from the French for "putting in place."

Off Heat

A recipe instruction that indicates that a pot or dish should be removed from the heat source and placed on a trivet or cool, unused burner before continuing.

Panade

A paste of milk and bread that is typically used to help foods, like meatballs and meatloaf, hold their shape and moisture.

Pasteurized

The process of applying heat to a food product to destroy pathogenic (disease-producing) microorganisms and to disable spoilage-causing enzymes.

Proof

A stage in the rising of dough when a shaped loaf is set out for its final rise and fermentation before baking. The word "proof" can also be used to refer to the process of testing yeast to confirm that it is active.

Puree

To grind ingredients to a fine, uniform consistency, often in a food processor or blender. The resulting mixture is also called a puree.

Reduce

To heat sauce or stock in order to partially evaporate the liquids and reduce the volume, concentrate the flavors, and thicken the consistency.

Scald

To bring a liquid to the verge of a boil.

Score

To make long, shallow cuts on the surface of a food in order to maximize surface area, increase marinade penetration, or create a rough texture.

Shock

To move cooking food to an ice bath in order to quickly stop the cooking process. Often used for vegetables.

Sift

To put a powdered ingredient such as flour through a fine-mesh strainer or sieve to aerate and break up clumps.

Skim

To remove the fat that floats to the surface of pan drippings or braising liquids after roasting or braising fatty cuts of beef, pork, or poultry.

Sweat

To cook over gentle heat in a small amount of fat in a covered pot.

Temper

To gradually increase the temperature of a sensitive ingredient, such as dairy or eggs, in order to prevent it from breaking or curdling once added to a hot soup or sauce. Melted chocolate is also tempered by careful heating and cooling to ensure it maintains its shine and snap when solid.

Truss

To tie up a chicken, turkey, or other bird with twine in order to keep the wings and legs close to the body and encourage even cooking.

Umami

A quality of meaty savoriness that brings depth to dishes. Widely considered the fifth taste (after sweet, sour, salty, and bitter).

Water Bath

A setup where a dish of food is placed in a larger pan containing hot water during baking. The water lowers the temperature surrounding the dish (even if it boils, the water temperature will be cooler than the oven temperature) and prevents uneven cooking.

Whip

To quickly stir an ingredient, such as egg whites or cream, with a whisk or electric mixer in order to aerate and stabilize the ingredient and add volume.

EQUIPMENT SHOPPING GUIDE

Here you'll find shopping guidance for all the equipment called for or recommended in the book. (For the most essential items, see pages 4–8.) Our test kitchen has conducted copious rounds of testing products and has identified the most important attributes in every piece of equipment, so you'll know what to look for. And because we accept no support from manufacturers, you can trust our recommendations. Prices are based on shopping at online retailers and will vary.

KNIVES AND MORE	ITEM	WHAT TO LOOK FOR	TEST KITCHEN FAVORITES
	CHEF'S KNIFE	· High-carbon stainless-steel knife · Thin, curved 8-inch blade · Lightweight · Comfortable grip and nonslip handle	Victorinox Swiss Army Fibrox Pro 8" Chef's Knife $39.95
	SERRATED KNIFE	· 10-inch blade · Fewer broader, deeper, pointed serrations · Thinner blade angle · Comfortable, grippy handle · Medium weight	Mercer Culinary Millennia 10" Wide Bread Knife $22.10
	PARING KNIFE	· 3- or 3½-inch blade · Thin, flexible blade with pointed tip · Comfortable grip	Victorinox Swiss Army Fibrox Pro 3¼" Spear Point Paring Knife $9.47
	MANDOLINE	· Razor-sharp blade(s) · Hand guard to shield fingers · Gripper prongs to grasp food · Measurement-marked dial for precision cuts · Storage for extra blades	Swissmar Börner Original V-Slicer Plus Mandoline $29.99
	CUTTING BOARD	· Roomy work surface at least 20 by 15 inches · Teak board for minimal maintenance · Durable edge-grain construction (wood grain runs parallel to surface of board)	Proteak Edge Grain Teak Cutting Board $84.99 *Best Buy* OXO Good Grips Carving & Cutting Board $21.99
	CARVING BOARD	· Trenches can contain ½ cup of liquid · Large and stable enough to hold large roasts · Midweight for easy carrying, carving, and cleaning	J.K. Adams Maple Reversible Carving Board $69.95
	KNIFE SHARPENER	· Diamond abrasives and a spring-loaded chamber to precisely guide blade · Quickly removes nicks in blades · Can convert a 20-degree edge to a sharper 15 degrees	*Electric* Chef'sChoice Trizor XV Knife Sharpener $149.99 *Electric, Best Buy* Chef'sChoice Diamond Sharpener for Asian Knives $79.99 *Manual* Chef'sChoice Pronto Manual Diamond Hone Asian Knife Sharpener $49.99

POTS AND PANS	ITEM	WHAT TO LOOK FOR	TEST KITCHEN FAVORITES
	TRADITIONAL SKILLET	· Stainless-steel interior and fully clad for even heat distribution · 12-inch diameter and flared sides · Comfortable, ovensafe handle · Tight-fitting lid included · Good to have smaller (8- or 10-inch) skillets too	All-Clad d3 Stainless Steel 12" Fry Pan with Lid $96.85
	NONSTICK SKILLET	· Dark, nonstick surface · 12- or 12½-inch diameter, thick bottom · Cooking surface of at least 9 inches · Comfortable, ovensafe handle · Good to have smaller (8- or 10-inch) skillets too	OXO Good Grips Non-Stick 12-Inch Open Frypan $39.99
	CARBON-STEEL SKILLET	· Affordable · Thick, solid construction; ergonomically angled handle · Sides flared up just right for easy access but high enough to contain splashes	Matfer Bourgeat Black Steel Round Frying Pan, 11⅞" $44.38
	CAST-IRON SKILLET Traditional	· Thick bottom and straight sides · Roomy interior (cooking surface of 9¼ inches or more) · Preseasoned	Lodge Classic Cast Iron Skillet, 12" $33.31
	Enameled	· Balanced weight, wide pour spouts, and oversized helper handle for comfortable use · Durable, satiny surface that does not require preseasoning · Easy to clean	Le Creuset Signature 11¾" Iron Handle Skillet $179.95
	DUTCH OVEN	· Enameled cast iron or stainless steel · Capacity of at least 6 quarts · Diameter of at least 9 inches · Tight-fitting lid · Wide, sturdy handles	*Heavier* Le Creuset 7¼-Quart Round French Oven $359.99 *Lighter* All-Clad Stainless 8-Quart Stockpot $279.95 *Best Buy* Cuisinart 7 Qt. Round Covered Casserole $121.94
	SAUCEPAN Large	· Steady heating and good visibility to monitor browning · Stay-cool, easy-to-grip handle · Helper handle for extra grabbing point	All-Clad Stainless 4-Qt Sauce Pan $179.13 *Best Buy* Cuisinart MultiClad Unlimited 4 Quart Saucepan with Cover $65.12
	Small	· Heavy, solid, well priced · Easy to control · Shallow shape and generous diameter	Calphalon Contemporary Nonstick 2½ Quart Shallow Saucepan with Cover $39.95
	RIMMED BAKING SHEET	· Light-colored surface (heats and browns evenly) · Thick, sturdy pan · Dimensions of 18 by 13 inches · Good to have at least two	Nordic Ware Baker's Half Sheet $14.97

POTS AND PANS	ITEM	WHAT TO LOOK FOR	TEST KITCHEN FAVORITES
	BAKING DISH Broiler-Safe	· Large easy-to-grip handles · Straight sides for easy serving · Lightweight porcelain	HIC Porcelain Lasagna Baking Dish $37.49
	Glass	· Dimensions of 13 by 9 inches (8-inch square dish is also useful) · Lightweight with large handles for easy grip and maneuvering	Pyrex Easy Grab 3-Quart Oblong Baking Dish $7.29 Pyrex 8-Inch Square Glass Baking Dish $9
	STOCKPOT	· 12-quart capacity · Thick bottom to prevent scorching · Wide body for easy cleaning and storage · Flat or round handles that extend at least 1¾ inches	All-Clad Stainless 12-Quart Stock Pot $389.95 *Best Buy* Cuisinart Chef's Classic Stainless 12-Quart Stock Pot $69.99
	ROASTING PAN	· At least 15 by 11 inches · Stainless-steel interior with aluminum core for even heat distribution · Upright handles for easy gripping · Light interior for better food monitoring	Calphalon Contemporary Stainless Roasting Pan with Rack $99.99 *Best Buy* Calphalon Commercial Hard-Anodized Roasting Pan with Nonstick Rack $59.99
	V-RACK	· Fixed, not adjustable, to provide sturdiness · Tall, vertical handles positioned on long sides of rack	All-Clad Nonstick Large Rack $24.95

HANDY TOOLS	ITEM	WHAT TO LOOK FOR	TEST KITCHEN FAVORITES
	KITCHEN SHEARS	· Take-apart scissors (for easy cleaning) · Supersharp blades · Sturdy construction · Work for both right- and left-handed users	Shun Multi-Purpose Shears/ Kershaw Taskmaster Shears $26.30
	TONGS	· Scalloped edges · Slightly concave pincers · Length of 12 inches (to keep your hand far from heat) · Open and close easily	OXO Good Grips 12-Inch Locking Tongs $12.95
	WOODEN SPOON	· Slim yet broad bowl · Stain-resistant bamboo · Comfortable handle	SCI Bamboo Wood Cooking Spoon $2.40
	SLOTTED SPOON	· Wide, shallow, thin bowl · Long, hollow, comfortable handle · Steep, ladle-like angle between handle and bowl	Cuisinart Stainless Steel Slotted Spoon $9.12
	SPIDER SKIMMER	· Long handle for protection from hot water and oil · Well balanced and easy to maneuver	Rösle Wire Skimmer $41.68 *Best Buy* WMF Profi Plus Spider Strainer 14" (5" dia.) $19.95

HANDY TOOLS	ITEM	WHAT TO LOOK FOR	TEST KITCHEN FAVORITES
	ALL-AROUND SPATULA	· Head about 3 inches wide and 5½ inches long · 11 inches in length (tip to handle) · Long, vertical slots · Good to have metal spatula to use with traditional cookware and plastic for nonstick cookware	*Metal* Wüsthof Gourmet Turner/Fish Spatula $44.95 *Metal, Best Buy* OXO Good Grips Flexible Turner—Steel $7.99 *Plastic* Matfer Bourgeat Pelton Spatula $8.23
	SILICONE SPATULA	· Firm, wide blade for efficient scraping and scooping · All-silicone design for easy cleanup	*All Purpose* Di Oro Living Seamless Silicone Spatula–Large $10.97 *Large* Rubbermaid 13.5" High-Heat Scraper $14.50
	OFFSET SPATULA	· Flexible blade offset to roughly 30-degree angle · Enough usable surface area to frost the radius of 9-inch cake · Comfortable handle	*Large* OXO Good Grips Bent Icing Knife $9.99 *Small* Wilton 9-Inch Angled Spatula $4.79
	ALL-PURPOSE WHISK	· At least 10 wires · Wires of moderate thickness · Comfortable rubber handle · Balanced, lightweight feel	OXO Good Grips 11" Balloon Whisk $9.99
	LADLE	· Stainless steel · Hook handle · Pouring rim to prevent dripping · Handle 9 to 10 inches in length	Rösle Hook Ladle with Pouring Rim $34 *Best Buy* OXO Good Grips Brushed Stainless Steel Ladle $9.99
	PEPPER MILL	· Easy-to-adjust, clearly marked grind settings · Efficient, comfortable grinding mechanism · Generous capacity	Cole & Mason Derwent Gourmet Precision Pepper Mill $40
	CAN OPENER	· Intuitive and easy to attach · Smooth turning motions · Dishwasher-safe	Fissler Magic Smooth-Edge Can Opener $29
	GARLIC PRESS	· Conical holes that press garlic through efficiently · Solid stainless-steel construction · Comfortable handle	Kuhn Rikon Epicurean Garlic Press $44.95
	VEGETABLE PEELER	· Sharp carbon-steel blade · 1-inch space between blade and peeler to prevent jamming · Lightweight and comfortable	Kuhn Rikon Original Swiss Peeler $3.50
	RASP-STYLE GRATER	· Sharp teeth (require little effort or pressure when grating) · Maneuverable over round shapes · Soft, grippy, secure handle	Microplane Premium Classic Zester/Grater $14.95

HANDY TOOLS	ITEM	WHAT TO LOOK FOR	TEST KITCHEN FAVORITES
	GRATER	· Sharp, large holes and generous grating plane · Rubber-lined feet for stability · Comfortable handle	Microplane Specialty Series 4-Sided Box Grater $34.95
	MANUAL CITRUS JUICER	· Directs juice in steady stream with no splattering or overflowing · Large, rounded handles that are easy to squeeze	Chef'n FreshForce Citrus Juicer $23.04
	MEAT POUNDER	· At least 1½ pounds in weight · Vertical handle for better leverage and control	Norpro GRIP-EZ Meat Pounder $17.50
	ROLLING PIN	· Moderate weight (1 to 1½ pounds) · 19-inch straight barrel · Slightly textured wooden surface to grip dough for easy rolling	J.K. Adams Plain Maple Rolling Dowel $13.95
	MIXING BOWLS Stainless Steel	· Lightweight, durable, and easy to handle · Conducts heat well for double boiler	Vollrath Economy Stainless Steel Mixing Bowls $2.90–$6.90
	Glass	· Tempered to increase impact and thermal resistance · Can be used in microwave · Durable	Pyrex Smart Essentials with Colored Lids $27.98 for 4-bowl set
	MINI PREP BOWLS	· Wide, shallow bowls · Easy to hold, fill, empty, and clean · Microwave-safe and ovensafe	Anchor Hocking 6-Piece Nesting Prep Bowl Set $11
	PASTRY BRUSH	· Bristles of moderate length and density · Comfortable handle · Loses few bristles	Winco Flat Pastry and Basting Brush, 1½ inch $6.93
	COLANDER	· 4- to 7-quart capacity · Metal ring attached to bottom for stability · Many holes for quick draining · Small holes so pasta doesn't slip through	RSVP International Endurance Precision Pierced 5 Qt. Colander $25.99
	FINE-MESH STRAINER	· Stiff, tightly woven mesh · Capacity of at least 5 cups with large, durable handle for support over bowls and pots	Rösle Fine-Mesh Strainer, Round Handle, 7.9 inches, 20 cm $45
	FAT SEPARATOR	· Bottom-draining model · Detachable bowl for easy cleaning · Strainer for catching solids	Cuisipro Fat Separator $33.95
	WINE OPENER	· Durable waiter's corkscrew design · Teflon-coated worm · Ergonomically curved body and hinged fulcrum	Pulltap's Classic Evolution Corkscrew by Pulltex $39.95 *Best Buy* Trudeau Double Lever Corkscrew $12.99

HANDY TOOLS	ITEM	WHAT TO LOOK FOR	TEST KITCHEN FAVORITES
	POTATO MASHER	· Solid mashing disk with many small holes · Comfortable grip · Long handle	Zyliss Stainless Steel Potato Masher $12.99
	POTATO RICER	· Large hopper with many holes so more food can travel through · Comfortable, ergonomic handles · Easy to assemble and clean	RSVP International Potato Ricer $13.95
	SALAD SPINNER	· Ergonomic and easy-to-operate hand pump · Wide base for stability · Flat lid for easy cleaning and storage	OXO Good Grips Salad Spinner $29.99
	STEAMER BASKET	· Collapsible stainless-steel basket with feet · Adjustable and removable center rod for easy removal from pot and easy storage	OXO Good Grips Stainless Steel Steamer with Extendable Handle $17.95
	DISH TOWELS	· Thin cotton for absorbency and flexibility · Dries glassware without streaks · Washes clean without shrinking	Williams-Sonoma Striped Towels, Set of 4 $19.95

MEASURING EQUIPMENT	ITEM	WHAT TO LOOK FOR	TEST KITCHEN FAVORITES
	DRY MEASURING CUPS	· Accurate measurements · Easy-to-read, durable measurement markings · Stable when empty and filled · Stack and store neatly · Handles perfectly flush with cups	OXO Good Grips Stainless Steel Measuring Cups $19.99
	LIQUID MEASURING CUP	· Crisp, unambiguous markings that include ¼- and ⅓-cup measurements · Heatproof, sturdy cup with handle · Good to have in variety of sizes (1, 2, and 4 cups)	Pyrex 2-Cup Measuring Cup $5.99
	ADJUSTABLE MEASURING CUP	· Plunger-like bottom (with tight seal between plunger and tube) that you can set to correct measurement, then push up to cleanly extract sticky ingredients (such as shortening or peanut butter) · 1- or 2-cup capacity · Dishwasher-safe	KitchenArt Adjust-A-Cup Professional Series $12.95
	MEASURING SPOONS	· Long, comfortable handles · Rim of bowl flush with handle (makes it easy to "dip" into dry ingredient and "sweep" across the top for accurate measuring) · Slim design	Cuisipro Stainless Steel Measuring Spoons Set $11.95

MEASURING EQUIPMENT	ITEM	WHAT TO LOOK FOR	TEST KITCHEN FAVORITES
	DIGITAL SCALE	· Easy-to-read display not blocked by weighing platform · At least 7-pound capacity · Accessible buttons · Gram-to-ounce conversion feature · Roomy platform	OXO Good Grips 11 lb Food Scale with Pull Out Display $49.95 *Best Buy* Ozeri Pronto Digital Multifunction Kitchen and Food Scale $11.79

THERMOMETERS	ITEM	WHAT TO LOOK FOR	TEST KITCHEN FAVORITES
	INSTANT-READ THERMOMETER	· Display auto-rotates · Wakes up when unit is picked up and lights up in low light · Long stem that can reach interior of large cuts of meat · Water-resistant	ThermoWorks Thermapen Mk4 $99 *Best Buy* ThermoWorks ThermoPop $29 *Best Midpriced* The Javelin Duo Pro $49.99
	OVEN THERMOMETER	· Clear temperature markings · Wide, sturdy base · Fairly easy to read	CDN Pro Accurate Oven Thermometer $8.70
	DEEP-FRY THERMOMETER	· Digital model · Easy-to-read console · Mounting clip (to attach probe to pan)	ThermoWorks ChefAlarm $59 *Best Buy* Polder Classic Digital Thermometer/Timer $24.99

BAKEWARE	ITEM	WHAT TO LOOK FOR	TEST KITCHEN FAVORITES
	SQUARE BAKING PAN	· Straight sides · Light gold or dark nonstick surface for even browning and easy release of cakes · Good to have both 9-inch and 8-inch square pans	Williams-Sonoma Goldtouch Nonstick 8-Inch Square Cake Pan $21
	METAL BAKING PAN	· Dimensions of 13 by 9 inches · Straight sides · Nonstick surface for even browning and easy release of cakes and bar cookies	Williams-Sonoma Goldtouch Nonstick Rectangular Cake Pan, 9" x 13" $32.95
	ROUND CAKE PAN	· Straight sides · Light finish for tall, evenly baked cakes · Nonstick surface for easy release	Nordic Ware Naturals Nonstick 9-Inch Round Cake Pan $14.32
	PIE PLATE	· Ceramic nonstick coating · Golden-hued metal plate bakes crusts without overbrowning · Produces crisp and flaky bottom crusts · Nonfluted lip allows for maximum crust-crimping flexibility · Good to have two	Williams-Sonoma Goldtouch Nonstick Pie Dish $18.95

BAKEWARE	ITEM	WHAT TO LOOK FOR	TEST KITCHEN FAVORITES
	LOAF PAN	· Light gold or dark nonstick surface for even browning and easy release · Good to have both 8½ by 4½-inch and 9 by 5-inch pans	Williams-Sonoma Goldtouch Nonstick Loaf Pan $21
	SPRINGFORM PAN	· Tall sides make for easy grip · Gold-toned pan for evenly baked crusts · Wide, raised base for support	Williams-Sonoma Goldtouch Springform Pan, 9" $49.95 *Best Buy* Nordic Ware 9" Leakproof Springform Pan $16.22
	MUFFIN TIN	· Gold nonstick surface for perfect browning and easy release · Wide, extended rims and raised lip for easy handling	OXO Good Grips Non-Stick Pro 12-Cup Muffin Pan $24.99
	BUNDT PAN	· Heavyweight cast aluminum · Thick, easy-to-grip handles · Clearly defined ridges for elegant cakes · 15-cup capacity	Nordic Ware Anniversary Bundt Pan $30.99
	COOLING RACK	· Grid-style rack with tightly woven bars · Six feet on three bars for extra stability · Should fit inside standard 18 by 13-inch rimmed baking sheet · Dishwasher-safe	Libertyware Half Size Sheet Pan Cooling Rack $15.99 for set of two
	BISCUIT CUTTERS	· Sharp edges · A set with variety of sizes	Ateco 5357 11-Piece Round Cutter Set $14.95

SMALL APPLIANCES	ITEM	WHAT TO LOOK FOR	TEST KITCHEN FAVORITES
	FOOD PROCESSOR	· 14-cup capacity · Sharp and sturdy blades · Wide feed tube · Should come with basic blades and disks: steel blade, dough blade, shredding/slicing disk	Cuisinart Custom 14-Cup Food Processor $199.99
	STAND MIXER	· Planetary action (stationary bowl and single mixing arm) · Powerful motor · Bowl size of at least 4½ quarts · Slightly squat bowl to keep ingredients in beater's range · Should come with basic attachments: paddle, dough hook, metal whisk	KitchenAid Classic Plus Series Stand Mixer $199.99 *High-End* KitchenAid Pro Line Series 7-Qt Bowl Lift Stand Mixer $549.95

SMALL APPLIANCES	ITEM	WHAT TO LOOK FOR	TEST KITCHEN FAVORITES
	HANDHELD MIXER	· Lightweight model · Slim wire beaters without central post · Variety of speeds	KitchenAid 5-Speed Ultra Power Hand Mixer $69.99 *Best Buy* Cuisinart PowerSelect 3-Speed Hand Mixer $26.77
	BLENDER	· Mix of straight and serrated blades at different angles · Jar with curved base · At least 44-ounce capacity · Heavy base for stability	*Midpriced* Breville The Hemisphere Control $199.95 *Inexpensive* Black + Decker Performance FusionBlade Blender $80.26 *High-End* Vitamix 5200 $449
	IMMERSION BLENDER	· Easy to maneuver and lightweight with slim, grippy body · Well-designed blade and cage · Detachable handle for easy cleanup	Braun Multiquick 5 Hand Blender $59.99
	WAFFLE IRON	· Indicator lights and audible alert · Makes two waffles at a time · Six-point dial for customizing waffle doneness	Cuisinart Double Belgian Waffle Maker $99.95
	SPICE/COFFEE GRINDER	· Electric, not manual, grinder · Deep bowl to hold ample amount of coffee beans · Good to have two, one each for coffee grinding and spice grinding	Krups Fast-Touch Coffee Mill $19.99

CLEANING AND CARING FOR YOUR EQUIPMENT

We've created our share of messes in the test kitchen and have had a few cooking snafus that required tons of cleanup. Along the way, we've learned a few tricks to get those pans shining like new again.

CLEANING EVERYDAY MESSES

1. BOIL WATER To clean a dirty traditional skillet (this usually isn't necessary for nonstick pans), fill it halfway with tap water. Bring to a boil, uncovered, and boil briskly for two or three minutes. Turn off the burner.

2. SCRAPE OFF RESIDUE Scrape the pan with a wooden spatula, pour off the water, and let sit briefly. Residue will start to flake off as the pan dries. Wash the skillet with hot water and dishwashing liquid, and dry.

CLEANING STUBBORN MESSES

1. SPRINKLE ON CLEANSER To clean stuck-on gunk, moisten the pan with water, then shake on powdered cleansers, like Cameo (for stainless steel, anodized aluminum, or nonstick surfaces) and Bar Keepers Friend (for stainless steel or nonstick surfaces).

2. SCRUB THE PAN Using a copper scrubber for stainless-steel skillets and a nylon scrubber for nonstick or anodized aluminum skillets, scrub the pan with circular motions. Finish by washing the pan with hot water and dishwashing liquid, then dry.

DUTCH OVENS

Enameled Dutch ovens are prone to staining, and while we're not concerned with keeping our cookware pristine, staining can be problematic if the bottom of the pot darkens so much that we can't monitor browning. We found that the best way to deep-clean a stained pot is to let it soak overnight in a solution of 1 part bleach to 3 parts water and then wash it thoroughly with soap and water.

A Dutch oven's enameled surface is very durable, but it's not completely impervious and can be subject to chipping. To help keep the enamel intact, don't subject your pot to dramatic temperature changes, especially near moisture. Don't clear food from utensils by whacking them on the pot's rim. Don't scrape metal utensils—specifically, sharp ones—along the bottom.

CUTTING BOARDS

Routine cleaning is essential; scrub your board thoroughly in hot, soapy water (or put it through the dishwasher if it's dishwasher-safe) to kill harmful bacteria, then rinse it well and dry it completely. For stubborn odors, scrub the cutting board with a paste of 1 tablespoon of baking soda and 1 teaspoon of water, then wash with hot, soapy water. To remove stubborn stains from plastic boards, mix a solution of 1 tablespoon of bleach per quart of water in the sink and immerse the board, dirty side up. When the board rises to the surface, drape a kitchen towel or two over its surface and sprinkle the towel with about ¼ cup of the bleach solution. Let it sit overnight, then wash it with hot, soapy water.

If using a wood or bamboo board, maintain it by applying a food-grade mineral oil every few weeks when the board is new, and a few times a year thereafter. (Don't use olive or vegetable oil, which can become rancid.) The oil soaks into the fibers of the board, creating a barrier to excess moisture. Avoid leaving wood or bamboo boards resting in water, or they will eventually split.

NONSTICK PANS

Nearly all nonstick pans rely on a top coat of polytetrafluoroethylene (PTFE) that keeps the surface slick and prevents food from sticking. Cooking over high heat, using abrasive pads, or washing the pan in the dishwasher will all cause this polymer to wear away. To prolong the nonstick coating's life, wash nonstick pans gently with a nonabrasive pad, and once they are dry, we recommend storing them using one of the following two methods.

A. SEPARATE AND STACK The surface of a nonstick skillet can chip or scratch easily, especially if you stack it with other pans. To protect the nonstick surface, place a double sheet of paper towels, bubble wrap, or a cheap paper plate between each pan as you stack them.

B. SEAL AND STACK Alternatively, before stacking smaller nonstick pans, slide them into large zipper-lock bags (2-gallon size for 10-inch pans and 1-gallon size for 8-inch pans). The plastic will protect the nonstick surface. Note that a 12-inch skillet will not fit in a zipper-lock bag.

BLENDERS AND FOOD PROCESSORS

After you're done using your blender, clean it by "blending" a warm soapy water mixture until the blades and jar are mostly clean, then rinse out the blender.

A similar technique works for your food processor. To quickly rinse the workbowl between tasks, add a few drops of dish soap and warm water to the liquid fill line, run the machine for a few seconds, and rinse the bowl well. To give a dirty processor bowl a good soak, put a wine or champagne cork in the center hole so you can fill the bowl all the way to the top.

EMERGENCY SUBSTITUTIONS

*No one wants to run to the market for just one ingredient. Below is a
list of ingredients commonly called for in recipes and the items you
are likely to have on hand that will work as substitutions.*

TO REPLACE	AMOUNT	SUBSTITUTE				
WHOLE MILK	1 cup	⅝ cup skim milk + ⅜ cup half-and-half ⅔ cup 1 percent low-fat milk + ⅓ cup half-and-half ¾ cup 2 percent low-fat milk + ¼ cup half-and-half ⅞ cup skim milk + ⅛ cup heavy cream				
HALF-AND-HALF	1 cup	¾ cup whole milk + ¼ cup heavy cream ⅔ cup skim or low-fat milk + ⅓ cup heavy cream				
HEAVY CREAM	1 cup	1 cup evaporated milk *Not suitable for whipping or baking, but fine for soups and sauces.*				
EGGS	Large	Jumbo	Extra-Large	Medium		*For half of an egg, whisk the yolk and white together and use half of the liquid.*
	1	1	1	1		
	2	1½	2	2		
	3	2½	2½	3½		
	4	3	3½	4½		
	5	4	4	6		
	6	5	5	7		
BUTTERMILK	1 cup	¾ cup plain whole-milk yogurt or low-fat yogurt + ¼ cup whole milk 1 cup whole milk + 1 tablespoon lemon juice or distilled white vinegar *Not suitable for raw applications, such as a buttermilk dressing.*				
SOUR CREAM	1 cup	1 cup plain whole-milk yogurt *Nonfat and low-fat yogurts are too lean to replace sour cream.*				
PLAIN YOGURT	1 cup	1 cup sour cream				
CAKE FLOUR	1 cup	⅞ cup all-purpose flour + 2 tablespoons cornstarch				
BREAD FLOUR	1 cup	1 cup all-purpose flour *Bread and pizza crusts may bake up with slightly less chew.*				
BAKING POWDER	1 teaspoon	¼ teaspoon baking soda + ½ teaspoon cream of tartar (use right away)				
LIGHT BROWN SUGAR	1 cup	1 cup granulated sugar + 1 tablespoon molasses *Pulse the molasses with the sugar in a food processor, or simply add it along with the other wet ingredients.*				
DARK BROWN SUGAR	1 cup	1 cup granulated sugar + 2 tablespoons molasses *Pulse the molasses with the sugar in a food processor, or simply add it along with the other wet ingredients.*				
CONFECTIONERS' SUGAR	1 cup	1 cup granulated sugar + 1 teaspoon cornstarch, ground in a blender (not a food processor) *Works well for dusting over cakes, less so in frostings and glazes.*				
TABLE SALT	1 teaspoon	1½ teaspoons Morton kosher salt or fleur de sel 2 teaspoons Diamond Crystal kosher salt or Maldon sea salt *Not recommended for use in baking recipes.*				
FRESH HERBS	1 tablespoon	1 teaspoon dried herbs				

TO REPLACE	AMOUNT	SUBSTITUTE
WINE	½ cup	½ cup broth + 1 teaspoon wine vinegar (added just before serving) ½ cup broth + 1 teaspoon lemon juice (added just before serving) *Vermouth makes an acceptable substitute for white wine.*
UNSWEETENED CHOCOLATE	1 ounce	3 tablespoons unsweetened cocoa powder + 1 tablespoon vegetable oil 1½ ounces bittersweet or semisweet chocolate (remove 1 tablespoon sugar from the recipe)
BITTERSWEET OR SEMISWEET CHOCOLATE	1 ounce	⅔ ounce unsweetened chocolate + 2 teaspoons sugar *Works well with fudgy brownies. Do not use in a custard or cake.*

ingredient assumptions we make in our recipes

Unless a recipe in this book specifically states otherwise, you should assume the following ingredients rules are being observed.

Flour	Unbleached, all-purpose
Sugar	Granulated
Salt	Table
Kosher salt	Diamond Crystal (see Emergency Substitutions chart, Table Salt, opposite, if using Morton)
Pepper	Freshly ground black
Spices	Ground
Herbs	Fresh
Butter	Unsalted
Eggs	Large
Dairy	Whole milk, or full-fat (although low-fat will generally work; skim won't)

CONVERSIONS & EQUIVALENTS

Baking is a science and an art, but geography has a hand in it too. Flours and sugars manufactured in the United Kingdom and else-where will feel and taste different from those manufactured in the United States. So we cannot promise that a cookie you bake in Canada or England will taste exactly the same as a cookie baked in the States, but we can offer guidelines for converting weights and measures. We also recommend that you rely on your instincts when making our recipes. Refer to the visual cues provided. If the dough hasn't "come together in a ball" as described, you may need to add more flour—even if the recipe doesn't tell you to. You be the judge.

The recipes in this book were developed using standard U.S. measures following U.S. government guidelines. The charts below offer equivalents for U.S. and metric measures. All conversions are approximate and have been rounded up or down to the nearest whole number.

Example

| 1 teaspoon | =4.9292 milliliters, rounded up to 5 milliliters |
| 1 ounce | =28.3495 grams, rounded down to 28 grams |

VOLUME CONVERSIONS

U.S.	METRIC
1 teaspoon	5 milliliters
2 teaspoons	10 milliliters
1 tablespoon	15 milliliters
2 tablespoons	30 milliliters
¼ cup	59 milliliters
⅓ cup	79 milliliters
½ cup	118 milliliters
¾ cup	177 milliliters
1 cup	237 milliliters
1¼ cups	296 milliliters
1½ cups	355 milliliters
2 cups (1 pint)	473 milliliters
2½ cups	591 milliliters
3 cups	710 milliliters
4 cups (1 quart)	0.946 liter
1.06 quarts	1 liter
4 quarts (1 gallon)	3.8 liters

WEIGHT CONVERSIONS

OUNCES	GRAMS
½	14
¾	21
1	28
1½	43
2	57
2½	71
3	85
3½	99
4	113
4½	128
5	142
6	170
7	198
8	227
9	255
10	283
12	340
16 (1 pound)	454

CONVERSIONS FOR COMMON BAKING INGREDIENTS

Because measuring by weight is far more accurate than measuring by volume, and thus more likely to produce reliable results, in our recipes we provide ounce measures in addition to cup measures for many ingredients. Refer to the chart below to convert these measures into grams.

INGREDIENT	OUNCES	GRAMS
Flour		
1 cup all-purpose flour*	5	142
1 cup cake flour	4	113
1 cup whole-wheat flour	5½	156
Sugar		
1 cup granulated (white) sugar	7	198
1 cup packed brown sugar (light or dark)	7	198
1 cup confectioners' sugar	4	113
Cocoa Powder		
1 cup cocoa powder	3	85
Butter†		
4 tablespoons (½ stick or ¼ cup)	2	57
8 tablespoons (1 stick or ½ cup)	4	113
16 tablespoons (2 sticks or 1 cup)	8	227

* U.S. all-purpose flour, the most frequently used flour in this book, does not contain leaveners, as some European flours do. These leavened flours are called self-rising or self-raising. If you are using self-rising flour, take this into consideration before adding leaveners to a recipe.

† In the United States, butter is sold both salted and unsalted. We recommend unsalted butter. If you are using salted butter, take this into consideration before adding salt to a recipe.

OVEN TEMPERATURE EQUIVALENTS

FAHRENHEIT	CELSIUS	GAS MARK
225	105	¼
250	120	½
275	135	1
300	150	2
325	165	3
350	180	4
375	190	5
400	200	6
425	220	7
450	230	8
475	245	9

CONVERTING TEMPERATURES FROM AN INSTANT-READ THERMOMETER

We include doneness temperatures in many of the recipes in this book. We recommend an instant-read thermometer for the job. For temperatures not represented in the chart above, use this simple formula:

To convert °F to °C: Subtract 32 from the Fahrenheit number, then divide the result by 1.8 to find the Celsius temperature.

Example
"Roast chicken until breast registers 160 degrees."

To convert 160°F to Celsius:
160°F − 32 = 128
128 ÷ 1.8 = 71.11°C, rounded down to 71°C

INDEX

Note: Page references in *italics* indicate photographs of finished recipes.

A

Acids, finishing dishes with, 47
Adjustable measuring cup
    for kitchen starter kit, 4
    shopping guide, 448
African Sweet Potato and Peanut Stew,
    266, 266–67
Aïoli, Garlic, 102
Aïoli Burger, 303
Al dente, about, 293, 440
All-Morning Energy Bars, *112*, 112–13
All-Purpose Whipped Cream, *420*, *420*
Almond(s)
    All-Morning Energy Bars, *112*, 112–13
    -Apricot Muffins, 140
    -Cherry Smoothies, 114
    French Toast Casserole, *138*, 138–39
    Granola with Dried Fruit, 110, *110*
    and Paprika, Sautéed Green Beans
        with, 54
    Pears, Goat Cheese, and Dried
        Apricots, Arugula Salad with, 152
    and Raspberries, Skillet Apple Crisp
        with, 409
Almost Hands-Free Risotto
    with Fennel and Saffron, 293
    with Parmesan and Herbs, *292*,
        292–93
    with Porcini, 293

Almost No-Knead Bread, *434*, 434–35
American Cheese and Sausage
    Breakfast Sandwiches, 117
American Sandwich Bread, *436*, 436–37
Anchovies, for recipes, 14
Apple(s)
    Celery Root, and Celery Slaw, 200
    Cheddar, and Hazelnuts, Brussels
        Sprout Salad with, 156
    choosing, for baking, 409
    -Cinnamon Steel-Cut Oatmeal, 108
    coring, 34
    Crisp, Skillet, *408*, 408–9
    Crisp, Skillet, with Raspberries and
        Almonds, 409
    Crisp, Skillet, with Vanilla, Cardamom,
        and Pistachios, 409
    Dried, Spiced Walnut Granola
        with, 110
    Kohlrabi, and Radicchio Slaw, 200
    -Walnut Coffee Cake,
        Make-Ahead, 147
Appliances, 8
Appliances, small, shopping guide,
    450–51
Apricot(s)
    Aged Gouda, and Pistachios, Quinoa
        Pilaf with, 77

Apricot(s) *(cont.)*
    -Almond Muffins, 140
    Dried, Pears, Almonds, and Goat
        Cheese, Arugula Salad with, 152
Aromatics
    about, 119
    in mirepoix, 273
    in sofrito, 273
Artichoke(s)
    Pasta with Garlic, Oil, and, 78
    Pepper, and Chickpea Tagine,
        312, 312–13
Arugula
    Roquefort, and Walnuts, French
        Potato Salad with, 161
    Salad with Figs, Prosciutto, Walnuts,
        and Parmesan, *152*, 152–53
    Salad with Pears, Almonds, Goat
        Cheese, and Dried Apricots, 152
Asiago and Dates, Grown-Up Grilled
    Cheese with, 301
Asian noodles
    about, 175
    soaking, 177
Asian pantry ingredients, 171
Asian Pear, Carrot, and Radish Slaw,
    200, 200–201